THE KINGFISHER
ILLUSTRATED
NATURE
ENCYCLOPEDIA

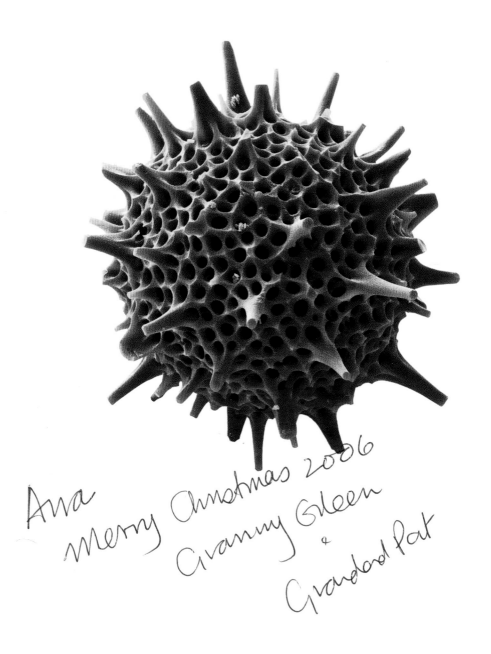

Ava
Merry Christmas 2006
Granny Gleen
&
Grandad Pat

Editors: Miranda Smith, Russell Mclean, Paula Borton

Senior designer: Malcolm Parchment

Designers: Peter Clayman, Carol Ann Davis, Sam Combes

Editorial assistance: Jennifer Schofield, Carron Brown, Sheila Clewley

Picture research manager: Cee Weston-Baker

Senior production controller: Nancy Roberts

DTP coordinator: Sarah Pfitzner

Artwork archivists: Wendy Allison, Jenny Lord

Illustrations: Julian and Janet Baker

Indexer: Sue Lightfoot

KINGFISHER
Kingfisher Publications Plc
New Penderel House
283–288 High Holborn
London WC1V 7HZ
www.kingfisherpub.com

First published by Kingfisher Publications Plc 2004
1 3 5 7 9 10 8 6 4 2
1TR/1103/TIM/GRS(GRS)/128MA(3.2GB)

Note to readers:
The website addresses listed in this book are correct at the time of going to print. However, due
to the ever-changing nature of the Internet, website addresses and content can change. Websites
can contain links that are unsuitable for children. The publisher cannot be held responsible for
changes in website addresses or content, or for information obtained through third-party
websites. We strongly advise that Internet searches should be supervised by an adult.

A CIP catalogue record for this book is available from the British Library.

ISBN 0 7534 0825 2

Printed in China

THE KINGFISHER
ILLUSTRATED
NATURE
ENCYCLOPEDIA

By David Burnie

KINGFISHER

Stages in the formation
of planet earth, about
4.7 billion years ago

CONTENTS

The fossilized skeleton of
Archaeopteryx, an early kind of bird

Campylodiscus diatoms –
types of microplant that
have a protective case
built from silica

A colony of African fruit bats roosting in a cave

A wild cat hissing and baring its teeth to repel an enemy

Leafcutter ants carrying pieces of leaf back to their nest in a South American rainforest

On the lookout for prey, a puma peers over a cliff in Navajo Tribal Park, Arizona, USA. Also known as the cougar or mountain lion, the puma hunts on its own, and deer are among its favourite food.

INTRODUCTION

For almost four billion years, life has flourished on planet earth – as far as we know, the only life-supporting world in a seemingly barren and inhospitable universe. From the simplest viruses to the largest land animals, the living things that inhabit the earth have always formed highly complex relationships between themselves and with their environments. *The Kingfisher Illustrated Nature Encyclopedia* celebrates this incredible diversity, bringing to life the wonders of the living world and exploring every major plant and animal group on the planet.

The encyclopedia is divided into three parts. The first, 'A Planet Apart', introduces earth, exploring the formation of our planet and the earliest origins of life. Since then, the unpredictable process of evolution has created a limitless variety of life-forms in every habitat – and also caused the extinction of 99 per cent of the world's species along the way.

Part two, 'The Living World', leads the reader through the five kingdoms of life – animals, plants, fungi, protists and bacteria. No one knows exactly how many different types of living things exist on earth, but scientists have identified more than 2.5 million species, a number that is growing all the time.

The third part, 'Wildlife Habitats', is a remarkable journey through the many different environments that support life on earth. From the bitter cold of the highest mountains to the blackness and extreme pressure of the ocean floor, living things have adapted to survive in almost every habitat that our planet has to offer, however unpromising the conditions. Species profiles highlight animals and plants of particular interest, such as the gnarled *Welwitschia* plant of the Namib Desert, and the Arctic bumblebee – one of the northernmost insects in the world.

The Kingfisher Illustrated Nature Encyclopedia presents a fascinating picture of life on earth, and, at a time when the living world is increasingly threatened by human activity, no subject is more vital to understand.

Seen from space, the earth and the moon look very different.
The moon is dry and barren, but the earth is cloaked by swirls of
cloud, showing that it has an atmosphere. Sunshine glints from the
surface of the oceans, while a patchwork of green and brown reveals
some of the habitats found on land. No other planet in the solar
system looks anything like this, and none – as far as we know – is
home to living things.

PART 1
A PLANET APART

INTRODUCING THE EARTH

DESPITE YEARS OF SEARCHING, ASTRONOMERS HAVE YET TO FIND ANYWHERE IN THE UNIVERSE THAT REMOTELY RESEMBLES THE EARTH. OUR PLANET IS ONE OF NINE IN THE SOLAR SYSTEM, BUT AS FAR AS WE KNOW, IT IS THE ONLY ONE THAT IS HOME TO LIVING THINGS.

Compared to most of the outer planets, the earth is small. Jupiter is more than 140,000 km across, and it could swallow the earth 1,300 times. Mercury, Venus and Mars are much more like the earth in size, but they are either roasted by the sun, or steeped in bitter cold. The earth alone is somewhere in between – a planet awash with water, and brimming with life.

A WORLD OF WATER

Water is a substance that makes the earth unique. It exists elsewhere in the solar system, but is nearly always frozen. Most of the earth's water is liquid. It slowly circulates to spread the sun's heat, and it evaporates to form clouds and rain. Without water, the earth's surface would be as dusty and lifeless as the moon's.

About 97 per cent of the world's water is in the oceans, while two per cent is locked up

△ *The earth's magnetic field protects us from particles given off by the sun. In the Arctic and Antarctic, these particles create shimmering curtains of light called auroras.*

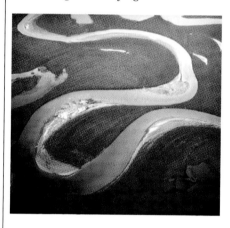

△ *Powered by warmth from the sun, the earth's water keeps moving. Rainwater flows over land in rivers, and also through it, in soil and porous rocks. Underground water can take thousands of years to reach the sea.*

in glaciers and polar ice. Freshwater makes up almost all of the rest. Only a tiny amount − just 0.001 per cent − consists of water vapour in the air.

THE ATMOSPHERE

On the moon, the sky looks black. Down on earth, the sky is blue. That is because the earth is surrounded by the atmosphere, which scatters light rays coming from the sun. But the atmosphere does more than make the sky an attractive colour. It protects living things from harmful radiation, and it helps keep the surface of the planet warm. It also contains gases that are essential for living things.

Nitrogen makes up nearly four-fifths of the atmosphere. All living things need this gas, but only microbes can collect it directly from the air. They build it into chemicals that plants and animals can use.

Oxygen is even more important, because living things use it to release energy. It makes up about a fifth of the atmosphere and, because it dissolves in water, oceans, lakes and rivers contain plenty too. A third gas − carbon dioxide − is far rarer. It makes up just 0.033 per cent of the atmosphere, but all the world's plants, and many of its microbes, need it to grow.

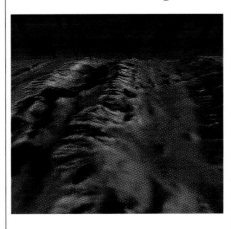

△ *Some of the surface features on Mars look as if they may have been formed by flowing water. Today, the surface of Mars is dry, although there are ice-caps at the Martian poles.*

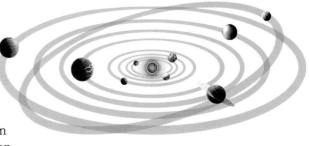

△ *Earth is the third planet from the sun in the solar system. Our nearest neighbours are Venus and Mars. Venus has an acidic atmosphere and is very hot, while Mars has a thin atmosphere and is cold.*

EARTH'S CHANGING SURFACE

The average temperature on earth's surface is a comfortable 14° C. But in the earth's core, it is at least 4,500° C. Heat from the core flows upwards towards the surface, melting rock, triggering volcanic eruptions and keeping continents on the move. Some of these changes make life dangerous for earth's inhabitants, but they create opportunities too. Without them, life on earth would probably be much less varied today.

▽ *Earth's atmosphere is over 400 km thick, but most of its water vapour is in the lowest 12 km, in a zone called the troposphere. Conditions there are always changing, as weather fronts track across the earth.*

HOW THE EARTH FORMED

COMPARED TO THE ENTIRE UNIVERSE, THE
EARTH IS STILL YOUNG. IT FORMED ABOUT
4.7 BILLION YEARS AGO, WHEN A CLOUD OF
GAS AND DUST SHRANK UNDER THE PULL OF
GRAVITY, AND THE SOLAR SYSTEM WAS BORN.

The newly formed earth was completely different to the
planet that we know today. It had no atmosphere or water,
and it was as lifeless as the moon. But as the earth aged,
heat built up inside it and the planet began to change. Heavy
elements, such as iron, sank downwards into the earth's core,
while lighter ones drifted up towards the surface. As the surface
cooled, minerals began to crystallize, producing earth's first solid
rocks. The heat also triggered violent volcanic eruptions –
a development that paved the way for life.

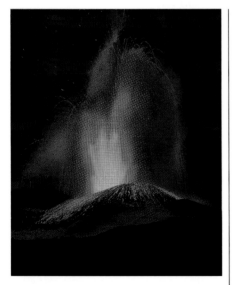

△ *Unlike the moon, the earth is studded
with volcanoes. About 600,000 years ago,
an eruption in North America produced
1,000 cubic kilometres of lava and ash. Even
bigger eruptions occurred in the distant past.*

AIR AND WATER

Earth's rocky crust formed about 4.5
billion years ago. Volcanoes were far
more active than they are now, and
they produced vast beds of lava that
poured out over the surface of the
planet. At the same time, volcanic
eruptions released immense clouds
of gas and water vapour. Light gases,
such as hydrogen, drifted into space,
but heavier ones were held in place
by the earth's gravity. These formed
a primitive atmosphere that contained
lots of nitrogen, carbon dioxide and
water vapour, but hardly any oxygen.

By about four billion years ago, the
world had cooled enough to allow
some water vapour to condense. At
first, the vapour formed tiny droplets,
shrouding the world in clouds. But
once the vapour had built up to a
critical level, the first rains began

△ *After the earth formed, its surface
gradually cooled, allowing solid rock to
develop. Earth's inner core is kept hot by
pressure and by natural radioactivity.
It will take hundreds of millions of years
for this internal heat to fade away.*

to fall. Some downpours may have
lasted for thousands of years, and so
much water fell that seas and then
oceans began to appear. These oceans
were the birthplace of living things.

UNDER BOMBARDMENT

The young earth was frequently hit
by debris from space. Most of this
material consisted of dust, but from
time to time devastating meteorites

slammed into the surface. Shortly after the crust formed, another planet may even have crashed into the earth, increasing its weight by half and almost smashing it apart.

Some scientists think that the moon was produced in the aftermath of this impact. According to this theory, a huge amount of rock was flung into space and then recaptured by the earth's gravity. Another possibility is that the moon was captured intact, after nearing the earth from another part of space.

THE ROCK CYCLE
On the moon, meteorite impacts leave permanent craters because there is nothing to wear them away.

The earth's surface, however, is constantly reshaped by wind, rain and ice. Volcanic activity creates even bigger changes, because it builds up mountains and keeps continents on the move.

These changes have been happening ever since the oceans and atmosphere first appeared. They break down rocks into tiny particles, which are then washed down rivers into the sea. Here, the particles form sediment that builds up on the seabed. After thousands of years, the sediment turns into solid rock. If this is forced upwards, it can turn into dry land, and the rock cycle begins again.

In many parts of the world, the earth's crust is like a giant sandwich, made up of layers of sedimentary rock dating back millions of years. The layers act like a record of the earth's past, showing what conditions were like when the rock formed. The fossils trapped inside them also show what was alive at the time.

THE OXYGEN REVOLUTION
No trace is left of the earth's first rocks, because they were destroyed long ago. The oldest rocks ever found date back about 3.9 billion years.

These rocks do not contain fossils, but even so, scientists think it is quite likely that life was already underway when they were made. These primitive life-forms lived in a world where oxygen was very rare. But over the next two billion years, the atmosphere's oxygen level began to rise, until it reached about 21 per cent – the level where it stands today. Amazingly, this change was brought about entirely by living things.

The creatures responsible for this transformation were microscopic bacteria. Using light, water and carbon dioxide, they developed a way of living called photosynthesis (see pp. 84–85). The bacteria took carbon dioxide from the air and released oxygen as a by-product. Each bacterium released only a tiny amount, but over trillions of generations, oxygen poured into the air. Without these early bacteria, the atmosphere would be unbreathable and animal life would not exist.

▽ *In the Grand Canyon, river water has sliced its way downwards through 1.6 km of rock – the greatest depth visible in one place anywhere on earth. The oldest rocks, at the bottom of the canyon, date back two billion years.*

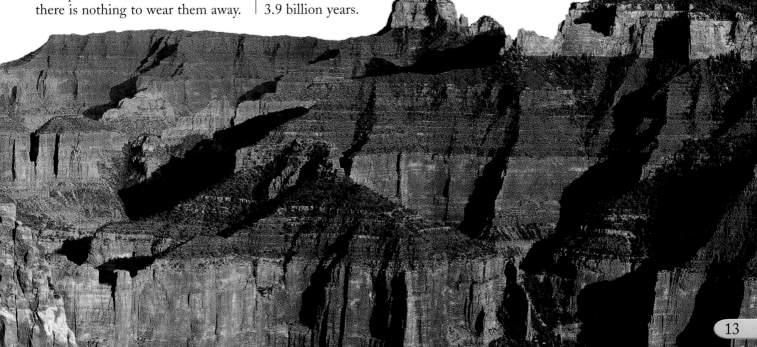

How
LIFE BEGAN

NOBODY KNOWS HOW LIFE STARTED ON
EARTH, OR WHERE THIS AMAZING EVENT TOOK
PLACE. BUT EACH YEAR, SCIENTISTS COME A LITTLE
CLOSER TO FINDING OUT. TWO THINGS SEEM CERTAIN –
LIFE APPEARED A LONG TIME AGO, AND THE FIRST LIVING
THINGS WERE FAR SIMPLER THAN ANYTHING ALIVE TODAY.

Some people believe that living things were specially created, and that life on earth dates back only a few thousand years. But almost all of the world's scientists disagree. They think that life dates back nearly four billion years, to a time when our planet was still quite young. They believe that life began through random chemical reactions, which eventually built up living things. This process may not have happened only on earth – elsewhere in the universe, other planets may have living things too.

△ *Every year, the earth is hit by hundreds of meteorites. In 1996, a team of NASA scientists investigated meteorite ALH84001, which is known to have come from Mars. They announced that they had discovered bacteria in the meteorite, but since then, other scientists have questioned their find.*

△ *These microscopic fossils from Canada are about two billion years old. They show the outlines of cell membranes – one of the key features of all known living things.*

ESSENTIAL EQUIPMENT
Living things are incredibly varied, but deep down they use the same working parts to stay alive. They all consist of cells, and each cell contains a complete set of chemical instructions, or genes. Cells are like microscopic bubbles, and they are surrounded by special membranes that protect them from the outside world. Cells can use energy from their surroundings, and they can also multiply and grow. Genes are even more important. They contain all the information needed to build cells and to make them work. They are able to copy themselves, and they are handed on when cells reproduce.

To understand how life began, scientists have tried to guess how cells and genes came about. Both are very complicated, which makes it highly unlikely that they could have appeared, ready-made, by chance. They might have developed step by step, however, from much simpler beginnings. Over a long time, random chemical reactions could have built up the equipment needed for life.

MYSTERIOUS WORLDS

Over 50 years ago, an American chemist called Stanley Miller carried out an experiment designed to imitate conditions on the early earth. Through completely random reactions, the test produced some of the carbon-based chemicals that are found in living things. Miller's results were sensational, but since then, scientists have made even more remarkable discoveries. Carbon-based chemicals have been detected in meteorites and comets, and even in 'empty' space. These chemicals are far simpler than any gene, and they are certainly not alive. But they are the chemical nuts and bolts from which living things are made.

Recently, some researchers have suggested that chemicals from space may have helped to kick-start life on earth. A few have even proposed that living microbes could have arrived in this way. But most scientists favour the idea that life on earth is 'home grown' – that it developed gradually

▽ *A scientist adjusts equipment during a re-run of Stanley Miller's famous experiment on the origin of life. The original test ran for many days.*

in sheltered surroundings, as carbon-containing chemicals became more varied and complex.

On the early earth, the continents were rocked by volcanic eruptions, so any complex chemicals on land would soon have been destroyed. But the seas were much less hostile. Seawater is good at dissolving chemicals and allowing them to react. Over millions of years, rain would have washed chemicals into the sea, and many carbon-based substances could have built up. The result was a promising brew that is often known as the 'primeval soup'.

THE CHEMICAL WORKSHOP

The open sea is good at mixing up chemicals, but it is not an ideal place for complex molecules to survive.

△ *Volcanic gases bubble up from a hydrothermal vent on the ocean floor. Vents like these may have been some of the places where the first living things appeared.*

Many scientists think that the chances would have been better on the seabed or in cavities inside rocks. Rock crystals may have acted as chemical work surfaces, allowing big molecules to form. At the same time, dissolved minerals could have supplied the energy needed to link

their atoms together. Hydrothermal vents are rich in these minerals, which is why some biologists believe they could have been the cradle of life.

Before life actually began, during a long 'pre-life era', random chemical

△ *Living stromatolites line the shore of Australia's Shark Bay. Fossil stromatolites are among the oldest signs of life on earth.*

reactions produced all kinds of carbon-containing molecules. Some of these molecules may have acted as catalysts, speeding up reactions thousands or millions of times. But at some point, a momentous event took place – a molecule appeared that could copy itself, and that could survive long enough to 'breed'. From this moment on, life was underway.

SHARING THE PAST

So far, all this is guesswork, and none of it can be proved. But once life did appear, evidence shows that it soon spread through the seas. Fossilized bacterial mounds, called stromatolites, have been identified that date back 3.4 billion years. Although their heyday is long past, living stromatolites still exist today.

During life's long history, millions of different species have evolved. But all of them have the same kind of cell membranes, and their genes work by using exactly the same chemical code. This makes it almost certain that today's living things share a single far-off ancestor, which came to life in the sea long ago.

THE BIOSPHERE 1

OVER THE LAST 3.7 BILLION YEARS, LIVING THINGS HAVE MANAGED TO SPREAD ALL OVER THE EARTH. THEIR HOME IS THE BIOSPHERE – A LAYER OF LIFE THAT CIRCLES THE ENTIRE PLANET.

The earth measures over 12,000 km across, but the biosphere is never more than about 25 km from top to bottom. If the earth were the size of a football, the biosphere would be no thicker than a sheet of paper. But packed into this layer is every single thing that lives on our planet, from the tallest trees and heaviest animals right down to the smallest microbes. Some parts of the biosphere teem with life, because living conditions there are almost ideal. Others have far fewer inhabitants, because extreme heat or cold makes it difficult to survive.

LIFE HIGH UP

If a space probe parachuted to earth searching for living things, the first concrete signs of life would appear about 20 km up in the air. Nothing actually spends its entire life this high up, but microbes, spores and pollen grains can all be carried here by the wind. Once they have reached these great heights, it can take them days or even weeks to drift back down to the ground.

At an altitude of about 1 km, flying animals start to become common. This part of the biosphere is home to insects and birds, which use the air as a highway. Birds are the most powerful fliers, but insects outnumber them many times. A single swarm of locusts can contain more than 70,000 tonnes of insects, fluttering on billions of filmy wings.

LIFE ON LAND

If the probe touched down on land, it would almost certainly find life straight away. In fact, some parts of the biosphere are so full of life that it might not reach the ground at all. Near the equator, trees thrive in the bright sunshine, heavy rain and year-round warmth. The result is dense tropical forest, which is one of the richest habitats on earth.

Farther away from the equator, the biosphere becomes less crowded and habitats start to change. Earth's weather patterns mean that tropical forest gives way to shrublands, and shrublands give way to desert. Here, life is thinly spread, particularly in places where there is less than 5 cm of rain a year. Farther north and south, in the world's temperate regions, the climate is much more moist. This part of the biosphere is full of plants and animals, although there are fewer species than in warmer areas of the world.

In polar regions and mountains, strong winds and intense cold make life difficult. Drought can also add to the problem. In Antarctica's 'dry valleys', for example, no rain or snow has fallen for more than a million years. These desolate places are the most lifeless parts of the biosphere, and earth's closest equivalent to the surface of Mars.

UNDERGROUND EARTH

The biosphere does not stop at the ground – instead, it continues beneath the surface. Fertile soil teems with animals, fungi and microbes that recycle dead remains. Living things also flourish in caves, while some bacteria survive in water-filled cracks in rocks deep underground. Experimental drills have found these bacteria at depths of 2 km, and some experts think that life below ground could go deeper still.

2

1

▽ *This view of the earth's surface shows a slice through the biosphere, together with living things from a variety of habitats on land. To find out about habitats in water, turn over the page.*

1 *Earthworms live in soil, where they help to recycle the dead remains of plants. Soil is an important part of the biosphere on land, because most plants need soil to grow.*

2 *In deserts, some plants come to life only after it has rained. Others survive drought by storing up water in their stems or roots.*

3 *In mountains, the yellow-billed chough lives at altitudes of up to 6,000 m. Birds are good at surviving high up because their plumage keeps them warm.*

4 *Pollen grains are produced by flowers. They are small and light, and some are specially shaped so that they drift for long distances through the air.*

5 *Temperate forests grow in parts of the world where it never gets very hot or very cold.*

Most of the trees lose their leaves in autumn and grow a new set in spring.

6 *Grasslands are home to the largest herds of mammals that live on land. The biggest grasslands are in warm parts of the world.*

7 *In the soil, amoebas eat other microbes, as well as the remains of larger living things.*

THE BIOSPHERE 2

IF YOU PICK A RANDOM POINT ANYWHERE ON THE EARTH'S SURFACE, IT IS TWICE AS LIKELY TO BE AT SEA THAN ON LAND. THE OCEANS MAKE UP AN ENORMOUS PART OF THE BIOSPHERE, AND LIVING THINGS ARE FOUND THROUGHOUT THEM, FROM THE SURFACE TO MORE THAN 10 KM DOWN.

The earth has five oceans and many smaller seas. Unlike land habitats, they are all connected, and the water they share is constantly on the move. Near the surface, currents can flow as fast as rivers, while in the oceans' depths they usually move at a dead-slow crawl. Because the oceans are linked, water life has been able to spread to every corner of the world. Even so, the oceans are divided into different habitats in the same way as the land.

SHELVES AND REEFS

Altogether, the world's coasts are at least 500,000 km long. On some coasts, the seabed drops away very steeply, so the water is soon thousands of metres deep. In other places, the seabed slopes much more gently – for example, halfway between Australia and New Guinea the seabed is as little as 70 m down. These shallow areas are formed by continental shelves – vast underwater ledges reaching out from the land.

Continental shelves cover only a small part of the oceans, but they are important habitats. Bottom-dwelling fish feed on animals that live on the seabed, making continental shelves some of the most fertile fishing grounds in the world. Tropical coral reefs have even more inhabitants. They are among the busiest parts of the entire biosphere.

LAYERS IN THE SEA

Although ocean water moves about, it does have built-in boundaries, such as the division between the sunlit surface water and the perpetual blackness below. Another boundary is called the thermocline – a zone where the water temperature rapidly drops as you go deeper down. These two boundaries are not far from the surface, and they often coincide. Together, they split the oceans into two different layers.

The top layer contains only two per cent of the world's saltwater, but it is home to all the water life that needs daylight to survive. In this vital part of the biosphere, microscopic algae collect light and use it to grow.

Deeper down, the cavernous dark layer contains everything that can exist without light. Here, animals live in a world of intense pressure and constant cold. The only warm places are hydrothermal vents, where volcanically heated water gushes up through the ocean floor.

DESCENT TO THE DEPTHS

The middle depths of the oceans are some of the emptiest parts of the biosphere. But even at the greatest depths, there is a lot of life on the seabed. This is because the seabed collects all the dead remains that drift down from high above. These remains form ocean sediment – a sticky substance that animals sift or burrow through, looking for food.

Seabed sediment builds up extremely slowly, but it can be up to 500 m thick. Even beneath the sediment, bacteria live in cracks in the ocean crust, surviving at depths of several kilometres. Where they fizzle out, life – and the biosphere – gradually comes to an end.

2

1

▽ This view of the biosphere shows ocean habitats, together with some of their inhabitants. The oceans are always changing, because the ocean floor is created and destroyed by earth's volcanic heat. About 250 million years ago, there was just one ocean, but it was as big as all of today's oceans added together.

1 Remote islands often have unique land plants and animals, and distinctive wildlife in the surrounding sea.

2 The surface waters of the oceans teem with microscopic algae, as well as animals that feed on them. Together, they make up the plankton – a huge collection of living things that drifts with the current.

3 Rocky coastlines are important breeding grounds for seabirds and marine mammals, particularly where steep cliffs keep predators away.

4 Coral reefs grow in regions where the water is shallow, clear and warm. They are home to a large share of the world's fish.

5 Some parts of the seabed are carpeted with brittlestars. These animals catch particles of food with their slender arms.

6 Bacteria live around hydrothermal vents, and also in water-filled cracks that reach deep beneath the ocean floor.

THE WORLD OF WATER

LIFE STARTED IN WATER AND SINCE THEN, LIVING THINGS HAVE SPREAD TO EVERY WATERY HABITAT ON EARTH. TODAY, GIANT ANIMALS CRUISE THROUGH THE OCEANS WHILE MICROSCOPIC CREATURES TEEM IN PONDS AND POOLS. HERE, THE STRUGGLE FOR SURVIVAL CAN BE INTENSE.

All living things need water, but for many it doubles up as a habitat too. Water life ranges from the smallest and simplest creatures to the world's longest and fastest-growing living things. So why does water make such a desirable home? One answer is that conditions in water are much more stable than on dry land. Another is that there is so much of it. The world's oceans alone contain over 1.4 billion cubic kilometres of water, making them by far the largest habitat on earth.

This lifestyle works because water is packed with drifting life. Some of the smallest drifters are single-celled algae, which live by soaking up the energy in sunshine. They are the key to life in open water, because they make the food that animals can eat. But even in the clearest water, sunlight only reaches a depth of about 250 m. As a result, algae live near the surface, so most animals live there too.

△ *Giant kelp is the world's longest and fastest-growing seaweed. It can shoot up from the seabed for more than 60 m before it hits the surface. Its leafy fronds have gas-filled floats to keep the plant upright.*

▷ *The biggest animals in the oceans all live by filtering food from the water. This is a basking shark – measuring up to 10 m long, it is the world's second-largest fish. It has small teeth, and traps food by using its gills as a sieve.*

Freshwater is often shallow, so light can reach all the way to the bottom. In summer, it can be packed with microscopic life, which is why pond water often looks green.

FLOATING FOOD

For many water animals, eating involves swimming through their food. Using all kinds of body parts, from trailing tentacles to gaping mouths, they scoop up food as they swim along. For a sea gooseberry, the daily catch may weigh less than a gram, but for whales it can be more than a tonne.

KEEPING AFLOAT

Land animals use a lot of energy working against the pull of gravity. But in water, life is much easier. Freshwater is over 750 times more dense than air, so it is very good at buoying up living things. Many soft-bodied animals simply float along with the current – a leisurely way of life that has no equivalent on land.

△ *Sea gooseberries, or ctenophores, are soft-bodied animals that catch food by trailing two slender tentacles lined with sticky cells. They swim by beating rows of 'paddles' that reflect sunshine like tiny mirrors.*

whipped up by storms, most of the planet's water moves very slowly, creating a world that is always calm.

But water's density has some disadvantages as well. Compared to air, it is very thick or viscous, so it takes a lot of effort to push through it. That explains why wading through water can be hard work. It also explains why nature's fastest swimmers are streamlined, because a smooth body shape helps the water to slip past them as they move.

VITAL INGREDIENTS

Pure water is very rare in nature, because water is very good at dissolving things. It dissolves minerals when it flows through the ground, and gases when it falls through the air. This is good news for water life, because plants and animals need dissolved substances to survive.

One of the most important of these is oxygen, which gets into water from the air. Dissolved oxygen is invisible, but it is vital for almost all living things. The colder water is, or the more stirred up it becomes, the more oxygen it dissolves. Another important ingredient is salt. Freshwater contains only a small amount, but each kilogram of seawater contains

Some water plants and animals also have adjustable buoyancy tanks. Using these, they can make sure that they grow upwards towards the surface, or float at the right level.

Water has some other benefits too. Because it is dense, it takes a long time to heat up or cool down. This is good for water life, as it means that there are no sudden temperature changes, unlike on land. It also takes a lot of energy to start water moving. Although rivers rush down mountainsides and the oceans are

△ *When sunlight shines through water, it gradually fades away. The red and orange parts of sunlight are absorbed first, while blue travels farthest of all. Below about 250 m, the water in oceans and deep lakes is always dark.*

▽ *Some water animals breathe air, but most take their oxygen from the water around them. This sea slug, or nudibranch, gets oxygen through a tuft of feathery gills on its back.*

roughly 35 grams of salt. If all this salt were spread across the seabed, it would make a layer 56 m thick. Some water animals can travel between freshwater and seawater, but most kinds of water life have adapted to a particular salt level, and cannot survive if they are switched between the two.

LIVING ON LAND

LAND IS HOME TO NEARLY ALL OF THE WORLD'S
FLOWERING PLANTS AND TO A LARGE SHARE
OF ITS ANIMALS. MANY KINDS OF
MICROSCOPIC LIFE EXIST HERE TOO.
BUT COMPARED TO LIVING IN
WATER, SURVIVING ON LAND IS A
SURPRISINGLY DIFFICULT BUSINESS.

△ *Conditions on land vary much more than in water. This plant is growing in ground that has cracked open during a drought – unless it rains soon, the plant will not survive.*

△ *A tough body case enables beetles to crawl through narrow spaces without damaging their wings. Because the case is waterproof, it stops beetles drying out.*

▷ *African elephants are the largest land animals alive today. For animals this heavy, lying down is a lengthy business, but wallowing in mud or bathing is often part of a herd's daily routine.*

Because we live on land, it is easy to imagine that it makes an ideal home for living things. But nothing could be further from the truth. Life on land is tough, and it takes special adaptations to survive. To make up for this, earth's land surface is amazingly varied, so land-dwellers have been able to develop a bewildering variety of different lifestyles.

TAKING THE WEIGHT

When astronauts return from space, they have to get used to earth's gravity. Something similar happened long ago, when earth's first land-dwellers emerged from the sea. Gravity has very little effect on water life, but on land it can make living things collapse.

Plants and animals avoid this fate by having special strengthening systems. In plants, these include wood – a tough but springy material that supports the world's tallest things.

Animals support themselves with skeletons made of even harder substances, including shell and bone. An insect's skeleton works like a case, but a bony one holds up an animal's body from inside. Some dinosaur skeletons supported animals weighing more than 50 tonnes, which shows just how successful this system can be. But skeletons do not have to be big to be strong. The hero shrew, from Africa, has such a tough spine that it can survive having a person step on its back.

DRY TIMES

Gravity is not the only problem land-dwellers have to deal with. Just as important is the threat of drying out. One way to get around this is to live in damp places, a tactic used by frogs and toads, as well as by animals that live in the soil. But damp habitats are not always easy to find, and they often dry out themselves. To be really successful on land, animals and plants need ways of keeping hold of the water that they contain.

In mammals, birds and reptiles, this job is done by skin. Skin works like a raincoat in reverse, because it stops water escaping to the air outside. Every day, we need to drink

△ *Flying is a very efficient way of moving about – in a day, these carmine bee-eaters of central Africa can travel more than 100 km to find food.*

to top up our moisture levels, but many desert animals can get all the water they need from their food. Insects are even better at managing their 'water budget', because their body cases also double up as a water barrier. Many of them eat dry food, and never drink a single drop of water in their lives.

Because plants do not move, they can store up water when it is wet, and use it when the weather turns dry. Cacti often store enough water to fill a bath, and the water stored in a baobab tree (see p. 202) could fill a small swimming pool.

BREEDING ON LAND
Lastly and most importantly, plants and animals have to produce young that can survive on land. Flowering plants do this by growing seeds – packages of cells that are designed

to survive heat, cold and drought. Many land animals lay waterproof eggs, but most mammals have a very different way of reproducing. Their young develop in the watery surroundings of their mother's womb, hidden away from the outside world.

△ *Taking its first glimpse of the world, a young green tree python emerges from its egg. Reptiles were the first animals to evolve waterproof eggs, helping them to live in dry places.*

◁ *Arching its neck, a giraffe takes a drink. Unlike humans, giraffes get most of their water from their food, so they can go without drinking for several days.*

ENERGY FOR LIFE

EACH DAY, THE SUN BOMBARDS OUR PLANET WITH
ENOUGH ENERGY TO KEEP A CAR RUNNING FOR
OVER A TRILLION YEARS. THIS ENERGY POWERS THE
WEATHER AND WARMS THE EARTH AND, MORE
IMPRESSIVELY, IT KEEPS LIVING THINGS ALIVE.

Just like machines, living things need energy to work. They use
energy to power their cells, and once these are running, they
can do all kinds of other things, including growing and moving
about. But this energy has to come from somewhere, and it has
to be replaced whenever it is used. Since life began, living things
have developed two different ways of getting their energy supplies.
Some collect it directly, usually by gathering light. Others –
including ourselves – get it second-hand, by digesting food.

POWERING UP

Most people enjoy relaxing in the
warm sunshine, but our bodies
cannot do much with light energy.
We use it to see and to produce
vitamin D, and that is where the list
comes to an end. But for many
bacteria, and almost all the world's
plants, light energy is vital for
survival. The bacteria and plants
soak it up, like living solar panels,
and use it to make themselves work.
This process is called
photosynthesis –
you can find
out about it
on pages
84–85.

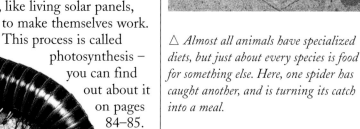

△ *Almost all animals have specialized
diets, but just about every species is food
for something else. Here, one spider has
caught another, and is turning its catch
into a meal.*

◁ *Measuring up to 28 cm long,
millipedes are some of the largest creatures
that feed on plant remains. Not only are
millipedes slow movers, but they
are also cold-blooded. This
combination makes
them very
economical
with energy.*

Plants collect about one per cent
of all the light energy that reaches
the earth. That may not sound a lot,
but it is more than 300 times the
energy generated by all the power
stations in the world. This energy
creates billions of tonnes of plant
matter, from roots and leaves to
flowers and seeds. Some energy is
used up when plants grow, but a lot
is built into the plants themselves.
This built-in energy is passed on to
animals whenever they eat plant
food. Once the energy has made this
jump, it is passed on whenever one
animal eats another.

FEEDING TIME

To release energy from food, animals
have to break it down. They do this
by combining it with oxygen – the
same chemical change that takes
place when things catch fire. Fire
releases energy very quickly, and in
dangerous amounts. If animals used
this way of getting energy, their
bodies would be cooked from the
inside. Instead, they release it in a
series of carefully controlled steps,
so that not too much heat is
produced. This way of releasing
energy is called cellular respiration,
because it uses oxygen and takes
place inside cells.

Animals are not the only living
things that respire. Respiration is
carried out by all living cells when

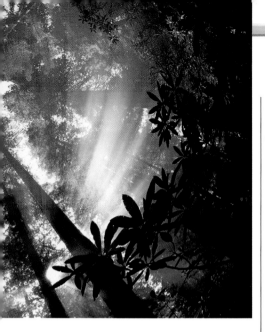

they break down food. Plant cells respire, because they make food by photosynthesis, and then break it down when energy supplies are low.

FAST AND SLOW

In the animal world, each species uses up energy at different rates. Shrews, for example, seem to run

▽ *This diagram shows how much energy different mammals use for each unit of body weight. The rate for humans is set at one. Small mammals use energy quickly because their bodies lose heat more rapidly.*

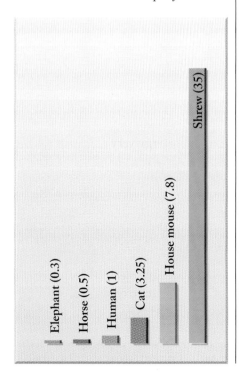

Elephant (0.3)
Horse (0.5)
Human (1)
Cat (3.25)
House mouse (7.8)
Shrew (35)

◁ *As sunlight floods down through this forest, it is collected by leaves. Trees invest energy in building up tall trunks so that they can catch even more light.*

their lives in fast-forward. They are always on the move, always eating, and hardly ever take a rest. Snakes and crocodiles, however, are very different. They seem to spend their time lazing about, and they can rest for several weeks after a large meal.

These differences result from each animal's metabolism, which is the sum total of its body chemistry. Shrews have a very fast metabolism, because they use up lots of energy keeping their tiny bodies warm. Snakes and crocodiles, on the other hand, are cold-blooded. Their metabolism is slow because they need much less energy to stay alive. Humans, like most large mammals, are somewhere in between.

At any moment, an animal's metabolic rate depends on what it is doing. When animals are active, their metabolic rate goes up, but when they are sleeping, it goes down. When animals hibernate, their metabolic rate drops further still. A hibernating bat uses energy 40 times more slowly than an active one, so the food reserves in its body can last for many weeks.

BOTTOM OF THE HEAP

Energy is not only passed on in living things, but it is also found in dead remains, such as the dead bodies of animals, rotting plants, and all kinds of natural waste – animal droppings and fallen leaves, for example. Many forms of life tap into this energy source. They include animals that scavenge for food (see pp. 132–133), as well as fungi and bacteria. Together, these living things are known as decomposers, because they break down and dispose of waste.

Decomposing is a reliable way of obtaining energy, because sooner or later, all living things die. It is also very thorough, because once it is finished, every scrap of available energy is released. Decomposition comes to an end when there is no energy left to pass on.

CHEMICAL TRICKS

Without sunlight to make plants grow, humans would not survive for very long. The same is true for other animals, and most fungi and bacteria.

△ *Without decomposers such as fungi, plants would still be able to collect energy from sunlight, but they would run out of the nutrients that they need to grow.*

However, in some of the world's remotest places – such as submerged rocks and deep-sea vents – bacteria live by collecting dissolved minerals and making them react. Unlike everything else in the living world, these tiny creatures do not need solar energy at all. These bacteria are known as lithotrophs, which literally means 'rock-eaters'. Some of them survive on a diet of manganese or iron, while others process sulphur. Lithotrophs are of great interest to scientists because it is just possible that lithotrophs live on other planets, as well as our own.

CHANGING CLIMATE

FOR THE LAST 50 YEARS, OUR PLANET HAS BEEN WARMING UP, BUT CLIMATE CHANGE IS NOTHING NEW. THROUGHOUT THE EARTH'S HISTORY, LIVING THINGS HAVE HAD TO ADAPT TO THESE CHANGES.

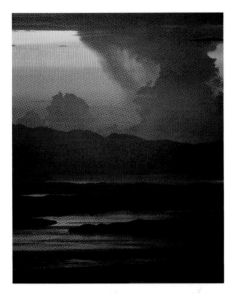

△ *The world's climate is shaped by lots of different things. One of them is cloud cover. Clouds reflect sunshine back into space, but they also work like a blanket, keeping in the earth's heat.*

Earth's climate is like an incredibly complex machine, with billions of separate parts. Predicting what it will do next is very difficult. Looking back is easier, however, thanks to evidence that the climate leaves behind – such as the thickness of tree rings or the make-up of ancient air, trapped deep in polar ice. They show that the world's climate is very variable, and that major changes can happen much faster than scientists once thought.

ICE AGES

Twenty thousand years ago, earth was a very different place. Immense glaciers covered much of the northern hemisphere, reaching as far south as present-day London and New York. Even in places such as New Guinea, glaciers flowed down from the highest mountains. So much water was locked up in ice that the sea level was over 100 m lower than it is now.

For plants and animals, these cold conditions had far-reaching effects. On the positive side, there was much more land because so much of the former seabed was high and dry. This made it easier for animals and plants to spread, because they could travel between places that are now separated by the sea. But on the negative side, life could be extremely cold and harsh. To keep warm, Ice Age mammals depended on deep layers of body fat and long, shaggy fur.

WHY THE CLIMATE CHANGES

This Ice Age was not the first that the earth has experienced, and it is unlikely to be the last. As far back as scientists can look, the earth's climate has swung between warm periods, called interglacials, and times when it has been much colder. Many experts believe that these climate swings

▷ *This chart shows how the world's average temperature has changed over the last million years. There have been several major warm periods, called interglacials – some brief, others more long-lasting. We are living in an interglacial today.*

Temp. (°C)

17 –	
16 –	Previous Ice Ages / Last Ice Age
15 –	Interglacials
14 –	
13 –	
12 –	
11 –	
10 –	Glacials
9 –	Thousands of years ago

| 800 | 700 | 600 | 500 | 400 | 300 | 200 | 100 | Present |

broke

are caused mainly by variations in the earth's orbit, but other factors are involved as well – volcanic eruptions and continental drift, for example.

Continents have been on the move ever since land first formed. Powered by volcanic heat, they creep across earth's surface at the rate of a few centimetres each year. This movement is much too slow for us to notice but, over millions of years, it can completely change the way the earth looks. And because the continents move, the oceans change shape as well.

Oceans play a key part in shaping the world's climate, because they store heat from the sun. Most of the heat is stored in the tropics and then carried north and south by warm currents. But if continents move and block these currents, the far north and south start to cool down. This cooling may be enough to trigger an Ice Age, which can last for hundreds of thousands of years.

STRANDED BY TIME

The last Ice Age ended about 10,000 years ago, when the earth warmed and glaciers began to retreat. Since then, the global climate has been fairly stable, but it has not stayed exactly the same. Average temperatures have risen and fallen, and rainfall patterns have changed too. In places such as the Sahara Desert, these changes have had some dramatic effects.

Today, the Sahara is one of the driest and least fertile regions in the world. But 5,000 years ago, its climate was much more moist. At that time, elephants and antelope fed in open woodland, and hippos lived in the region's lakes and rivers. During the next 3,000 years, the Sahara's climate became steadily drier. The desert began to expand, and many of the region's plants and animals dwindled and then disappeared. But they did not all vanish. Hidden away in the Sahara's mountains, where the climate is slightly more moist, olive trees and freshwater fish still manage to survive.

△ ▽ The Tassili Mountains, in southern Algeria, are in the heart of the Sahara Desert. Rock engravings – such as the antelope below – show that this dry and remote region was full of wildlife a few thousand years ago.

◁ Polar ice works like a diary of the world's climate, because it traps dust, pollen and bubbles of air. By drilling down through the ice, scientists can collect samples dating back thousands or millions of years.

△ *As the days lengthen in spring, this English oak tree suddenly starts to grow. Its buds burst open, producing thousands of bright green leaves.*

△ *By midsummer, the oak's leaves have turned dark green and have finished growing. Among them, the year's crop of acorns is starting to form.*

△ *During autumn, the leaves change colour from green to yellow, and begin to fall. The acorns are almost ripe – soon they will start to fall too.*

△ *In winter, the tree is leafless, so it is not harmed by the cold. It will stay like this until winter is over, and the warmer days of spring arrive again.*

SEASONS AND WEATHER

INSTEAD OF BEING UPRIGHT, THE EARTH TILTS AT AN ANGLE AS IT CIRCLES AROUND THE SUN. THIS TILT IS SMALL, BUT IT HAS A HUGE IMPACT ON LIVING THINGS BECAUSE IT IS THE REASON WHY THE SEASONS CHANGE.

Along the equator at midday, the sun is almost directly overhead, and each day is almost exactly 12 hours long. But farther north and south, the sun is lower and the earth's tilt has much more effect. In winter, the tilt is away from the sun, so the days are short and cold. In summer, the tilt is in the opposite direction, so the days are long and warm. Near the poles, it never gets warm, but summer days are so long that the sun never sets at all.

◁ *Earth's tilt means that the northern and southern hemispheres experience the same seasons, but six months apart. This diagram shows a complete year, with the northern summer on the left and the southern summer on the right.*

A YEARLY DELUGE
In the tropics, there is no such thing as winter, so plants and animals never have to face real cold. But they do have to cope with changing weather, because the seasons often alternate between wet and dry. During the wet season, rain can be incredibly heavy. For example, in Cherrapunji in northeast India,

over 9 m of rain has been recorded in a single month – 15 times more than London receives in an entire year. But at the height of the dry season, places such as Cherrapunji often have no rain at all.

Tropical plants and animals have to adapt to this topsy-turvy weather. Grazing animals feed up in the wet season, when there is lots to eat. But during the dry season, life becomes much tougher, because many plants stop growing and lose their leaves. Predators and scavengers, on the other hand, may do better in the dry season, because prey that is hungry or thirsty finds it harder to escape.

THE FOUR-SEASON WORLD

In the world's temperate regions, there are usually four seasons – spring, summer, autumn and winter. In spring, the days lengthen rapidly and plants put on an impressive burst of growth. This is also a busy time for animals, with millions of migrating birds arriving to breed. By midsummer, most plants have stopped growing and are producing seeds. Autumn is a time of preparation, as the days shorten and temperatures begin to fall. By the time winter arrives, the migrant birds have gone and most of the trees have lost their leaves.

Temperate regions never get very hot or very cold, but their weather is often changeable and difficult to predict. Dry summers may be followed by wet ones, and warm spring weather can often be followed by frost and snow. Plants and animals have to be ready for these changes, so that they can survive whatever the weather brings. Many of them use changes in day length as a guide to when to start growing or when to begin hibernation. Unlike the weather, day length always varies exactly in step with the seasons – so it is a perfect way of keeping time.

ENDLESS LIGHT

Along the Arctic and Antarctic Circles, the sun never sets on midsummer's day, and it never rises in midwinter. Beyond here, spring and autumn become shorter and shorter, and the difference between summer and winter becomes more extreme. At the poles themselves, the sun shines for six months without a break and then sets for a six-month winter rest. In midwinter, the moon is often below the horizon too, so the only light comes from the stars.

As well as coping with darkness and cold, polar wildlife has to put up with extremely strong winds. In earth's windiest place, on the coast of Antarctica, gales can gust at more than 300 km/h, and they keep blowing for days on end. Fortunately, most polar animals live in the seas, where they are sheltered from this icy blast.

△ *These wildebeest may look miserable, but they depend on rainy season downpours to survive. If the rains are light, they will not have enough food to last them the year.*

▽ *This 24-hour sequence was taken on midsummer's day, just north of the Arctic Circle. The sun sinks low in the sky around midnight, but rises again before it has set.*

DEALING WITH DISASTER

IN NATURE, DISASTER CAN STRIKE AT ANY TIME.
UNLIKE HUMANS, PLANTS AND ANIMALS CANNOT
CALL FOR OUTSIDE HELP – INSTEAD, THEY HAVE
TO DEAL WITH DISASTER THEMSELVES.

On 27 August 1883, the biggest volcanic eruption in history blasted apart the Indonesian island of Krakatoa. On nearby islands, forests disappeared under 75 m of burning ash, while on Krakatoa itself, not a single plant or animal is thought to have survived. Fortunately for the earth's wildlife, this kind of catastrophe is very rare. But every year, living things have to cope with all sorts of other hazards, from extreme weather to forest fires.

△ *In the American Midwest, tornadoes cause severe damage each year. Amazingly, insects and other small animals may survive being sucked up inside a tornado's funnel.*

◁ *This lava flow in Hawaii buried a village and obliterated roads. Animals can usually escape slow-flowing lava, but plants are incinerated before being engulfed.*

▽ *At this wildlife refuge in California, lakes often dry up in summer, so animals have to be well prepared. Many freshwater animals shed their eggs in the mud – these hatch when the water returns.*

DEADLY STORMS

When a storm is on the way, the air pressure drops. Some wild animals can sense this, but unless they can fly, they have little chance of escape. For plants the situation is worse still, because they are stuck in one place. So what happens to wildlife when a really powerful storm strikes?

The answer is that it survives surprisingly well. Animals instinctively seek shelter to avoid the worst of the weather and, unlike people, they do not venture out until the storm is over. Floods are more of a problem, because it can be hard to find high ground. For plants, being flexible is often the key to survival. Some palm trees can bend almost horizontal without snapping in two. After the storm, they gradually recover, sprouting new leaves to replace the ones that have been torn away.

EARTHQUAKES AND FIRE

For humans, earthquakes can be deadly, striking without warning and making buildings collapse. But despite their awesome power, they are much less dangerous for wildlife. This is because earthquakes rarely do much damage out in the open.

Fire is a much more serious hazard, so most wild animals take emergency action as soon as they smell smoke. Grazing mammals run away, while burrowing animals head underground. Honeybees return to their nests to

▽ *When floodwaters rise, grazing mammals can find themselves in trouble. Wild mammals can swim to safety, but these farm animals will have to be rescued.*

collect as much honey as they can before abandoning their home.

Compared to animals, plants are often better at surviving the flames, even though their leaves may be burned away. In dry habitats such as shrublands (see pp. 204–211), some plants actually depend on fire to keep other species in check.

DROUGHT-BUSTERS

Natural disasters do not always strike suddenly. Drought is one of the most serious hazards, and it builds up over months or even years. Most dryland species – such as cacti and camels – are good at collecting and conserving water, but they cannot keep going forever if their supplies run out. The champion drought-busters are tiny animals that dry out themselves. Called water bears or

△ *With flames flickering behind them, a group of mules and horses heads away from a fire. Most animals react instantly to the smell of smoke, waking up if they are asleep.*

tardigrades (see p. 155), they can survive droughts that last for years.

WINNING FORMULA

Even after a catastrophe as big as the Krakatoa eruption, wildlife eventually recovers. Within five years, Krakatoa's shattered remains were coming back to life, and today the island is covered by forest once more. Plants and animals can do this because they are good at producing young, and because their young are designed to spread. For living things, breeding is the best kind of insurance, as it gives each species the best chance of survival.

THE EVOLUTION OF LIFE

BY EXAMINING FOSSILS, SCIENTISTS CAN LOOK BACK AT LIFE IN THE DISTANT PAST. THIS RESEARCH SHOWS THAT LIVING THINGS GRADUALLY CHANGE – OR EVOLVE – AS TIME GOES BY.

Evolution happens extremely slowly, so it is hard to see it taking place. But it has left behind a wealth of tell-tale clues. Fossils are the most important, because they tell us about extinct species, and about the way living things have changed. Today's living things also provide clues, because evolution shows up in all kinds of features, from skeletons right down to genes.

THE GREAT DEBATE

Two hundred years ago, most naturalists believed that the world was just a few thousand years old. They also thought that living things, or species, always stayed the same. But as scientists examined rocks and fossils all over the earth, it became clear that the planet is very old, and that all sorts of species had lived in the past and then become extinct. In 1859, an English naturalist called Charles Darwin published a book that made sense

△ *Prehistoric cave paintings, such as this one at Lascaux in France, show that our ancestors lived alongside animals that are now extinct.*

of these discoveries. Called *The Origin of Species*, it put forward the evidence for evolution, and also explained why it occurs.

Since then, evolution has been at the centre of a great debate. On one side, some people reject the entire idea, because it does not fit with their religious beliefs. On the other, many people – including the vast majority of the world's scientists – are equally convinced that evolution does occur.

CHANGE AND ADAPTATION

Two years after Darwin published his book, workers in a German quarry discovered one of the most famous fossils in the world. Known as *Archaeopteryx*, it had wings and feathers, but it also had teeth, fingers with claws, and a long bony tail. *Archaeopteryx* was an early kind of bird, but its teeth, fingers and tail make it different from any bird alive today. Palaeontologists – scientists who study fossils – recognized that *Archaeopteryx* was an extraordinary find that backed up Darwin's ideas. It had clearly evolved from reptiles, but its features showed that it was not a reptile itself.

◁ *Like a crashed plane,* Archaeopteryx *lies spread out in a slab of limestone. This famous fossil is a classic 'intermediate' species – one that links different groups of living things.*

When species evolve, adaptations develop that make them better at particular ways of life. For *Archaeopteryx*, feathers were a key adaptation, because they enabled it to glide, or perhaps to fly. They would also have kept its body warm, and they might even have been used to scoop up dragonflies and other flying insects, which *Archaeopteryx* used as food.

WINNERS AND LOSERS

Adaptations are the nuts and bolts of evolution. They can shape almost any feature of a living thing, from the way it looks to how it behaves. But as Darwin realized, they do not appear in a single lifetime. Instead, they evolve gradually over many generations, through a process called natural selection. Adaptations build up extremely slowly but, given enough time, they can become so important that new species are formed.

△ *Fossils not only show what living things looked like – they can also show when they lived. This palaeontologist is studying the fossil of a* Titanosaurus, *a dinosaur that died out around 66 million years ago.*

Evolution started when life began, and living things started to compete with each other to survive. This process is still at work, creating new adaptations that can help living things to succeed. Extinction is part of evolution, because it clears away the 'losers' and gives new and better-adapted species a chance to prove themselves. Ninety-nine per cent of the world's species – including *Archaeopteryx* itself – are now extinct. But although *Archaeopteryx* died out, other feathered fliers survived, and their descendants now fill the skies.

▽ *Chimps and humans look very different, but we share the same ancestors. About five million years ago, the line that led to humans and the one that led to chimps split apart.*

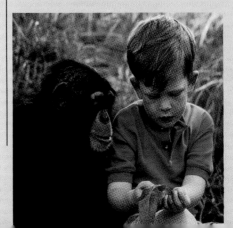

TIMELINE OF LIFE 1

IF EARTH'S ENTIRE HISTORY COULD BE SHRUNK INTO A SINGLE DAY, THE FIRST SIGNS OF LIFE WOULD APPEAR LONG BEFORE DAWN. BUT IT WOULD BE 9.30 IN THE EVENING BEFORE ANIMALS STARTED TO RESEMBLE ANYTHING ALIVE TODAY.

To make sense of earth's immensely long past, scientists divide it up into different stages. The longest of these stages are called eras. Eras are split into periods, and periods are sometimes divided into shorter stages called epochs. During each stage, living things evolved, and they left behind fossils when they died. On these two pages, you can find out how life evolved during the most distant part of the earth's history, from its beginnings until the end of the Paleozoic era, 245 million years ago.

THE ARCHEAN ERA

This part of the earth's history began about 3.8 billion years ago – the age of the oldest known rocks. It lasted for 1.3 billion years, which is just over a quarter of the earth's total existence. Life appeared early in the Archean era, and the earliest definite signs of it are chemical traces found in rocks 3.7 billion years old. The microscopic organisms that left these traces were single-celled, like bacteria today.

THE PROTEROZOIC ERA

Proterozoic means 'earlier life'. In this era, microbes evolved that grew by collecting the energy in sunlight. Known as cyanobacteria or blue-green algae, their descendants are still alive today. Cyanobacteria lived in shallow seas. Some formed large mounds called stromatolites, which left fossils in Proterozoic rocks.

3,800–2,500 mya (million years ago)	PRE-VENDIAN PERIOD 2,500–650 mya	VENDIAN PERIOD 650–540 mya	CAMBRIAN PERIOD 540–505 mya

Sulfolobus
(*heat-loving bacterium*)

Cyanobacteria

Stromatolite

Charnia

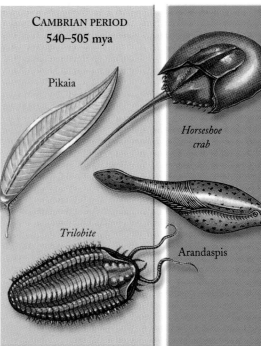

Pikaia

Horseshoe crab

Trilobite

Arandaspis

About one billion years ago, life took a major step forward when the first animals appeared. At first they were tiny, but they were more complex than earlier life-forms because their bodies contained many cells. By the Vendian period, at the end of the Proterozoic era, animal life had become diverse. These early animals included *Charnia*, which looked like a feathery tuft on the seabed.

THE PALEOZOIC ERA

The Paleozoic era – a word that means 'ancient life' – is divided into six periods. The first one, called the Cambrian, was one of the most extraordinary times in earth's history, when animals evolved shells and other hard body parts – a biological revolution that created many new ways of life. These animals included trilobites and other arthropods, molluscs, and early chordates such as *Pikaia*. Chordates had a strengthening rod along their bodies, and they were the ancestors of all animals with backbones, including ourselves.

Marine life continued to expand in the Ordovician period. Some of the largest animals were the nautiloids – a group of molluscs related to today's octopuses and squids. Horseshoe crabs and other arthropods were common, and at the end of the Ordovician, some of these animals took their first steps onto land.

Sea scorpions were the giants of the Silurian period, at nearly 3 m long. Fish such as *Jamoytius* were also common. Early fish had no jaws, but during the Silurian, fish with hinged jaws evolved. Unlike earlier kinds, these could bite off pieces of food.

By the Devonian period, fish had taken over as the largest sea animals.

The 4 m-long *Dunkleosteus* had plate-like teeth that could slice prey in two. But this period brought even bigger developments on land. Four-legged amphibians, which had evolved from fish, adapted to life out of water. *Ichthyostega* was one of the earliest.

During the Carboniferous period, immense forests were home to the earliest flying insects, including cockroaches and giant dragonflies. The first reptiles date from this time, and during the Permian period they became the dominant land animals. *Dimetrodon* and *Edaphosaurus* were two of the biggest. Both had 'sails' on their backs, which they used to regulate their body temperature. The late Permian also saw the rise of the therapsids – reptile-like animals that were the ancestors of mammals – but it ended with a mass extinction that devastated life on earth (see p. 51).

ORDOVICIAN PERIOD
505–438 mya

Nautiloid

SILURIAN PERIOD
438–408 mya

Sea scorpion

Jamoytius

DEVONIAN PERIOD
408–360 mya

Dunkleosteus

Ichthyostega

CARBONIFEROUS PERIOD
360–286 mya

Dragonfly

Lepidodendron (tree-sized clubmoss)

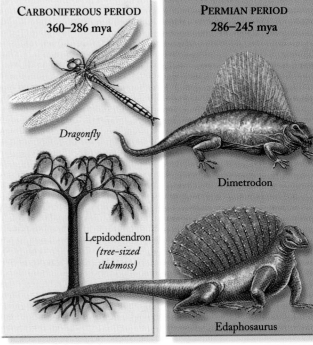

PERMIAN PERIOD
286–245 mya

Dimetrodon

Edaphosaurus

TIMELINE OF LIFE 2

OVER THE PAST 245 MILLION YEARS, ANIMALS AND
PLANTS HAVE LEFT A HUGE TREASURY OF FOSSIL
REMAINS. THEY INCLUDE AWE-INSPIRING RELICS
FROM THE AGE OF REPTILES AND FRAGMENTS
OF EARLY HOMINIDS – APE-LIKE ANIMALS THAT
EVENTUALLY GAVE RISE TO HUMAN BEINGS.

Compared to the timeline on the previous two pages, the one shown here is short. If earth's history were squeezed into a day, it would cover a little over an hour. But during this time, an astounding variety of living things evolved, from flowering plants to the largest animals ever to have existed on land. The timeline covers two geological eras: the Mesozoic, which ended 66 million years ago, and the Cenozoic, which continues into modern times.

THE MESOZOIC ERA

The Mesozoic, or 'middle life' era, is often known as the age of reptiles. Many other animals lived in this era, but reptiles became the largest in the sea, in the air, and on land. Scientists split the Mesozoic into three periods. The first one – known as the Triassic – opened after the Permian mass extinction, a disaster that erased about three-quarters of the animal species on earth.

At the beginning of the Triassic, most of the world's land was joined together in a supercontinent called Pangaea. The climate was warm, and tree ferns, conifers and cycads were common plants. Triassic reptiles included some of the first gliding vertebrates. Evolution also produced bizarre animals such as *Tanystropheus*, which probably used its amazingly long neck to fish from the shore.

TRIASSIC PERIOD
245–208 mya
(million years ago)

Tanystropheus

Tree fern

JURASSIC PERIOD
208–144 mya

Ichthyosaur

Archaeopteryx

Allosaurus

CRETACEOUS PERIOD
144–66 mya

Velociraptor

Magnolia

TERTIARY PERIOD
Paleocene epoch
66–58 mya

Mesohippus

TERTIARY PERIOD
Eocene epoch
58–36 mya

Diatryma

Grass

Dinosaurs evolved towards the end of the Triassic, but the Jurassic period marked the height of their reign. As the climate became more moist, some plant-eating species reached an incredible size. These herbivores provided prey for some equally impressive predators, including *Allosaurus*, which weighed up to three tonnes. Birds evolved from feathered dinosaurs, and the earliest ones date back to Jurassic times.

Flowering plants appeared in the Cretaceous period, triggering a burst of evolution in the insect world. Flying reptiles, called pterosaurs, soared through the sky on leathery wings. One species, *Quetzalcoatlus*, had a wingspan of 12 m, making it almost certainly the largest flying animal ever. Among the dinosaurs, small hunters, such as *Velociraptor*, lived alongside tyrannosaurs, the

largest land predators of the time. But 66 million years ago, earth was struck by a giant meteorite, bringing the age of reptiles to a cataclysmic end.

The Cenozoic era

During this era, life recovered from the Cretaceous mass extinction. Mammals began to fill the roles that reptiles had taken before, becoming so successful that the Cenozoic is often known as the mammal age.

The earliest mammals fed on insects and other small animals, but in the Tertiary period, large plant-eating kinds evolved. Grasses developed early in the Tertiary, enabling some mammals to adopt herding lifestyles in open grassland and wooded savanna. These animals included the forerunners of today's horses, as well as far bigger animals, such as *Brontotherium*, and the first

elephants. Birds also gained from the disappearance of the dinosaurs. The large, flightless *Diatryma* was almost certainly a predator, ripping prey to pieces with a massive hooked beak. Towards the end of the Tertiary, primates called australopithecines appeared in Africa. One of these ape-like animals was our direct ancestor.

During the early Quaternary period, the climate became colder and a long Ice Age began. Mammals adapted to the changing conditions, and some highly specialized kinds evolved. One was *Smilodon*, a sabre-toothed cat that killed its prey with serrated teeth up to 18 cm long. Humans first appeared about 500,000 years ago. At first, they collected wild food and hunted, but by the end of the Ice Age, 10,000 years ago, they began to farm. Since then, our species has changed the world.

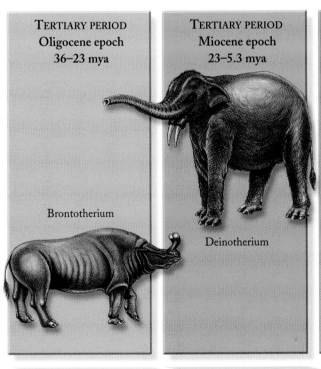

TERTIARY PERIOD
Oligocene epoch
36–23 mya

Brontotherium

TERTIARY PERIOD
Miocene epoch
23–5.3 mya

Deinotherium

TERTIARY PERIOD
Pliocene epoch
5.3–1.6 mya

Australopithecus

QUATERNARY PERIOD
Pleistocene epoch
1.6 mya–10,000 ya

Smilodon

Irish elk

QUATERNARY PERIOD
Holocene epoch
10,000 ya–present

Modern human

Domestic dog

CENOZOIC ERA

How evolution works 1

FOSSILS SHOW THAT LIVING THINGS EVOLVE, BUT THEY DO NOT EXPLAIN HOW OR WHY EVOLUTION OCCURS. AS CHARLES DARWIN DISCOVERED, THE ANSWERS TO BOTH QUESTIONS CAN BE FOUND BY LOOKING CLOSELY AT THE NATURAL WORLD.

△ *For both the largest and the smallest creatures, every day is a struggle for survival. For these tadpoles, life has got off to a particularly difficult start, because their pond is starting to dry up.*

In the mid-1800s, when Charles Darwin wrote *The Origin of Species*, he showed that evolution takes place and he explained why it happens. Darwin's breakthrough came when he realized that living things struggle to survive, and that in this struggle, some will be better than others at surviving and producing young. Because these 'winners' leave more offspring, their features will become more common. In other words, their species will slowly change.

TOUGH TIMES AHEAD
A female common frog lays about a thousand eggs and from the moment the eggs hatch, an intense struggle for survival begins. Some of the tadpoles die within hours because they are attacked by waterborne fungi, or because they cannot find enough food. Others meet their end when they are swallowed by fish and other predators. By the time the tadpoles have turned into frogs, only a few dozen will be left. But even for the survivors, life is not simple. Some will die of hunger, while those that wander too far from water will die by drying out. Even if they avoid these fates, they still run the risk of being eaten by foxes or birds. After three or four years, only a handful of frogs will be left alive and ready to become parents themselves.

But who are these winners? The answer is quite simple – they are those which are 'fittest' and have what it takes to survive.

INHERITED VARIATIONS
To us, one common frog looks very much like another. The same is true of almost all living things. But because most things have two parents, they inherit a mixture of genes (see p. 42). This gives them different features so that they have a variety of strengths and weaknesses in the struggle to survive. Useful genes are likely to be passed on, because their owners are more likely to breed.

(see p. 42)

On the other hand, unhelpful genes are less likely to spread, because many of their owners will not survive to breed at all.

▽ *Because life is hazardous, parents in nature always produce plenty of young. A dandelion plant can grow up to 30 seed-heads, or 'clocks'. Each one contains enough seeds for over 100 new dandelion plants.*

△ *For lynx and hares, speed is essential to survive. Lynx have evolved muscles for sprinting, but hares have extremely sharp eyesight and hearing, so they often have a head start in the race to escape.*

Although Darwin knew nothing about genes, he knew a lot about the variations in living things. He realized that these variations could be inherited and that useful ones could build up over time. Variations create adaptations – features that help living things to survive. Over time, as these adaptations build up, species evolve.

NATURAL SELECTION

In the struggle for survival, nature favours those that are good at caring for themselves and producing young. Darwin called this process natural selection. Natural selection works automatically without anything at the controls. Sometimes natural selection favours individuals that are extra strong or fast. For example, lynx have been 'selected' for their speed because they sprint to catch their food. But being strong and fast is not always a recipe for success. Many insects are successful because they are so small. They often succeed because they keep still, instead of running or flying away.

Natural selection can also favour different ways of raising a family. Many species – from oak trees to frogs – put all their energy into producing lots of young, but none into helping them survive. Mammals are the opposite. They have smaller families and they work hard to give their young a successful start in life.

NEW SPECIES

Natural selection is constantly picking its way through all the tiny variations in living things. In the short term, the changes are so small that they do not have a noticeable effect. But given more time, they can have a much bigger impact. For example, one original species can evolve into several, each adapted for a different way of life.

Charles Darwin stumbled across a famous example of this when he visited the Galapagos Islands in 1835. He found a dozen species of finch, all different, but at the same time they were suspiciously similar. As Darwin later realized, the finches had all evolved from a single species, which had become stranded on the islands long ago.

▽ *Near the remains of a fallen tree, a young coconut sprouts its first leaves. Like all living things, its chances of survival will depend on two things – the genes that it inherited from its parents, and luck.*

▽ *Female scorpions carry their young until they are ready to live on their own. Caring for a family makes life harder for parents, but it improves the chances that some of their young will survive.*

HOW EVOLUTION WORKS 2

UNLIKE A HUMAN DESIGNER, EVOLUTION NEVER STARTS FROM SCRATCH. INSTEAD, IT TAKES FEATURES THAT ALREADY EXIST AND ADAPTS THEM FOR NEW WAYS OF LIFE. AS A RESULT, EVERY LIVING THING CONTAINS REMINDERS OF ITS EVOLUTIONARY PAST.

Humans are great planners. Before we make something, we decide how it is going to work and then we select the best possible materials for the job. But evolution works in a very different way because the force that drives it – natural selection – cannot plan ahead at all. As a result, evolution follows an unpredictable path. It can turn one adaptation into many different ones, and it can also backtrack, dropping something that it has previously made.

△ *The speed at which evolution works varies. The coelacanth has changed very little in the last 65 million years. Slow-changing species, known as 'living fossils', include plants, microbes and animals.*

LOOKING AT LIMBS

One of the best examples of the ingenuity of evolution can be seen in vertebrate limbs. Vertebrates are animals with backbones, and their limbs include legs, flippers, fins and wings. From the outside these limbs look very different, and they work in different ways. But vertebrate limbs are all built on the same plan, and in scientific terms they are said to be 'homologous'. This means that they all contain the same underlying skeleton inherited from the same distant ancestor that lived long ago – regardless of whether the limbs are long, short, fat or flat. Homologous structures provide strong evidence that different species are related.

Analagous structures are ones that do similar jobs, but which are built in different ways. For example, both birds and bees have wings, but birds' wings are made of bones and feathers, while bees' wings are made of a filmy substance called chitin. These two very different patterns show that birds and bees are not close relatives.

▽ Unlike some flightless birds, ostriches still use their wings. They raise or lower them to adjust their body temperature. Male ostriches also spread them out to attract females.

DROP IT!

In evolution, adaptations have to pull their weight. When an adaptation stops being useful, natural selection starts to act against it, and it falls out of use. Eventually, an adaptation can stop working altogether, although it takes a long time for it to disappear completely.

This is exactly what happened with ostriches and other flightless birds. Millions of years ago, their ancestors could fly, but as time went by they developed lifestyles that involved less time in the air. The forerunners of ostriches took up life on Africa's open plains, and instead of flying away from danger, they started to run away. Over many generations, natural selection built up their leg muscles and shrank the muscles that flapped their wings. Today, ostriches have very weak wing muscles and their flight feathers are soft and fluffy, instead of stiff and strong. Even with its wings outstretched, an ostrich has no hope of getting off the ground.

PRECISION ENGINEERING

The natural world is full of adaptations that have been jettisoned in this way. Some reptiles have no legs, while many cave-dwelling animals have only tiny eyes. Humans also have a collection of evolutionary leftovers – for example, some of our scalp muscles were originally used to move our ears.

But how did really complicated organs, such as eyes and ears, evolve in the first place? Could natural selection ever produce something as sophisticated as these? The answer – most biologists believe – is a definite 'yes'. Like all other adaptations, eyes and ears would have evolved

Seal

Bat

△ Although seals and bats are very different from one another in appearance, and their bones are also different in shape and size, they both have skeletons that follow the same underlying plan. This similarity in skeleton shows that they have evolved from the same ancestors, which lived long ago.

in a series of tiny steps, and at each stage, they would have been a useful feature to have. A look at today's animals shows that eyes vary enormously – some are so simple that they can only tell light from dark. But in the distant future, natural selection could convert these into eyes just as complex as our own.

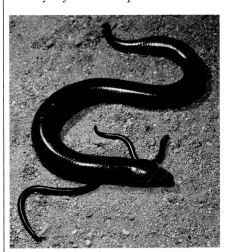

△ Some lizards have gradually lost their legs to suit a burrowing lifestyle. The giant legless skink, from southern Africa, can reach a length of 55 cm. This adult female is flanked by two of her young.

GENES AND DNA

WHEN SCIENTISTS FIRST STUDIED EVOLUTION, THEY HAD NO IDEA HOW LIVING THINGS INHERIT FEATURES FROM THEIR PARENTS. TODAY, AFTER 50 YEARS OF GROUND-BREAKING RESEARCH, WE KNOW THAT IT IS THROUGH GENES AND DNA.

Nucleus

Y ou do not have to be a scientist to know that cats produce kittens and that hens produce chicks, and not the other way around. But what makes young animals – or plants – like their parents? And why are some features, such as eye colour, passed on without being blended together and mixed up? Until the 1950s, these questions were difficult to answer, because no one knew how cells store the instructions' needed to make living things. Then, in 1953, scientists unravelled the structure of DNA, and the answers fell into place.

△ *The two strands in a DNA molecule spiral around each other like a twisted ladder. Each rung in the ladder is made by chemicals called bases, which fit together in pairs. The bases work like letters, spelling out the instructions that the DNA contains.*

HOW DNA WORKS
DNA, or deoxyribonucleic acid, is a remarkable substance. It is the only chemical that can copy itself, and it is also one of the few that can store information. DNA is found in all living cells, and it copies itself when cells divide, so that its instructions can be handed on.

Most chemicals always have the same structure – in other words, their atoms are always arranged in exactly the same way. But DNA is different. Its molecules have a 'backbone' of two spiral strands, held together by chemicals called bases. The spiral strands are always the same, but there are four different types of base, and they can be arranged in any order. These bases work like a four-letter alphabet, spelling out instructions. Before a cell divides, the two strands unwind and each one makes a new partner strand. In this way, the instructions are passed on.

FOLLOWING INSTRUCTIONS
Unlike a set of printed instructions, a DNA molecule is not divided up by paragraphs or by headings. But DNA does have its own punctuation. Special sequences of bases act like start and stop signs.

△ *Animals inherit a set of genes from each of their parents. This cat has inherited genes for a tabby coat and ones for green eyes. It will pass them on when it breeds.*

△ *This cat has inherited a gene that gives high levels of melanin in its coat. Melanin is a black pigment that is common in fur, feathers and skin.*

◁ *In most cells, DNA is stored inside the cell's nucleus, or control centre. Each cell has several DNA molecules, packaged up in X-shaped structures called chromosomes.*

Cell

△ *These trees belong to the same species, but each one has inherited slightly different versions of the same genes, giving each tree different chances in the struggle for survival.*

The same cat might also inherit white paws from one of its grandparents, even though neither of its parents has white paws themselves. This happens because some alleles can be masked by others disappearing for a generation or more until they are unmasked again.

THE FULL STORY
Genes control a huge range of features, but they do not decide exactly how everything looks and lives. The outside world plays a part as well. For example, if an animal is well fed it will reach its maximum possible size, but if it goes hungry it will be underweight. Animals inherit instinctive behaviour, which is programmed by their genes. But many animals also learn some of their behaviour, and this depends on experience. Plants are even more variable. Their shape depends partly on their genes, but also a great deal on the conditions where they grow.

showing where each instruction begins and ends. These instructions are known as genes. There can be several thousand genes in a single DNA molecule. Together, a complete set of genes contains all the information needed to build up a living thing, and to keep it running.

The instructions programmed by genes are extremely varied. Some genes decide physical features,

inherit a unique collection of alleles, which are slightly different versions of the same genes. As a result, they have their own different characteristics. This kind of variation is very important, because it allows species to evolve.

such as the colour of eyes or skin. Many control the speed of chemical processes, while some act as 'master' genes, by turning other genes on or off. A few come into action only in emergencies – for example, suicide genes make cells self-destruct if they come under attack by a virus.

NATURAL VARIATIONS
If two animals or two plants have the same genes, they will be identical in almost every way. This does happen in nature, but it is not common. Instead, most living things

Genetic variation comes about mainly through sexual reproduction. In this kind of reproduction, alleles from two parents are combined and shuffled, creating a new combination that is handed on. For example, a cat may inherit black fur from one parent and green eyes from the other.

▷ *Unlike most cells, bacterial cells have a single, looping DNA molecule. This bacterium has been specially treated to make its DNA spill out of its single cell. DNA molecules are extremely slender, but they can measure several centimetres long.*

ADAPTING TO SURVIVE 1

THERE ARE MORE THAN TWO MILLION KINDS –
OR SPECIES – OF LIVING THINGS ON EARTH,
AND NO TWO ARE EXACTLY THE SAME. THAT
IS BECAUSE EACH ONE HAS FOLLOWED ITS OWN
PATH IN EVOLUTION, AND DEVELOPED DIFFERENT
ADAPTATIONS FOR SURVIVAL.

If living things were perfectly equipped for their way of life, they would never need to change. But in nature, nothing is ever perfect. Instead, natural selection works all the time, giving a boost to any feature that helps in the struggle for survival. It has been doing this for more than three billion years, so it has had time to come up with an amazing variety of adaptations. Wherever you look in the natural world, these adaptations are all around. Some are eyecatching and easy to understand, but others are harder to spot, and work in unexpected ways.

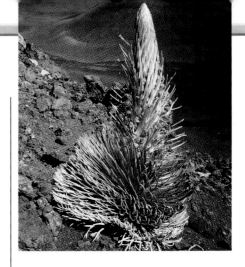

△ The silversword plant has evolved adaptations for life high up, where the sunlight can be intense. Thanks to these, silverswords can live in a habitat where few other plants are able to survive.

LIGHT WORK
The ash-strewn slopes of a volcano and the swirling water off a rocky coast could hardly be more different habitats – which is why their plants and animals have evolved in

△ Crouching on a leaf, this spider looks exactly like a bird dropping. This kind of adaptation makes the spider less likely to be eaten.

▷ Each one of a giant kelp's leafy fronds has an inbuilt, gas-filled float. The floats hold up the whole plant, which can be dozens of metres long.

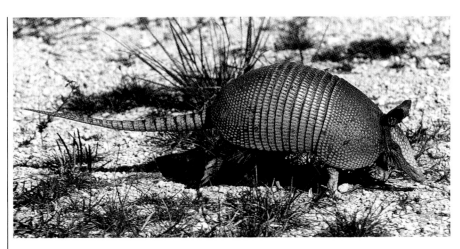

different ways. In the Hawaiian Islands, the silversword plant grows on some of the highest volcanoes on earth. Its leaves are covered with fur-like hairs, which help to stop it being burned by the dazzling sunshine. But off the rocky coast of California, a seaweed called giant kelp has the opposite problem. To reach light, it needs to grow upwards through 50 m of water. How does it do this? By forming gas-filled floats, which keep the plant upright as it grows.

ANIMAL ADAPTATIONS

Evolution has been even more inventive in the animal world. Unlike plants, animals move, and they also eat food, so natural selection has been able to develop

△ *Aye-ayes use their unusual fingers to forage for food after dark. Like many highly specialized animals, they are easily harmed when humans interfere with their habitat.*

some very specialized adaptations for their different ways of life.

Our fingers are one example, as they allow us to pick up and hold things in countless different ways. But when it comes to fingerwork, even we do not match up to the aye-aye – a strange-looking primate from the forests of Madagascar. Like us, the aye-aye has four fingers and a thumb. But the middle finger is much longer and thinner than the rest, and the aye-aye uses it like

a bony drumstick, tapping on branches as it climbs through trees. If the sound is promising, the aye-aye picks away the wood and tweaks out insect grubs living inside.

HIDING AWAY

Natural selection has created all kinds of unusual body parts, from skinny fingers to mouthparts that work like harpoons. But it can work with whole bodies too. The animal world is full of species that are incredibly well camouflaged, thanks to specially adapted body cases, shells or skin. Some species blend in with their background, while others mimic something that is either inedible or dangerous to eat.

Animal camouflage can be amazingly convincing, but it is not too hard to work out how it evolves. If an animal is better at hiding than its relatives, it is less likely to be spotted and eaten, so it will leave more young. In the next generation, the best camouflaged animals will also be best at surviving. Repeated thousands or millions of times, this process has created the extraordinary disguises that animals have today.

ANIMAL ARMOUR

During the history of life, armoured animals have evolved many times. Today, they include animals such as pangolins, armadillos and tortoises.

△ *Protected by its portable armour, an armadillo takes a stroll. The armour is made of small, bony plates that cover most of the armadillo's body except its underside.*

In the past they included much bigger species such as glyptodonts, which were built like living tanks. Because animal armour has evolved so often, scientists say that there is a strong selection for it. In other words, it is an adaptation that gives a very good chance of success.

But unlike armour, some animal adaptations are shown by only a few species, or even just one. The aye-aye's fingers are one example, and so are the shells of molluscs called piddocks. The shells have sharpened edges, and a piddock uses them like a drill bit to bore a tunnel through wood or rock. Humans use drills all the time but, as the piddock shows, nature got there first.

△ *Piddocks filter their food from seawater, and they use their sharp-edged shells to drill themselves a safe home. An adult piddock cannot leave its burrow, because its shell is wider than the entrance.*

ADAPTING TO SURVIVE 2

ADAPTATIONS DO NOT ONLY AFFECT THE WAY LIVING THINGS LOOK. IN ANIMALS, SOME OF THE MOST IMPORTANT ADAPTATIONS ARE ONES THAT INVOLVE BEHAVIOUR.

△ *Hibernation is an adaptation of behaviour. It helps dormice to survive through the winter, when food is scarce.*

Unlike longer legs or sharper teeth, behaviour may not sound like an adaptation. You cannot pick up and examine it, and it does not fossilize when animals die. But behaviour can be inherited, which means it may change or evolve over time. This kind of behaviour is known as instinct, and it is programmed into an animal's genes. Like all other adaptations, instinct has developed over millions of years, and it helps animals survive.

FITTING IN

When animals first evolved, their behaviour was extremely simple. They moved towards food, and away from anything that might be dangerous. But as animals started to become more complicated, their behaviour became more complicated too. They evolved sense organs to find out about their surroundings, and patterns of behaviour that gave them the best chance of survival.

Millions of years later, these patterns – or instincts – still control the way most animals live. Spiders rush towards struggling flies, but if they are threatened, they head for somewhere dark. Honeybees fly towards the smell of flowers, but away from the smell of smoke. In autumn, many animals go into hibernation – a deep sleep that lasts

▽ *Spiders use complicated behaviour to spin webs and catch prey. This orb-weaver spider has caught an insect, and has stopped it struggling by wrapping it up in a bag of silk.*

until the following spring. Animals do not have to learn this kind of behaviour, because it comes built-in.

Just like other adaptations, behaviour often reveals glimpses of a species' past. For example, pet dogs often walk around in a circle before lying down – behaviour inherited from their ancestors, which used it to flatten plants into a comfortable bed.

BEHAVIOUR AND BODY PARTS

In the animal world, behaviour and body parts often evolve together.

▽ *A Weddell seal's breathing hole is its lifeline – without it, survival is impossible. The seal starts the hole when the ice is shallow, but by the end of the winter it can be up to 2 m deep.*

△ *Beavers seem to understand a lot about dam building, but they work entirely by instinct. They can make a tree fall in exactly the right direction by chewing through the opposite side.*

Just like body parts, these building skills have evolved as well. When birds first appeared, for example, they almost certainly laid their eggs on the ground – just like most reptiles do today. But as time went by, and birds became more agile, some of them started to nest off the ground. Today, more than 100 million years later, birds include some of the best builders on earth.

uses for standard animal equipment. This has happened with the Weddell seal. Its ancestors moved into the seas off Antarctica about 15 million years ago, when the climate was much warmer than it is now. As Antarctica became colder, more and more of the sea became covered by winter ice. The Weddell seal survives in this frozen habitat thanks to its teeth, which it uses for gouging out breathing holes in the ice. Without this behavioural adaptation, most Weddell seals would die out.

BRANCHING OUT
Evolution also affects the way animals build. The first animals built nothing, but as time went by, their descendants evolved special construction skills. Today's animals build all kinds of shelters, nests and traps – find out about some of them on pages 150–151.

This makes good sense, because without the right behaviour, many body parts would be no use at all. Complicated behaviour controls legs and wings, but some of the most intricate kinds are used for catching food. Spiders, for example, use several different types of silk to make their webs, but they do not have to be taught which type goes where. When they make a catch, they identify their prey by its movements, instinctively recognizing the difference between a fly and a wasp with a dangerous sting.

Sometimes, evolution creates new

▷ *Sometimes, an animal's behaviour allows it to make use of new opportunities. White storks originally nested in trees, but in Europe they often nest on rooftops instead. Many other birds – including swallows and swifts – nest inside buildings.*

SHARED SOLUTIONS

IN THE LIVING WORLD, SPECIES THAT LIVE IN
SIMILAR WAYS OFTEN EVOLVE SIMILAR ADAPTATIONS.
THIS CREATES SOME REMARKABLE LOOKALIKES –
ONES THAT EVEN SCIENTISTS CAN MUDDLE UP.

▽ *The baseball plant (top) and the golden barrel cactus (below) are amazingly alike. But the baseball plant comes from southern Africa – a part of the world where wild cactuses do not exist. It is short and dumpy, but some of its relatives from wetter places grow into shrubs and trees.*

Take a close look at the two plants in the centre of this page. Both have a barrel-like shape and are protected by spines. They both live in deserts and store water in their stems. Unless you are an expert on desert plants, you would think that they are close relatives. In fact, they are very different. One is a cactus from Mexico, the other is a baseball plant from southern Africa. They look the same because they have adapted to a very similar way of life.

△ *Mantis flies (top) and praying mantises (bottom) both have front legs that grab and stab prey, but they are not closely related. They have developed the same leg design separately, through convergent evolution.*

NATURE'S COPYCATS

Like an inventor that never runs out of ideas, evolution is good at creating adaptations. It can even produce the same adaptation in two quite different things. This usually happens when different species share a similar lifestyle, so that natural selection works on them in similar ways. The result is called convergent evolution – a gradual change that makes two species look more and more alike.

The cactus and the baseball plant are two examples of species that have 'converged', even though they live thousands of kilometres apart. Their rounded shape helps them to conserve water, while their spines keep hungry animals at bay. They have other similarities too – both have long roots, and neither grows leaves. Altogether, these adaptations help them to survive in a habitat that can be dry for months at a time.

HIDDEN HISTORIES

The world is full of convergent species – some are illustrated on these two pages. Many look only slightly similar, while others are close enough for people to confuse them. For example, whales and dolphins look very much like fish, because they have streamlined bodies, and flippers instead of legs. Several centuries ago, most people thought they were all the same.

Deep down, however, convergent species are always different, because they have evolved from different starting points. Fish are cold-blooded, and they breathe by collecting oxygen through gills.

◁ *Limpets (left) and barnacles (right) both live in exposed places, where they are often pounded by waves. Limpets are protected by a shell, but barnacles have a case made up of separate plates. Although it is not built like a shell, the barnacle case does the same job.*

But the ancestors of whales and dolphins were warm-blooded land mammals that took up life in the sea. Over millions of years, these mammals adapted to their new habitat, and they gradually developed a fish-like shape.

But evolution could not disguise their past. That is why whales and dolphins still raise their young on milk, and why they come to the surface to breathe air.

CAUSING CONFUSION

Convergent evolution can create problems when scientists try to classify living things. It is not too hard to work out that a dolphin is a mammal, but some lookalikes are more convincing than this. For example, barnacles spend their adult lives fastened to rocks, and they have pointed shells that protect them from the waves. They look like molluscs, and early naturalists believed that is exactly what they were. However, young barnacles start life in the open sea, and they are equipped with lots of legs. A close look shows that barnacles are actually crustaceans – in other words, relatives of lobsters and crabs.

Things get even more tricky when related species evolve in the same way, because they have lots in common to begin with. To unravel their ancestry, scientists cannot rely on appearances – instead, they often track the path of evolution by looking at their DNA.

CONVERGENCE PAST AND PRESENT

Today's lookalikes are only part of the story, because convergent evolution has been at work for a very long time. In prehistory, animals called pyrotheres looked very similar to elephants, while further back in time, reptiles called placodonts looked just like turtles because they evolved the same rounded, scale-covered shells. But some of the best examples of convergence occur in

pouched mammals, or marsupials. Sabre-toothed marsupials, from South America, looked just like sabre-toothed cats, and marsupials called borhyaenids looked amazingly similar to wolves and bears. The most recent of these carnivorous

△ *A dolphin (top) and a tuna (below) both have streamlined, muscle-packed bodies, and both feed on fish in open water. But dolphins are relative newcomers to life in the sea. The fact that they breathe air shows that their ancestors once lived on land.*

lookalikes died out in the 1930s. Called the Tasmanian wolf, or thylacine, this unusual animal was the largest marsupial predator to survive into modern times. To see what it looked like, turn the page.

EXTINCTION

WHEN SOMETHING DIES, ITS DESCENDANTS USUALLY LIVE ON. BUT WHEN THE LAST MEMBER OF A SPECIES DIES, THAT SPECIES VANISHES FOREVER. EXTINCTION IS A NATURAL PART OF EVOLUTION, AND EXTINCT SPECIES OUTNUMBER LIVING ONES BY ROUGHLY ONE HUNDRED TO ONE.

△ For more than 130 million years, pterosaurs were the world's largest flying animals, with wingspans of up to 12 m. Despite conquering the skies, these leathery-winged reptiles died out at the same time as the dinosaurs, about 66 million years ago.

During the history of life on earth, millions of species have evolved and millions have become extinct. Extinction is normally a slow process, so there is plenty of time for new species to evolve. But, just occasionally, huge numbers of species die out together when disasters or climate change strike. Today, extinction is a hot topic, because human activities are making species extinct at an ever-increasing rate.

FINAL EXITS
In the early 1800s, the thylacine was a common animal. This wolf-like marsupial lived in Tasmania, where it fed on wallabies, birds and other wild prey. But when farming began on the island, thylacines developed a taste for sheep. Farmers fought back to protect their flocks, and by the 1880s, thylacines were becoming rare.

▽ Although thylacines have vanished forever, we have a good idea of what they looked like. Some were stuffed and put in museums. One was even recorded on film.

By 1933, the situation reached crisis point. The thylacine population was down to one – an animal in Hobart zoo. When this sole survivor died three years later, Tasmania's marsupial 'wolf' became extinct.

In North America, the passenger pigeon suffered an even more dramatic fate. In 1810, it was the world's most numerous bird – one single flock was estimated to be two billion birds strong. These gigantic flocks migrated across the continent to feed, and when the pigeons roosted or nested, their weight could bring branches crashing to the ground. But passenger pigeons made easy targets, and large-scale hunting soon began. The last known specimen died in 1914.

◁ Before they were wiped out, passenger pigeons fed mainly on acorns, and nested in giant colonies up to 30 km across.

These two stories show how easy it is for species to die out. The thylacine and passenger pigeon were both well adapted, and had existed for hundreds of thousands of years. But evolution could not prepare them for a new enemy – humans carrying guns.

FADING OUT
In nature, it is very rare for species to die out as quickly as this. Instead, they normally go into a slow decline, which gives better-adapted species time to take their place. In the

◁ Clustered around a female, male golden toads fight for the chance to mate. This photograph was taken in the 1980s, in the Monteverde cloud forest of Costa Rica. A few years later, the species mysteriously disappeared.

elephant family, for example, dozens of different species have evolved and become extinct over the last 50 million years. They included giant mammoths and mastodons, as well as dwarf elephants just 1 m high. The most recent elephantine extinction involved the woolly mammoth, which died out only 6,000 years ago. It evolved during the last Ice Age, but did not manage to adapt when warmer times returned.

Species that live in small areas are particularly at risk if life gets tough or if humans change their habitat. This is what happened to the dodo, a giant flightless pigeon from the island of Mauritius. It was hunted by human settlers, and its young were eaten by introduced animals, such as cats. It became extinct in 1681. Species that live on 'islands' inland can also suffer. In Costa Rica, for example, the golden toad lived in one small patch of forest high up in the mountains. During the breeding season, hundreds of toads used to gather in forest pools, but in the early 1990s, the species disappeared.

▷ This chart shows how extinction rates have varied over the last 545 million years. Not all mass extinctions happened quickly – some probably took tens or even hundreds of thousands of years. Species in the sea were often harder hit than ones on land.

MASS EXTINCTIONS

Two possible explanations for why the golden toad vanished are disease and water pollution. But every so often in the earth's history, far more catastrophic events have wiped out a large slice of the living world. The most famous of these mass extinctions occurred about 66 million years ago, when a 10 km-wide meteorite slammed into the earth. Dinosaurs and pterosaurs died out completely, creating new opportunities for mammals and birds.

An even greater mass extinction occurred about 245 million years ago. Nearly three-quarters of the world's species disappeared. This extinction was probably caused by several factors, including volcanic eruptions, climate change and a record drop in sea levels. Life eventually recovered, but it took millions of years.

Despite the ever-present threat of extinction, the living world harbours some surprising survivors. Scientists were stunned to discover a living coelacanth (see p. 40) in 1938, because this fish was thought to have been extinct for millions of years. In the plant world, a tree called the dawn redwood was discovered in 1944 – another example of an 'extinct' species coming back to life.

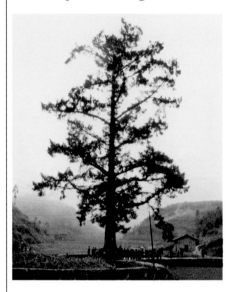

△ The dawn redwood was discovered by a forestry official in a remote part of China in the 1940s. Since then, examples of this 'living fossil' have been successfully grown in parks all over the world.

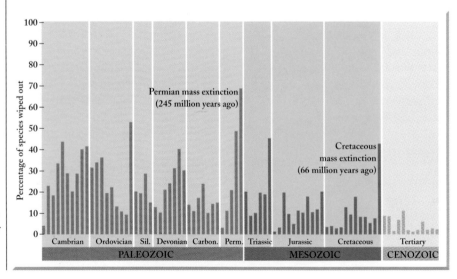

WILDLIFE UNDER THREAT

TODAY'S PLANTS AND ANIMALS LIVE IN A FAST-CHANGING WORLD. THERE ARE MORE PEOPLE THAN BEFORE, AND WE ARE HAVING AN EVER-INCREASING EFFECT ON OTHER LIVING THINGS. AS A RESULT, MANY SPECIES ARE FINDING IT HARD TO SURVIVE.

△ An Australian customs agent demonstrates a vest that has been specially adapted for smuggling parrot eggs. The vest keeps the eggs warm during their journey overseas.

∇ Every year, millions of seahorses are caught, dried and then exported to the Far East. They are easy to catch, and many tropical species are disappearing fast.

Fifty years ago, there were probably 100,000 black rhinos in Africa. Today, there are about 3,000. In 1900, there were eight different subspecies of tiger. Today, there are only five. Altogether, over 5,000 kinds of animals are in serious danger of extinction, along with at least as many plants. Numbers like this make grim reading. They explain why many people are concerned about the world's wildlife – and why we need to act urgently.

△ In England, the swallowtail butterfly once thrived in marshy places. But when marshes were drained to make way for fields, the swallowtail began to decline.

∇ Harpy eagles feed on monkeys and sloths. They can survive only in undisturbed tropical forest with tall nesting trees.

SHRINKING HOMES

The greatest threat facing wildlife is habitat change. Forests are cut down, marshlands are drained, and open spaces are covered by buildings and roads. A third of the earth's surface has already been changed in this way, and more is swallowed up each year.

All across the world, changes like this have hit animals and plants. Small animals, such as butterflies, are easily harmed by habitat change, but the real losers are animals like the harpy eagle, which need an immense amount of space. Harpy eagles are huge birds, and each breeding pair needs up to 250 square kilometres of forest to find enough food. At a time when tropical forests are being cut down, that much space is not easy to find.

THE WILDLIFE TRADE

People, as well as animals and plants, need living space. As the human population increases, we will need even more farmland to grow enough food. But habitat change is not the only problem facing the world's animals – many species are also targeted by the wildlife trade. Sometimes the victims are living animals, which are sold as performing animals or pets. But more often the trade is in body parts, which include all kinds of things, from horns and bones to skins and eggs.

At one time, spotted cats were high on the list of targets, because their fur was in demand for making coats. Fortunately, fur is not so fashionable now, but the demand for body parts still claims millions of animal lives each year. Black rhinos are killed for their horns, while elephants are hunted for their ivory. Tiger bones, bear paws, seahorses and snakes are all used in oriental medicines. Birds' eggs are bought by collectors who are more interested in eggs than in living birds. Much of this trade is illegal, but high prices on the black market make it difficult to prevent.

ANIMAL INVADERS

Poachers and collectors are usually aware that they are breaking the law. But wildlife can also be harmed accidentally, when people move plants or animals between different parts of the world. This is what happened in Australia, when European settlers introduced cats, rabbits and foxes about 200 years ago. These mammalian invaders spread quickly, and they had a devastating impact on small marsupials in Australia.

Many non-native animals are introduced deliberately, but some

▷ On the island of Borneo, a wildlife worker looks after a baby orang utan. The orang's mother was killed when her forest home was set on fire.

species hitch a lift instead. In North America, one of the most problematic is a small, stripy mollusc called the zebra mussel, which arrived from Europe in 1985. It travelled aboard a ship heading for the Great Lakes, and was flushed out when the ship emptied its ballast tanks. Since then, zebra mussels have managed to spread throughout the Great Lakes, clogging up the intakes of power stations, sinking buoys and swamping the feeding grounds of fish. If they spread much further, scientists think that several kinds of freshwater fish could eventually become extinct.

ENDANGERED PLANTS

Compared to animals, plants do not often hit the headlines, but many of them are endangered too. If anything, they are even more important, because animals often rely on particular plants for their food. Plants are threatened by being cut down or collected, and they can be at risk from other plants as well. In remote places, such as the Hawaiian Islands, introduced plants are a beautiful but deadly menace. Over 95 per cent of Hawaii's native plants are found nowhere else in the world, but already some are on the verge of extinction, as green invaders take over their home.

▷ Dark areas show the black rhino's range today, compared with its range in 1900 (light purple).

◁ Wildlife rangers examine the body of a black rhino that has been killed by poachers. The poachers started to cut off the rhino's horn, but were disturbed before they finished.

BACK FROM THE BRINK

WHEN A SPECIES IS ON THE EDGE OF EXTINCTION, EMERGENCY ACTION CAN SOMETIMES SAVE IT FROM OBLIVION. IT IS DEMANDING WORK, BUT RESCUE PROJECTS ARE NEVER SHORT OF VOLUNTEERS.

△ *Once common, prairie dogs now depend on human protection for survival.*

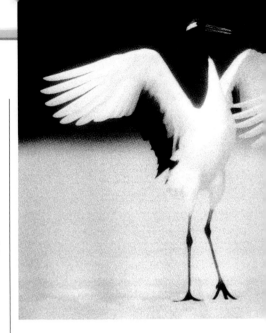

△ *Two Japanese cranes dance on a frozen lake. Japan's national bird, the crane nearly died out in the 1950s when most of its wetland habitat disappeared. Today, special refuges help it to survive.*

In 1980, there were just five Chatham Island black robins left on earth. Fortunately, the single female turned out to be good at laying eggs. Today, Chatham Island robins number about 250 birds so, for now at least, the species has survived its knife-edge scrape with extinction. No other animal has come back from such an all-time low, but many species are down to a few dozen or a few hundred animals. When populations become this small, great care is needed to bring them back from the brink.

the threat of attack. The gamble seems to have worked, because after several ups and downs, the total population now stands at about 80. But everyone who works with kakapos knows that they are not yet in the clear. For a species to be really safe, it needs to be able to survive on its own.

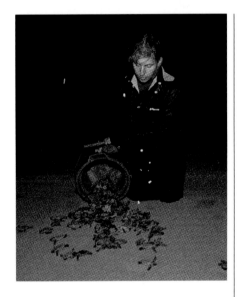

△ *A wildlife worker helps baby turtles on their way to the sea. By raising turtle eggs in special hatcheries, many more of their young are able to survive.*

LAST CHANCE

Today, nearly 200 species of birds are classified as critically endangered. Cranes, ibises and eagles all feature high on the list, but one of the rarest species – and certainly the strangest – is a parrot called the kakapo. Kakapos live in New Zealand, and they are the only flightless parrots in the world. Unfortunately, their ground-based lifestyle makes them easy prey for stoats and cats, which eat their young and eggs.

In the 1970s, the kakapo appeared to be doomed. A handful of birds were collected and kept in captivity, but none survived. During the 1980s, all surviving kakapos were transferred to offshore islands that were free from introduced mammals, so that the birds could live without

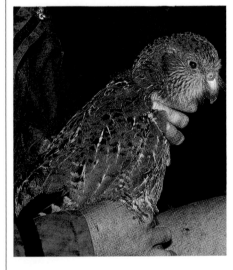

△ *Gripped by its neck and feet, an adult kakapo is given a check-up. Although they cannot fly, kakapos are good climbers. They use their beaks and toes to clamber into shrubs and trees.*

▷ *Pandas often give birth to twins, but it is rare for both of them to survive.*

very difficult to breed in captivity – scientists have been trying to improve their success rate for over 40 years.

Today, there are a few hundred giant pandas in the wild in China, and about 150 in captivity. Many have been loaned to foreign zoos in the hope of breeding young. Because pandas are popular, this also helps to raise funds. But some specialists think that the best way to conserve pandas is to protect their habitat, so that they can live and breed in the wild.

PROBLEMATIC PANDAS

Saving species can involve some difficult decisions. Moving kakapos might have harmed rather than helped them, which is why the operation had to be taken step by step. With other critically endangered species, another tactic is to breed animals in captivity, so that they can eventually be released. In some cases, this has been a big success. For example, there are now nearly 200 California condors, compared with 27 in the 1980s. But not all animals take to life in zoos. Giant pandas are

WINNERS AND LOSERS

Whales have a special place in the story of wildlife conservation. For hundreds of years, they were ruthlessly hunted – between 1904 and 1939, over half a million blue, fin and humpback whales were killed in the southern hemisphere alone.

But as whale stocks plunged, whaling quotas were agreed. Finally, in 1986, a complete ban on commercial whaling came into force. Since then, the world's largest whales have started to recover, prompting disagreements about what to do next. Many countries feel that whales should have permanent protection, but some are pressing for whaling to be resumed. For some species, however, the ban may have come too late. The northern right whale, for example, is down to about 300 animals. Because whales breed very slowly, most experts doubt that it will survive.

WORLDWIDE WORK

Most people are concerned about endangered mammals and birds. But threatened wildlife also includes many less glamorous species, such as snails, earwigs and ferns. All over the world, conservationists are working to protect these animals and plants, even though their efforts often go unnoticed. So why do they do it? The answer is because they are a part of nature, just like all species on earth. Conservation is not only about protecting the species that we like, or those that look good on television. Instead, it is about protecting the whole of the natural world.

▽ *Visitors come face to face with a grey whale off the coast of northwest Mexico. Grey whales were given protection in 1946. Since then, their population has risen to more than 20,000.*

Magnified over 20,000 times, these bacteria look harmless, but they can cause a dangerous lung infection called Legionnaire's disease. No one knows where this bacteria lives in the wild, but it thrives in water tanks and air-conditioning units, and it spreads to people when contaminated droplets get into the air. Fortunately, outbreaks of the disease are rare.

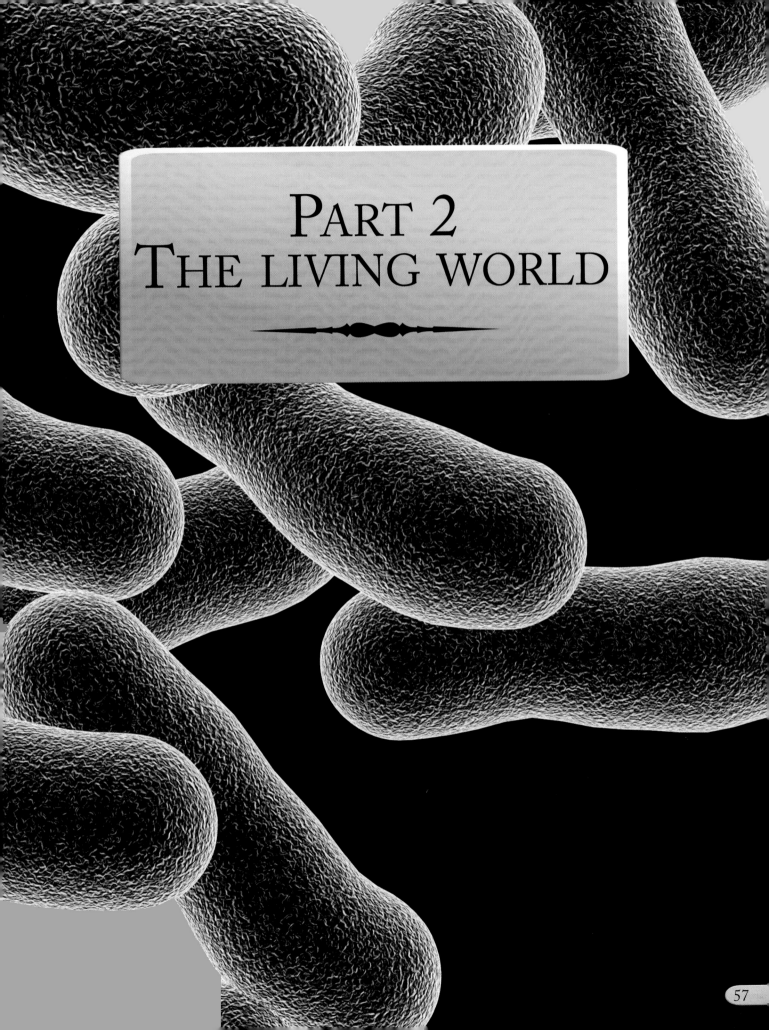

PART 2
THE LIVING WORLD

KINGDOMS OF LIFE

TO MAKE SENSE OF THE NATURAL WORLD, SCIENTISTS CLASSIFY LIVING THINGS IN GROUPS. THE SMALLEST GROUPS ARE SPECIES. THE LARGEST, CALLED KINGDOMS, ARE THE ULTIMATE 'DEPARTMENTS' OF LIFE.

During the early days of science, most naturalists thought that all living things were either animals or plants. But when microscopic life was discovered, it became clear that life is much more varied than this, and that two kingdoms were not enough. Since then, the number of kingdoms has expanded to five, but even this may not be the end of the story.

◁ *Many bacteria spend their lives fastened in one place, but some can glide or swim. This spiral-shaped swimmer is* Campylobacter jejuni, *a bacterium that causes food poisoning in humans.*

▷ *Magnified over 600 times, this intricate object is the skeleton of a radiolarian. Radiolarians are protists that live in the sea. They use sticky threads to trap their microscopic prey.*

SMALL-SCALE LIFE

The world's smallest living things are bacteria. They are simpler than all the other kinds of life, which is one of the reasons why they are classified in a kingdom of their own. Each one has a single cell containing just the bare essentials needed for staying alive. Around this is a tough wall that protects the cell from the outside world. Compared to other organisms, bacteria are not diverse, but they are incredibly abundant. Together, they vastly outnumber all other living things on earth.

The next kingdom, called the protists, also contains microscopic life, together with some species that can be seen with the naked eye. Like bacteria, most protists have only a single cell, but theirs are more complicated, and they contain a range of different working parts, just like our own. Protists usually live in water, and some behave like tiny

▷ *Some fungi grow mushrooms and toadstools when they reproduce, and are easy to spot. But many others are microscopic and spread invisibly through their food.*

◁ *Plants are vital for life, because they create food that other living things can eat. Some plants – like this barrel cactus – can survive without rain for months on end.*

THE WORLD OF ANIMALS

The last of the five kingdoms contains all the world's animals – an incredibly wide-ranging collection of living things with varied lifestyles to match. Like plants, animals contain lots of cells, but they need food to survive. Animal diets are almost as varied as animals themselves. Many feed on plants or other animals, but the animal kingdom also includes a host of scavengers and recyclers

animals, while others are like miniature plants. Over 100,000 species have been discovered, and they are so varied that some scientists think that they should be classified in several kingdoms, rather than just one.

FUNGI AND PLANTS

The next two kingdoms contain fungi and plants – living things that seem to have a great deal in common. Most of them sprout from the ground, and all of them spread by scattering spores or seeds. But fungi and plants are actually very different from each other. Fungi live by digesting substances around them, while plants do not need food at all. Plants collect energy directly, by soaking up sunshine with their leaves. Scientists have identified over 100,000 kinds of fungi, but the plant kingdom contains at least 400,000 species, and probably many more.

△ *Two fake 'eyes' make this moth caterpillar look much more dangerous than it is. Tricks like this are common in the animal kingdom, where animals run the risk of ending up as something else's prey.*

which live on nature's leftovers and on dead remains. Many living things can move, but animals move farther and faster than anything else. Some animals spend nearly all their lives in one place, but most need to move about to feed. They crawl, run, swim or fly through every habitat on earth, using a bewildering assortment of body parts, from muscular suckers and jointed legs to fins and feathery wings. About two million species of animal have been found so far. Many scientists think that the total could be five or even ten times that number.

◁ *No one knows exactly how many species there are on earth, but this chart shows how many have been identified so far. Animals make up by far the biggest slice, because they have evolved so many different ways of life.*

Fungi 100,000

Protists 100,000

Bacteria 10,000

Plants 400,000

Animals 2,000,000

CLASSIFYING LIVING THINGS

DURING THE NEXT 25 YEARS, A TEAM OF SCIENTISTS IS PLANNING TO DRAW UP A DATABASE OF ALL THE WORLD'S LIVING THINGS. IT IS A MAMMOTH TASK, BECAUSE NO ONE KNOWS HOW MANY SPECIES THERE ARE.

Long before science even existed, people recognized that living things fall into different groups. Birds, for example, have feathers and wings, while insects usually have six legs. Scientific classification continues this kind of work, but in a much more precise and orderly way. Once something has been classified, scientists can see how it is related to similar species, and where it belongs in the living world.

△ *By comparing DNA from different species, scientists can see how closely they are related. This chemical evidence helps in piecing together how different species have evolved.*

MAKING A NAME

When a new species is discovered, scientists compare it with known species, to make sure that it is a genuine new discovery. If it passes this test, the next step is to give it a scientific name. Unlike everyday names, scientific names are written in Latin, and they have two parts. The first part is the name of a genus – or group of species – to which the new discovery belongs. The second name identifies the species itself. For example, the North American swift fox is called *Vulpes velox*. The first part of this name means 'fox', while the second part means 'fast'.

Names like this sometimes look long and complicated, but they have

◁ *There are at least 20,000 species of crickets and grasshoppers, and probably many more. This museum collection shows just some of the species that live in the rainforests of Central America.*

several big advantages. One is that they are unique, so two different species can never get muddled up. Secondly, they can be recognized by scientists all over the world, whatever language they speak. The third advantage is that they work like signposts, showing how living things are related. This is easy to see using the Internet: search for the word *Vulpes*, and links to all the world's typical foxes will appear. In the plant world, the name *Quercus* produces links to all the world's oak trees.

LIFE'S FILING SYSTEM

Scientific names are like fingerprints, because no two species share the same one. But classification does not stop there. Individual species are organized into larger groups, which work like folders containing computer files. The first folder is the genus, and the next one up is

called a family. After this come order, class and phylum folders, and finally the top folder – a kingdom. Some folders contain just a single species, but the insect folder holds at least 800,000.

This filing system is very important, because it shows how closely different species are related. If two species are in the same folder, that means they have shared the same ancestors at some point in the past. In other words, they have evolved from the same branch of the living world.

CHANGING TRACK

If scientists could see back into the past, they would be able to classify all the species in the world in exactly the right way. But as this is not possible, they have to work from different kinds of evidence, including fossils and the features of living things. Classification is updated all the time, as the evidence is examined and new discoveries are made.

MICROLIFE

MORE THAN 99 PER CENT OF THE EARTH'S LIVING
THINGS ARE INVISIBLE TO THE NAKED HUMAN EYE.
TOGETHER, THEY MAKE UP THE CROWDED AND
BUSTLING WORLD OF MICROLIFE.

Without help, the smallest things that the human eye can spot are about 0.2 mm across – that's about one-fifth of the width of an average human hair. This may seem small to us, but it is actually much bigger than many living things. These miniature life-forms are known as microbes or microorganisms. Some microorganisms are only just invisible, while others are so small that they can be seen only if they are magnified over a thousand times. But small does not always mean simple, and microorganisms include some surprisingly complex creatures, as well as the most basic living things on earth.

WHO'S WHO

There are microorganisms in all the kingdoms of the living world, and micro size is often the only thing they have in common. As a rule, bacteria are the smallest and most numerous of them all, followed by larger, single-celled organisms

▽ Amoebas live in watery habitats, and the largest ones can be nearly 1 mm long. In theory, these can be seen without a microscope, but because they are transparent, they are actually very difficult to spot.

known as protists. The microworld also contains microscopic fungi, as well as thousands of species of microscopic animals and plants.

Although bacteria are the smallest living things, even smaller things sometimes show signs of life. These are viruses and viroids – packages of chemicals that survive by attacking living cells. Unlike other microorganisms, viruses and viroids cannot grow, and they cannot reproduce unless they manage to get inside a suitable host. For this reason – and several others – most scientists do not consider them to be fully alive.

A QUESTION OF SIZE

Where size is concerned, different kinds of microorganisms often overlap. For example, the world's smallest animals are much smaller than the largest bacteria, though they have complicated bodies with lots of moving parts. These animals are called rotifers, and they live in freshwater and the sea. Head-to-tail, it would take over 5,000 of the tiniest species to stretch across this page.

1 mm
0.1 mm   Alga (*Volvox*)

0.01 mm   Protozoan (*Didinium*)

0.001 mm   Human red blood cells

0.0001 mm   Bacteria (*Streptococcus*)

0.00001 mm   Virus (Common cold)

△ This chart shows some average sizes for microorganisms and other living cells. From the top, each step in the chart is ten times smaller than the one above it. Volvox is large enough to see with the naked eye.

◁ *The rings on these leaves are a sign of virus attack. Viruses are a serious problem for farmers and gardeners, because they infect many kinds of plants. Some viruses simply weaken plants, but others eventually kill them.*

At the other extreme, some protozoans (animal-like protists) are so big that they do not qualify as microorganisms at all. One of the bulkiest specimens alive today is a giant freshwater amoeba which can be seen easily with the naked eye. But even this is not a record, because millions of years ago, some single-celled protists managed to grow as large as a grapefruit.

MICROHABITATS

One of the great advantages of being small is that the list of possible habitats is almost endless. Microorganisms are found in them all. They find their way into the most remote and inaccessible places, and into every part of human homes. In general, most of the microorganisms live in water or in places that are damp. One of their particular favourites is soil, especially when it contains lots of dead remains. Other choice habitats are the moist surfaces and insides of larger living things. In animals, these include skin, mouths and teeth, and also the whole of the alimentary canal – the tube that absorbs water and digests food.

For animals, many of these microorganisms are harmless, while others are a positive help. Together they make up an animal's 'microbial flora', which is the collection of microbes that lives on or in the animal when it is in good health. But microorganisms also include species that target living things, and that use them as food. These invaders are often pathogenic – in other words, they cause disease. Over millions of years, animals in particular have evolved defences against these micro-attackers. Without these defences, they would soon be overrun.

LIVING IN THE MICROWORLD

For microorganisms, the world is a very different place to the one that we humans inhabit. For example, gravity has almost no effect on them, because there is so little for it to attract.

▷ *Like ants on the surface of a space rocket, hundreds of bacteria are clinging to the head of this pin. Bacteria like these often feed on microscopic patches of sweat left behind by human hands.*

If a microorganism moves, it reaches full speed almost straight away, but the moment it stops pushing, it comes to an instant halt. On land, microorganisms sometimes get blown into the air. Because they are so lightweight it can take days or weeks for them to come back to the ground. This means that it is difficult to keep anywhere completely microbe-free. In places where it really matters, such as operating theatres, the air is often kept under slight pressure, to prevent any microbes drifting inside.

MILLION-YEAR SLEEPERS

Microorganisms hardly ever build homes, and because they are small, very little stands between them and the outside world. However, many have a tough streak that helps them survive. They often cope with hard times by 'shutting down', and they can do this for years on end. Some micro-animals can stay dormant for a decade or more, but bacteria can do even better than this. In the right conditions, their dormant spores can survive for millions of years – much longer than the entire history of the human species.

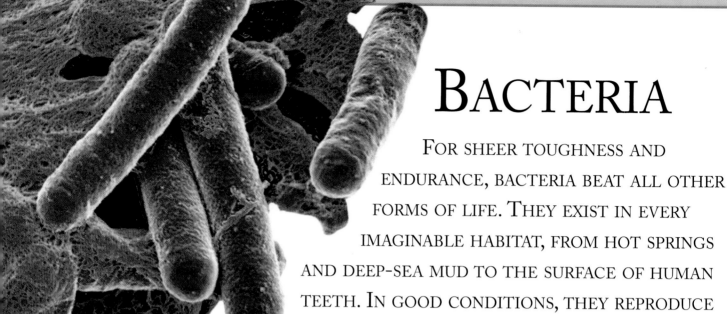

BACTERIA

FOR SHEER TOUGHNESS AND
ENDURANCE, BACTERIA BEAT ALL OTHER
FORMS OF LIFE. THEY EXIST IN EVERY
IMAGINABLE HABITAT, FROM HOT SPRINGS
AND DEEP-SEA MUD TO THE SURFACE OF HUMAN
TEETH. IN GOOD CONDITIONS, THEY REPRODUCE
FASTER THAN ANYTHING ELSE ON EARTH.

△ *These* Clostridium *bacteria normally live harmlessly in the soil. However, if they get into the body, they can have deadly effects, because they release one of the most powerful nerve poisons known.*

WHAT ARE BACTERIA?
Bacteria are the smallest fully living things, and also the most ancient forms of life on earth. Each one consists of a single cell, which is usually round, rod-shaped or spiral.

Bacteria have a bad reputation, because some kinds can cause disease. But if bacteria disappeared overnight, most other living things – including ourselves – would soon find it very difficult to survive. This is because bacteria are nature's chief recyclers. Many of them feed on dead remains, and the warmer it is, the faster they work. When they break down their food, they release nutrients that other living things need.

The cell has a tough wall, and it is often surrounded by a kind of glue or by sticky hairs, which help to anchor it in place. To reproduce, most bacteria simply divide in two. At top speed, they can do this every 20 minutes, which means that a single bacterium can soon turn into many millions.

MAKING A LIVING
Compared to other forms of life, bacteria make their living in many different ways. Some get their energy from sunlight while a few use chemicals from rocks – a trick that dates back to the

△ *These slender strands are formed by* Anabaena, *a cyanobacterium powered by sunlight.* Anabaena *and its relatives collect nitrogen gas from the air, helping to enrich or fertilize the soil.*

◁ *Individual bacteria are microscopic, but bacterial colonies can often be seen with the naked eye. This petri dish contains many colonies, growing on a thin layer of nutrient-rich jelly.*

earliest days of life on earth. But most bacteria absorb nutrients from dead matter, which can include anything from animal corpses to leftover food. Pathogenic bacteria are different, because they invade living things. These invasions, called infections, often produce disease.

VIRUSES

VIRUSES ARE THE SMALLEST THINGS THAT SHOW
SOME SIGNS OF BEING ALIVE. THEY ARE MUCH
SIMPLER THAN BACTERIA, AND THEY CAN ONLY
SURVIVE WITH THE HELP OF OTHER LIVING
THINGS. VIRUSES ARE GOOD AT SPREADING,
AND THEY CAN BE DIFFICULT TO CONTROL.

Most viruses are far smaller than bacteria, and they are
more like machines than living things. Instead of cells,
they have an exact number of chemical components,
which fit together in a specific way. Viruses do not feed or
grow, and they cannot reproduce on their own. Instead,
they hijack living cells, and force them to make copies
of themselves. Viruses attack all kinds of hosts,
including bacteria, plants and animals,
and many of them cause disease.

INSIDE A VIRUS
Viruses are built like containers, and
they carry an unusual cargo. This is
a collection of genes – chemical
instructions that build living things
and make them work. Normally, a
virus's genes are switched off, but if
the virus comes into contact with

△ Looking like a row of mushrooms, these
human immunodeficiency viruses (HIV)
are about to break out of their host cell.
HIV causes AIDS – a disease that has
swept the world in the last 20 years.

the right kind of
cell, that can quickly change.
First, the virus inserts its genes
into the cell, often leaving the empty
container outside. The viral genes
then switch on, and begin to take

control. Within minutes, the host
cell stops its normal work and
begins to assemble viruses instead.
Once these are complete, the cell
often bursts, letting the new viruses
escape. Viruses cannot move, so they
rely on outside help to travel. Some
are passed on by touch, while a few,
including flu viruses, are passed on
when people cough or sneeze.

△ Tobacco mosaic viruses (TMV)
look like slender rods. Each rod
consists of a coil of protein
molecules, protecting a payload of
genes that is tucked away inside.

◁ These bizarrely shaped
objects are bacteriophages,
or viruses that attack
bacteria. They help to keep
bacteria in check.

HALF ALIVE
Viruses are impossible to
avoid, and most living
things are attacked
by them every day.
Fortunately, most viruses do little
harm, but some can cause serious
disease. In humans, these include
yellow fever and AIDS. Exactly
where viruses came from no one
knows. One theory is that they are
renegade genes which have managed
to escape from living things and
develop a 'lifestyle' of their own.

The Grand Prismatic Spring, in Yellowstone Park, USA, gets its rainbow colours from cyanobacteria and other microbes. These bacteria live by collecting energy from sunshine, and are experts at coping with sizzling surroundings. The centre of this giant pool stays at a piping hot 86° C, thanks to volcanic heat from rocks below the surface of the ground.

PROTOZOANS

DESPITE THEIR TINY SIZE, PROTOZOANS INCLUDE SOME OF THE MOST VORACIOUS PREDATORS ON EARTH. MOST PROTOZOANS LIVE IN WATER, BUT SOME ARE FOUND INSIDE OTHER LIVING THINGS.

Seen through a microscope, protozoans often look like minute animals living at breakneck speed. Many of them swerve around obstacles and zoom away from danger, and they quickly gather wherever there is a chance of finding food. But protozoans are not animals, and they do not have eyes, mouths or even brains. Instead, they are protists – microorganisms with just a single cell. Unlike algae (see pp. 70–71), protozoans need to eat, and they get their food in different ways. Many are active predators, hunting for food, while others stay in one place and feed on anything edible that drifts nearby. Some form partnerships with much larger living things, but a few cause dangerous diseases.

△ *Looking like a prickly sculpture, this is the skeleton of a radiolarian – a protist that lives in the sea. In a living radiolarian, jelly-like threads reach out from the skeleton, and catch tiny creatures drifting nearby.*

Trichonympha, the hidden helper

Most plant-eating animals use microorganisms to help them digest their food. *Trichonympha* is one of these hidden helpers. It lives in the intestines of cockroaches and termites, and it feeds on tiny specks of wood that its host has swallowed. In return for this food, it produces energy-rich chemicals that its host can use. Without *Trichonympha*, most cockroaches and termites would starve to death.

Trichonympha engulfs a piece of wood.

The piece of wood is slowly digested.

LIFE ON THE MOVE

Protozoans are far too small to have legs or fins, but even so, they are amazingly good at getting around. Amoebas move by changing shape, a talent that is particularly useful for squeezing through tight spaces, such

△ *In a deadly duel, a predatory protist called* Didinium *(shown in brown) attacks* Paramecium *(green), its favourite prey.* Didinium *can stretch like a balloon, allowing it to swallow prey even bigger than itself.*

as the gaps between particles of soil. When the amoeba has tracked down its prey, it flows around it and engulfs it – a process like being swallowed by a living jelly.

Even when the amoebas are in a hurry, they cannot travel at more than about 2 cm an hour. However, in ponds and lakes, some protozoans zip along at over 30 or 40 times

▷ *Slime mould amoebas are among the strangest inhabitants of the microworld. They spend most of their lives on their own, but they gather together to reproduce. Over 50,000 amoebas may join together to form a 'slug' (right), which slowly creeps across the ground. When a slime mould 'slug' finds a suitable spot, it begins to change shape. Some of the amoebas form a slender stalk, while the ones on the top of the stalk make spores (far right). Eventually, the spores are scattered into the air. When they land, they hatch into new amoebas, and the cycle begins again.*

this speed. One of the fastest of all is *Paramecium*, a slipper-shaped organism that is covered with silky 'fur'. Unlike real fur, *Paramecium*'s hairs – called cilia – can move, beating in waves to speed this protozoan through its watery home. In fact, *Paramecium* moves so quickly that it is hard to see under a microsocope, unless a thickener is added to the water to slow it down.

PROTOZOAN PARTNERS

Most protozoans live in the sea, or in watery habitats on land. They often form part of the plankton, which makes them important in food chains. But some live in a very different environment – the intestines of plant-eating animals. Here, they help their host break down its food. These protozoans can be incredibly abundant – an elephant, for example, can have several billion of them living in its gigantic gut.

Living inside an animal has many advantages. The protozoans have an almost non-stop supply of food, and they are kept safe and warm. But there is one big drawback – like water in a river, their food is always on the move, and the protozoans eventually get washed downstream.

△ *This photograph shows a cluster of malaria parasites inside a human red blood cell. These parasites are spread by mosquitoes, which suck them up when they feed on blood.*

Many of them end up being digested by their host, although some pass out of its body unharmed.

PROTOZOAN PARASITES

Protozoan partners are useful to animals, but parasitic kinds are not. These unwelcome guests often arrive in water that animals drink, although some are injected by insects that feed on blood. Protozoan parasites affect almost all wild animals, and many do only minor harm. But they also include dangerous species, such as the ones that cause malaria. This serious disease affects humans and many other mammals, as well as reptiles and birds.

ALGAE

WHEREVER THERE IS WATER AND SUNLIGHT, ALGAE MAKE THEMSELVES AT HOME. THESE MICROPLANTS MAY BE SMALL, BUT THEY ARE SO NUMEROUS THAT THEY CAN SOMETIMES BE SEEN FROM SPACE.

Most algae are tiny green specks of living matter that drift in open water. They are simpler than real plants, but they live in the same way, by soaking up energy in sunshine. Although they are small, algae are vital for water life, because they make food that animals need to survive.

△ Volvox *is a freshwater alga that lives in ponds. Shaped like a hollow ball, it contains lots of cells, together with 'babies' that swim around inside it. The parent colony eventually breaks open to release the babies.*

GOING GREEN

Long before true plants first appeared on earth, algae were already flourishing in rivers, lakes and seas. Today, they thrive in many artificial habitats as well, from ponds and ditches to bottles that have filled with rain. In ideal conditions, they can multiply very rapidly, turning the water bright green.

Algae belong to the protist kingdom, and most of them have a single cell. But, unlike protozoans, algal cells often stick together to form groups called colonies. Algal colonies can look like microscopic space stations, stacks of miniature coins or even mats of slimy hair.

MAKING BABIES

Algae do not have flowers, and none of them makes seeds. Instead, the smallest ones often reproduce by dividing in two. This breeding technique is quick and efficient, and it boosts their numbers in record time. Algae divide most rapidly in spring, when the days are bright and long. The result is millions of tonnes of extra food that fish and other animals can use.

The bigger the algae, the more cells they contain, and the harder this dividing technique becomes. To get around this problem, larger algae reproduce by making spores. Spores are like seeds, but they are much smaller, and they can drift far away through water, or through the air. One ball-shaped alga, called *Volvox*, behaves like a floating nursery. It contains miniature 'babies', which swim around inside it until they are ready to take up life on their own.

△ *Green pond scum is often formed by* Spirogyra, *an alga whose cells grow in slender threads. Each cell contains a spiral band which collects energy from sunlight.*

ALGAE ON THE MOVE

Algae may be simple, but they have one remarkable talent – many of the smallest kinds can swim.

These micromovers swim in the same way as protozoans, by beating tiny hairs to move them through the water. They are too small to swim far, but they can propel themselves to where the light is brightest. Because bright light means more energy, this simple reflex helps them to thrive.

Many algae also have built-in floats that are often in the form of microscopic bubbles of oil. These floats keep them drifting near the surface – the best place to bathe in the sun. Together, these surface drifters make up the phytoplankton, a nutritious soup that protozoans and animals use as food.

LIVING IN A CASE

Most algae have tough cell walls, but some are also protected by a case. These cases are extremely small, but they include some of the most intricate and beautiful

△ Many diatoms are flat, but this species – called Campylodiscus – has a built-in twist. In some parts of the oceans, the empty cases of dead diatoms form layers of ooze many metres deep.

Dinoflagellates, dangerous drifters of the seas

Most algae are quite harmless, but one group, called dinoflagellates, includes some of the most lethal organisms afloat. Many of them produce powerful poisons which can kill anything nearby. When conditions are good, billions of dinoflagellates can build up in warm water along shallow coasts, forming swarms called red tides. As well as poisoning animals directly, red tides suffocate fish and seabed life when their algae die and rot away.

Dinoflagellates are often armour-plated, and some species have sharp spines. In *Ceratium*, which is shown here, the spines are extra long, which makes the alga harder for animals to swallow. Like all dinoflagellates, *Ceratium* swims by beating two long hairs. One of the hairs pushes it along, while the other one makes it revolve, like a microscopic rifle bullet spinning through the sea.

objects in the microworld. One group of algae, called diatoms, makes cases that have two almost equal halves. One half fits tightly over the other, like a box with a snap-on lid.

Diatoms build their cases from silica, the same substance that is used for making glass. But instead of heating the silica and then moulding it, they simply grow it into the

▽ Seaweeds often live in the zone between the tides, where they have to withstand dry air as well as pounding waves.

right shape. Diatoms collect silica from the water around them, and they are incredibly good at gathering it up. Sometimes, there is less than one part of silica to every million parts of water, but even so, diatoms manage to collect what they need.

OCEAN GIANTS

The algal world also includes some species that definitely do not qualify as microlife. These are seaweeds – algae that look like plants. Unlike real plants, seaweeds do not have roots or leaves. Instead, they fasten themselves in place with a holdfast – which often looks like a rubbery clamp – and they absorb sunshine through their leathery fronds.

Some seaweeds are quite delicate, but others are amazingly strong. Called wracks and kelps, they live on stormy coasts, where they have to withstand pounding by the waves.

Seaweeds can be just a few centimetres high, but some are many metres long. The longest of all is giant kelp, which grows along the west coast of North America. This huge seaweed is one of the fastest-growing living things on earth. The record depth for a seaweed is 268 m. At this depth, sunlight is 500,000 times weaker than at the surface.

FUNGI

WHEN PEOPLE THINK OF FUNGI, MUSHROOMS AND TOADSTOOLS ARE USUALLY THE FIRST THINGS TO COME TO MIND. BUT THESE COLOURFUL AND EYE-CATCHING OBJECTS ARE JUST A SMALL PART OF THE FUNGAL WORLD.

△ *These mushrooms have sprouted from a fungus that lives in the ground. They enable the fungus to spread, while the underground part of the fungus concentrates on collecting food.*

After bacteria and protists, fungi are the most common living things on earth. Most of them are microscopic, but they also include the largest single organisms that scientists have ever found. They live in all the earth's habitats, from forests and deserts to the bottom of the sea, and they even form part of the teeming microworld that flourishes on human skin. Unlike plants, fungi can grow in the dark, but they need food to survive. Most feed on dead leftovers, but some have a taste for living things. Despite this, fungi often go unnoticed, and very few have everyday names. That is because most of them live inside their food, and only become visible when they reproduce.

NATURE'S MISFITS

The reproductive parts of fungi include some of the strangest objects in the living world. Mushrooms and toadstools are odd enough, but other fungi look like nests, tufts of hair, or almost perfect replicas of human ears. They often sprout from the ground or from trees, and their job is to spread a fungus's spores.

Centuries ago, naturalists thought that these objects were plants, even though they do not have leaves. But since then, scientists have made a remarkable discovery – far from being plants, fungi are more closely related to animals instead.

△ *The red cage fungus produces sticky spores on the inside of its struts. Flies are attracted by its putrid smell, and they carry the spores away on their feet.*

FEEDING THREADS

There is no such thing as a typical fungus, because they come in so many different sizes and shapes. But fungi all have one thing in common – they survive by absorbing food.

△ *Orange peel fungus often sprouts on gravelly soil. Its eyecatching colour makes it very difficult to miss.*

Unlike animals, fungi do not swallow food and then digest it. They do things the other way around. A fungus digests its food on the spot, and then soaks up the nutrients that are released. The structures that do this work are minute threads called hyphae, which spread throughout a fungus's food.

△ *Bird's nest fungus, which is only 5 mm across, produces clusters of spores that look like tiny eggs. When it rains, the raindrops fall into the nest, throwing the 'eggs' up to 1 m through the air.*

▷ *Yeasts are microscopic fungi that consist of single cells. This is baker's yeast – the species that is used in the production of wine and beer, and to make dough rise.*

Hyphae can be incredibly fine, but they can spread for amazing distances. They often reach from the ground right to the tops of trees, and they form immense networks in the soil. Some wood-eating fungi can even spread from house to house all the way down a street.

DRUGS AND POISONS
Some fungi are good to eat, but others contain foul-tasting chemicals, or even deadly poisons. It takes skill and experience to tell which is which, because safe and dangerous species sometimes look alike. Stranger still, being poisonous does not 'run in the family', because some groups of fungi contain both safe and dangerous kinds.

The world's most poisonous fungus is a species called the death cap, which lives in woodlands across the northern hemisphere. Death caps look quite like edible mushrooms, but each one of them contains enough poison to kill an adult human being. To make matters worse, death cap poisons – called amatoxins – take up to 12 hours to start working. By the time someone starts to feel unwell, it is often

too late to save them. But strangely, fungi that are poisonous to human beings are often harmless to other animals. Slugs, for example, love toadstools, and they eat many poisonous kinds without suffering any problems at all.

△ *In the wild,* Penicillium *mould often lives on rotting fruit. It is one of the world's most famous fungi, because it was the original source of penicillin – the first antibiotic to be discovered.*

FUNGI AT WAR
Scientists do not really know why some mushrooms and toadstools are poisonous, but they do understand why poisons are produced by some moulds. These fungi often have to compete with bacteria, and they use poisons to stop their micro-rivals taking over their food. Their poisons are known as antibiotics. They are some of nature's most effective chemical weapons.

The first antibiotic was discovered in 1928, when a Scottish biologist called Alexander Fleming noticed mould in a laboratory dish. The dish was being used to grow bacteria, but the mould had killed all the bacteria growing around it. From the mould, *Penicillium*, scientists later managed to isolate the chemical, penicillin, that it uses to keep bacteria at bay. It is now one of the world's most important medical drugs.

HOW FUNGI FEED

FUNGI CANNOT MOVE, BUT THEY ARE EXTREMELY GOOD AT FINDING FOOD BY STEALTH. THEIR MENU INCLUDES ALL KINDS OF FARE, FROM FRUIT AND ROTTING WOOD TO FEATHERS AND HUMAN SKIN.

For fungi, feeding is a slow process. Instead of catching food, they normally grow through it. Their feeding threads, or hyphae, spread into their food and absorb the nutrients that it contains. Fungal threads are usually hidden away, but they can occasionally reach a giant size. Some fungi feed on living plants and animals, while others spread through the soil. From time to time, fungi also grow on something else – ourselves.

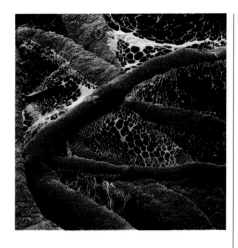

△ *Enlarged over 1,000 times, this photograph shows fungal threads or hyphae growing through their food. Together, the threads have a huge surface area – just what is needed for absorbing nutrients.*

FEEDING TIME

When animals feed, they usually swallow their food and then digest it. After this, they absorb the food's nutrients. Fungi are different, because they cannot swallow food at all. Instead, a fungus releases digestive enzymes that break down the food on the spot. Once the enzymes have done this, the fungus absorbs the substances that it needs.

A fungus's enzymes are specially tailored to deal with its food. Many fungi have enzymes that break down cellulose – the most important building material in plants. Some can also digest lignin, an even stronger substance that gives wood its strength. Fungal enzymes also include chemicals that can break down fats and proteins, which enable them to attack animals and their remains. Some highly specialized fungi produce an enzyme that breaks down keratin. This extra-tough protein is the main ingredient of fur, feathers, claws and nails, and the outermost layer of skin. Fortunately, our skin is well protected from fungal attack. If keratin-eating fungi do get a hold, they rarely cause us lasting harm.

ATTACK FROM WITHIN

Fungi are not fast feeders, but they can develop phenomenal appetites once they start to grow. As they feed, they often change their surroundings. They can turn ripe fruit soft and squishy, and they also turn fallen leaves into a mushy paste. Fungi even attack other fungi, making mushrooms and toadstools rot away. When fungi get to work on dead wood, they can weaken it so much that it falls apart. At first, the wood slowly cracks and splits, as its lignin is gradually destroyed. Eventually – often years later – it crumbles away completely, leaving nothing but a pile of dust.

Wood-eating fungi carry out important work, by breaking down fallen trees and branches so that their nutrients can be recycled. But

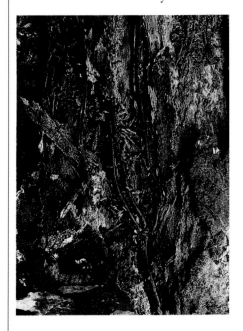

△ *In some fungi, hyphae join together to form much thicker strands. These black strands belong to a honey fungus, which is feeding on dead wood. Each strand is as thick as a shoelace.*

if they get into houses, they can cause serious damage. One notorious fungus, called dry rot, feeds on damp wood, and its long hyphae spread through gaps in bricks and concrete, like invisible tentacles in search of food. Dry rot is a common problem in some parts of the world, but strangely, it has hardly ever been seen in the wild.

◁ With its head trapped in a fungus's noose, this roundworm has no chance of escape. Its body will be digested as the fungus grows into its prey.

HOW LICHENS LIVE

In a lichen, the two partners work in different ways. The fungus collects minerals and other nutrients, and also anchors the lichen in place. Meanwhile, the algae gather energy from sunlight. They use it to carry out photosynthesis, which produces

△ Spreading over an ancient gravestone, these lichens may be several centuries old.

food that the fungus can use. Most lichens reproduce by growing small granules that are scattered by the wind or rain.

Lichens grow extremely slowly, but they make up for this by having very long lives. In extreme habitats, like Antarctica, they can be centuries old, but they often grow by less than a tenth of a millimetre a year.

On bare rocks, lichens often dry out completely for weeks or months at a time. Plants cannot cope with this, but lichens take it in their stride. When it rains, they soak up water like pieces of blotting paper, and almost immediately come back to life.

DEADLY SNARES

Many fungi attack living animals, often homing in on their skin. But some of the world's strangest fungi actually catch and kill their prey. Most of these fungal hunters live in the soil, where they trap microscopic worms. To catch their victims, the fungi use special snares, which are shaped like tiny rings. Each ring is made up of three curved cells, which are very sensitive to touch. If a worm accidentally wriggles into a ring, the cells instantly respond. They swell up, gripping the worm so that it cannot escape. Once the worm is dead, the fungus grows into its body and digests it from inside.

△ In 1992, scientists discovered a network of fungal threads covering 600 hectares of forest floor in the state of Washington, in northwestern USA. It is the largest single organism ever found. This map compares its size with downtown New York.

Predatory fungi do not only live in the soil. Some species live in freshwater, and go fishing for food with sticky lures. If an animal tries to feed on the lure, it gets glued into place. Once the animal is dead, the fungus digests the prey.

LICHENS

Fungi often feed on their own, but they can be even more successful when they team up with living partners. Often, these partners are microscopic algae. When fungi and algae team up, the result is a lichen – a living mixture that is much tougher than either of the partners on its own. Some lichens look like small bushes, but most are flat, and they grow by spreading over surfaces like a living crust. Unlike plants, they do not have roots or leaves, and they never flower.

There are over 10,000 kinds of lichens, and they live in an amazing range of habitats. Some grow on tree trunks, fallen branches or fence posts, while others live on windswept hillsides, or along the shore. Many of them grow on bare rocks in deserts, but they are just as much at home in towns and cities, where they spread over paving stones, concrete and bricks. Several kinds manage to cling to life in Antarctica's mountains, just a few hundred kilometres from the South Pole. Here, the wind can hit 150 km/h, and winter temperatures drop to −60° C, making it impossible for plants or animals to survive.

HOW FUNGI REPRODUCE

INSTEAD OF MAKING SEEDS, FUNGI REPRODUCE BY SCATTERING MICROSCOPIC SPORES. SPORES WORK LIKE SEEDS, BUT THEY ARE MUCH SMALLER AND SIMPLER. THEY CAN DRIFT FAR AND WIDE THROUGH THE AIR, OR THEY CAN TRAVEL IN OTHER WAYS – FOR EXAMPLE, BY HITCHING A LIFT ON AN INSECT'S FEET.

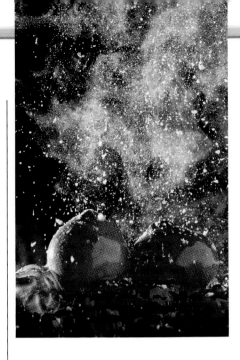

△ *Each time it rains, these tropical puffballs expel clouds of spores. Puffballs are common in woodlands and grasslands all over the world.*

Compared to animals and plants, fungi are some of the most prolific parents on earth. An ordinary mushroom can produce ten billion spores, as long as it is not picked too early. Some fungi are even more productive than this. Puffballs can produce over 5,000 billion – laid out end to end, enough to reach right around the earth! So why is the world not swamped by fungi? The answer is that each spore has only a tiny chance of survival.

△ *A spore print like this is easy to make. Cut the cap off a toadstool, lay it on a piece of glass or paper, and then cover it with a bowl. After a day, the spores will form a print showing the toadstool's gills.*

SPORE FACTORIES

A mushroom is like a living factory, and it does its work in record time. In only a week, it emerges from the ground, ripens its spores and sheds them into the air. The spores float away on the breeze, often landing nearby. Some travel hundreds of kilometres before they touch down.

Edible mushrooms make their spores in thin flaps, called gills, which are easy to see when a mushroom is turned upside-down. Operating at full stretch, they can release up to half a million spores a minute. The cap works like an umbrella, making sure that the gills stay dry. With so many spores on the move, it is important that they do not collide or stick together.

Scientists have discovered that each one has a minute electrical charge. This works like a magnet in reverse, keeping all the airborne spores apart.

LIFT OFF

Fungi have lots of different ways of sending spores on their way. Mushrooms shed their spores downwards, but puffballs give theirs a flying start by blowing them up into the air. When a puffball is newly grown, it feels hard and rubbery, like a ball. But as its spores begin to ripen, it dries out. The top of the puffball then opens up, forming a hole so that the spores can be released. If the puffball is hit by raindrops, the 'bag' is squashed, and a cloud of spores is puffed out.

Most puffballs are not much bigger than a golf ball, but some reach gigantic sizes. One of the largest specimens ever known, found in New York State in 1877, measured over 1.6 m across. Giant puffballs tear open when they are ripe, releasing their spores into the breeze. Sometimes, large chunks of them break away, like pieces of sponge that blow about in the wind.

Remains of giant puffballs have been found in archaeological digs. Long ago, people may have used them to carry fire, because they smoulder for several hours if they are set alight.

FUNGAL ARTILLERY

To survive and grow, spores have to land near food. The chances of this happening are extremely small, and many of them perish during their journey. But some fungi have ways of improving the odds. *Pilobolus* lives on cattle dung, and spreads by blasting packages of spores a few metres into the air. These packages stick on nearby blades of grass, where they are in just the right place to be eaten by cattle. If one of them is swallowed by a cow, it passes through its body unharmed, and emerges ready-planted in a perfect home.

△ *This electron micrograph picture shows* Pilobolus *growing on cattle dung. Each fruiting body is about 1 cm high, and ends in a swelling topped by a package of spores.*

they will begin to grow. One dung-dweller grows on the droppings of mice, and produces clusters of spores with long, sticky strands. If a mouse comes nearby, these strands glue themselves to its whiskers, and the mouse swallows the spores when it grooms itself.

SMELLY FUNGI

Mushrooms have a pleasant smell, but some fungi really reek. The most putrid are the stinkhorns. These woodland fungi grow long stalks topped by a mass of greenish slime. The slime attracts flies, and it sticks to their feet and mouthparts, ensuring that the spores are carried away.

Truffles also use smell to spread their spores, but their smell is quite different, and more appealing to humans. These woodland fungi grow underground, and they need animal help to spread. Ripe truffles attract

▷ *These flies are feasting on the slime produced by a stinkhorn fungus. They will 'plant' the spores when they next land on the ground.*

△ *Ripe* Pilobolus *fruiting bodies bend towards the light, and pressure inside builds up (1). The package of spores blasts off, travelling up to 2 m into the air (2).*

wild boar, which dig them up and scatter their spores. For centuries, truffles have been highly prized by cooks, and in Europe, professional truffle-hunters use specially trained dogs or pigs to track them down.

△ *Ink cap fungi have caps that digest themselves, turning into an inky-black liquid. In this picture, the tallest ink cap has almost finished self-digesting.*

CLEANING UP

Animal dung is a favourite habitat for fungi, and many kinds live on this kind of food. Most of them have special spores which need to pass through an animal's body before

◁ *This soldier termite is guarding a fungus garden, deep in an underground nest. The white objects are the parts of the fungus that the termites eat.*

FUNGI AND ANIMALS

FOR ANIMALS, FUNGI CAN BE EITHER USEFUL ALLIES OR DEADLY ENEMIES. SOME KINDS OF FUNGI PROVIDE ANIMALS WITH THEIR FOOD, WHILE OTHERS ARE STEALTHY INVADERS THAT ATTACK ANIMALS AND DIGEST THEM FROM INSIDE. BECAUSE THEY SPREAD BY USING SPORES, THESE KILLER FUNGI CAN ATTACK ALMOST ANYWHERE.

C ompared to plants, fungi do not play a huge part in human life, although we would miss them if they disappeared. But for some animals, fungi are vital for survival. Mushrooms and toadstools are eaten by slugs and insect grubs, but the real fungus specialists are animals that cultivate fungi as food. They harvest fungi, but they also work as their partners, by protecting them and helping them to spread. Unfortunately for animals, not all fungi are this useful, or this well-behaved. Some feed by breaking into animal bodies, and they can spread through them as quickly as mould through a slice of bread. A brush with one of these fungi can have fatal results.

THE FUNGUS GARDENERS

In warm parts of the world, termites chew their way through wood and grass, and carry millions of tonnes of it underground every year. Like most animals, the termites cannot digest this kind of food themselves. Instead, they rely on the help of tiny microbes which live in their intestines – one of these, called *Trichonympha*, is shown on page 68. But some species of termites are

▽ *Slugs often feed on mushrooms and toadstools. They rasp away at the fungi using a radula – a mouthpart that contains hundreds of microscopic teeth.*

△ *This female wood wasp, or horntail, is drilling into a tree to lay her eggs. Wood wasps carry fungi with them, but they usually pick trees that have already been damaged by fungal attack.*

even more efficient, because they have evolved an extra way of getting nutrients from their food.

In their underground nests, these termites swallow their food, and then gather up their own droppings. These droppings contain partly digested remains, and the termites build them into a spongy mass that

▽ *This Peruvian grasshopper has been killed by a fungus. The fungus has sprouted tiny 'mushrooms' which will soon scatter their spores.*

can be over 60 cm across. This is the termites' underground 'garden'. It is a perfect habitat for a particular fungus that the termites tend and eat. As long as the termites look after the fungus, it stays inside its underground home. But if the termites desert their nest, the fungus grows to the surface and produces mushrooms, enabling it to spread.

MOULDY TUNNELS

Many insect grubs bore their way through wood, using it as food. As they tunnel along, they often swallow fungi that are already in the wood. For them, fungi are like side dishes that help to make up a meal. But some wood-borers go further. Fungi make up most of their diet, while wood takes second place.

Wood wasp larvae grow up in this way. They often tunnel through conifers, and foresters dislike them because they can damage and weaken trees. Their burrows are lined with a fungal 'fur', and the grubs graze on the fungus as they crawl about in the wood. When adult wood wasps emerge from their burrows, they take some of the fungus with them. Females infect new trees when they lay their eggs, making sure that their grubs have the fungus that they need to survive.

THE INSECT-KILLERS

Humans sometimes suffer from fungal infections. Athlete's foot, for example, is one that people often catch at school. It is caused by a fungus that feeds on the surface of the skin, and that thrives in the warm and moist conditions inside sweaty trainers and tight-fitting shoes. Usually, these infections do little harm, although they take time to clear up. For wild animals, fungi are more of a threat. They can kill mammals, birds and fish, and they are particularly deadly to insects.

One way to spot these fungi is to look for insects that seem to be stuck on window-panes or on blades of grass. If an insect does not run or

△ *Fruit flies feed on sugary sap, and also on yeasts – microscopic fungi that feed on sugar themselves. Yeasts form a thin layer around some fruits, giving them a waxy feel.*

fly away, it may have been a victim of fungus attack. The attack begins when a single microscopic spore lands on an insect's body. Once it has dissolved its way through the body case, the fungus spreads inside, dissolving the insect's internal organs as well. Once an insect is infected, the fungus often changes the way that it behaves. It makes the insect settle out in the open – the perfect place for the fungus to spread its lethal spores.

FUNGI AND PLANTS

MOST TREES ARE EVENTUALLY KILLED BY FUNGI, AND FUNGI ALSO ATTACK MANY OTHER PLANTS. BUT FUNGI AND PLANTS ARE NOT ALWAYS ENEMIES. WITHOUT FUNGAL PARTNERS, MANY PLANTS WOULD FIND IT DIFFICULT TO SURVIVE.

△ *These tiny orange mounds are produced by a rust fungus living in a leaf. Each one will release thousands of spores.*

Plants are tempting targets for fungi, because they are full of food and cannot run away. Fungi attack plants above and below ground, seeking out any weak points in their defences. They break into roots and through wounds in bark, and through the microscopic pores or breathing holes that all plants have in their leaves. Once a fungus is inside a plant, the stage is set for a serious and sometimes lengthy struggle. Some fungi damage parts of plants, leaving their host weakened but alive. Others are much more dangerous, because they go for the kill.

▷ *Fungi attack living trees, and break down dead wood after a tree has died. These mushrooms are sprouting from a decaying branch in the Amazon rainforest.*

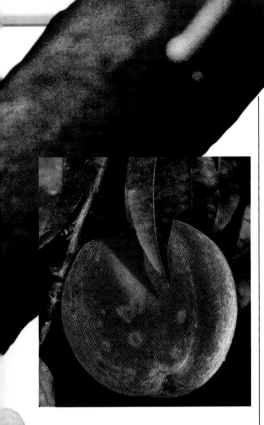

△ *This peach tree has been infected by a rust fungus. Although the fungus will not kill the tree, it will reduce the crop, and will probably spread to other trees nearby.*

MORTAL COMBAT

For plants, fungal warfare starts the moment that they germinate from their seeds. One fungus, a mould called *Pythium*, is often lying in wait for them in the soil. *Pythium* breaks into tender young shoots, and quickly dissolves their cells. In less than an hour, the shoot often topples over like a fallen tree – ending a plant's life almost before it has begun.

At the other extreme, duels between fungi and trees can go on for many years. This is because trees have many defences that prevent airborne spores from getting at their living wood. If this shield is breached, trees can also use chemical weapons, including sticky resins, that make it harder for fungi to spread. Even if a fungus does take hold, trees can take a long time to die. Each year, they surrender a little bit more of themselves, until finally no living wood is left.

When the battle is finally over, and the tree is dead, different fungi move in. They slowly break down the dead remains, weakening the tree until it falls. The trunk and branches then gradually turn to dust, and their nutrients are returned to the soil for future use.

FUNGUS EPIDEMICS

For farmers and gardeners, fungi are a constant problem. Cultivated plants are attacked by hundreds of different species, including moulds and mildews, wilts, rusts and smuts. Their names may sound funny, but their effects are not. Despite modern fungicides, they can get out of control and cause tremendous damage to crops. Fungi can even change the landscape. In the 1920s, for example, a fungal epidemic killed most of North America's chestnuts, while in the 1980s, Dutch elm disease killed most of the elm trees in the British Isles.

Further back in time, fungal diseases have sometimes caused even greater disasters. One of these occurred in the 1840s, when a fungus called late blight attacked Ireland's potato crop. Without this essential source of food, more than a million people starved to death.

UNDERGROUND ALLIES

With a record like this, fungi sound like nothing but trouble for plants. But fungi and plants have a strange relationship, and some fungi actually help plants to thrive. These 'good' fungi live in the soil, and they team up with plants by making contact with their roots. Instead of attacking the plant, the fungus supplies it with mineral nutrients that it collects from the soil. It is something that fungi are very good at, because their feeding threads spread so far. In return for this service, the plant

△ *In woodlands and forests, many toadstools are connected to nearby trees because their feeding threads spread underground to link up with tree roots.*

gives the fungus some of the sugary food that it makes.

Over millions of years, this private arrangement has proved to be amazingly successful. Orchids have developed such close partnerships with fungi that they depend on them to survive. Many trees also rely on fungi, and even those that do not rely on them grow much better when they have these partners underground. This explains why some mushrooms and toadstools always grow near particular trees – together they make up some of nature's most effective teams.

▽ *Burnt orchids, which live in Europe's meadows and grasslands, can spend their first ten years hidden underground. During this part of their lives they get food from a fungal partner, which wraps itself around their roots.*

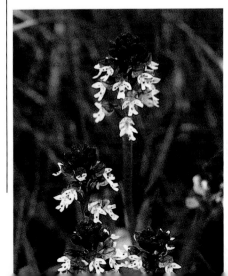

PLANTS

IF ALIENS WERE STUDYING EARTH FROM SPACE, PLANTS WOULD BE THE MOST VISIBLE SIGN OF LIFE. PLANTS LIVE ON LIGHT, AND ARE THE CORNERSTONE OF THE LIVING WORLD.

Plants are distant relatives of algae, and they live in a similar way by collecting energy from sunlight. Most plants grow on land. Here, they have adapted to all kinds of habitats, from deserts to the tundra near the poles. Plants first appeared over 400 million years ago, and they have evolved to include the tallest and most colourful living things on earth.

△ Duckweeds are the smallest flowering plants in the world. The tiniest species can fit through the eye of a needle, and their flowers can only be seen with a microscope.

◁ A hiker peers inside a giant sequoia's hollow trunk. These conifers are the world's heaviest plants – up to 2,500 tonnes. Their fireproof bark can be over 30 cm thick.

◁ *Ant plants in southeast Asia have spongy stems that ants use as a home. The plant lives off the ground, and gets nutrients from the ants' droppings, instead of the soil.*

plants make their seeds with the help of flowers. There are a quarter of a million kinds of flowering plants, many with spectacular blooms. Among them are all the world's grasses and every single one of the world's broadleaved trees.

GREEN ENGINEERING

Because plants cannot move about, they need equipment to survive. Their roots probe deep into the ground to search out water, and their leaves spread out to catch the sun. A plant's stem carries out the vital task of ferrying water upwards from the ground so that the leaves can do their work. If a plant's stem is cut or broken, the leaves soon shrivel and die. Some plant stems are short and stubby, but others tower over 50 m into the air. These giant stems are tree trunks – the heaviest pieces of engineering ever put together by

GOING GREEN

The world's first land plants were just ankle-high, and they reproduced by releasing tiny spores. Mosses still live like this and, like early plants, they need to be damp to grow. As time went by, plants became taller, tougher and more varied. The new plants included giant horsetails and tree-ferns, which grew in vast forests on swampy ground. The breakthrough came later, when some plants evolved seeds. Seeds turned out to be one of nature's greatest inventions, allowing plants to spread to some of the driest and coldest places on earth.

Today, seed-bearing plants include coniferous trees, which make their seeds in woody cones. But far more

▷ *The bird-of-paradise flower is pollinated by birds. If a bird lands on the blue perch, its feet collect pollen, and it carries this to the next flower.*

anything living on land.

Plants build themselves from little more than water and air. This amazing trick is photosynthesis, and it is powered by energy from the sun. Plants are not the only things that carry it out, but on land they are the only ones that use it on such a massive scale. Photosynthesis builds up every part of a plant, from tree trunks weighing thousands of tonnes to seeds smaller than dust.

△ *The hammer orchid lives in western Australia. When a wasp lands on the red hammer, the flower suddenly folds up, and dusts the visitor with pollen.*

WORKING PARTNERS

Over millions of years, animals and plants have become close partners. Many flowering plants depend on animals, but animals need plants even more. Without plants, there would be no food for plant-eaters, and without plant-eaters, predators would have nothing to hunt. But wild animals are not alone. Humans also depend on plants: without the food and raw materials that they supply, we would also find it impossible to survive.

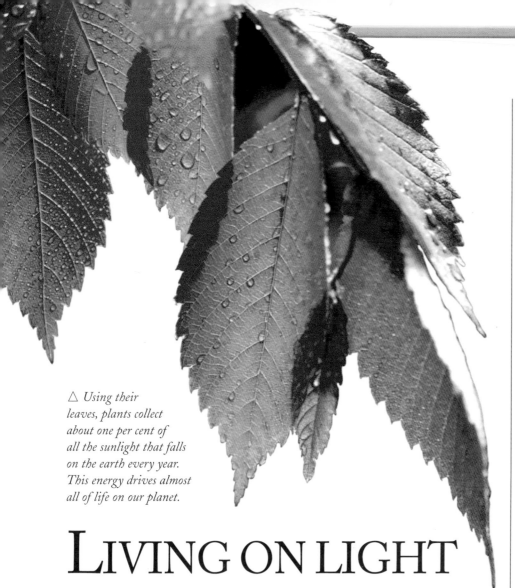

△ *Using their leaves, plants collect about one per cent of all the sunlight that falls on the earth every year. This energy drives almost all of life on our planet.*

LIVING ON LIGHT

PLANTS LEAD THE WORLD IN USING SOLAR POWER. THAT IS BECAUSE SUNLIGHT SUPPLIES ALL THE ENERGY THAT THEY NEED TO SURVIVE AND GROW.

Every three seconds, the sun supplies the earth with as much energy as the entire human race uses in a day. We are only just starting to tap into this gigantic resource, but plants have been using it since they first evolved. Their secret is photosynthesis – a process that captures light and sets it to work.

COLLECTING LIGHT
Light is pure energy. It cannot be eaten and it cannot be stored, but it can be collected and used. This is exactly what plants do. Through their leaves, they absorb the energy in sunlight, and they use it to power chemical reactions. These reactions work like digestion in reverse. They start with very simple substances, and use them to build up ones that are more complex. This process is called photosynthesis – a word that means 'building with light'.

Plants first have to collect the energy in sunlight, so that the cascade of chemical reactions can begin. They do this by using a substance called chlorophyll. Chlorophyll is very good at collecting the blue and red parts of sunlight, but not so good at collecting green. This unused light bounces back off leaves, or shines straight through them, which is why green is the colour of the living world.

ESSENTIAL INGREDIENTS
As well as light, plants need two simple substances before photosynthesis can start. One of these is water, which they normally take from the ground. Water travels up plants in a non-stop stream, through the roots and stems until it arrives in their leaves. The other essential ingredient is carbon dioxide – a gas that is present in air. Plants absorb carbon dioxide through their leaves. Once the gas is inside a leaf, it seeps into the cells where photosynthesis occurs. These leaf cells are microscopic factories, crowded with dozens of green blobs.

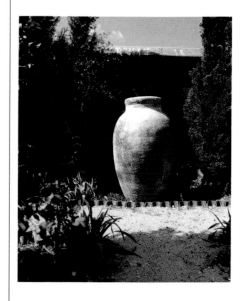

△ *Because plants use energy from the sun, they do not need food. Their roots absorb water and small amounts of minerals, but nothing else.*

These blobs, called chloroplasts, are where photosynthesis takes place. Inside each chloroplast is a stack of transparent membranes, which are packed with chlorophyll molecules. When sunlight shines through the membranes, the chlorophyll starts capturing energy.

PERFECT PARTNERS
With the help of energy from the sun, plants take water and carbon dioxide, and use them to build a sugar called glucose. Glucose is packed with energy, which means that plants can use it as a fuel. But even more importantly, it is a stepping-stone towards making hundreds of other substances that plants need when they grow.

Most chemical reactions produce some waste, and photosynthesis is no exception. In this case, the waste is pure oxygen, which escapes into the air. This makes animals and plants ideal partners, because animals need oxygen to survive. When animals breathe, they give off carbon dioxide, and plants use this when they grow.

GOING FOR GROWTH
To grow, plants use building materials that can cope with tough conditions. In the plant world, the number one building material is a substance called cellulose. Plants make cellulose by adding together glucose molecules to form long chains. A single chain can contain over 5,000 glucose molecules.

To use these chains as a building material, plants arrange them in special ways. They build the chains together into fibres, and then they lay the fibres down in crisscrossing sheets. The result is light but tough – exactly what is needed to keep plant cells in shape.

STORAGE FOR SURVIVAL
Plants need energy to keep going at night, and to survive when the weather turns dry or cold. Many plants store energy by turning glucose into a powdery substance

△ *Magnified over 500 times, this slice through a leaf shows chloroplasts inside living cells. The more chloroplasts a cell has, the more light it can collect.*

called starch. They stockpile starch in their roots or stems, and many also in their seeds. In seeds, this store gives young plants enough energy to germinate and grow.

Humans cannot digest cellulose, but starch is a vital part of our food. Wheat, corn and potatoes are packed with it. When we eat these, we get a large helping of energy – one stored away by living plants, using light from the sun.

This diagram shows the main steps that take place during photosynthesis. The 'ingredients' needed are shown on the left, and the results are shown below.

1 *Plant collects light energy with its leaves.*
2 *Plant collects carbon dioxide through its leaves.*
3 *Plant collects water through its roots.*

4 *Using solar energy, the chloroplasts combine the water and carbon dioxide to make glucose.*
5 *Glucose is an energy-rich sugar, or simple carbohydrate. The plant can turn glucose into many useful substances. One of these is cellulose – a carbohydrate that is a tough building material.*
6 *The plant uses cellulose fibres to construct new cell walls.*
7 *New cells make the plant grow.*

LEAVES

LEAVES ARE NATURE'S ANSWER TO A TRICKY
PROBLEM – HOW TO COLLECT THE LIGHT IN THE
MOST EFFICIENT WAY. THEY HAVE TO STAND UP
TO ALL KINDS OF DIFFERENT CONDITIONS, FROM
BAKING SUNSHINE TO TORRENTIAL RAIN.

Leaves work like solar panels, and their job is to collect the
light that plants need. Some are just a few millimetres long,
but the largest palm leaves would barely fit inside a bus.
Leaves can be as soft and delicate as a piece of tissue, or as hard as
plastic, with jagged edges, sharp points or an armoury of dangerous
spines. These designs have evolved over hundreds
of millions of years. They suit plants to different
habitats, and to very different ways of life.

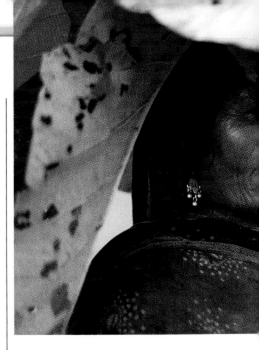

△ Tropical plants often have big, floppy
leaves, because they live in places where the
air is warm, damp and calm. In most other
parts of the world, leaves like this would
get ripped to pieces by the wind.

▽ Like many freshwater plants, water
crowfoot has two kinds of leaves – feathery
ones underwater, and rounded ones in the air.

◁ When leaves are held up against the
light, their veins are easy to see. Leaf
veins do two jobs – they support the leaf,
and they carry water to its cells. The highly
magnified picture (above left) shows a
single pore in a yew tree leaf. At night,
the brown guard cells close the pore, to
prevent the leaf losing too much water.

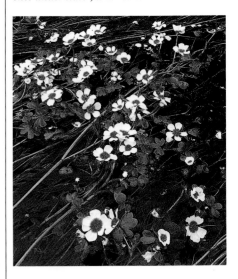

HOW LEAVES WORK
No matter what they look like,
leaves all work in a similar way.
They gather energy from sunlight,
and they use it to make substances
that plants need when they grow.
Leaves work by using photosynthesis
(see pp. 84–85). Photosynthesis
needs carbon dioxide and water, as
well as sunlight, so these must be

inside the leaf for things to start.
These substances arrive on site by
following two quite different paths.
Leaves get carbon dioxide from
the air, through microscopic pores
called stomata. These are surrounded
by special guard cells that can make
them open or close. Carbon dioxide
flows in through these pores, and
then makes its way into the cells
where photosynthesis takes place.
At the same time, oxygen flows out.
It may sound like breathing, but
plants do not have to put any effort
into making it work. That is because
their leaves are thin, so the gases can
seep in or out without any help.

WATER ON TAP
Unlike carbon dioxide, water often
has much farther to travel. It flows
into a plant's roots and along
a system of ultra-fine pipelines,
moving up the stem, into leaf stalks,
and finally into leaf veins. Once
it has arrived, most of the water
evaporates through the leaf pores,
and this pulls more water up the

plant to take its place. This water flow is called transpiration. The warmer, drier and windier it is, the faster transpiration works.

Cacti often use just a few drops of water a day, because they are specially adapted for life in dry places. But most plants get through far more than this. A single corn plant can drink up to 200 litres of water while it grows, which is enough to fill an average bath to the brim. Trees are even thirstier. A large oak can suck up over 500 litres in a single day. Poplar trees can dry out the soil so much that it shrinks, making buildings crack or collapse.

SPECIAL SHAPES

The ideal shape for collecting light is big and flat, like a solar panel. But leaves are not made of metal, and they are not bolted to the ground. They have to combine lightness and strength, and they have to work in all kinds of different habitats, from windswept mountainsides to the dimly lit rainforest floors. This is one of the reasons why leaves are so varied, and why no two species have leaves that are exactly alike.

Most plants grow simple leaves, which are ones that have a single blade. Compound leaves are different, because they are divided up into small leaflets, which look like leaves themselves. To make things even more complicated, the leaflets may be compound themselves, creating a mass of feathery foliage attached to a single stalk. Grass leaves are easier to recognize, because they are long and narrow, and do not have a stalk. In a grass leaf, the veins are parallel, but in most other plants they spread through the leaf like a net.

LEAF LIFESPANS

Leaves do not only differ in shape and size – their surface varies too. Some leaves are shiny and smooth, but others feel sticky, or have a covering that feels like fur. A few are even dangerous to touch. Nettle leaves are covered with stinging hairs, while poison ivy leaves contain a toxic resin that can stick to skin and clothes. These different features help to protect leaves against rain,

△ *Scabweed, from New Zealand, has just what it takes to survive on rocky mountain slopes. Its leaves are tiny, and packed together tightly to protect them from the wind.*

strong sunshine and drying winds, and also against animals that use leaves as food. In southwest Africa, the *Welwitschia* plant (see p. 184) has just two leaves, and they are built to last for hundreds of years. But with most other plants, leaves have a much shorter life. Once their work is done, the plant cuts off their water supply, and they flutter – or sometimes crash – to the ground.

FULL CIRCLE

Every year, evergreen trees shed their leaves gradually, but deciduous trees lose all of them at the same time. In autumn, fallen leaves are everywhere, but by the following spring, most have disappeared. This vanishing trick is the work of bacteria and fungi, which feed on dead leaves, turning them into smaller and smaller fragments which eventually mingle with the soil. These dead remains fertilize the ground, helping more plants – and more leaves – to grow.

◁ *The raffia palm has the world's biggest leaves. They can be up to 23 m long, and each one lasts for up to ten years. Raffia fibre is made from the leaf stems.*

FLOWERS

PEOPLE ARE FASCINATED BY FLOWERS. WE PAINT THEM
AND PHOTOGRAPH THEM, AND OFTEN HAVE THEM IN
OUR HOMES. BUT FLOWERS DO NOT GROW JUST FOR
US TO ENJOY. INSTEAD, THEY HAVE A DIFFERENT
MISSION – TO ENABLE PLANTS TO REPRODUCE.

It is difficult to imagine a world without flowers.
They grow in every natural habitat on land,
and a few very special kinds even 'bloom'
beneath the sea. Flowers brighten up gardens
and roadsides, and some of the smallest ones
manage to survive in cracks in pavements,
just beneath passing feet. Flowers have a
bewildering variety of shapes and colours,
but they all carry out the same essential
tasks. They allow female cells to be
fertilized by male pollen. Once this
has happened, they make a plant's seeds.

ANATOMY OF A FLOWER

The best way to find out about flowers
is a drastic one: starting at the outside,
simply pull a flower apart. In most
flowers, the first things to come away
are green flaps called sepals, which
protect the flower while it is still a
bud. Next come the petals. Usually,
they are the most eyecatching parts
of flowers, and their job is to attract
animals so that pollen can be
transferred from plant to plant.
With the sepals and petals out of the
way, only the innermost parts of the
flower are left. First is a circle of
stamens. These are the flower's male
parts, and their function is to produce
pollen. In the very centre are the
flower's female parts, or carpels.
Their role is to collect pollen
arriving from other
flowers, and then to
use it to make seeds.

*With its petals folded back,
this tropical passionflower is an
irresistible attraction for visiting
insects. Its intricate shape
ensures that insects are dusted
with pollen as they feed.*

2 *The bright red flowers attract insects, which bring pollen from other poppy flowers.*

1 *Poppy flowers open in the morning, when their sepals fall off and their petals open up.*

3 *The petals drop off, leaving a case that contains hundreds of developing seeds.*

ANIMALS AND WIND

That, in a nutshell, is how most flowers are made. But because there are so many kinds of flowering plants, there are also thousands and thousands of different flowers. Most flowers are like living shop windows, and they lure animals with the promise of food. This food is usually sugary nectar, although some flowers reward their visitors with other things, such as pollen itself. These flowers need to be noticed, which is why they have bright colours and tempting smells. But not all flowers are like this. Many plants do not need to attract animals, because they spread their pollen by the wind. Their flowers are often green and small, and easy to overlook.

THE SEX LIFE OF PLANTS

Animals are usually male or female, but in the plant world, things are not always so straightforward. Because most flowers have male and female parts, their owners are male and female at the same time. Plants like these usually swap pollen with their neighbours, but if they have to, they can often pollinate themselves – a useful trick if they are growing on their own, with no available partners close by.

But many other plants, such as pumpkins, have separate male and female flowers. Their flowers grow on the same plant, but only the female ones produce fruit and seeds. Finally, there are plants which are more like animals, with separate sexes on separate plants. The kiwi fruit is one of these. To produce kiwi fruit, farmers have to grow male and female plants, so that pollination can occur.

POLLINATION

UNLIKE ANIMALS, PLANTS CANNOT PAIR UP
TO REPRODUCE. THEY GET TOGETHER
IN ANOTHER WAY, BY SWAPPING
MICROSCOPIC GRAINS OF POLLEN.

For plants, reproduction is a tricky business. Male and female cells are needed, and if possible these need to come from different parent plants. But plants cannot move, so the parents can never meet. This is where pollen comes in. This dust-like substance contains a plant's male cells, and it is small and light enough to travel from plant to plant. When male pollen lands on the female parts of a flower, it fertilizes the female cells, or ova. Once this vital step has taken place, the female cells can start to develop into seeds.

△ *In summer, a quick shake is enough to make a pine tree release clouds of yellow pollen. These pollen grains have microscopic sails which help them float away.*

POLLEN ON THE MOVE

Pollen grains are made by stamens, or the male parts of flowers. Once their pollen is ripe, they release it, so that it can travel from plant to plant. The journey may be as far as a next-door plant, or some kilometres away. Each plant has its own 'brand' of pollen, and it can only fertilize plants of the same kind.

Pollen gets about in two quite different ways. Some plants simply shed their pollen into the air. The pollen floats away in the breeze and, with luck, some of it lands on the female parts of other flowers. This method is used by all the world's grasses, and by lots of broadleaved trees. It is also used by conifers, although they make their pollen in cones, rather than in flowers.

Because wind-pollination is so hit-and-miss, a huge amount of pollen is needed to make it work. On warm

△ *Pollen grains are as distinctive as fingerprints. Each plant produces its own kind, and scientists sometimes identify plants by looking at their pollen alone.*

summer mornings, wind-pollinated plants release billions of pollen grains into the air. The grains are far too small to be visible, but they give many people hay-fever and runny eyes.

POLLEN CARRIERS

The world's earliest seed-producing plants were all pollinated by the wind. But when flowering plants appeared, some of them developed much smarter ways of sending pollen on its way. They evolved flowers that attract animals. In return for a reward of food, these visitors act as a private courier service, delivering pollen to its destination. The first pollinating

◁ *Bees help to spread pollen, but they also use it as a food. They scrape pollen off their bodies, and pack it into special 'pollen baskets' on their legs.*

animals were probably beetles, which clamber about in flowers to feed. Today, pollinating animals include many different kinds of insects, as well as birds, bats and marsupials. During their long partnerships, flowers and their visitors have evolved so they fit almost like a lock and key. When an animal arrives at a flower, the flower's male parts, or stamens, dust its body with pollen. The animal carries this to the next flower it visits, where the flower's female parts are waiting to collect it. Once a pollen grain arrives at its destination, it grows a slender tube into the flower's

▷ Hummingbirds are the only pollinating birds that hover as they feed. Pollen sticks to their faces, and is transferred from flower to flower.

ovaries, which are the chambers where the female cells are held. Each pollen grain fertilizes a single female cell and, after this, the cell grows into a seed.

ANIMALS AT WORK

By looking at a flower, it is often easy to work out what animal pollinates it. Insect-pollinated flowers are usually brightly coloured and sweet-smelling, because insects are attracted by bright colours and sugary smells. Flat flowers are often pollinated by flies and wasps, while tube-shaped ones are visited by butterflies and bees, because they have longer tongues. They can reach right into the bottom of the flower, where the reward of nectar is waiting. Moth-pollinated flowers – such as honeysuckle – have a similar shape, but they give off their perfume at night, which is when most moths are on the wing.

Because most insects are small, insect-pollinated flowers are also small. But birds or bats often use flowers as landing pads, so it is important the flowers are tough. A bird or a bat can drink far more nectar than a bee, so their flowers produce nectar for days at a time, which guarantees lots of callers.

PARTNERS

Many pollinating insects visit a range of plants, but some kinds concentrate on just one kind.

These insects get all their food from the plant, as well as somewhere to raise their young. In return, they provide the plant with a private delivery service. In warm parts of the world, fig trees are pollinated in this way. There are over a thousand species of fig trees in the world, but amazingly, each one has its own kind of pollinating wasp.

▽ Banana flowers have a musky smell that attracts bats after dark. Here, a short-nosed fruit bat is lapping up nectar, and is getting covered in pollen as it feeds.

FLOWERHEADS

FOR PLANTS, THE BEST WAY OF
ATTRACTING ANIMALS IS TO PUT ON
A REALLY IMPRESSIVE SHOW. THIS IS
THE REASON WHY SO MANY PLANTS
GROW THEIR FLOWERS IN GROUPS.

O n their own, single flowers can be tricky to spot –
imagine searching for a single poppy in a field.
But if a plant has hundreds or thousands of flowers,
the combined display is much harder to miss. Plants stage this
show by having lots of separate flowers, or by growing the flowers
in clusters, which are known as flowerheads. Flowerheads are
almost as varied as flowers themselves, and some of the world's
best-known 'flowers' are actually flowerheads in disguise.

△ *Lotus plants have large single flowers.
Like the world's first flowers, they are built
on a simple circular plan, so their different
parts are easy to see. Flowerheads are more
complicated, and their individual flowers
are sometimes hidden away.*

FLORAL LOOKALIKES

To find one of the commonest kinds
of flowerhead, look no further than
the nearest patch of grassy ground.
This is the favourite habitat of
daisies – some of the most successful
and widespread weeds in the world.
Daisy plants look as though they

have individual flowers, but each
'flower' is actually made up of
dozens of mini-flowers, or florets.
In this kind of flowerhead, the
florets are arranged as if they were
on a plate. The ones in the middle
of the plate produce pollen and
seeds, while the ones around the

△ *Orchids have complicated flowers, with
colours and scents that attract particular
animals. Some orchids grow single flowers,
but most have eyecatching flowerheads.*

rim each have a single extra-large
petal, which makes the flowerhead
bright and easy to see.

Daisies belong to a gigantic family
of plants that is at least 25,000
species strong. Their relatives
include dandelions, goatsbeards,
thistles and sunflowers, as well as
many garden plants. Each species
is different and unique, but their
flowerheads are all built on the
same winning plan.

Lily		a.m.
Open 24 hours a day		p.m.
Evening primrose		a.m.
Open from dusk to dawn		p.m.
Goatsbeard		a.m.
Open in morning only		p.m.

◁ *Flowers often
have different
opening times,
shown in yellow
on these 12-hour
clocks. Lilies never
close. Evening
primroses, which
are pollinated by
moths, open at
night and close by
day. Goatsbeard
flowerheads have
one of the shortest
opening times –
they open around
sunrise, but close
by midday.*

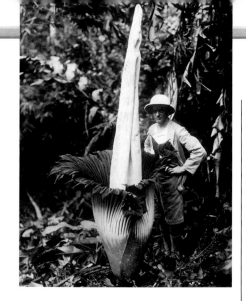

△ *The titan arum's flowerhead can be over 2.4 m tall, and up to 4 m around its rim. Rare in the wild, it has been successfully cultivated in botanical gardens.*

SPIRES AND UMBRELLAS

Daisy florets are not much wider than a human hair. But many flowerheads have much larger flowers, spaced much further apart. In foxgloves, for example, the flowers are as big as thimbles – the ideal size for bumblebees to squeeze their way inside.

In a foxglove flowerhead, the lowest flowers open first. So, when a bumblebee arrives to look for nectar, it starts at the bottom of the flowerhead and works its way up. Foxgloves take advantage of this behaviour, because the first flowers that a bee visits, at the bottom, contain only ripe female parts. These collect any pollen that the bee is carrying, and use it to make seeds. Higher up, where the flowers are younger, only the male parts are ripe. They dust the bee with pollen, and it flies away, carrying the pollen to another foxglove plant.

Lots of other plants have flowers in spires, but plants in the carrot family have flowerheads shaped more like umbrellas. Each umbrella has a set of spokes, topped with a set of flowers. For insects, these flowerheads make handy feeding platforms, and also great places for basking in the sun. Hoverflies are particularly fond of them, and they guard their umbrellas fiercely, zooming towards rivals and chasing them away.

STATELY BUT SMELLY

The world's tallest flowerhead belongs to a plant called *Puya raimondii*, which grows in the Bolivian Andes. It can be more than 10 m high, and it contains nearly 10,000 small white blooms. A *Puya* plant can take 100 years to grow, but it blooms just once, for about three months, and then dies. But for a combination of size and smell, nothing beats the titan arum, or devil's tongue, which grows in rainforests on the Indonesian island of Sumatra. Its flowerhead sprouts from a giant underground tuber, and it looks like a soft, fleshy spire towering out of a leathery cup.

Unlike the *Puya* flowerhead, this colossal object blooms for just four or five days, and it produces a powerful odour that smells like a mixture between burned cooking and rotting fish. Flies love the smell, but people find it so repulsive that it can even make them faint. The titan arum's flowers are tiny and well hidden. The only way to see them is to take a deep breath, get up close, and peer inside.

▽ *When sunflowers bloom, their outer florets open first. Because they have lots of florets, they stay in flower for many days.*

SEEDS AND FRUIT

INSIDE EVERY SEED IS AN EMBRYO PLANT, WAITING
FOR THE CHANCE TO GROW. SEEDS PROTECT
THIS IMPORTANT CARGO, WHILE FRUITS HELP
SEEDS TO SPREAD FAR AND WIDE. SOME SEEDS
CAN BE SMALLER AND LIGHTER THAN SPECKS
OF DUST, BUT THE LARGEST FRUITS OF ALL
CAN WEIGH ALMOST HALF A TONNE.

Seeds are designed to last, and they are the toughest objects in the entire plant world. If they are kept dry, they can survive for years, and if they are deep-frozen, they can often survive for a century or more. But as soon as outside conditions are right, a seed germinates, which means that the embryo inside it starts to grow. A fruit is a container that holds seeds. It shelters the seeds while they develop, and it often helps them spread.

SEED OR FRUIT?

Seeds and fruits are two quite different things, but they are easy to get muddled up. Seeds are usually small and hard, and each one always contains a single embryo plant. Most seeds also have a store of pre-packed food. This food keeps the embryo alive until it germinates. After this, it lets a young plant grow until it is able to make food of its own.

In everyday life, a fruit is something soft and juicy that is good to eat. But to scientists, a fruit is anything that contains seeds, as long as it is produced by a single flower. That means that fruits include not only apples, oranges and grapes, but also all sorts of other things, from cucumbers, coconuts and tomatoes to pea-pods and poppy-heads. The world's heaviest fruits are pumpkins: the largest specimen on record weighed a monstrous 481 kg.

◁ *Goosegrass fruits have tiny hooks, which cling to the fur of passing animals. These fruits break off easily if the animal brushes past.*

SEEDS IN STORAGE

Although seeds often look small and fragile, they can cope with conditions that would kill adult plants. They do not need light, and they can survive with almost no water or air. Also, seeds are not harmed by the cold. Low temperatures simply slow down their onboard chemistry, so putting seeds in a fridge keeps them fresh. Once they are brought out, warmed

◁ *These four pictures show a wheat seedling germinating. Seedlings need water, so their number one priority is to grow a root that collects water from the soil.*

△ *This is the winged fruit of a climbing plant called* Alsomitra macrocarpa, *which grows in the rainforests of southeast Asia. With 'wings' that are 15 cm across, it can take over a minute to flutter to the ground.*

up and wetted, they miraculously come back to life. Cold storage is a method used by conservationists to protect many of the world's endangered plants. In the past ten years, seeds from thousands of rare plants have been collected, dried out and stored in special seed banks in different parts of the world. They are kept at a temperature of about −20° C, which is about the same as in a deep freeze. In these chilly conditions, seeds can last a long time. Most of the ones in store today will be alive and well in the year 2100 and beyond.

GERMINATION

Seeds need warmth and moisture before they can start to grow. But to be on the safe side, they wait for the right moment before breaking their dormancy or sleep. In places where the winters are cold, most seeds do not germinate until they have been 'primed' by several weeks of frost. This means that they come to life when winter is properly over, rather than during mild periods in between. In deserts, many seeds are triggered into life by sudden storms, while in shrublands, they are often primed by natural chemicals formed during bushfires. This ingenious system means that they start growing as soon as a fire is over, when the ground is covered with fertile ash.

AGAINST THE ODDS

Despite their toughness, individual seeds have only a tiny chance of growing into adult plants. For some, disaster strikes early on, when they get eaten before they have left their parent plant. For many others, a similar fate lies in store on the ground. Small birds often feed on seeds, and rodents are fond of them too. Seeds can also be attacked by diseases and by moulds. With this long list of dangers, it is not surprising that so few survive.

To make up for all these casualties, plants produce seeds on a massive scale. A single grass plant can produce hundreds of seeds, while an oak tree can grow more than a hundred thousand acorns a year. And, unlike a grass plant, an oak tree goes on doing this for two centuries or more.

But the champion seed-producers are orchids that grow high up on tropical trees. Just one of these plants can produce over ten million seeds. These orchid seeds are the smallest and lightest in the world, and it would take almost a billion of them to weigh as much as a pea.

SEEDS ON THE MOVE

YOUNG PLANTS NEED TO GET AWAY
FROM THEIR PARENTS, SO THAT THEY
HAVE ENOUGH LIGHT AND SPACE TO GROW.
OVER MILLIONS OF YEARS, PLANTS HAVE COME
UP WITH SOME AMAZING WAYS TO SCATTER
THEIR SEEDS FAR AND WIDE. SOME DO IT ALL
ON THEIR OWN, BUT MANY RELY ON OUTSIDE HELP.

△ These jackal berry seedlings
are germinating in a pile of elephant
dung. Jackal berry seeds are primed to
germinate by being swallowed, and then
passing through an animal's intestines.

△ In the rainforests of Central America,
the quetzal feeds on fruits with large seeds
or stones. The bird digests most of the fruit,
but it drops the stones on the forest floor.

Plants are incredibly good at spreading, even though they
cannot move. They quickly take over newly cleared ground,
whether it is in someone's back garden, or on remote islands
far out at sea. Plants set up home on other plants, and a few even
manage to take root in walls and on rooftops, high above city
streets. Plants can get to these places because their seeds are natural
travellers. Thanks to them, hardly anywhere is beyond their reach.

CATAPULTS AND BOMBS
The world's heaviest seed belongs
to the coco-de-mer, a rare palm that
grows in the Seychelles (see p. 155).
Its seeds can weigh a massive 20 kg.
When they are ripe, they simply
crash to the ground, roll a few
metres, and then come to a halt. But
many seeds travel a lot farther than
this. To get going they rely on fruits,
because these natural containers are
designed to help seeds to disperse.
   Plants with dry fruits often get
their seeds off to a flying start.
For example, poppy-heads work like
miniature pepperpots, scattering
their seeds when the wind blows
past. Pods are more like catapults.
Once they have dried out in the
sunshine, they split open with a
snap, flinging their seeds across the

ground. One unusual fruit, called the
squirting cucumber, behaves like a
miniature bomb. This bristly object
explodes when ripe, blasting seeds
and juice several metres into the air.

DRIFTERS AND FLOATERS
Snapping and bursting works well
enough, but seeds travel even farther
when they drift or float away.
Many of the world's most successful
weeds – including dandelions and
thistles – have feathery fruits that
are blown away by the wind. Each
fruit contains a single seed, and a
bristly parachute that helps it along.
In forests, plants often have fruits
with wings, which helicopter their
way to the ground. Some are not
much bigger than a fingernail,
but giant ones, such as *Alsomitra*

macrocarpa (see p. 95), can have a 'wingspan' as large as some birds'.

Coastal plants, like the coconut palm, often have waterproof fruits that float. If a coconut is caught by a current, it can drift across an entire ocean to germinate on a faraway shore. The same is true of a plant

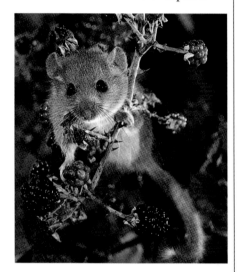

△ *Common dormice feast on blackberries, helping to scatter the seeds. Soft fruit like these change colour when they are ripe, letting animals know they are ready to eat.*

called the sea bean, which grows on coasts around the Caribbean Sea. Its heart-shaped seeds often cross the Atlantic, and they are sometimes washed up north of the Arctic Circle.

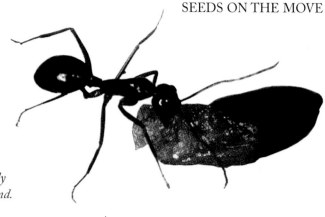

▷ *This ant has made a useful find – a seed with a special parcel of food. Back in their nest, the ants eat the food parcel but abandon the seed, unintentionally 'planting' it underground.*

ANIMAL HELPERS

These travels are impressive enough, but they are only half the story. Just as plants use animals to carry their pollen, they also use them to spread their seeds. Many of their fruits have hooks or barbs, which work by latching onto fur and skin. Some of these fruits are also good at sticking to socks or fastening themselves to shoes. Fortunately, most of these hitchhikers are small, but a few reach a serious size. In Africa, the devil's claw has hooks up to 8 cm long – just the thing for snagging onto antelope hooves.

Juicy fruits also use animals, but they work in a more roundabout way. When these fruits are ripe, they become brightly coloured, which attracts animals looking for a meal. Animals are less fussy than humans, and they do not bother to pick out the seeds as they feed. Instead, they

swallow the fruit whole, taking in the seeds. The fruit's flesh soon gets digested, but the seeds are much tougher. Unless they are chewed, they will pass through animals unharmed. Digestive juices often prime them to germinate and, without animals, some of them cannot begin to grow.

Fruit-eating animals include many kinds of birds, as well as mammals and even some fish. Most of them make good seed-spreaders, because they are always on the move. For plants, they are doubly useful, because they often scatter seeds in a ready-made fertilizer – a pile of droppings or dung.

▽ *When tumbleweeds have finished flowering, their roots shrivel up and break away. The dead plants then roll along in the wind, scattering seeds as they go.*

PLANTS WITHOUT FLOWERS

NO MATTER HOW HARD YOU LOOK, YOU WILL NEVER FIND A MOSS OR A FERN IN FLOWER. PLANTS LIKE THESE BREED WITHOUT NEEDING TO FLOWER – JUST LIKE THE EARLIEST PLANTS ON EARTH.

Until the end of the age of the dinosaurs, flowers did not exist. There was no grass – because grasses are flowering plants – and no broadleaved trees. All plants bred by shedding tiny spores or by making primitive seeds. Since then, the world has changed a great deal. The dinosaurs have vanished, and flowerless plants have been pushed aside by ones that have blooms. But flowerless plants still survive, and some are a great success.

◁ *Mosses grow their spores in slender capsules, which are usually just a few centimetres high. One of these capsules has opened up, so that it can scatter its spores into the air.*

MOSSES AND LIVERWORTS

One of the best places to see these flowerless survivors is by fast-flowing streams. The rushing water creates a cool and damp habitat – exactly the sort of place where mosses thrive. Mosses are basic plants, without true leaves or roots. They often look like bright green

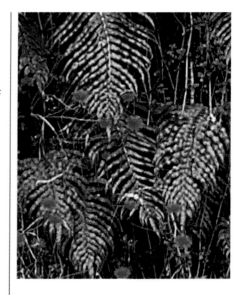

△ *Filmy ferns get their name because their leaves are just one cell thick. These delicate plants can grow only in very humid places, because they dry out easily.*

◁ *Liverworts spread by making spores, and by growing cups containing miniature 'eggs'. The eggs jump out of their cups when they are hit by rain. Exactly the same technique is used by the bird's nest fungus (see p. 73).*

cushions, although some underwater kinds are like trailing hair. Unlike flowering plants, they are small and compact. The world's tallest species, from Australia, is only 60 cm high.

To grow, mosses have to be wet, and many of them can hold water like a sponge. But although they like streamsides and boggy places, they do not have to be permanently damp. Some mosses grow on rocks and walls, where they can dry out for weeks or months at a time. These dried-out mosses look grey and dead, but when it rains, they quickly come back to life.

Streamsides are also a favourite habitat for liverworts – the simplest plants in the world. Some look like small green tongues, while others are more like ribbons with tiny leaves. Liverworts creep along instead of growing upwards, and branch by splitting in two. Many grow over damp rocks, but in rainforests they also live on other plants' leaves. They do not damage their host plant, but they do steal some of its light.

FERNS

There are over 11,000 species of ferns, which makes them the largest group of non-flowering plants. The smallest kinds could easily fit in an egg cup, but the world's tallest species – tree ferns – can be up to 25 m high. Most ferns are rooted in the ground, but some clamp onto tree trunks, while a few float on the surface of ponds. Some species of ferns are rare, but one kind, called bracken, is a troublesome weed.

Compared to mosses and liverworts, ferns are more like flowering plants. They have true roots as well as stems and leaves, and they also have internal pipelines that carry water up from the soil. But ferns do not have flowers, and they spread by making spores rather than seeds. Their life cycles switch between two very different kinds of plants (see p. 101).

CONIFERS AND THEIR RELATIVES

Seeds and flowers usually go together, but in the history of plants, seeds were actually developed first. That explains why conifers can have seeds, although they do not have flowers. There are only about 550 kinds of conifers in the world, compared to 250,000 kinds of flowering plants, but they are still very successful in places where it is dry or cold. In the far north, they make up the boreal forest – the largest forest in the world.

Conifers also have some relatives that are harder to find. They include cycads – which look like palm trees – and the ginkgo, or maidenhair tree. This 'living fossil' comes from the Far East, and has leaves that look like bright green fans. Another conifer relative, called *Welwitschia* (see p. 184), is a leading candidate for the title of strangest plant in the world. It lives in the deserts of southwest Africa, and it often looks like a pile of rubbish rather than something that is alive.

△ *Conifers have two types of cones. Male cones make pollen, but female cones make seeds. These are young female cones from a larch tree. They are still soft, but they will turn hard and woody when they are ripe.*

PLANT LIFE CYCLES

TWO OR THREE TIMES EVERY CENTURY, MILLIONS OF
BAMBOO PLANTS IN CENTRAL CHINA BURST INTO
BLOOM, SET SEED AND DIE. THIS FINAL FLOURISH IS
NOT AN ACCIDENT – INSTEAD, IT IS JUST ONE OF THE
MANY WAYS IN WHICH PLANTS ORGANIZE THEIR LIVES.

Compared to animals, plants have amazingly varied
lifespans. At the one extreme, some live for a few
weeks, but bristlecone pines can keep going for
more than 5,000 years. Creosote bushes may sail past their
10,000th birthday, because each clump keeps on spreading
long after its oldest part is dead. A few – including many
bamboos – bloom in a single, suicidal burst. But whatever
their lifespan, plants divide up their lives in different ways.

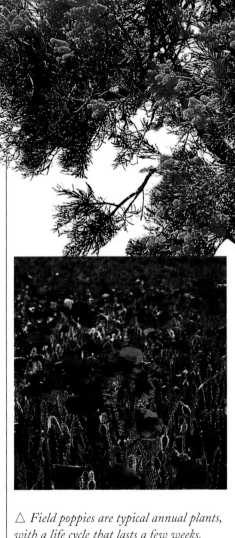

A SPEEDY START
For most weeds, the important thing
in life is speed. These plants often
grow on disturbed ground, and they
need to flower and set seed before
larger plants squeeze them out.
Instead of storing away food for
hard times, they put all their energy
into flowering and, after this, they
die. These plants are known as
annuals, because they complete their
whole life cycle in less than a year.
Annuals include poppies and other
wayside weeds, as well as plants that
spring up in deserts soon after it rains.

A LIFE IN TWO HALVES
In places where the winters are
cold, many plants follow a different
timetable. They live for two years,
and in the first year, concentrate on
growing and storing up food. In the
second year, they use up all their
food reserves to grow flowers. Then
their lives usually come to an end.
These plants are known as biennials.

△ *Mulleins are biennial plants. During
the first year (top photograph) the plant
is low-growing, and has a rosette of
leaves. In the second year, it puts all
its energy into growing an impressive
flowerhead, which can be over 2 m high.*

△ *Field poppies are typical annual plants,
with a life cycle that lasts a few weeks.
They do not live long as plants, but their
seeds can survive for many years in the soil.*

△ *In mountain pastures, many perennial plants grow from tubers or bulbs. These orchids are flowering in the Pyrenees.*

Biennials often store food in roots or tubers, because there is less chance of being eaten underground. Carrots are biennials – they are dug up after their first year, before they have a chance to flower and go to seed.

PERMANENT PLANTS

Annuals and biennials are 'temporary' plants. They are quick to appear, but they never grow in the same place for long. The reason why they keep on the move is that they have to compete against plants which are designed to last. These permanent plants are called perennials. They include ones that die down to ground level at the end of each year, as well as all the world's shrubs and trees. Compared to annuals and biennials, perennials play a long-term game. They often grow slowly, and it can take them years to reach adult size. But once they are mature, they keep faster-growing plants in the shade. Unlike their smaller rivals, most perennials keep flowering year after year.

GRAND FINALE

Over 99 per cent of all the world's plants follow one of these life cycles. The ones that do not are the plant world's real eccentrics, which save all their energy for a once-in-a-lifetime explosion of flowers. These plants include many different kinds of

△ *Agave flowerheads can be more than 15 m high. Something this big takes a huge amount of energy to grow, which is why agaves flower just once, then die.*

bamboos, as well as agaves, many bromeliads, and the famous talipot palm (see p. 105). Talipot palms grow until they are about 75 years old, and then they produce one of the biggest flower shows in the world. Although the tree dies, this grand finale is not in vain, because it produces a gigantic crop of seeds.

△ *The Australian Christmas tree is a woody perennial. As long as it gets enough water, it grows bigger every year. At Christmas, it produces a stunning display of flowers.*

▷ *Ferns have complicated life cycles that involve two separate types of plant. 'Adult' ferns release spores, which germinate to produce plants called gametophytes. These make male and female sex cells, which come together to produce the next generation of adult plants. Fern gametophytes are paper-thin and often smaller than a stamp.*

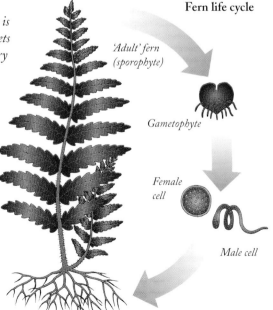

Fern life cycle

'Adult' fern
(sporophyte)

Gametophyte

Female
cell

Male cell

TREES

TREES ARE THE TALLEST AND HEAVIEST
LIVING THINGS THAT HAVE EVER EXISTED
ON EARTH. FOR THOUSANDS OF YEARS, PEOPLE
HAVE USED THEM FOR WOOD AND FOR FOOD,
BUT EVEN TODAY, NEW KINDS ARE STILL BEING
DISCOVERED IN REMOTE PARTS OF THE WORLD.

△ *This picture shows magnified cells deep inside an oak tree's trunk.*

People often talk about trees and plants as if they were different things. It is easy to see why, because trees reach such an impressive size. But trees are plants, although they are built on a gigantic scale. The feature that makes trees special is that they have trunks and branches made of wood. Wood is the plant world's strongest building material. It takes time and energy to make, but it enables trees to tower above other plants. This gives trees an unbeatable advantage in the struggle to collect light.

REACHING FOR THE SKY
The world's tallest trees are coast redwoods, which grow in northern California. Helped by the mild and foggy coastal climate, these majestic conifers can be more than 110 m high. In the past, some trees were even taller than this. In 1885, the giant trunk of a fallen mountain ash was discovered in Australia.

▷ *This giant fig tree, from the Kakamega Forest in Kenya, is held up by huge buttress roots which snake their way across the ground. Figs are broadleaved trees, and they grow mainly in warm parts of the world.*

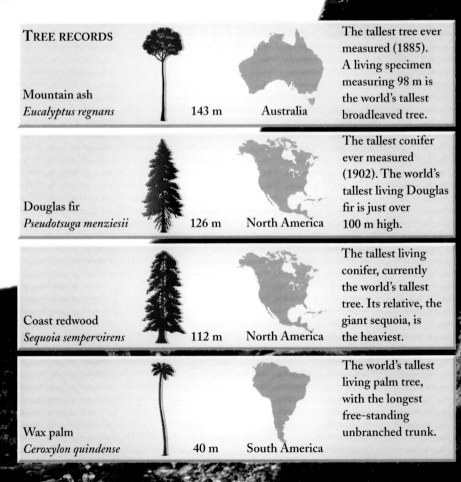

TREE RECORDS

Mountain ash *Eucalyptus regnans*	143 m	Australia	The tallest tree ever measured (1885). A living specimen measuring 98 m is the world's tallest broadleaved tree.
Douglas fir *Pseudotsuga menziesii*	126 m	North America	The tallest conifer ever measured (1902). The world's tallest living Douglas fir is just over 100 m high.
Coast redwood *Sequoia sempervirens*	112 m	North America	The tallest living conifer, currently the world's tallest tree. Its relative, the giant sequoia, is the heaviest.
Wax palm *Ceroxylon quindense*	40 m	South America	The world's tallest living palm tree, with the longest free-standing unbranched trunk.

When this tree was alive, it probably towered over 140 m above the ground. But some dendrologists – or tree experts – believe prehistoric trees may have reached 175 m, in other words about 25 storeys high. When architects design skyscrapers, they know exactly how tall the finished building will be, but a tree keeps growing upwards until something stops it or makes it fall down. The threats that face trees include lightning, drought and wind, and the taller a tree grows the more dangerous they become.

△ *California's upright coast redwoods are a tempting target for woodcutters. Over the years, conservationists have battled to stop these conifers from being cut down.*

TYPES OF TREES

With a few rare exceptions, all the world's trees belong to just two groups of plants. The first contains conifers, which are trees that grow their seeds in cones. Most of these trees are evergreen, with scaly or needle-shaped leaves. Conifers grow quickly and often have dead-straight trunks – something that makes them very useful as timber trees. There are only about 550 species of conifers, which is very few compared to the total number of plant species in the world. But conifers are very common, and because they are planted for their wood, they are becoming more widespread all the time.

The second group contains broadleaved trees. Not all of them actually have broad leaves, but they do all grow flowers. Some have flowers that are pollinated by wind, but many have eyecatching blooms that attract animal visitors. In the tropics, broadleaved trees are usually evergreen, but in places with dry seasons or cold winters, their branches are bare for several months each year. Broadleaved trees are amazingly varied, and they live in all kinds of habitats, from deserts to seashore mud. Over 10,000 species have been identified, but no one knows how many kinds there are in total.

1   **2**   **3**

△ *Broadleaved trees all have flowers, but they are pollinated in different ways. Oak trees (1) have catkins pollinated by the wind. Judas trees (2) and horse chestnuts (3) have flowers pollinated by insects.*

◁ *Trees growing in exposed places often develop a lopsided shape. This happens because the prevailing wind kills buds on one side of the tree, making it grow in the opposite direction. This windswept shape protects the tree.*

HOW TREES GROW

TREES CAN KEEP GROWING FOR CENTURIES, SO THEY HAVE TO BE BUILT FOR STRENGTH. MOST TREES STEADILY REINFORCE THEMSELVES AS THEY GROW, SO THE OLDER AND TALLER THEY ARE, THE STRONGER THEY BECOME.

In the tropics, some trees rush upwards at the rate of 5 m a year – that is about 100 times faster than humans grow during their teens. In other parts of the world, trees grow more slowly, but some still put on a metre or more every spring. For trees, growing is a complicated business, and it has to be carefully managed. That is because each extra metre increases the risks of getting blown down or falling apart.

SAPWOOD AND HEARTWOOD

Trees do not simply grow upwards – most of them grow outwards at the same time. This outward growth is produced by the cambium – a layer of living tissue only a few cells thick. The cambium is just beneath the bark, and it covers the whole of the tree like an invisible film. Trees grow

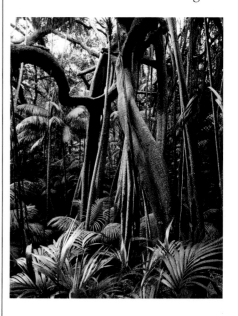

△ *Banyan trees sprout roots that can turn into extra trunks. The world's largest banyan tree has over 1,700 trunks, and covers an area bigger than a football pitch.*

▽ *In mountains, the higher trees are, the more slowly they grow. The tree line marks the point where conditions become too tough for them to survive.*

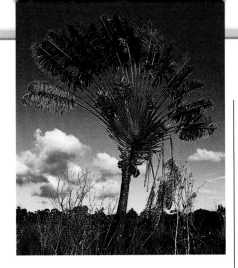

△ *The traveller's tree, from Madagascar, grows a gigantic fan of leaves. The youngest leaves are at the top of the fan, and the oldest ones at the sides.*

when the cells in their cambium start to divide. On the inside face of the cambium, the cells produce new wood which makes the trunk and the branches expand. On the outside face, they produce new bark, which pushes outwards, making the old bark split or fall away. These two kinds of growth fatten up a tree, giving it the extra strength it needs.

Because the cambium stays near the surface, this is where a tree's youngest wood is found. Called sapwood, it is sometimes so full of sap that it feels slippery and wet if it is cut. But as each year's sapwood gets older, it gradually starts to change. It stops carrying sap, because its cells become blocked with resins and oils. This turns it into heartwood – old wood that is heavy and hard. Heartwood strengthens trunks and branches like an inner skeleton. But unlike bone, heartwood cannot grow, because almost all of its cells are dead.

GROWTH RINGS

In places where it is always wet and warm, trees can grow all year round. But where the winters are cold, all the year's wood is formed in a single burst during spring and early summer. These bursts of growth create rings in the wood, which can be seen when trees are cut down.

By counting growth rings, it is easy to work out a tree's age. But growth rings can reveal much more than this. Because they are thick when growing conditions are good, and thin when they are bad, they also show what the weather was like in the past. By examining growth rings from the world's oldest trees, dendrochronologists – or tree ring experts – have been able to piece together a climate record for the world dating back more than 5,000 years.

△ *Talipot palms, from southeast Asia, bloom once and then die. Each tree can have over a quarter of a million creamy yellow flowers.*

PALM TREES

Most trees have a 'wrap-around' cambium, but palms and their close relatives are built in a quite different way. They have just a single growing point, at the very tips of their trunks. The growing point builds the trunk, and as it moves upwards, growth beneath it stops. If the top of a palm is cut off, the tree stops growing and dies.

This unusual growth technique means that palm trunks get taller without getting any stouter – one of the reasons why they are such graceful trees. Palm trunks do not

have true bark, which means that they cannot heal cuts in the same way as other trees. People who harvest coconuts make use of this. The steps that they cut into a coconut palm in order to climb it last for the whole of its life.

CHANGING SHAPES

Palm trees never have branches, but with other trees, new branches often shade out the old ones lower down. To deal with this problem, trees often carry out their own tree surgery, by shedding the branches nearest the ground. This surgery starts when a tree is young, and it continues year after year. As a result, the remaining branches move higher and higher, and the tree develops a crown. Some of the world's greatest branch-shedders grow in tropical forests. Here, the tallest trees end up with smooth, branchless trunks up to 30 m high, soaring upwards like pillars from the forest floor.

Trees respond to their surroundings in other ways. They grow taller if they are crowded, and they often lean away from the prevailing wind. In shady conditions, they often have larger leaves. These different growth patterns help to explain why no two trees are exactly the same.

Conifers usually have short branches and keep their upright shape as they grow.

Palms have no branches. They grow taller, but their trunks do not become thicker.

Most broadleaved trees change shape as they get older, developing a rounded crown.

PLANT DEFENCES

PLANTS CANNOT BITE BACK AT HUNGRY ANIMALS, BUT THEY HAVE PLENTY OF WEAPONS THAT CAN STOP THEM IN THEIR TRACKS, OR EVEN KILL THEM.

△ *Poison ivy contains a chemical called urushiol, which causes skin inflammation. The poison can be spread on clothes, and even in smoke if the plant is burned.*

△ *Stings give nettles protection from plant-eating mammals. Cattle and horses eat lots of other wild plants, but they leave nettles well alone.*

In the animal kingdom, vegetarians outnumber predators by at least ten to one. From insects to elephants, they add up to billions of mouths, all hungry for their share of food. Without protection, the world's plants would be helpless, and every last trace of them would soon disappear. But plants manage to thrive. That is because evolution has given them ingenious – and sometimes painful – ways of fighting back.

SECRET SHIELDS

The commonest weapons in the plant world can be seen only through a microscope. They are tiny hairs, and they cover many plants like miniature forests, just a few millimetres high. Some of these hairs are branched, and are designed to snap off and

clog up insects' mouths. Others produce blobs of sticky substances, which trap aphids and other sap-suckers before they have a chance to feed. Hairs are particularly important for protecting new stems and leaves, which is why these often have a silky or sticky feel.

To fend off much larger animals, bigger weapons are needed. On their stems and leaves, nettles have hollow hairs made of silica, which work like hypodermic needles. If an animal – or person – touches one of these hairs, the tip snaps off and injects a collection of toxic chemicals, including formic acid, the same substance found in ant stings.

△ *Cholla cacti have brittle stems covered with spines. If an animal touches one of these plants, pieces of stem break off and fasten themselves to its skin.*

▷ *Animals often use camouflage to avoid attack, but this tactic is much harder for plants. These living stones, found in the deserts of southwest Africa, masquerade as pebbles in their gravel-covered home.*

Stings from the common nettle hurt for a few hours and then fade away, but some species – such as the New Zealand nettle tree – have much more powerful stings that have been known to kill farm animals. However, these stings are too large to bother insects, which is why many caterpillars grow fat on a diet of nettle leaves.

SPINES AND THORNS

In dry habitats, animals use plants for water as well as for food. Here, plants often defend themselves with an armoury of vicious spines. Acacia trees have woody spines that are up to 15 cm long, but the most painful spines are ones that belong to cacti. Some cacti spines have overlapping scales that point backwards towards the plant. If one of these gets into an animal's skin, the scales make it very hard – and uncomfortable – for the spine to work its way out. If this were not enough, cacti also have another defence, because their spines sit in tufts of slender hairs. These hairs look harmless, but they

△ Many plants produce latex – a milky sap containing defensive chemicals. Here, latex is being tapped from a rubber tree by cutting into the wood.

easily break off. Once in skin, they cause an irritation that can last for days.

Spines give animals an instant warning, making them move away, but thorns often have the opposite effect. Because thorns are curved, they hook into an animal's skin, making it difficult for the animal to escape. While the animal struggles to extract itself, it learns a painful lesson. With luck, it remembers not to tangle with the plant a second time.

CHEMICAL WEAPONS

If an animal does breach a plant's outer defences, it may have an unpleasant surprise in store. This is because many plants use chemical weapons to avoid ending up as food. Some of these substances simply make leaves taste bitter or become difficult to digest, but they also include some deadly poisons. For example, a common garden shrub called cherry laurel can produce cyanide in its leaves. Normally, the leaves are quite harmless because they contain the ingredients for making cyanide, rather than the poison itself. But if an animal starts to feed on them, cyanide starts to form. Its sickly sweet smell warns the animal that it is dicing with death.

Most plant poisons have to be swallowed or breathed in before they work, but some are dangerous even if they touch the skin. Poison ivy is one of the most notorious, because it produces a toxic resin that can stick to clothes and shoes. Even months later, its effects can still be felt.

▷ For plants, animals can be allies as well as enemies. These South American ants live inside cecropia trees. In return for a home, they attack anything that tries to feed on the trees' leaves.

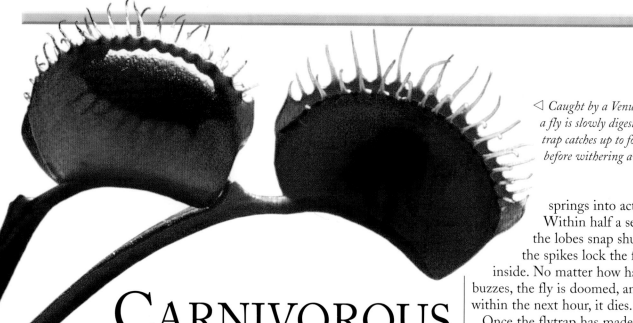

△ Caught by a Venus flytrap, a fly is slowly digested. Each trap catches up to four insects, before withering away.

CARNIVOROUS PLANTS

TO AN UNWARY FLY, A VENUS FLYTRAP SEEMS LIKE A GOOD PLACE TO LAND. BUT IT IS A DEADLY MISTAKE, BECAUSE THE FLYTRAP IS CARNIVOROUS AND IT USES FLIES AS FOOD.

Plants grow by using sunlight, but they also need simple nutrients, just like we need salt and other minerals. Most plants get these from the ground, but carnivorous plants get some of theirs by catching and digesting animals. These plants have evolved sophisticated lures and traps, and most of them catch insect prey.

OPEN AND SHUT
The Venus flytrap is barely more than ankle-high, but it is one of the strangest plants in the world. Each of its leaves is divided into two flat lobes, bordered by a row of spikes. The lobes join at a hinge, but they are normally held wide open, to make an inviting landing platform for passing flies. The platform has a special attraction: it produces sugary nectar that insects use as food. But if a fly lands to feed, it brushes against special trigger hairs, and the trap

springs into action. Within half a second, the lobes snap shut, and the spikes lock the fly inside. No matter how hard it buzzes, the fly is doomed, and within the next hour, it dies.

Once the flytrap has made a catch, its digestive enzymes set to work. They break down the fly's body, so that the plant can absorb the nutrients that it contains. Several days later, the remains of the fly fall out, and the trap is ready to make another catch.

STUCK FAST
Venus flytraps are amazingly sensitive, and they can tell the

◁▽ Climbing pitcher plants have traps at the ends of their leaves. Each trap has a lid and a funnel. The pool of digestive fluid often contains dead remains.

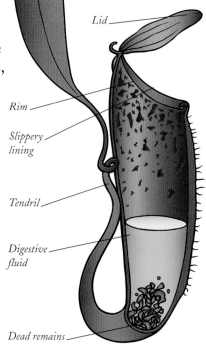

Lid

Rim

Slippery lining

Tendril

Digestive fluid

Dead remains

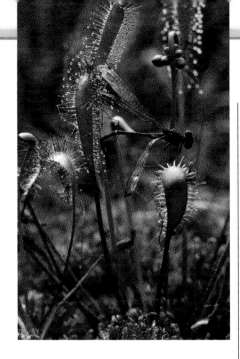

△ *There are over 100 species of sundews, which is about a quarter of all the world's carnivorous plants. This one – growing in a peat bog – has caught a damselfly.*

difference between appetizing insects and inedible objects that fall into their traps by chance. But most of the world's carnivorous plants 'hunt' in a different way. They lure insects into sticky situations that make it very difficult for them to escape. Some of the commonest of these plants are called sundews. They live all over the world, particularly on mountains and in boggy places. A sundew's leaves are covered in sticky hairs, which carry drops of glue-like fluid. If an insect lands on a sundew leaf, the hairs fold over it and it cannot escape.

DEATH BY DROWNING

Insects are often attracted to sweet-smelling drinks, and sometimes they fall into them and drown. Pitcher plants use exactly the same principle to catch their prey. There are several kinds of pitcher plants, and they grow in many habitats, from marshland to tropical forests. Although they belong to different plant families, their traps work in much the same way. Each pitcher is like a vase, and it has a slippery rim that gives off a rotting scent. If an

insect lands on the rim to investigate the smell, it slips over and tumbles inside. The bottom of the pitcher contains a pool of digestive juice, which turns insects into meals.

Some pitcher plants are just a few centimetres high, and have traps that sit on the ground. But the world's largest species, from Southeast Asia and Australia, can be over 6 m long, and climbs upwards through trees and shrubs. One of the rarest of these plants, called *Nepenthes rajah*, lives in the rainforests of northwest Borneo. Its pitchers can hold over a litre of fluid, and they are so large that rats have been known to fall into them and drown.

BLIND EXIT

Most pitchers have flaps that work like umbrellas, stopping rainwater getting inside. But a plant called the cobra lily, from California and Oregon, has hooded pitchers with protruding tongues. The tongues produce nectar, and this attracts flies searching for food. When a fly lands, it walks along the tongue and into the pitcher's mouth. Here, it sees a collection of tiny windows above it. The insect flies up towards the windows, but finds it cannot escape.

△ *The Albany pitcher plant grows in southwest Australia. Its pitchers are close to the ground – the ideal place for catching beetles and ants looking for food.*

Soon it becomes exhausted, and drops into the deadly fluid below.

UNDERWATER HUNTERS

The Venus flytrap reacts amazingly quickly, but some even faster hunters set their traps in ponds and lakes. These plants are called bladderworts, and they catch tiny

△ *These balloon-shaped objects are a bladderwort's underwater traps. Although they look harmless, they are a deadly threat to small animals that come too close.*

water animals, such as worms and water fleas. Bladderworts drift across the water's surface, and as well as upright stems, they have curling underwater stems that look very much like roots. These underwater stems carry the plant's hunting equipment. Each one bears dozens of traps, which look like tiny balloons. Each trap has a small trapdoor, which is normally kept tightly shut. To prime the traps, the plant pumps out some of their water, so that the pressure in them is lower than the water outside. If an animal swims too near a trap, it touches a set of bristles that are attached to the door. The door flicks open, and the trap sucks in water, carrying the animal inside. The door then snaps shut. Once the victim has been digested, the trap is reprimed, so that it is ready for another catch.

PASSENGERS AND PARASITES

MOST PLANTS RELY ON THEIR OWN RESOURCES IN THE DAILY STRUGGLE TO SURVIVE, BUT SOME USE THEIR NEIGHBOURS AS WELL. THESE PLANTS INCLUDE HARMLESS PASSENGERS, AND SOME DAMAGING OR DEADLY PARASITES.

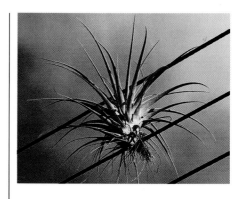

△ *Unlike most epiphytes, air plants can survive in places where the climate is dry. This one has managed to set up home on a telephone wire.*

In the plant world, light is the key to success. Individual plants grab as much as they can, but the competition is tough, particularly if there are trees nearby. Plants called epiphytes have evolved a way around this problem – they perch on other plants. Parasitic plants are more ruthless. They attack their hosts, stealing their water and food.

△ *There are about 20,000 kinds of orchids in the world, and over half of them are epiphytes that grow on other plants. This king orchid, from Queensland, Australia, is growing on a tree trunk.*

FREE RIDES

Epiphytic plants are specialists in life off the ground. Most of them live on trees, because this gives them a solid perch where they can grow safely for many years. In temperate regions – such as North America and Europe – the most common epiphytes are mosses and ferns, but in the tropics, trunks and branches are often draped with flowering plants as well. These high-rise flowerers include some of the world's most beautiful orchids, as well as spiky plants called bromeliads, which can grow to be larger than a supermarket trolley, and can weigh more than an adult man.

Despite their differences, epiphytes share a number of interesting adaptations for their unusual way of life. They hang on with specialized roots or stems, and they also use these for collecting water when it rains. They get nutrients from airborne dust, or from dead leaves that fall on them from above.

UNWELCOME APPROACH

Epiphytes do not do any harm to their host plants, although if there are too many of them, their weight can sometimes bring branches crashing to the ground. Parasitic plants are different, because they live at their hosts' expense. There are different levels of this sneaky lifestyle: some parasites merely steal from their neighbours, others grow on them, but a few actually spend their lives hidden away inside them.

The Australian Christmas tree (see p. 101) is an example of a parasite that robs its neighbours. Its roots break into ones grown by nearby plants, so that it can siphon off

△ *Rafflesia plants have no roots and no leaves, but gigantic flowers. Their seeds are spread by large forest animals, including elephants.*

their water and sap. Its commonest hosts are grasses, but it will try to break into almost anything that is shaped like a root, including buried cables.

Because roots are hidden away, it is difficult to recognize parasites that steal underground. Above-ground

parasites are much easier to spot. One of the commonest is a plant called dodder, which is found in many parts of the world. Its spaghetti-like stems swarm over its host, producing small growths that steal water and nutrients by breaking into its stems. Dodder starts life on the ground, but its roots soon wither

△ *Dodder stems wind around their host plants, seeking out places where they can break in and steal water and nutrients.*

away. It can leap from host to host, creating a tangled web a number of metres across.

PLANT INVADERS

Mistletoe is a parasite that many people have heard of, because it is often gathered and hung up at Christmas time. It lives on trees, and spreads by growing berries that contain sticky seeds. Birds eat the berries, but the seeds often stick in their beaks. When they clean their beaks on branches, the seeds are left behind. Dwarf mistletoe, from North America, spreads in an

△ *Witchweeds are parasites that attack many crops, including maize, rice and sugar cane. Here, a witchweed seed – coloured orange – is germinating, and has started to attack a plant.*

explosive way. Its berries burst open when they are ripe, firing their seeds sideways at speeds of up to 100 km/h. The world's most impressive parasite – giant rafflesia – lives in the forests of Sumatra. It attacks vines, and its flowers are the largest of any in the world. But this is the only part of the plant that is ever seen, because the rest is hidden away inside its unlucky host.

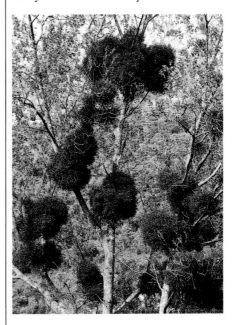

△ *This old poplar tree has been attacked by dozens of mistletoe plants. With so many parasites stealing its nutrients, the tree will find it difficult to grow.*

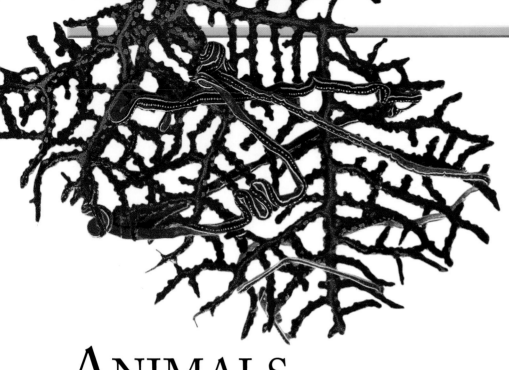

ANIMALS

THE WORLD TEEMS WITH ANIMALS. THEY LIVE IN EVERY HABITAT, FROM TROPICAL FORESTS TO POLAR ICE. SO FAR, SCIENTISTS HAVE IDENTIFIED ABOUT TWO MILLION DIFFERENT KINDS, BUT MILLIONS MORE ARE STILL WAITING TO BE DISCOVERED.

There is no such thing as a typical animal, because animals are the most varied living things on earth. Some kinds are as soft as jelly, and hardly look like animals at all, while many have much more complex bodies, with tough skeletons, keen senses and weapons, such as teeth, claws or stings.

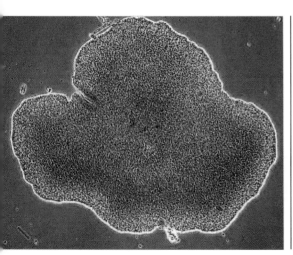

◁ *Placozoans were discovered in 1883 by a sharp-eyed scientist who found them in a saltwater aquarium. They are not the world's smallest animals, but they are the simplest. They have no close relatives.*

ANIMAL FEATURES

The world's simplest animals are so tiny that they can only just be seen with the naked eye. Called placozoans, they are shaped like miniature pancakes, and their paper-thin bodies are just 2 mm across. Placozoans live in water, and they

◁ *Ribbon worms are the longest animals in the world. One record-breaking specimen measured over 55 m from its head to the tip of its tail – making it over 50 per cent longer than the biggest blue whale.*

do not have eyes, fins or even mouths. They creep over rocks and grains of sand, and they reproduce by breaking into separate pieces which take up life on their own.

It would take 15,000 placozoans, lined up end to end, to stretch the full length of a blue whale. This sea-going mammal is the largest animal that has ever lived, with a weight of up to 190 tonnes. Despite this incredible difference in size, placozoans and whales do have some things in common. Like all animals, their bodies are made up of lots of cells. They have to eat to survive, and they are able to move.

CELLS AND SKELETONS

Placozoans have just a few hundred cells, but most animals – including humans – have millions or billions. In an animal's body, cells are divided into different types, and each type carries out different kinds of work. Some cells protect an animal's body from the outside world, while others help it to absorb and digest its food. Most animals also have nerve cells, which keep their bodies coordinated, and muscle cells, which enable them to move. Sense organs are also part of the nervous system. They let animals keep track of changes around them, so they can escape from danger or find food.

▷ *Mammals dominate life on land, but they make up less than three per cent of all the animal species on earth. These gemsboks are experts at living in dry habitats – they can get all their water from their food.*

Unlike plant cells, animal cells are soft and flexible, because they do not have cell walls. But some animal cells produce hard substances which give them extra strength. These substances include chalky minerals, which make up shells and bones, and also chitin, which makes insect body cases. Chitin looks and feels like plastic, and it is tough, waterproof and extremely light.

◁ *Keen eyesight and sharp talons make the sparrowhawk a highly effective predator. This one is feeding on a bird that it has attacked and killed.*

FOOD AND FEEDING

No matter how or where they live, all animals need food. Food provides them with energy, and with the substances that they need to grow. Most animals feed either on plants or on other animals, but some have much more unusual diets, based on leftovers or dead remains. For example, museum beetles feed on mummified corpses that have dried out in the sun. These scavengers do a very useful job in nature, but they can cause havoc when they attack stuffed animals in museums.

Because animals do not need light to survive, they can live in far more places than plants. Many animals live in darkness, either in the soil, in caves, or in the depths of the sea. Lots more animals are active at night, when there is less chance of being spotted and attacked.

ANIMALS ON THE MOVE

Compared to other living things, animals are expert movers. They run, crawl, burrow or swim, and some of them can fly or glide. Whales, birds and butterflies can journey thousands of kilometres each year, and even slow movers, such as snails, manage an impressive distance during their lives. Some animals have lots of stamina, and can keep on the move for days. Swifts, for example, eat and sleep on the wing, and fly without a break until they are three or four years old. But on land, many predators move in short bursts, because they use speed and surprise to catch their prey.

Animals are not the only things that can move about – many microorganisms can as well. But animals are by far the biggest and fastest travellers in the natural world. However, the animal kingdom also contains plenty of creatures that spend their adult lives fixed in one place. These animals include corals, barnacles and giant clams. Because they live in water, they can survive by just sitting and waiting for food to drift their way.

SHAPES AND SKELETONS

ALL ANIMALS NEED TO KEEP IN
SHAPE. SOME OF THEM ARE AS SOFT
AS JELLY, BUT MANY HAVE A HARD
FRAMEWORK THAT HOLDS THEIR
BODIES TOGETHER.

◁△ *Living sponges often
feel hard and crunchy,
because they have skeletons
made of mineral spicules.
The object on the left is a
single spicule, enlarged
thousands of times.*

The world's simplest animals are all soft-bodied. Most of them live in the sea, where water helps to buoy them up. On land, being soft is not nearly such a good idea, because gravity can make soft things collapse. This is one of the reasons why most large animals have hard skeletons. These hold their bodies together, so that they can stay in shape and move about. Skeletons can also make an animal more difficult to attack.

ANIMALS UNDER PRESSURE
Soft-bodied animals are not difficult to find. They include lots of seashore creatures, such as sea anemones and jellyfish, and also a very common land animal: the earthworm. An earthworm has no hard body parts, but it has no trouble pushing its way through the ground. If it is picked up, it can squeeze its way between a person's fingers with surprising strength.

How does something soft manage to do this? The answer is that an earthworm's body is divided into dozens of compartments, and each one is under pressure, like a tyre. This pressure comes from a fluid, and it pushes outwards against the worm's skin, keeping it in shape. When the worm wants to move, it makes its compartments stretch and contract. Normally, this pushes the worm forwards, although it can just as easily go in reverse.

SPONGY SKELETONS
When animals evolved skeletons, they came up with several different kinds. Some of the most unusual ones belong to sponges. These primitive animals do not have heads or brains, but they do have internal scaffolding, made up of microscopic particles of silica and other minerals. These particles are called spicules. Some spicules are straight, while others are shaped like hooks or even tiny stars. A single sponge has millions of them, and they are often linked together by fibres that help to give a sponge its shape. A bath sponge is a complete skeleton, without the sponge's living cells. Before it can be sold, it has to be cleaned, because sponges often have sand and small animals inside them.

LIVING IN A CASE
Unlike sponges, the world's most successful animals are often on the

◁▽ *Flatworms (left) and sea anemones
(below) have soft bodies. Like many soft-bodied animals, they can move – but only
slowly. Flatworms ripple through the
water, while sea anemones creep over rocks.*

move. Called arthropods, they include an incredible array of creatures that hop, scuttle, run, swim or fly. The most common arthropods are insects, but this huge group of animals contains many other species, such as spiders, scorpions and crustaceans, and also centipedes and millipedes.

Arthropods are extremely varied, but they have one feature in common – a skeleton that works like a case. The case is made of separate

△ *This spider has almost finished moulting. It is hanging beneath its old body case, which is attached to a leaf by its empty legs.*

plates which meet at flexible joints. It fits around the animal's entire body, with tubular plates for its legs, and transparent ones for its eyes. The case keeps an animal in shape, and stops it drying out. Because it is flexible, it lets its owner move.

Arthropod body cases are almost as varied as arthropods themselves. In crabs and lobsters, they are like suits of armour, protecting them from attack. Scorpions also have tough cases, but because they live on land, theirs combine lightness with strength. A mosquito's body case is ultra-thin, because it spends most of its life in the air.

SHELLS AND BONES

Body cases are one of nature's most successful 'inventions', but they have two serious drawbacks. The first is that they are heavy and cumbersome if they are too big. That is why most of the world's arthropods are only a few centimetres long. Secondly, a body case cannot grow. Instead, it has to be discarded or moulted from time to time, and a replacement grown in its place.

Shells do not have this disadvantage, because they can grow in step with their owners. They are very good at protecting the animal inside, but not much help for moving about. But there is a kind of skeleton that can move and also grow. It is the kind that we have, and it is made of bone.

FLEXIBLE FRAMEWORK

Vertebrates are the only animals that can grow bones, so they are the only ones with bony skeletons. They include fish, amphibians, reptiles and birds, and also mammals – such as ourselves. Unlike body cases,

△ *The giant African land snail is the largest shelled animal that lives out of water. Its spiral shell can measure over 25 cm long.*

a vertebrate's skeleton is on the inside. It has flexible joints that allow it to move, but it is also very strong.

Bones contain living cells, and they grow in step with the rest of an animal's body. This means that vertebrates do not need to moult. Better still, a bony skeleton can grow very large without making it difficult to move. That is why the world's largest animals are all vertebrates – on land, in the sea, and in the air.

▷ *A gibbon's skeleton contains over 200 separate bones. The joints in its arms are extremely flexible. It can swing beneath branches almost as fast as a person can run, and it can leap over 10 m from tree to tree.*

BREATHING

WHEN A WHALE COMES TO THE SURFACE AFTER A DEEP DIVE, ITS NUMBER ONE PRIORITY IS AIR. ON AVERAGE, WE BREATHE ABOUT 15 TIMES A MINUTE, BUT MANY WHALES CAN HOLD THEIR BREATH FOR OVER AN HOUR.

Animals breathe, or respire, because their bodies need to take in oxygen and get rid of carbon dioxide. Some small animals, such as flatworms, simply let these gases flow through their skin. But most animals need much more oxygen, particularly if they lead active lives. They get it with the help of respiratory organs, which include gills and lungs. These organs have a rich blood supply. Blood flows through them to collect oxygen, and then delivers it to where it is needed.

△ *Like many freshwater insects, diving beetles have to come to the surface to breathe air. These beetles store air under their wing cases, so they have to swim hard to dive.*

△ *After a dive, a humpback whale blasts a jet of oily-smelling breath into the air. Most whales have a pair of blowholes, but sperm whales have just one, on the left side of their snouts.*

BREATHING UNDERWATER

Water contains lots of dissolved oxygen, particularly if it is cold. Mammals cannot breathe this oxygen – even ones that are full-time swimmers, such as seals and whales. But fish breathe it all the time, because they are equipped with gills.

Gills are collections of flaps or filaments that are surrounded by water. They have a large surface, but they are also very thin, so oxygen can easily flow into them, while carbon dioxide flows out. Most fishes' gills are hidden away in hollow chambers just behind their heads. When a fish swims, water flows in through its mouth, past its gills, and then out through slits or holes. The faster the fish moves, the more oxygen its gills take up. When a fish is still, it often 'gulps' water to keep up its oxygen supply. A few fish, such as the mudskipper, can survive in the air. But for most fish, being hauled onto land spells certain death. Their gills stick together, preventing them from getting the oxygen they need.

BREATHING TUBES

Fish are not the only animals with gills – tadpoles have them too. So do lobsters, crabs and clams, as well as some insects that swim or dive. But insects were originally land animals. This explains why most of them have to come to the surface, so that they can breathe air.

Insects have a unique system for getting oxygen into their bodies. Instead of lungs, they have a set of breathing tubes called tracheae. The tubes open to the outside through holes called spiracles, which are along an insect's sides. Inside the animal, each tube divides into thousands of microscopic branches, which supply oxygen to individual cells. Small insects let oxygen flow through their tubes unaided, but large ones – such as grasshoppers –

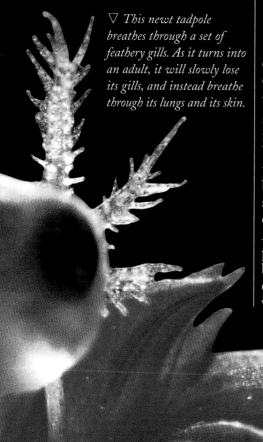

▽ *This newt tadpole breathes through a set of feathery gills. As it turns into an adult, it will slowly lose its gills, and instead breathe through its lungs and its skin.*

often contract their muscles to help it on its way.

When an insect sheds its skin, it has to shed the lining of all its breathing tubes as well. As the skin

△ *Magnified hundreds of times, this picture shows a single spiracle belonging to a caterpillar. Spiracles are normally arranged in a line along an insect's sides.*

falls away, the linings are pulled inside out, just like discarded socks.

TAKING A BREATHER

Tracheae work well for insects, because their bodies are small. But animals with backbones, apart from fish, all breathe by using lungs. Unlike gills, lungs are hollow, and they are hidden away inside the body. They contain millions of small air spaces, which make it easy for oxygen to flow into the blood. A shrew's lungs are smaller than peas, while a whale's are often bigger than a car. Despite this enormous difference in size, they work in a very similar way. When

a mammal takes a breath, muscles make its chest expand. This makes the lungs expand as well, and they suck in air from the outside. To breathe out, the animal lets its chest muscles relax. As its chest contracts, the lungs shrink, and used air is squeezed out. But if an animal is highly active, its chest muscles work much harder. They suck in up to five times as much air as normal, and also force much more of it out.

HIGH FLIERS

After a two-hour dive, elephant seals only need about five minutes at the surface to catch their breath. But the real experts at collecting oxygen are birds. A bird's lungs are connected to hollow chambers called air sacs, which reach right inside their bones. Air flows through a bird's lungs in a one-way stream, allowing them to collect as much oxygen as possible. Birds need highly efficient lungs because flying uses up so much energy – up to ten times as much as when they are sitting on a perch. Extra-efficient lungs also enable them to fly at high altitudes, where the air is thin. Some birds can fly at altitudes of over 10 km, a height that would leave human beings gasping for breath.

▽ *Thanks to their extra-efficient lungs, yellow-billed choughs manage to live and breed at over 6,000 m in the Himalayas.*

HOW ANIMALS MOVE

FOR MOST ANIMALS, MOVEMENT IS VITAL FOR SURVIVAL. SOME MOVE SO SLOWLY THAT THEY WOULD TAKE AN HOUR TO CROSS THIS PAGE, BUT THE FASTEST CAN OUT-ACCELERATE A CAR.

△ *A frog's back legs work in two ways – they can be used for jumping, and also for swimming.*

Animals are not the only living things that move, but nothing can beat them for stamina and speed. Some birds can fly more than 1,000 km in a single day, while in a whole lifetime, a grey whale swims double the distance to the moon. Animals move by using muscles, and they control them with their nerves and brains.

swimmer of all is the sailfish, which can hit speeds of over 100 km/h. Its muscle-packed body is beautifully streamlined, and its powerhouse is a stiff, knife-shaped tail fin that slices its way through the sea.

△ *If it is threatened, the basilisk lizard can run across the surface of rivers and ponds. Once it has travelled a few metres, it swims away.*

IN THE SWIM
Three-quarters of the world is covered with water, so swimming is an important way of moving around. The tiniest swimmers are planktonic animals, which live near the surface of the sea. Some of them simply drift along, but many move by beating feathery legs, or minute hairs that work like oars. Planktonic animals cannot make much headway against the current, but many of them carry out daily journeys down into the sea's depths, to keep out of the way of predatory fish.

FAST MOVERS
In water, most large swimmers move using fins or flippers. The fastest

Compared to the sailfish, whales move much more slowly. The grey whale, for example, migrates over 12,000 km a year, but its average speed is not much faster than a person taking a walk. But dolphins and porpoises can swim fast – some of them reach speeds of 55 km/h.

Fins and flippers are not the only way of swimming in a hurry. Octopuses escape from danger by sucking up water, and then squirting it backwards through a funnel. This makes the octopus zoom off in the opposite direction – a kind of underwater jet propulsion.

MOVING ON LAND
Some ways of moving in water also work on land. For example, land snails move in just the same way as their watery relatives, by crawling on a single sucker-like foot. To make sure that its sucker sticks, a snail

◁ Most fish beat their tails when they swim, and use their other fins for steering. Sharks are different, because they swim by bending their bodies from side to side.

△ Several desert snakes – including this African viper – move by 'sidewinding'. Instead of slithering, these snakes throw themselves forwards over the sand.

produces lots of slimy mucus, which forms a trail behind it as it moves. Snails can climb up vertical surfaces, and they can also move upside down. But this way of getting about is not fast – at top speed, a garden snail moves at about 0.008 km/h.

LEGS
Legs were developed by animals that originally lived in water, and that later crawled out to take up life on land. Today, there are two quite different groups of leg-bearing animals on land. The first are the vertebrates, which are animals with backbones, such as ourselves. The second are the arthropods – animals that include insects, spiders and their relatives.

Vertebrates never have more than four legs. Arthropods often have six or eight, but some have many more. The record, held by a millipede, is an amazing 750. At the other extreme, some vertebrates have gradually lost some of their legs, and move on their bodies instead. A rare reptile called the ajalote has just one pair of legs, but all the world's snakes have no legs at all.

QUICK MOVERS
Because arthropods are small, they do not have high top speeds. The fastest are cockroaches, which can run at just over 5 km/h. But as these animals weigh very little, they can perform some remarkable feats. Almost all of them can run upside down, and some can jump dozens of times their own length. They can also start and stop almost instantly – one of the reasons why people find 'bugs' alarming.

By comparison, vertebrates take longer to get moving, but they are much faster overall. For example, a red kangaroo is able to cruise at 50 km/h. Cheetahs – the world's fastest land animals – can hit double this, although they cannot keep up this speed for more than 30 seconds at a time.

▽ Although it is fast, this hare is no match for a cheetah. Cheetahs move too quickly to pounce on their prey – instead, they trip it up with a blow from one of their front paws.

GLIDING AND FLYING

ANIMALS FIRST TOOK TO THE SKIES OVER 350 MILLION YEARS AGO. TODAY, THE AIR TEEMS WITH ANIMALS THAT GLIDE OR FLY. SOME ARE LARGE AND POWERFUL, BUT OTHERS ARE ALMOST INVISIBLE.

∇ *The barn owl hunts small rodents, and is a specialist at slow flight. When searching for food, it moves at about 10 km/h – slower than a human jogger. Here, an owl swoops down and opens its talons, ready to grab its prey.*

M any animals can glide, but only insects, birds and bats can truly fly. They use muscle power to flap their wings, so they can take off and land whenever they like. Insects outnumber other fliers millions of times, and their small size makes them extremely good at manoeuvring in the air. Bats fly far and fast, but birds are the best aviators in the animal world. Some of them carry out airborne journeys that literally cross the earth.

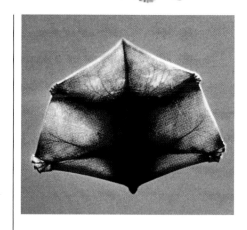

△ *Flying lemurs, or colugos, are some of the world's largest gliding mammals. With their legs stretched out, their skin flaps make them look like living kites.*

GREAT GLIDERS

Gliding animals include an amazing array of creatures, from rodents and marsupials to snakes, frogs and fish. Some glide just a few metres before they drop back to the ground, but expert gliders – such as flying fish – can stay in the air for 300 m or more. Many of these animals use gliding as an emergency escape, but for some, such as the flying lemur,

gliding is a practical way of moving around – even for mothers who have to carry their young on board.

Gliding animals do not have true wings. Instead, they have flat body parts that cushion their fall once they have launched themselves into the air. Flying fish glide on one or two pairs of extra-large fins, while flying frogs use their outstretched feet, which work like small parachutes. Gliding mammals use flaps of elastic skin that stretch between their legs, and often their tail. When not in use, these conveniently fold away.

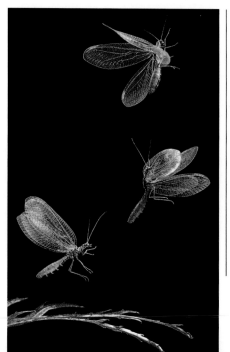

◁ *Flapping its delicate wings, a lacewing launches itself into the air. This slow-motion sequence shows the moment of take-off, with two pairs of wings beating together.*

△ *Flying fish glide to escape predators. They spread their fins like wings, and some species use their tails like an outboard motor, helping to launch them into the air.*

In North America, monarch butterflies often migrate over 3,000 km to breed, while in Europe, clouded yellow butterflies often cross the Arctic Circle in summer as they search for a place to lay their eggs.

FEATHERED FLIERS

Bats can fly at up to 40 km/h, but that is slow compared to some birds. Geese can exceed 90 km/h in level

over 11 km up, and it is possible that they can actually fly higher still. Birds set these flight records because they have hollow, lightweight bones and extra-efficient lungs. But their feathers are even more important. They give birds a streamlined shape, and help them to speed through the air.

Arctic terns travel up to 50,000 km a year, which is probably more than any other animal in the world. But

AIRBORNE INSECTS

Unlike gliders, flying insects put a lot of muscle power into staying in the air. A dragonfly beats its wings about 30 times a second, while a housefly beats its 200 times or more. Flies have just one pair of wings, but most other insects have two. In butterflies and moths, the front and back wings beat together, but in dragonflies they beat in opposite directions at once. This allows dragonflies to hover, and even to fly in reverse.

Most insects do not fly far, and many are so small that they are easily blown off course by the wind. But the insect world does include some true long-distance travellers.

flight, while peregrine falcons reach 200 km/h when they dive after their prey. Vultures have been seen from aircraft

sooty terns are even more impressive. They can stay airborne for over five years. Their epic flights end on tropical islands, when they eventually land to breed.

▷ *For an earwig, getting ready to fly is a lengthy job. The hindwings are packed away under the much smaller forewings (1), and they are folded up over 30 times to make them fit. Once the earwig has unfolded them, the wings are surprisingly big (2).*

1   2

ANIMAL SENSES 1

ANIMALS HAVE TO FIND FOOD, BUT THEY ALSO HAVE TO STEER CLEAR OF DANGER. THEY DO THIS BY USING SENSES, WHICH KEEP THEM IN TOUCH WITH THE OUTSIDE WORLD.

△ *Jumping spiders have four pairs of eyes. One pair is extra large, and faces forwards like a pair of headlights. The spider uses these eyes to judge distances before it jumps.*

For humans, vision and hearing are the most important senses in daily life. They tell us an immense amount about our surroundings, and help us to pinpoint things that are on the move. But we are not alone, because many animals rely on these two senses as well. Predators often use vision or hearing to track down their prey, while prey animals often use the same senses to make a quick escape. Our senses may be keen, but some animals' are keener still.

SEEING AHEAD

A flatworm's eyes are so simple that they can only tell the difference between light and dark. Eyes like these are no good for spotting food, but they give flatworms advance warning if a predator is lurking overhead. But most animal eyes do much more than this. They gather light and then focus it, so that their owner can form an image of the surrounding scene.

Our eyes have a single lens, which focuses light onto a curved screen called a retina. All mammals have eyes like these, and so do other vertebrates or animals with backbones. Because we have two eyes, we see the same scene from slightly different viewpoints, and this enables us to judge depth. This is very important for animals that hunt, which is why almost all of them have forward-pointing eyes as well. Plant-eaters, on the other hand, often have eyes that point sideways. This allows them to keep a lookout all around, so that they get the earliest possible warning of

△ *For its size, the tarsier has the largest eyes of any mammal. Each one is larger than its brain. Tarsiers live in tropical forests, and hunt insects after dark.*

approaching danger. Chameleons get the best of both worlds. Their eyes can swivel independently, so they can look in two quite different directions at once.

SEEING IN DETAIL

Eyes work because their retinas contain special receptor cells. These cells intercept light, and convert it into electrical signals that travel to the brain. Some receptors respond to colour, while others work in black and white. The more receptors there are, the more detail an eye can see.

A human eye has up to 200,000 receptors in each square millimetre of its retina, but some birds of prey have five times more. This gives them extremely sharp eyesight, allowing them to spot small animals from high up in the air. These birds are very good at seeing things that move, but they find it much harder to see things that are still. Many other predators are the same, which is why prey animals often 'freeze' if they are seen.

COMPOUND EYES

When we look at other mammals, similar eyes look back at us. But coming eye-to-eye with an insect is a very different experience. That is because insect eyes are built on an entirely different plan. Instead of having a single lens, they have hundreds or even thousands. Each one leads into a separate

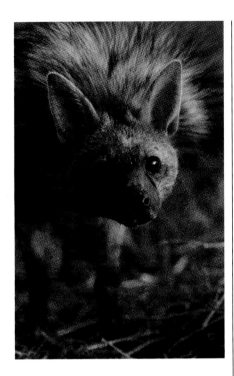

△ *Aardwolves eat termites, and search for them after dark. Their highly sensitive ears pick up the sound made by termites as they move across the ground.*

compartment, and these combine together to produce the image that the insect sees.

Such eyes are known as compound eyes, and their size and shape varies hugely throughout the insect world. Worker ants often have minute eyes with fewer than 50 compartments, but a dragonfly's eyes have up to 25,000. Its eyes are so big that they cover most of its head. Eyes this size are good at spotting movement – just what a dragonfly needs to snatch up other insects in mid-air.

PRIVATE CALLS

Vision has one serious drawback – it does not work in the dark. That is why many nocturnal animals rely on hearing instead. Hearing does not provide so much detail, but it works even when there are obstacles in the way. Many animals use sound to communicate, because they can call while they are safely hidden away. In tropical rainforests, cicadas produce deafening calls that can be heard from a distance of almost 1 km. Despite this, cicadas are extremely difficult to find. At the other end of the sound spectrum, elephants communicate by rumbles that are too deep for humans to hear. These sounds carry far and wide, allowing different herds to keep in touch.

HUNTING BY SOUND

Some animals find their food by sound. They do this by producing high-pitched noises, and then listening for the echoes that come back. If something is nearby, the echoes return quickly, helping the hunter to home in on its food. This system is called echolocation, and it is most highly developed in bats. In one famous experiment, a bat was released in a pitch-black room, which was divided in two by a transparent fishing net. The bat flew through the net by closing its wings, showing that it could tell where the net was.

▽ *To escape being eaten, some moths give off high-pitched sounds. These 'jam' the echolocation signals used by bats, throwing them off course.*

▽ *Colour vision varies between different animals. Some see a wide range of colours, but many deep-sea fish are limited to bluish-green. Some snakes can see infrared, using special detectors that are described on page 127.*

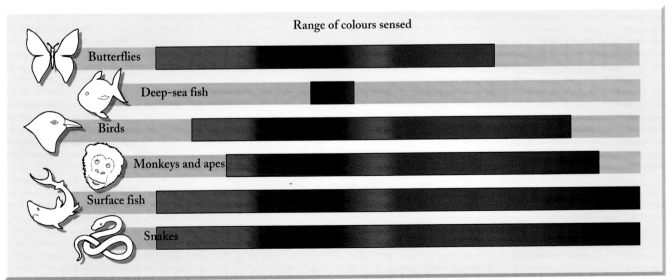

Range of colours sensed

Butterflies

Deep-sea fish

Birds

Monkeys and apes

Surface fish

Snakes

ANIMAL SENSES 2

WITHOUT VISION AND HEARING, HUMANS WOULD
HAVE PROBLEMS DEALING WITH EVERYDAY LIFE,
BUT IN NATURE MANY ANIMALS USE COMPLETELY
DIFFERENT SENSES TO FIND THEIR WAY ABOUT
AND TO TRACK DOWN THEIR FOOD.

△ *Cave crickets use their long antennae,
or feelers, to find their way through the
darkness. Their antennae are very sensitive
to air currents, warning the crickets if
predators are nearby.*

Humans have five main senses – vision, hearing, smell, taste
and touch. We also have a sense of balance, which is often
overlooked. Our sense of touch is good, but compared to
many animals, our senses of smell and taste are very poor. Many
animals use smell and touch when they move about, and some have
mysterious extra senses that detect things we cannot sense at all.

Animals use taste to test things
they can touch, but the sense of
smell can work much farther away.
Some male moths can detect the
scent of a female when she is more
than 5 km off. At this distance, the
female's scent is so diluted that it
makes up only a million-billionth of
the air. Even so, the male's antennae
can pick up the scent molecules.

NAVIGATION BY SMELL
Animals use smell to keep in
touch, and often to find their food.
Mammals are very good at this,
and many species – from foxes to
antelope – use scent to mark their
territories. These scent marks cannot
be seen, but they last for days or

weeks, letting would-be rivals know
that the area has already been
claimed. On the whole, birds do not
have a good sense of smell, but there
are some exceptions. American
vultures are attracted by the smell
of rotting flesh, for example.

For land animals, smell and taste
are two different senses, but in water
they merge. Most people can tell the
difference between bottled water and
tap water, but fish and turtles can
sense incredibly small variations in
water's chemical composition. As
well as tasting these differences, they
also remember them, so that they
can use them like points on a map.
Salmon use this sense to find their
way across the sea, and back into the
very same rivers where they hatched.

△ *Butterflies, houseflies and honeybees can
all taste with their feet. These butterflies
have settled on some animal dung, and
are sucking up the salts that it contains.*

TASTE AND SMELL
When a butterfly lands, it can taste
what is underfoot without having to
unroll its tongue. Butterflies can do
this because they – and some other
insects – have chemical sensors built
into their legs. This remarkable
system allows flies to home in
on their food, and it also helps
butterflies to find the right plants
on which to lay their eggs.

▷ *Male moths
have feathery
antennae, which
are good at collecting
minute amounts of
scent from the air.
The females' antennae
are much smaller
and simpler.*

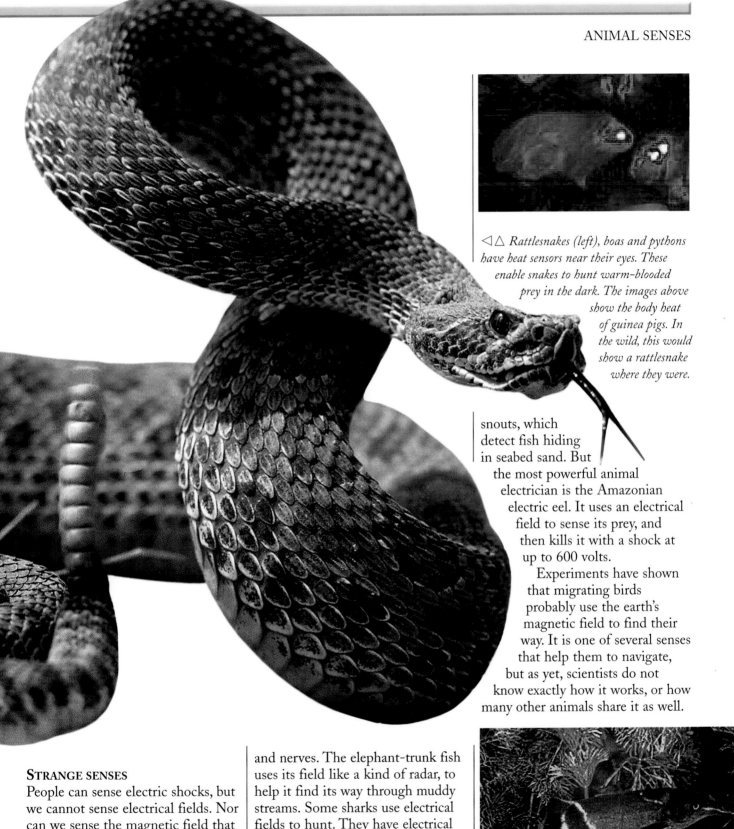

◁△ *Rattlesnakes (left), boas and pythons have heat sensors near their eyes. These enable snakes to hunt warm-blooded prey in the dark. The images above show the body heat of guinea pigs. In the wild, this would show a rattlesnake where they were.*

snouts, which detect fish hiding in seabed sand. But the most powerful animal electrician is the Amazonian electric eel. It uses an electrical field to sense its prey, and then kills it with a shock at up to 600 volts.

Experiments have shown that migrating birds probably use the earth's magnetic field to find their way. It is one of several senses that help them to navigate, but as yet, scientists do not know exactly how it works, or how many other animals share it as well.

STRANGE SENSES

People can sense electric shocks, but we cannot sense electrical fields. Nor can we sense the magnetic field that surrounds the whole of the earth. But for some animals, both play a part in everyday life.

Most animals have their own electrical field, because they generate electrical impulses in their muscles and nerves. The elephant-trunk fish uses its field like a kind of radar, to help it find its way through muddy streams. Some sharks use electrical fields to hunt. They have electrical sensors around their mouths and

▷ *The elephant-trunk fish finds its way by using its own electrical field. Like most fish, it also has a line of pressure sensors along its sides.*

PLANT-EATERS

HERBIVORES, OR PLANT-EATERS, OUTNUMBER PREDATORS BY AT LEAST TEN TO ONE. THEY RANGE IN SIZE FROM THE LARGEST LAND MAMMALS TO TINY GRUBS THAT CAN COMFORTABLY FIT INSIDE A LEAF.

Plant food has two big advantages – it is often easy to find and, better still, it cannot run away. For small animals there is another plus – plants make good places to hide from prying eyes. But eating plants does have some drawbacks, because this kind of food takes a long time to eat, and it can be difficult to digest.

△ *In proportion to their weight, caterpillars eat more food than elephants. These tropical caterpillars have spikes to protect them from birds.*

SECRET ARMIES

Elephants can eat a third of a tonne of food a day, and they often smash down trees to get at their leaves. Wild boar use different tactics, bulldozing their way through soil to reach juicy roots. But despite their size, animals like these are not the most important plant-eaters in the world. Instead, insects and other invertebrates are far out in front.

In tropical grasslands, ants and termites often outweigh all other plant-eaters put together. They collect seeds and pieces of leaves, and carry them underground. In woodlands and forests, many insects feed on living wood, while caterpillars chew through the leaves overhead. They have voracious appetites, and if they get into parks or plantations, they can be serious pests.

Mammals often eat a wide range of plants, and so do slugs and snails. But small plant-eaters are usually much more fussy about their food. For example, hazelnut weevils always feed on hazelnuts, while

△ *This wandering trail shows where a leaf-mining caterpillar has chewed its way through a leaf. The dark patches in the trail are the caterpillar's droppings.*

▽ *Snails rasp away at plants using a set of microscopic teeth. They usually eat young plants, because their leaves are thin and tender.*

red admiral caterpillars feed on nettle leaves. If these caterpillars are put on any other plant, they starve to death. Such fussiness might seem strange, but for plant-eaters it sometimes pays. That is because specialists are extra-efficient at dealing with their normal food.

SEEDS AND STORES

There are very few plant-eating reptiles, but lots of plant-eating birds. Only a small number eat leaves – instead, most

◁ Naked mole rats live underground,
and feed on plant tubers and roots. These
African rodents are almost blind, and
hardly ever come to the surface.

concentrate either on flowers, or on fruit and seeds. Hummingbirds visit flowers to gather nectar, while some parrots collect pollen, which they lap up with their brush-tipped tongues. But fruit- and seed-eating birds are much more common and, unlike hummingbirds and parrots, they live all over the world.

Seeds are an ideal food, because they are packed with nutritious oil and starch. That is why lots of birds eat them, and why rodents feed on them too. Seed-eating rodents are particularly common in dry places, where food can be hard to find.

△ *Like many other small rodents,
kangaroo rats use their cheek pouches
to carry seeds back to their nests.*

Unlike birds, rodents are able to survive difficult times by collecting food and storing it underground. In central Asia, some gerbils store up to 60 kg of seeds and roots. This massive larder can keep them well-fed for months.

EATING GRASS
Seeds are easy to digest, which is one reason why they make up an important part of most people's diet. But grass and other leaves are not nearly as easy for animals to

break down. That is because they contain cellulose (see p. 85), a tough substance that humans are not able to digest. We are not alone, because grazing mammals cannot break down cellulose either, even though it makes up a large part of their food.

So how do these animals survive? The answer is that they use microorganisms to do this work for them. These organisms include bacteria and protozoans, and they have special enzymes that can split cellulose molecules apart.

Mammals keep these microorganisms in their digestive systems, where the warmth and moisture create ideal conditions for their work. Many grazing animals house them in a special stomach chamber, called the rumen, which works like a fermentation tank. These grazers, known as ruminants, include antelope, cattle and deer. All of them 'chew the cud', which means that they regurgitate their food after they have swallowed it, then chew it a second time. This mashes the food up, which makes it easier for the microorganisms to break it down.

△ *Grazing mammals often live in herds,
because this gives them a better chance
of spotting predators before they have
the opportunity to attack.*

FULL-TIME FEEDERS
Rumination is very efficient, but takes a long time to work. Eating grass is also time-consuming, since each mouthful has to be bitten off and then thoroughly chewed. As a result, grazers do not have much

Red fox
Searching for food: 35% of each day
Inactive 60%
Feeding 5%

Roe deer
Searching for food 5%
Inactive 40%
Feeding 55%

△ *Compared to predators, such as the
red fox, plant-eaters spend much less time
looking for food but far longer eating it.
For example, a roe deer usually feeds for
more than 12 hours each day.*

time off. Instead, they are kept busy collecting and digesting their food.

The same is true for plant-eating insects, although their feeding habits often change once they become adults. Caterpillars are busy feeders, but adult butterflies or moths spend most of their time looking for partners or laying eggs. Many of them visit flowers, but a few do not eat at all. Mayflies take things to even greater extremes – as adults, they do not have working mouths.

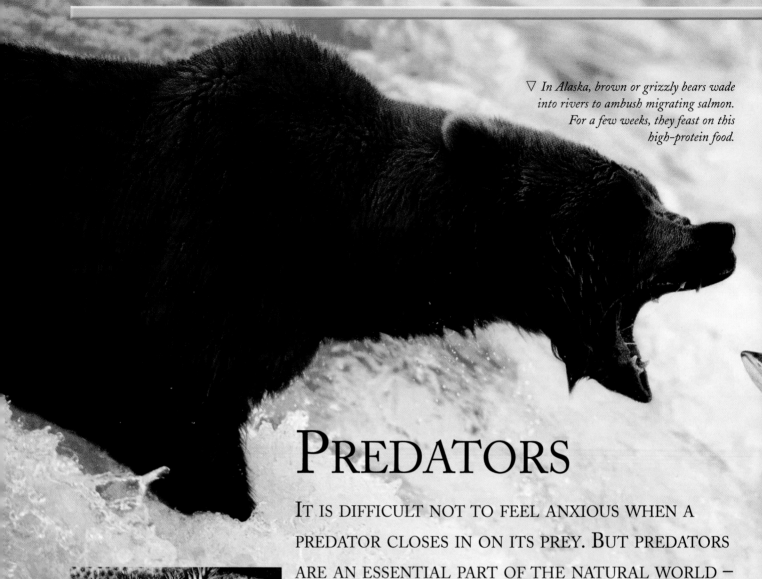

In Alaska, brown or grizzly bears wade into rivers to ambush migrating salmon. For a few weeks, they feast on this high-protein food.

PREDATORS

IT IS DIFFICULT NOT TO FEEL ANXIOUS WHEN A PREDATOR CLOSES IN ON ITS PREY. BUT PREDATORS ARE AN ESSENTIAL PART OF THE NATURAL WORLD – WE ARE SOMETIMES PREDATORS OURSELVES.

Compared to eating plants, being a predator is a gamble, because there is always a chance that the prey will escape. To make up for this, meat is a highly nutritious food. To hunt successfully, most predators have keen senses and rapid reflexes. They overcome their victims by using specialized weapons, such as poisonous stings, powerful claws or sharp teeth.

△ *The crown-of-thorns starfish feeds on living corals. It crawls over coral reefs, digesting the soft parts of the coral polyps.*

SLOW-MOTION HUNTERS
When people think of predators, fast-moving animals – such as cheetahs – are often the first ones that come to mind. But many predators are not like this. For example, starfish move more slowly than snails, but they prey on animals that cannot get away. For a starfish, finding food is not difficult. The hard part comes when it has to pull a shell apart, to get at the animal inside.

In water and on land, many

▷ *With its jaws gaping open, a rat snake swallows a bird. Snakes always swallow their prey whole, so they need powerful digestive juices to break down their food.*

predators do not chase anything at all. Instead, these hunters lie in wait for prey to wander within range. Many of them are superbly camouflaged, and some improve their chances by building traps or using lures. Lie-in-wait hunters include anglerfish, praying mantises, spiders and many kinds of snakes. Most of them are cold-blooded, which means that they do not need lots of energy from their food. As a result, they can survive without food for days or even weeks.

△ *Using its small but powerful jaws, a praying mantis feeds on a cricket. Large praying mantises sometimes catch lizards and even frogs.*

MAMMALS THAT HUNT
Birds and mammals are warm-blooded, so they need lots of energy to keep their bodies working. For a brown bear, that energy comes from all kinds of food, including insects, fish and sometimes other bears. Weighing up to 1,000 kg, this huge animal is the world's largest land-based predator. Normally it is wary of humans, but if it does attack, the results can be deadly.

Mammalian carnivores – or meat-eaters – have specialized teeth to deal with their food. Near the front of their mouths, they have pointed canine teeth, which are used to grip their prey. Once they have killed a victim, their carnassial teeth set to work. These teeth are near the back of the jaw. They have long, sharp edges, and they slice through flesh like a pair of scissors. Some carnivores, such as wolves, use them for cracking open bones so that they can reach the marrow inside.

AIRBORNE ATTACK
Birds of prey do not have teeth, and instead they hunt with their talons, or claws. Once they have made a kill, they usually carry the victim back to a favourite perch or to their nest. Some of the largest species can lift amazing weights – in 1932, a white-tailed sea eagle in Norway carried off a four-year-old girl. Amazingly, she survived.

Talons are good for catching prey, but birds of prey use their hooked beaks for tearing up food. Birds that hunt small animals have a different technique. They manoeuvre their

◁ *An African fish eagle carries off its prey after snatching it from the water's surface. It will swallow the fish after it lands on a perch.*

food until it is pointing head-first down their throat. Then they swallow it whole.

MASS MURDERERS
Some of the world's most efficient hunters feed on animals that are much smaller than themselves. In the Southern Ocean, whales hunt shrimp-like animals called krill by filtering them out of the water. Their giant catches are the largest made by any predator, and a single mouthful can weigh over a tonne. Grey whales dig up molluscs on the seabed, while humpback whales ambush shoals of fish by making 'nets' from bubbles. This forces the shoal into a small space, where it is much easier prey. But the best fishers of all are humans – we catch millions of tonnes a year.

▽ *By blowing air from its blowhole, a humpback whale surrounds a shoal of fish with a column of rising bubbles. The whale then swims up through the centre of the column, swallowing the fish that are trapped inside.*

SCAVENGERS

THOUSANDS OF KINDS OF ANIMALS FIND RICH PICKINGS IN WASTE AND DEAD REMAINS. THEY HELP TO RECYCLE MATTER, SO THAT NUTRIENTS CAN BE RE-USED.

△ *This giant earthworm, from Australia, is bigger than many snakes. Fortunately, it is a harmless scavenger that helps to improve the quality of the soil.*

▽ *Male fiddler crabs use their small pincer to pick up particles of food. Once they have chewed the particles, they leave pellet-shaped leftovers on the mud. The large pincer is too unwieldy for feeding – instead, it is used for signalling during courtship.*

In the animal world, scavenging is a good way of making a living. That is because other animals generate a constant supply of dead bodies, along with droppings, skin flakes, feathers and fur. None of this appeals to us, but for scavengers it makes up a nutritious and reliable source of food. Without scavenging animals, dead remains would still be broken down by microbes, but they would take much longer to be cleared away.

PARTICLE FEEDERS
To find some of the world's most successful scavengers, the place to look is the nearest muddy shore. This is prime scavenger habitat, because it is full of tiny particles containing animal and plant remains. Many of these particles come from the sea itself, but others flow down rivers and then settle on the shore. The result is a rich layer of sediment – the ideal place for small scavengers to set up home.

Many of these particle feeders burrow through the sediment –

△ *With its tentacles extended, a fanworm collects drifting particles from the sea. Each tentacle is covered with fine hairs that move food towards the worm's mouth.*

a good way to avoid hungry birds. These burrowers include shrimps and snails, and also heart urchins, which have spines that look like fur. Fanworms have a different feeding technique – they collect the particles as they drift by. In warm parts of the world, fiddler crabs emerge onto the mud when the tide goes out, picking up the particles with their claws. Every time the tide comes in, it drops more particles, so the crabs rarely run out of food.

SCAVENGERS IN SOIL
On dry land, scavengers are everywhere, living unseen in the soil. Many of them are microscopic, but in some parts of the world – such as South Africa and Australia – they include earthworms over 4 m long. Earthworms are outstandingly useful animals because they help to mix up and fertilize the soil. Without them, the ground would be far less fertile, making it much more difficult to grow food.

◁ By shaping animal dung into a ball, dung beetles can roll it away to a suitable spot for burial. They push the ball along with their feet.

Earthworms drag fallen leaves into their burrows, but some insects bury other things underground. Burying beetles dig 'graves' for small mammals and birds, and they lay their eggs on them before covering them up. When the beetle grubs hatch, they feed on the corpse. Dung beetles do the same thing, although their grubs hatch inside a private ball of animal droppings that their parents have rolled away and then buried.

WINGED SCAVENGERS

Burying beetles deal with small corpses, but large ones attract very different scavengers. In Africa, hyenas are quickly lured by the scent of rotting flesh, while in Tasmania, carcasses attract a scavenging marsupial called the Tasmanian devil. It has a formidable bite, allowing it to slice through dry skin, gristle and even bones. But in many parts of the world, the most important scavengers are ones that arrive by air.

Many birds home in on dead remains. Crows and magpies, for example, often gather to feed on animals that have been hit by cars. Gulls feed on dead remains that have been washed up on the shore, and also on waste food that humans throw away. But in the bird world, vultures are the real specialists at the scavenging way of life. They fly by soaring high up on warm air currents − a technique that enables them to scan enormous areas in their search for food. Vultures also keep a close eye on each other, and if one drops down to feed, others soon follow from far around.

For a vulture, survival depends on being able to eat a lot of food in a short space of time. Sometimes, these birds eat so much that they have to wait several hours before they can fly away.

△ Many insects feed on dead remains. This stag beetle grub will spend several years feeding on dead wood before it turns into an adult.

▽ In Africa's grasslands, this carcass is surrounded by jostling vultures. Although they have weak claws, their powerful beaks can rip holes in rotting skin.

ANIMAL DEFENCES

ONCE THEY ARE ADULT, SUPER-PREDATORS SUCH AS THE GREAT WHITE SHARK HAVE NO NATURAL ENEMIES. BUT FOR OTHER ANIMALS, DANGER CAN STRIKE AT ANY TIME AND GOOD DEFENCES ARE VITAL FOR SURVIVAL.

In the animal world, predators are always on the lookout for food. Compared to them, prey animals often look vulnerable, but in fact, things are not quite as one-sided as they seem. Prey species have evolved all kinds of defences – without them, they would not exist. These defences are not totally foolproof, but for every animal that gets killed and eaten, lots more manage to outwit their enemies and escape.

◁ *Rodents keep out of danger by staying out of sight, often in dense vegetation. Caught out in the open by a bobcat, this mouse has only a small chance of survival.*

QUICK EXITS

When danger threatens, many animals react by trying to make a rapid escape. Some antelope can run at over 60 km/h, while hares can cruise at over 50 km/h – an impressive feat for animals that weigh about a tenth as much as a man. But for getting out of trouble, acceleration is sometimes as important as speed. Cockroaches have a top speed of only about 5 km/h, but they accelerate amazingly quickly from a standing start. As they scuttle away from danger, they often change direction – a trick that makes them even harder to catch.

Animals that cannot move quickly often use camouflage to blend in with their surroundings. Insects are particularly good at this, which is fortunate for them, because their predators include sharp-eyed birds. For camouflage to work, an animal normally has to stay completely still, but some stick insects blend in even better by swaying slightly, just like twigs blowing in the breeze.

TRICKSTERS AND CHEATS

One of the best ways to put off an attacker is to carry a dangerous weapon. For example, most predators will not touch wasps or hornets, because these insects have

▽ *Few animals can beat insects when it comes to camouflage. This photograph shows two superbly camouflaged katydids on the bark of a rainforest tree in Peru.*

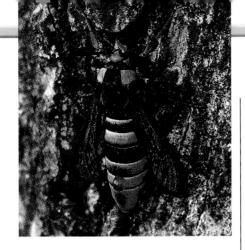

△ The hornet clearwing moth bears an astonishing resemblance to a real hornet. However, despite its black and yellow warning colours, it does not have a sting.

dangerous stings. But not all 'wasps' and 'hornets' are exactly what they seem. Some harmless flies and moths imitate these insects, and they do it so convincingly that few predators – or people – can tell them apart. The moths have transparent wings, and some of them even make a wasp-like buzzing sound when they fly.

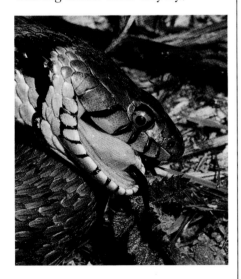

△ With its mouth open and its tongue hanging out, this grass snake looks quite dead. Grass snakes are not poisonous, and they use this defence if they cannot escape.

This defence technique is called mimicry, and it is widespread in the insect world. Spiders are also good mimics. Several kinds mimic stinging ants, and they move in an ant-like way across the forest floor. Spiders have eight legs, while ants have six legs. But birds cannot count, so they are fooled by the spiders' disguise.

PLAYING DEAD
Scavengers are not fussy about their food, but many predators only hunt prey that moves. They show little interest in animals that are still, and even less in ones that are dead. This gives prey animals a remarkable last-ditch defence – if they can pretend to be dead, there is a chance that a predator might leave them alone.

Not many animals can do this, but they include some of the best actors in the living world. The grass snake lies on the ground with its mouth gaping open, while the Virginia opossum collapses on its side. It can stay like this for up to six hours, and does not react in any way if it is touched. But once the coast is clear, the 'dead' opossum comes back to life and runs away.

UNEATABLE MEALS
Another way to keep out of trouble is by being difficult or dangerous to eat. This is the defence used by tortoises, and other animals that have hard shells. Tortoises pull in their legs and head if they are threatened, but box turtles can shut up their shells completely once they have withdrawn inside. Some armadillos roll themselves into a ball, while the porcupine fish inflates itself by swallowing water, so that it swells up like a spiny ball.

All these animals are edible, which is bad news for them if their defences fail. But animals with built-in poisons do not need shells or spines. Some of the most potent poisons are produced by tiny poison-

△ By baring its teeth and hissing, a wild cat tries to make itself look as dangerous as possible. If it is cornered, it responds by going on the attack.

arrow frogs, which live in tropical forests. In one species, a single frog contains enough poison to kill a thousand people, even though it is less than 4 cm long.

▽ Surrounded by vicious spines, a fully inflated porcupine fish is a meal few animals would want to tackle. Once it is inflated, the fish can hardly move.

PARTNERS AND PARASITES

TEAMING UP WITH ANOTHER SPECIES IS OFTEN A RECIPE FOR SUCCESS. IN MANY ANIMAL PARTNERSHIPS, BOTH SPECIES BENEFIT, BUT PARASITIC PARTNERS TAKE WHAT THEY CAN, AND GIVE NOTHING IN RETURN.

When ants meet aphids, a strange ritual takes place. Instead of attacking the aphids, the ants tap them with their antennae, and the aphids respond by producing droplets of sugary fluid, called honeydew. For the aphids, life is much safer with the ants acting as guards. In return, they give the ants a useful supply of food. Partnerships like this are common in the animal kingdom, but ones involving parasites are even more widespread.

◁ *Ants are aggressive towards most insects, but they look after aphids in return for food. Some ants even build mud shelters to protect these sap-sucking insects.*

EQUAL SHARES
The clear waters above coral reefs are the setting for one of the most remarkable partnerships in the world. Here, fish queue up and wait to be cleaned. The cleaners are often brightly coloured shrimps, which pick their way carefully over fishes' scales. Cleaner shrimps feed on dead scales and encrusting animals, and they sometimes venture right inside their clients' mouths. Once a fish has been cleaned, it swims off, and another one takes its place.

Animals cannot plan ahead, so their partnerships do not involve

△ *Most shrimps are well camouflaged, but cleaner shrimps have bright colours to attract clients. Fish remember where they live, and return regularly for a clean.*

agreements like they would in the human world. Instead, each animal behaves in ways that make its partner respond. For example, cleaner shrimps 'advertise' themselves by having bright colours,

△ *Before a female tick can lay her eggs, she needs a meal of blood – the only time she eats during her adult life. By the time she finishes feeding, her abdomen has swollen up like a balloon.*

and by sitting in a prominent place. Client fish keep still while they are being cleaned, and they resist the temptation to swallow the cleaner while it is busy at its work.

TAKING ADVANTAGE
Shrimps are not the only animals that make their living by cleaning. Some fish do, and so do oxpeckers on land. These African birds scuttle over buffalo, rhinos and other large

△ *Perched on a lion's face, a moth sips tears from its eye. In warm parts of the world, several kinds of moth feed on tears, and some even try their luck on humans.*

mammals, removing insects and other pests. But oxpeckers also do something else – they peck at wounds, and feed on their host's blood. As well as helping their host, oxpeckers also harm them, so they

are not quite the perfect partners that they seem. With parasites, things are even more unequal, because a parasite does nothing to help its partner, or host. Instead, it uses it as a source of food, and often as a place to live. Parasites are extremely common in the animal kingdom, and they include thousands of species of invertebrates, such as worms, fleas, flies, lice and ticks. In the wild, almost all animals harbour parasites of some kind, and despite modern medicine, many people have to put up with them too.

MOVING ON
Fleas live on the outside of animals, so it is not too difficult for them to spread from host to host. The adults scatter their eggs in nests and in bedding, and the eggs hatch into tiny, white legless grubs. When the grubs are about two weeks old, they seal themselves in a cocoon, and turn into adults. But a flea cocoon does not open as soon as an adult flea is ready to emerge. Instead, it waits for weeks or months until an animal – or person – walks close by. Alerted by the vibration, the cocoon pops open, and the newly emerged flea jumps onto its host.
Ticks have a different way of finding a host. They climb to the

▷ *Lampreys are among the few parasitic vertebrates (animals with backbones). Using its sucker-like mouth, this one has fastened itself onto a trout, so that it can feed on its blood.*

ends of twigs and grassblades, and wait patiently for animals to walk nearby. If they feel warmth from a moving body, they quickly climb on board. Like fleas, ticks can carry disease, so walking in grassy places can be hazardous if ticks are around.

INTERNAL PARASITES
Parasites that live inside animals have more complicated life cycles, because it is harder for them to spread from host to host. Human tapeworms alternate between two hosts – humans and

△ *This caterpillar is surrounded by cocoons made by tiny parasitic wasp grubs. The grubs grew up inside the caterpillar, and fed on it while it was still alive.*

pigs – while some parasites even have three. But because the chances of reaching a new host are so small, these parasites often produce incredible numbers of eggs. Tapeworms release up to half a million every day, and they can continue producing eggs for several years. This makes them the most prolific egg-layers on the planet.

ANIMAL REPRODUCTION

BREEDING TAKES TIME AND ENERGY, BUT IT IS THE MOST IMPORTANT TASK IN AN ANIMAL'S LIFE. SOME ANIMALS CAN BREED ON THEIR OWN BUT, FOR MOST, BECOMING A PARENT MEANS FINDING A MATE.

▽ *Most insects have to mate before the female lays her eggs. Here, a male grasshopper is using his hooked feet to cling to the female while mating.*

Compared to humans, many animals start breeding at a very early age. Lemmings can become pregnant at the age of two weeks, but some insects grow up even faster, becoming parents at the age of eight days. But successful reproduction is not just a matter of speed. Future parents often have to compete to win a partner. They also have to avoid being spotted by predators during this dangerous but crucial moment of their lives.

△ *Tugging in different directions, two halves of a sea anemone are about to become separate animals. This way of reproducing is common among microorganisms, but much rarer in the animal kingdom.*

SINGLE PARENTS

When sea anemones are fully grown, they can reproduce by tearing themselves in half. This drastic step is the simplest way of reproducing, because only one parent is involved. But it only works for very simple animals. Most species, including ourselves, cannot work if we are divided in two.

This does not mean that lone parents are rare, however. Many small insects can also reproduce on their own, although they do it in a different way. The females produce egg cells, and these develop into young without the mother having to mate. This is called parthenogenesis, or 'virgin birth'. In spring, female aphids, or greenfly, use it to produce enormous families without any help from males.

BEING DIFFERENT

In the animal world, one-parent families have a big drawback – the young are all identical. They share exactly the same genes, which means that they share the same features – both good and bad. Normally, this is not a problem. But if food runs short, or if disease breaks out, the young are equally at risk, and entire families can die.

Sexual reproduction makes this kind of calamity less likely. That is because it involves two parents. The parents' genes are shuffled like a pack of cards, and a different combination is passed on to each of their young. Because the young are all slightly different, there is a better chance that at least some will survive. This advantage explains why sexual reproduction is so common.

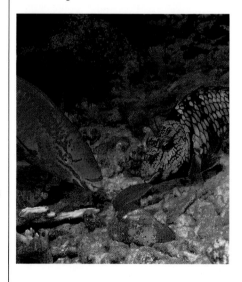

△ *Most animals are either male or female, but parrotfish often start as females, and then change to males in later life. This photograph shows a male (left) and a female (right).*

GETTING TOGETHER

For sexual reproduction to work, two partners have to get together, so that a male's sperm cells can fertilize the female's eggs. It can be a dangerous job –

especially for male spiders, which are often ten times smaller than their mates. The male courts the female extremely carefully, signalling by waving his front legs, or by tugging on her web. It is vital that his courtship signals get across, because if they do not, the male is likely to end up as a meal.

Not many animals run this kind

of risk, but in every species partners have to track each other down. Often, the males court the females – either by their colours and patterns, or by the way they behave. Birds and frogs often use sound as a signal, and so do many insects. But fireflies use their own light, and each kind flashes on and off for a different length of time. Their message is a simple one: 'I'm here, I belong to your species, and I would make an ideal mate.'

THE RIVALS

In most species, the female gets to choose a partner from the available males. As a result, males often compete with each other, like rivals in a talent contest. Male birds sometimes compete by singing or parading their plumage, but weaver birds show off a different skill. Each male builds an elaborate nest, and then shows it off whenever a female flies past. If a female is impressed, she will move in, mate, and lay her eggs. But if the nest does not attract

△ *Male elephant seals battle ferociously for control of a stretch of beach. The winner assembles a group of females, and chases any rival males away.*

attention, the male eventually abandons it, and starts another one nearby. For male weaver birds, this kind of contest creates lots of work, but rival males very rarely come to blows. But with mammals, the

△ *With its throat swollen up like a balloon, a frog broadcasts a call that will attract any females nearby.*

breeding season involves serious combat. Male deer charge each other with their antlers, while male elephant seals rip into their rivals with their teeth. The winner mates with lots of females, while the loser backs off – often biding its time until the following year.

◁ *Male fireflies use light to signal to females waiting on the ground. Each species has its own sequence of flashes, creating different patterns as the males fly through the sky. Four sequences are shown here.*

STARTING LIFE

WHEN SNAKES LAY EGGS, THEY USUALLY ABANDON THEM,
SO THEIR YOUNG HAVE TO FEND FOR THEMSELVES.
BUT MANY ANIMALS CARE FOR THEIR OFFSPRING
UNTIL THEY ARE READY TO LIVE ON THEIR OWN.

Parental care is an essential part of human life, because we take an exceptionally long time to grow up. Other mammals also care for their young, protecting them and feeding them on milk. But in the rest of the animal world, family styles vary enormously from one species to another. Birds often feed their young, but Komodo dragons do exactly the opposite. These giant lizards are cannibals, and they eat any young that make the mistake of coming too close.

△ *After tearing open its egg, a green mamba takes its first look at the outside world. It will be fully independent from the moment it slithers out of the shell.*

EGGS AND EMBRYOS

Practically all the world's animals – including ourselves – start life as eggs. In all mammals, except platypuses and echidnas, the eggs stay inside the mother's body. Here, they develop into embryos, and the mother eventually gives birth to living young. With birds, the start of life is very different. Birds lay their eggs, and the embryos develop as soon as the mother sits on the eggs. This is called incubation, and it

▽ *Young shrews follow their mother by forming a line and gripping each other with their teeth. But shrews have poor eyesight, and these ones have latched on to a toy instead.*

◁ *When the coast is clear, a male mouthbrooder fish lets his young swim out to feed. They dart back into his mouth at the first sign of danger.*

keeps the developing embryos warm. Laying eggs makes good sense for birds, because it would be hard for them to fly with young on board. But in other groups in the animal kingdom, things are not quite so clear cut. For example, pythons lay eggs and then incubate them, but many other snakes keep their eggs inside their bodies until the moment they are ready to hatch. These eggs often tear open as they are laid, making the snakes look as though they are giving birth. Most fish also

lay eggs, but some sharks – including the great white – give birth to live young. In some species, life gets off to a gruesome start, because the largest embryos eat the smallest ones before they are born.

PARENTS ON GUARD

Ocean sunfish can lay over 100 million eggs each time they spawn. The eggs drift away in

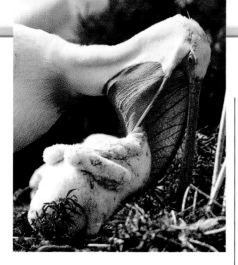

△ *With its head deep inside its parent's throat, a young pelican takes a fishy meal. Fish-eating birds often regurgitate food rather than carrying it back to the nest in their beaks.*

the water, and only a tiny number of them survive for more than a few days. Sunfish make no attempt to look after their eggs – it would be an impossible task with such a gigantic brood.

Animals like the sunfish put all their energy into mass production. At the other extreme, animals that produce much smaller families often devote an immense amount of energy to looking after their eggs and young. Male seahorses collect the female's eggs, and carry them in a pouch, while mouthbrooding fish hold their eggs and hatchlings in their mouths. Albatrosses spend up to ten weeks sitting on their eggs, but female octopuses are even more devoted. They watch over their eggs for several months, cleaning them and keeping guard. During this time, the octopus eats nothing, and when the eggs hatch, she dies.

FAMILY LIFE

Once an animal's eggs have hatched, life can become busier still. Young snakes and lizards find their own food, but newly hatched birds often

▷ *Young dolphins often stay with their mothers for more than a year. As they grow up, they learn to recognize other dolphins by their calls.*

depend on their parents to bring them what they need. Adult blue tits have up to 12 nestlings. The young are blind and helpless when they hatch, and it takes them nearly three weeks to become ready to fly. Until then, the two parents search for food, making over a thousand trips back to the nest each day.

Because young birds are so vulnerable, the parents are always on the alert for danger. This is particularly important for wading birds, such as lapwings and killdeer, because they nest on the ground.

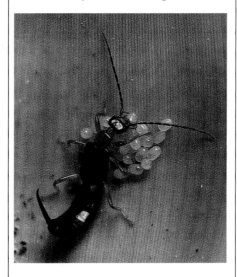

△ *Earwigs are among the few insects that take care of their eggs. The female periodically cleans them to prevent them being attacked by mould.*

If a predator heads towards the nest, the female stages a special display to put it off the scent. She moves out into the open and then walks away, pretending to drag a broken wing. With luck, the predator follows her. Once she has lured it far enough from the nest, she flies up and away.

MAMMAL FAMILIES

Because mammals feed their young on milk, the bond between the mother and her baby is very strong. Most mammals recognize their own young by their scent, and they look after them with great care. At this time of life, adult males can be a threat, so many female mammals bring up their offspring on their own. Young mammals often cling to their mothers, but young marsupials are even better protected, because they travel in their mother's pouch.

During their time together, young mammals watch how their parents feed. This is a vital part of growing up, because it teaches the young how to behave. Predatory mammals watch how their parents hunt, while the brainiest mammals – such as dolphins and chimps – learn sounds and gestures that enable them to communicate with their own kind. For humans, this is even more important, because language allows us to exchange skills and ideas.

GROWING UP

WHEN ANIMALS START LIFE, THEY SOMETIMES LOOK VERY DIFFERENT FROM THEIR PARENTS. MANY CHANGE COLOUR AS THEY GROW UP. BUT SOME ANIMALS CHANGE MUCH MORE DRAMATICALLY, WHEN THEIR BODIES ARE COMPLETELY REBUILT.

Young mammals look quite similar to their parents, even though their bodies are not yet fully developed. But with some animals, it is hard to see any resemblance at all. Caterpillars look nothing like butterflies, while young lobsters are transparent, and do not have any claws. Young animals like these are known as larvae. They live in different ways to their parents, but once their 'childhood' comes to an end, they develop an adult shape and an adult way of life.

◁ *Like most crustaceans, lobsters start life as larvae that live in the plankton. This four-week-old larva has a transparent body case, which makes it harder for predators to spot.*

LARVAL LIFE

Insects often have larvae, but the best place to find them is in watery habitats – particularly the sea. Here, thousands of kinds of animals start life as larvae that hatch from eggs. They are produced by some fish, and also by a huge range of invertebrates, from lobsters and barnacles to clams, sea urchins and starfish. Most of these larvae look nothing like their parents and, in the past, scientists sometimes mistook them for completely separate species.

Unlike young mammals or young birds, larval animals are fully independent, and they have

important tasks to carry out. For caterpillars, that task is feeding – something that they do round the clock. By feeding up, caterpillars collect all the raw materials that are needed to build an adult butterfly. For marine larvae, the mission is quite different. These larvae are often produced by slow-moving animals, or ones that spend their adult lives fastened in one place. They usually drift in the plankton, travelling far and wide and helping their species to spread.

Tadpoles are larvae, and so is the axolotl – a pink amphibian from Mexico that is sometimes kept as

a pet. This remarkable animal can breed while it is still a larva, but for most larvae, breeding cannot begin until they are adults.

METAMORPHOSIS

The change from a young shape to an adult shape is known as metamorphosis. In the sea, most larvae metamorphose gradually, so that their bodies alter step by step. A larval lobster changes slightly each time it sheds its skin. By its fourth moult, it has well-developed legs and antennae, and small but

▽ *Emperor angelfish change colours and patterns as they grow up. This photograph shows an adult fish (top), with a young fish below it.*

effective claws. At this stage, the young lobster is less than 2 cm long, but its life in the plankton is already nearing its end. Tadpoles also change gradually. Their gills shrink, their legs appear, and their tails are slowly absorbed. During metamorphosis, their diet changes as well. Newly hatched tadpoles normally feed on plants, but they slowly switch to a diet that includes animal food. By the time they become adult frogs or toads, they are 100 per cent carnivorous, and never touch plant food again.

SLOW CHANGE

Many insects change in stages as well. Just like young lobsters, young grasshoppers become more like their parents each time they moult. A newly hatched grasshopper has a large head, short body and stubby legs. It cannot fly, because it has no wings. But as it grows and moults, wing buds start to appear on the sides of its body. By its sixth and final moult, the adult grasshopper is fully developed and, once its wings have hardened, it can fly away.

This kind of development is called incomplete metamorphosis, because the changes are limited. Many other insects, including dragonflies, beetles and bugs, also develop in this way. But for butterflies and moths – as well as flies, bees and wasps – metamorphosis is much more drastic. Instead of changing slowly, these insects change suddenly when their larval life comes to an end.

BUILDING A BUTTERFLY

The first sign of this change comes when a caterpillar loses interest in its food, because it now has other priorities instead. It builds a protective case, called a chrysalis, which is sometimes surrounded by a silk cocoon. To do this, moth caterpillars often clamber down from their food plants, so that they can build their chrysalis underground. Butterflies usually make theirs in the open, hanging from leaves or stems.

Once the chrysalis is complete, remarkable events start to take place. The caterpillar's body is slowly dismantled into a soup of living cells. If the chrysalis is opened at this stage, there is no sign of anything living inside. But within days, major reconstruction work is under way, as the body of an adult moth or butterfly is assembled. When the adult insect is complete, it breaks out of its protective case. A brand-new moth or butterfly emerges. This kind of change is known as complete metamorphosis, because the caterpillar's body is totally transformed.

△ *Swallowtail butterflies begin life as eggs, laid singly on food plants. The egg darkens when the caterpillar inside is about to hatch.*

△ *The caterpillar feeds, doubling in size every four or five days. At this stage in life, its main enemies are insect-eating birds.*

△ *After feeding for about a month, the caterpillar spins a chrysalis. The chrysalis splits open when the butterfly is complete.*

INSTINCT AND LEARNING

SPIDERS CANNOT DESIGN OR PLAN, BUT THEY STILL
MANAGE TO BUILD COMPLICATED WEBS. UNLIKE
OUR BEHAVIOUR, THEIRS IS CONTROLLED BY
INSTINCT – A BUILT-IN PROGRAMME THAT IS
HANDED ON FROM PARENTS TO THEIR YOUNG.

Instinct is the invisible guide that keeps the animal world working
smoothly. With simple animals like spiders and insects, it controls
everything that the animal does, and usually the way that it
does it. Instinct allows these animals to carry out some amazingly
complicated tasks, even though they have tiny brains. Animals
with bigger brains also have instincts, but their behaviour is more
flexible. This is because they are able to learn through experience.

*△ When a spider spins a web, it does
not have any idea of how it should look.
The spider simply carries out instinctive
actions, and the web gradually takes shape.*

WHAT IS INSTINCT?
An animal's instincts make it behave
in set ways in everyday situations.
Young birds instinctively beg for
food when their parents arrive at
the nest, while young mammals
instinctively suckle milk. Later in
life, instincts control all kinds of
behaviour, from courtship and
migration to web-building and
nest-making. Because instinctive

behaviour does not have to be
learned, an animal can carry out
all these tasks without ever having
done them before, and without
having to understand any of the
steps that are involved.

Sometimes, instinctive behaviour
is so impressive that animals really
seem to know what they are doing.
For example, beavers construct
amazingly elaborate dams and
channels (see p. 150),
while termites build
large and complex
nests. But unlike human
builders, these animals

cannot come up with new designs.
They simply carry out the instructions
that are held by their genes.

MAKING THE RIGHT RESPONSE
Instinctive behaviour is always
sparked off by some kind of trigger.
For example, toads instinctively
lunge at prey that is on the move,
but they will ignore the same animal
if it is still. Fish in a shoal bunch
together if they are threatened, and
then fan out again when the danger
has passed. Behaviour can also be
sparked off by environmental factors,
such as the change of seasons or the
shifting tides. Fiddler crabs, for
example, have an inbuilt 'clock' that

*▽ When threatened by a snake, a fire-
bellied toad instinctively arches its back.
This reveals bright markings, warning
the snake that the toad's skin is poisonous.*

is set by the tide. They come out to feed at low tide, even if they are moved far from the shore. Instincts like these are very important, because they help animals to survive. But sometimes instincts can go wrong. Moths navigate by using the moon, for example, but this instinct also makes them spiral towards lights after dark. This is a big disadvantage of instinctive behaviour – it cannot adjust to anything new.

LEARNING FROM EXPERIENCE

Humans have some instincts, but most of our behaviour is learned.

△ *Squirrels bury surplus acorns in the autumn. They do not understand about seasons, but this instinctive behaviour provides them with food for the winter ahead.*

We learn not only from our own experience, but also from other people's, and we are so good at it that we pick up new skills all the time. In the rest of the animal world, animals often carry out tasks by instinct, but learning can sometimes make them better.

▷ *These young chimps are using grass stems to fish termites out of their nest. The chimps have learned how to do this by watching adults and copying the way they behave. This kind of learning is unusual in wild animals, but humans use it all the time.*

▷ *This female goose will be followed by her goslings wherever she goes. The goslings recognize their mother by a kind of learning called imprinting.*

Nest-building is a good example of how these two kinds of behaviour blend together. When a bird makes its first nest, it follows an instinctive plan. The nest may not be perfect, but it will be the right size and shape. But if the bird lives long enough, it will become a better builder. It will learn where the best materials can be found, and discover which places are good for building nests. This experience will often make it better at attracting mates.

ANIMAL INTELLIGENCE

It is very difficult to compare animals' intelligence with ours. Many animals are capable of using simple tools, but very few actually make them for themselves. Some birds can count up to five or six, but numbers seem to play no part in their daily lives. Octopuses are even 'brainier'. In experiments, they have worked out how to take the stoppers off bottles

to reach food inside. But our closest relatives are much brighter still. Orang utans have learned how to operate machinery, while chimps communicate using a language that has more than 30 separate 'words'.

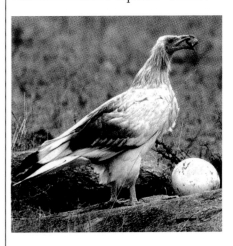

△ *Egyptian vultures use stones to break open ostrich eggs. Although they look intelligent, they sometimes throw the stone beside the egg, instead of against its shell.*

Life in a lion pride is usually peaceful, but fighting can break out when one pride meets another. Here, in Kenya's Masai Mara National Park, lionesses from one pride are defending their territory against some intruders. These fights look dangerous, but most of the aggression is just for show – serious injuries are rare.

LIVING IN A GROUP

SHOALS, SWARMS, FLOCKS AND HERDS ARE A FEATURE OF THE ANIMAL WORLD. BUT WHY DO SOME ANIMALS GATHER TOGETHER, WHEN OTHERS SPEND MOST OF THEIR LIVES ON THEIR OWN?

Animals do not live together simply because they enjoy each other's company. Instead, they do it because group life improves their chances of survival. Some gather together for a specific reason and then go their separate ways. At the other extreme, social animals – such as ants and termites – depend on life in a group and cannot survive alone.

△ *During the day, striped grunts live in tightly packed shoals. At night, the shoal splits up as the fish feed on the seabed.*

TEMPORARY GROUPS

On warm spring evenings, clouds of midges often dance in the air. Each cloud contains hundreds of male midges, which gather together to attract female partners. When a female approaches the swarm, the males rush towards her, and one of them usually succeeds in luring her away to mate. The other males return to their dance, but for the happy couple, group life is at an end.

Midge swarms are temporary groups – the kind that usually happen at particular times of the year. Spring is the season when frogs and toads gather at their breeding pools, and when some birds gather at traditional courtship grounds called leks. Animals also get together in winter, when they take refuge against bad weather. Ladybirds cluster together under bark, while wrens crowd together in nest-boxes and tree holes. But these animals do not become permanent companions. As soon as the days lengthen, they disperse and sometimes never meet again.

LIFE IN A HERD

An antelope herd is a very different kind of group, because animals stay

△ *Ladybirds often gather together when they hibernate. Their bright colours warn that they taste bad – a message that is even clearer when lots of them are packed together.*

△ *Kookaburras live in extended families. Instead of leaving the nest when they can fly, the young stay behind and help their parents to raise further broods.*

in it for life. Antelopes live in herds to protect themselves, because they have less chance of being attacked if they stick together than if they live alone. The same is true with many fish, because predators often find it difficult to pick out prey from the fast-moving shoal. In these groups, animals really do behave like 'one of the herd', because they often do the same thing at the same time.

But just because animals live together, it does not mean that they help each other too. In fact, if an antelope is attacked by a predator, the other members of the herd often seem unconcerned. The reason for this is that animals put their relatives first. If a calf is attacked, its mother will defend it fiercely, but she will not do anything to protect a calf belonging to another animal.

EXTENDED FAMILIES

Life in an elephant herd could hardly be more different, because the group is held together by very close family ties. The herd is led by an old female called a matriarch, and most of the other females in the herd are her daughters, or relatives of some kind. The matriarch has many years' experience of the best places to find water and food, and as the younger elephants grow up, they visit these places themselves. By the time the matriarch dies, another female is ready to take her place.

Unlike antelopes, elephants bond with all the other members of their herd. If an elephant is sick, the herd slows down, and healthy herd members may protect it from attack. When a female is about to give birth, older females – known as 'aunts' – stay close by, and make sure that the calf does not stray.

And when a herd member dies, all the elephants seem to be distressed and upset. Compared to antelopes, elephants seem much more like us.

GIANT COLONIES

Group living reaches its peak among social insects, which include ants and termites, as well as many kinds of bees and wasps. These animals live in giant families called colonies, which can be over two million insects strong. In a colony, only one member breeds. She is known as the queen, and she devotes her entire life to laying eggs. The rest of the colony consists of workers. They build and defend the nest, collect food and raise the young.

For a colony to operate, the workers have to carry out exactly the right tasks at the right time. Their 'orders' come in the form of chemical scents, called pheromones, which are issued by the queen.

As long as she produces these chemicals, the workers go about their daily routine. Workers can also give off some pheromones themselves – if they are attacked, for example. When a worker releases 'attack pheromone', others quickly gather round to fight off the threat.

△ *A queen termite can lay 30,000 eggs in a day. Her sausage-shaped body is so large that she is unable to feed herself – instead, workers bring food to her.*

Colonial life is extremely successful, but sometimes intruders manage to break in. Certain kinds of ants invade other colonies and capture their workers, while some caterpillars feed inside ants' nests.

The caterpillars feel and smell just like ants – a trick that fools the ants into thinking they are friend rather than foe.

▽ *Meerkats live in groups that contain two or three families. These sociable animals always stick together, and take turns to watch for danger. If they spot trouble, they make a loud call.*

ANIMAL ARCHITECTS

LONG BEFORE HUMANS LEARNED HOW TO MAKE BRICKS AND CONCRETE, ANIMALS WERE BUILDING HOMES OF THEIR OWN. SOME OF THEIR HOMES WOULD FIT IN AN EGG CUP, BUT OTHERS WEIGH OVER A TONNE.

Animals are well adapted to outdoor life, so most of them do not need homes for themselves. But animals often build homes to protect their young. Nests keep young animals dry and warm, and they also conceal them from predators looking for an easy meal. Animals build other structures as well. These include traps for catching food, and also bizarre structures called bowers, which some birds use to attract their mates.

△ *A female hummingbird fastens her nest to a twig using strands of spiders' silk. Like many female birds, she is the builder – the male gives her no help at all.*

Beavers make dams to create somewhere safe to live. Water builds up behind the dam, forming a freshwater lake. In the deepest part of the lake, the beavers construct a mound called a lodge, which has their living quarters hidden away inside. The walls of the lodge can be over a metre thick, so even during the winter, the central chamber stays warm. The only way of getting into the lodge is through underwater tunnels – a security feature that keeps most predators at bay.

To make their dams, beavers gnaw through young trees and then float the wood into place. As the wooden framework builds up, they add

THE DAM-BUILDERS

The largest structures made by animals are coral reefs. They can be hundreds of kilometres long, but they are not built in an organized way. Beaver dams, on the other hand, are purpose-built, and they are the largest pieces of engineering in the animal world. The longest one on record measured 700 m from end to end. It was strong enough to support human sightseers, and even people on horseback.

▽ *Using their sharp front teeth, beavers can gnaw through trees 30 cm thick. Like other animal architects, they instinctively know what building materials to use, and how to fit them together.*

Paper walls

Cells

1 **2** **3** **4**

△ *Common wasps make their nests by chewing wood fibres, and spreading it into papery layers. Figures 1 and 2 show a new nest that has been started by a queen wasp. Figures 3 and 4 show the same nest three months later. It has been expanded by the workers, who have added lots of extra 'floors'. These floors contain cells that hold developing grubs.*

vegetation and mud to make it watertight. Once the dam is complete, these natural engineers keep a lookout for leaks, and carry out repairs. A well-built dam can last for decades, so generations of beavers use the lodge as their home.

MAKING AN ENTRANCE

Birds are famous for their building skills and, unlike beavers, many of them start afresh each year. Hummingbirds make their nests out of mosses and lichens, fastening them together with spiders' webs. The result is warm and surprisingly strong – a perfect nursery for the smallest nestlings in the world. Larger birds often build with twigs and sticks, but some specialize in using mud. Swallows often make mud nests shaped like cups, but the rufous ovenbird, from South America, makes one that looks like a large balloon. It has a side-entrance that leads into a curving passage, making it hard for predators to reach the eggs or chicks. Weaverbirds and oropendolas have a different way of keeping out unwanted visitors. Their

nests are made of woven leaves, and they have tubular entrances. These hang downwards like trunks, and can be almost a metre long.

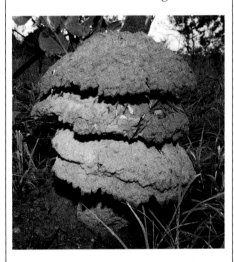

△ *This termite's nest has overlapping roofs that keep it dry. It is built on the ground, but many termites nest in trees, using chewed-up wood as their building material.*

HAND-ME-DOWNS

Nests like these take a long time to build, but even so, many of them are used just once. The reason for this is that nests get dirty, and they can harbour parasites, such as ticks and fleas. But birds of prey do not seem to be put off by these hygiene problems, because they often use

▷ *In Australia and New Guinea, male bowerbirds build amazingly elaborate structures to attract females. The owner of this bower is decorating it with red berries to increase its appeal.*

the same nest year after year. Sometimes, a nest is passed on down the generations, and each new pair of owners makes it bigger still.

The largest tree nests are built by bald eagles, using branches as thick as a person's arm. Their nests may be over 6 m deep and weigh twice as much as a family car. Despite these vast constructions, bald eagles lay just two eggs each time they breed.

INSECT NESTS

The insect world contains some exceptional builders as well. Potter wasps make miniature mud flasks to house their grubs, while some caddisflies fish for food by spinning underwater nets. But the most impressive insect nests are made by social species, which include ants, bees, wasps and termites. The tiny pharaoh ant makes nests smaller than golfballs, but some termites make mounds up to 9 m high. Built of mud, these insect fortresses bake rock-hard in the tropical sun.

△▽ *Grasslands are one of more than a dozen ecosystems that exist on land. Most ecosystems do not have sharp boundaries – instead, they merge into one another. Together, they make up the biosphere, which is home to all life on earth.*

ECOLOGY

LIVING THINGS ARE LIKE PIECES IN A GIANT AND EVER-CHANGING JIGSAW PUZZLE. ECOLOGISTS INVESTIGATE HOW THE PIECES FIT TOGETHER – WITH EACH OTHER AND THE WORLD AROUND THEM.

The natural world is full of connections. For example, owls eat mice, and bumblebees use old mouse nests, so the fewer owls there are, the more chances bumblebees have of finding a home. Zebras eat grass, but because they also nibble away at other plants, they actually help grass to spread. Connections like these make nature work.

△ *Africa's grasslands and its wildlife form one of the most distinctive ecosystems on earth. This ecosystem is famous for its large herds of grazing mammals.*

WHAT IS ECOLOGY?

When scientists first started to study nature, they concentrated on individual living things. They travelled the world, sending specimens back to museums so that they could be catalogued and identified. Today, this work still goes on, but scientists also study the way living things interact. This research is particularly important, because it helps us to understand how the changes humans bring – such as pollution and deforestation – can affect the living world.

Ecology is the study of these connections. It involves living things themselves, and the raw materials and nutrients that they use. Energy is also important in ecology, because it is the driving force that keeps living things alive.

CLUBBING TOGETHER

When researchers investigate wild animals, they sometimes get to know them extremely well. Experienced researchers can identify chimps by their faces, and humpback whales by the patterns on their tails. Individuals can be fascinating to follow, but ecologists are more interested about how life works on a bigger scale.

Moving upwards from individuals, the first important level is a population. This is a group of living things belonging to the same species, that live in the same area at the same time. Some populations contain just a handful of members, while others have thousands, and they also change in different ways. A population of elephants or oak trees changes slowly, because these species take a long time to breed, and live for many years. But a population of grasshoppers changes very quickly, because insects have much shorter and faster lives.

In some populations, individuals are spread out at random, but more often they live in scattered groups. This can be a problem for scientists trying to monitor wildlife, because it makes populations difficult to count. Things get even trickier with animals that are always on the move, such as tigers and whales.

COMMUNITY LIFE

After populations, the next level up is called a community. This contains populations of several different species, mixed together like neighbours in the same part of town.

In nature, community life is always busy, but it is not always as peaceful as it sounds. That is because the species have very different lifestyles. Some get on extremely well, but others use their neighbours as prey.

Living communities vary hugely from region to region. In the tropics, they often contain thousands of species which fit together in extremely complex ways. But in the world's most hostile habitats, the list of species does not even fill a page. For example, deep-sea vents teem with bacteria, but there is no plant life of any kind, because there is no light. In these difficult conditions, fewer than a dozen kinds of animals make vents their permanent home.

HABITATS AND ECOSYSTEMS

A community is a collection of living things, and nothing else. But the next step up – called an ecosystem – includes their home, or habitat, as well. Ecosystems include all kinds of habitats and their wildlife, from coniferous forests and tundra to coral reefs and caves.

Ecosystems need energy to work, and this usually comes from the sun. Plants collect sunlight on land, while algae collect it in the surface layers of the sea. Once they have gathered this all-important energy, they use it to grow, and this makes food that other living things can use. Each time something gets eaten, this energy passes from one species to another. Deep-sea vents are among the few places where life is fuelled in a different way. Here, bacteria collect energy from minerals dissolved in water, and they create the food that keeps animals alive.

Added together, the world's ecosystems make up the biosphere, which is the largest ecological level of all. This incredibly varied stage – with all its teeming inhabitants – includes every place on earth where living things can be found.

◁▽ *All the zebras in an area make up a population. They mix with each other all the time, so they interbreed. In a zebra population, all the individual animals have slightly different patterns, but it takes an expert eye to tell one individual from another.*

△ *Together with different plants and animals, zebras form a community – a living mixture of different species that live in the same area, and that use each other for survival. Zebras need grass for food, but they help it to spread by nibbling away other plants.*

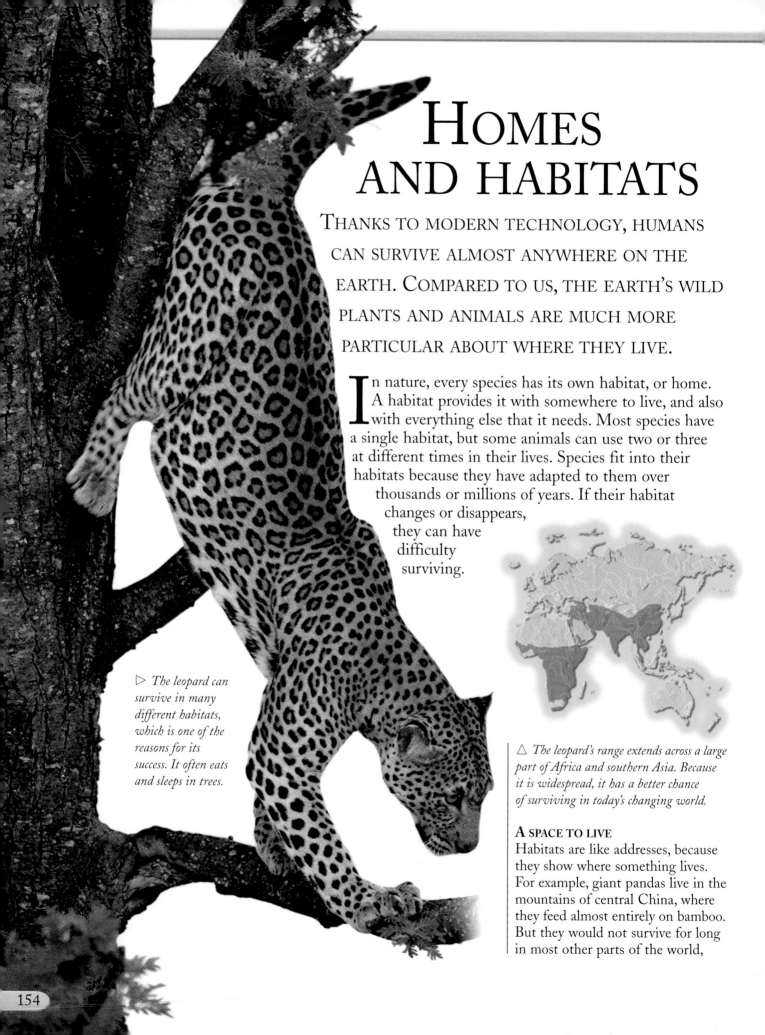

HOMES AND HABITATS

THANKS TO MODERN TECHNOLOGY, HUMANS CAN SURVIVE ALMOST ANYWHERE ON THE EARTH. COMPARED TO US, THE EARTH'S WILD PLANTS AND ANIMALS ARE MUCH MORE PARTICULAR ABOUT WHERE THEY LIVE.

In nature, every species has its own habitat, or home. A habitat provides it with somewhere to live, and also with everything else that it needs. Most species have a single habitat, but some animals can use two or three at different times in their lives. Species fit into their habitats because they have adapted to them over thousands or millions of years. If their habitat changes or disappears, they can have difficulty surviving.

▷ The leopard can survive in many different habitats, which is one of the reasons for its success. It often eats and sleeps in trees.

△ The leopard's range extends across a large part of Africa and southern Asia. Because it is widespread, it has a better chance of surviving in today's changing world.

A SPACE TO LIVE

Habitats are like addresses, because they show where something lives. For example, giant pandas live in the mountains of central China, where they feed almost entirely on bamboo. But they would not survive for long in most other parts of the world,

▽▷ Water bears, or tardigrades, live in damp 'microhabitats' throughout the world. If their home dries up, they pull in their legs and dry out as well. Once they are dormant, they can survive for years until it turns wet once more.

because pandas depend on bamboo. Without it, they cannot feed.

Compared to the giant panda, the leopard is much more flexible about what it eats and where it is at home. It can survive on open grassland and in tropical forest, and even in farmland quite close to towns. This helps to explain why the leopard is the most successful big cat alive today. But some of the world's most widespread animals live in habitats that most people do not even realize are there. Microscopic creatures called water bears live in pools, puddles and gutters, and even in the thin film of water between individual particles of soil. Habitats like these can be found all over the world, which is why water bears live worldwide as well.

SPECIAL HOMES

Long ago, our ancestors spread northwards out of Africa – a journey that eventually carried them all over the globe. But in nature, some species evolve in one place, and never manage to spread anywhere else. This is often because they are isolated on remote islands, or in valleys high in mountains.

Species like these are called 'endemics'. They include thousands of unusual plants, such as the coco-de-mer, and also a large collection of extraordinary animals, from the lemurs of Madagascar to the famous giant tortoises of the Galapagos Islands. The kiwi, from New Zealand, is an endemic species, and so are almost all of Hawaii's native birds and snails.

Endemic species are often rare, because their natural home is usually small. This makes them very vulnerable. If their habitat changes, or if humans bring in new species from outside, they can disappear in a remarkably short space of time. Many endemic species have already become extinct. In places such as New Zealand and Hawaii, conservationists are trying hard to protect the ones that still remain.

△ *These plants have moved into a brand-new habitat – a field of lava produced by a volcanic eruption. As time goes by, soil will start to form and more plants will grow.*

NEW HABITATS

Most of the world's habitats are fully stocked with wildlife, but sometimes, completely new habitats open up. If a river changes course, or a wildfire breaks out, plants and animals waste no time moving into newly vacant ground. Sometimes, big disasters create opportunities on a far larger scale. In the American northwest, for example, Mount St Helens erupted in 1980. The eruption flattened thousands of trees and coated the ground with a deep layer of ash. But just three years later, the ash was covered with flowers and insects, and today, the forest is rapidly returning.

▽ The coco-de-mer palm is a unique tree that grows the largest seeds in the world. It can only live where the ground is fertile, and where the temperature is warm throughout the year.

Seychelles
Islands

Southern
Africa

△ *The coco-de-mer has a tiny range compared to most other trees. In the wild, it grows in a few valleys in the Seychelles Islands in the Indian Ocean, and nowhere else in the world.*

LIVING TOGETHER

WHEN LIONS SHARE THE SAME HABITAT WITH ZEBRAS, IT IS EASY TO GUESS WHAT HAPPENS. BUT SPECIES LIVE TOGETHER IN MANY WAYS – SOMETIMES, THEY HELP EACH OTHER TO SURVIVE.

◁ *Bats eat lots of insects, but insects breed much faster than bats. This is one of the reasons why prey species survive despite being hunted.*

Habitats provide living things with a home, but they do not guarantee them an easy time. In each habitat, food and space is limited, so each species has to work hard to get its share. In this struggle, some species compete head-on, some join forces, and some do not affect each other at all. The result is a complicated world, where things are not always quite as they seem.

△ *Chased by a lioness, this zebra is in serious danger. But for zebras as a whole, being hunted is much less of a problem than running out of food.*

HUNTERS AND HUNTED

For zebras in Africa's grasslands, being hunted is a fact of life. A single adult lion needs to eat up to 20 large animals a year, and zebras often feature on their menu. As well as coping with lions, zebras have to put up with other predators. These include leopards and hyenas on land, and crocodiles that lurk in rivers and waterholes, waiting for animals to come within range.

With all these enemies, an individual zebra's life can be cut short at any time. But for an entire species, predators are not a major threat. Most predators target young animals, or ones that are injured or ill. While these stragglers are picked off, the healthiest animals survive. Far from endangering their prey, predators help to keep the species in good condition, by ensuring that the fittest animals breed. Predators actually need animals to escape, because if they did not, they would eventually run out of food.

JOINING FORCES

In every habitat, some species form partnerships that help them to survive. This is called symbiosis, and it can be a temporary arrangement, or something that works full-time. In Africa's grasslands, one of the strangest short-term partnerships involves a mammal called the ratel or honey-badger, and a bird called the honeyguide. The honeyguide feeds on insects, and it is good at finding bees' nests, but it cannot break them open. Instead, it looks for help. The honeyguide attracts a ratel by flying towards it, and making a clicking sound. Once the ratel takes an interest, the bird leads it towards the nest. When the ratel has broken into the nest and eaten its fill, the bird feeds on the insects, honey and wax that are left behind.

Honeyguides and ratels can survive quite well without each other. But full-time partners are quite different. They often depend on each other completely, and cannot survive on their own. Figs and fig wasps are partners like this (see p. 91). So are yuccas and yucca moths, which live in the deserts of the American southwest. Yuccas grow creamy-white flowers, and these provide food and shelter for the yucca moth's caterpillars, which grow up hidden inside them. In return, the adult moths pollinate yucca flowers. Yuccas are often grown in gardens in other parts of the world, but without their moths, they hardly ever produce seeds.

BATTLES FOR SURVIVAL

If different species compete head-on, a battle breaks out. This is what happened about three million years ago, when North and South America joined together, after millions of years of being apart. Once the two continents were linked, a two-way traffic of species

△ *These butterflies have gathered on a tropical riverbank to collect nutrients in the mud. They look like an easy target for birds, but there are so many of them that most will manage to escape if they are attacked.*

began, as animals moved north and south. In the tough competition that followed, North America's grassland mammals proved to be a big success. They spread so far and so fast that many of South America's home-grown species died out. But some of South America's forest mammals managed to make a home in the north. Marsupials were among them, which explains why North America still has a few marsupial mammals today.

▷ *In the coniferous forests of the American northwest, Douglas firs are home to many different types of birds. By living at different levels, and eating different food, the birds share the same habitat without competing head-on.*

MAKING ROOM

Extinction is perfectly natural, but it does not always happen when two species find themselves in a head-on clash. That is because species can adjust to each other. Instead of eating the same food, or using the same homes, they slowly change as time goes by. As a result, they end up being able to live side by side.

This is exactly what researchers find in long-established habitats, where species have had plenty of time to adjust to their neighbours. In forests, for example, different types of birds often live in the same trees, and seem to feed on the same food. But a closer look usually shows that each species lives at a different level, and has a slightly different diet.

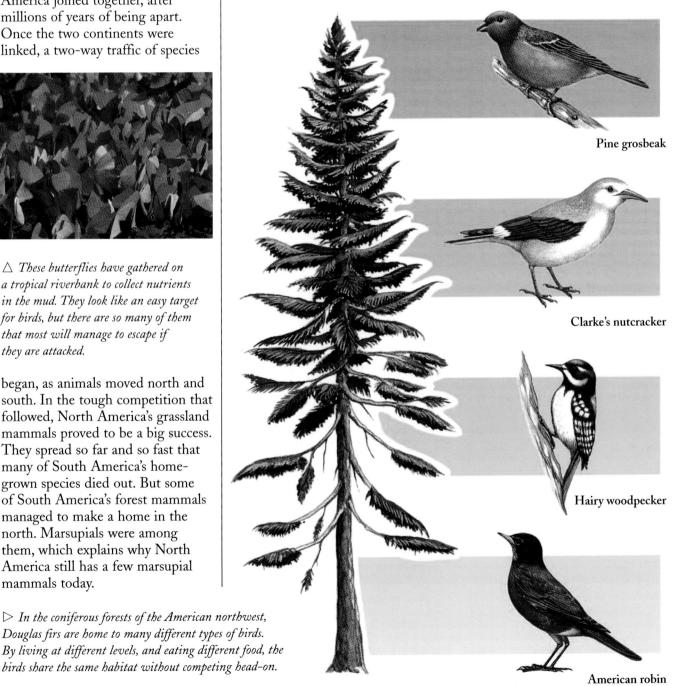

Pine grosbeak

Clarke's nutcracker

Hairy woodpecker

American robin

FOOD CHAINS AND WEBS

IN NATURE, FOOD IS ALWAYS ON THE MOVE. WHEN A BUTTERFLY FEEDS ON A FLOWER OR WHEN A SNAKE SWALLOWS A FROG, FOOD MOVES ONE STEP FURTHER ALONG A FOOD CHAIN. SO DOES THE ENERGY THAT IT CONTAINS.

Food chains are not something that you can pick up or touch, but they are an essential part of the living world. That is because food is passed on whenever one thing eats another. Eaters often end up being eaten themselves, and when this happens, food is passed on again. The result is a food chain. Most living things play a part in several different chains. Added together, the food chains make up food webs – networks that can involve hundreds or even thousands of different species.

HOW FOOD CHAINS WORK
On this page and the one opposite, you can trace your way through a tropical food chain. Like almost all food chains on land, it starts with a plant. Plants collect energy directly

△ The photographs on these pages show a food chain in the rainforest of Central America, beginning with a flower. A heliconid butterfly becomes species two in the chain when it feeds on the flower. The butterfly is the first food-eater in the chain.

from sunlight, so they do not need to eat. But plants do make food, and this is passed on when they are eaten by herbivores, or plant-eating animals.

Many herbivores feed on roots, leaves or seeds. But in this food chain, the herbivore is a butterfly, which settles on the plant's flowers to drink nectar. Nectar is rich in energy, so it makes an ideal fuel. Unfortunately for the butterfly, it is preyed upon by a green lynx spider – the third species to join the chain. Like all spiders, this one is strictly carnivorous, and it is an expert at catching insects. But to hunt butterflies, the spider has to risk moving about during the day. Its movements attract the attention of a glass frog, which swallows the spider, becoming species number four. Glass frogs have many enemies, and one of them is the eyelash pit-viper – a small but highly poisonous snake that often lurks near flowers.

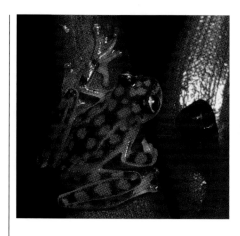

△ A glass frog is species number four in the chain. It lives in trees, and feeds on many different animals – some are plant-eaters, but many are predators like itself.

When it eats the frog, it becomes species number five. But the snake is also vulnerable, and its life is cut short when it is spotted by a rare harpy eagle, which joins the chain as species number six. The harpy eagle has no natural enemies, so the food chain comes to an end.

FOOD CHAINS AND ENERGY
Six species may not sound very many, particularly in a habitat that teems with life. But it is actually more than average – many food chains have just three or four. So why do food

△ A green lynx spider catches the butterfly, and collects food energy from its prey. The spider is species number three in the food chain, but it is the first predator so far.

△ *An eyelash pit-viper spends most of its life off the ground, and it catches animals feeding near flowers. It is species number five, and the third predator in the chain.*

chains run out so soon? The reason is to do with energy.

When animals eat food, they use its energy in two different ways. Some gets built in to their bodies, but most of it is used in making their bodies work. Built-in energy can be handed on, but working energy is lost once it has been used. With active animals, such as birds and mammals, working energy makes up about 90 per cent of the total, so only ten per cent is left as potential food. By the time a food chain reaches its fourth or fifth species, not much energy is left. When it reaches the sixth, there is hardly any at all.

PYRAMIDS OF LIFE

This rapid drop in energy explains another feature of food chains – in most, the species near the bottom of the chain are much more numerous than those at the top. If the chain is arranged in layers, the result is a 'pyramid of numbers', like the one shown on the right.

This particular pyramid shows a single food chain in a freshwater habitat. Working

up from the bottom, the most common animals are tadpoles and water beetles. Further up the chain, predatory fish are less common, and fish-eating birds rarer still. The same kind of pyramid works for almost all habitats, from grasslands to Arctic tundra. It explains why 'top predators', such as herons, lions and harpy eagles, need a lot of space to survive.

WORLDWIDE WEBS

Food webs are more complicated than food chains, because they involve many different species. As well as prey and their predators, they also include species that live by breaking down dead remains. In a food web, some species have just a few connections. Others have dozens, because they eat many kinds of food.

Elaborate food webs are often a sign of a healthy environment, because they show that lots of

△ *A harpy eagle is the last species in the chain. Nothing hunts it, but when the eagle dies, its remains will enter a separate food chain where they will be broken down by decomposers.*

species are living side by side. If a habitat is damaged – by pollution or deforestation, for example – food webs can be disrupted, because some of their species disappear.

A food chain pyramid in a freshwater habitat

Grey herons hunt alone. Standing still in shallow water, they watch patiently for movement, and strike with a sudden lunge of their dagger-like bill.

Perch are predatory fish. They eat a wide range of prey, including water insects, frogs and other fish.

Great diving beetles hunt tadpoles, seizing them with their front legs before slicing them up in their jaws.

Tadpoles feed on waterplants when they are young. They switch to a meat-eating diet as they grow older.

Floating waterplants form the bottom of the pyramid. They create food that can be passed up a food chain.

A boat heads downriver in Bowling Green Bay National Park, a wetland habitat in northeast Australia. In this part of the world there is a long dry season each year, so trees can only survive if they grow close to the riverbank. Crocodiles lurk in the murky water, and the narrow strip of forest teems with birds.

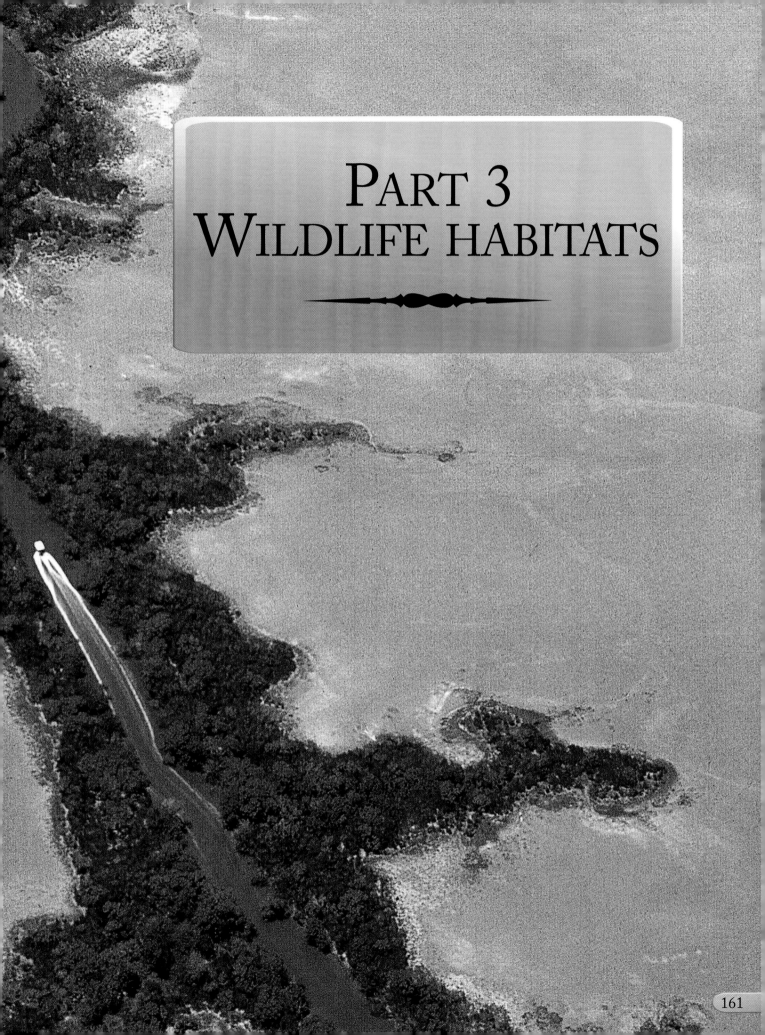

PART 3
WILDLIFE HABITATS

BIOMES OF THE WORLD

THE HUMAN WORLD IS SPLIT UP INTO NATIONS, BUT THE NATURAL WORLD IS ORGANIZED IN A VERY DIFFERENT WAY. ITS 'COUNTRIES' ARE CALLED BIOMES, AND EACH ONE HAS A DISTINCTIVE MIX OF LIVING THINGS.

From the air, biomes are easy to spot. Deserts are dry and brown, while tropical forests look like dark green carpets. Tundra is open, bleak and bare, while wetlands are often full of waterlogged vegetation. In everyday language, biomes are often known as habitats – a word also used to mean the exact surroundings that a species uses as its home.

THE BIOME MAP
On land, there are ten major biomes. They are shaped mainly by climate, because that affects the kind of plants which can grow. For example, tropical rainforest is found in places that are always warm and wet, while desert forms where it is too dry for trees to survive. Each biome is found in several different parts of the world, wherever the climate is the same. The plants in each biome vary from place to place but, because they grow in the same conditions, they often have the same shape and even the same kind of leaves.

Animal life depends on plants, so it is divided into biomes too. Most of the world's grazing mammals live in grasslands, and a massive slice of its insect life is found in tropical and temperate forests. Deserts are one of the most important biomes for snakes and lizards, although shrublands are good places for them too. A big fraction of the world's fish live in coral reefs – the nearest thing to a biome in the sea.

BIOMES ON THE MOVE
Because biomes are shaped mainly by the climate, they often do not have clear-cut frontiers. Instead,

ARCTIC

Lincoln Sea

Beaufort Sea

Baffin Bay

Arctic Circle

Hudson Bay

Gulf of Alaska

Labrador Sea

NORTH AMERICA

ATLANTIC OCEAN

Tropic of Cancer

Gulf of Mexico

Caribbean Sea

Equator

PACIFIC OCEAN

SOUTH AMERICA

Tropic of Capricorn

Key
- Polar (The Arctic/Antarctica)
- Arctic tundra
- Mountains
- Coniferous forests
- Temperate forests
- Grasslands and savanna
- Shrublands
- Deserts
- Wetlands
- Tropical forests
- Coral reefs

Antarctic Circle

neighbouring biomes usually merge. In the far north, coniferous forest gradually gives way to tundra, while in the tropics, shrublands give way to desert. In places, the boundary zones between two biomes can be hundreds of kilometres wide.

Climate patterns slowly shift, so biomes shift too. Deserts expand when the climate turns drier, then contract again when wetter times return. The further back in time you go, the bigger these changes become.

At the height of the last Ice Age, tundra covered large parts of North America, Europe and Asia. Tropical rainforests shrank, because the climate was cool and dry, and with the forest on the retreat, rainforest animals had to retreat as well.

PEOPLE AND BIOMES

The map below shows where the world's biomes are today. What it does not show are the changes that have been caused by human beings.

Ever since we learned how to farm, about 10,000 years ago, we have had a growing impact on the world's biomes. Forests have been cut down, grasslands ploughed up and wetlands drained. In some parts of the world, desert conditions have spread, because farmland soil has been washed or blown away. If none of this had happened – or if it somehow went into reverse – the world's biomes would look exactly as they are shown here.

O C E A N

Greenland Sea

Kara Sea

Laptev Sea

Barents Sea

East Siberian Sea

Norwegian Sea

Arctic Circle

North Sea

EUROPE

Bering Sea

Sea of Okhotsk

Black Sea

Caspian Sea

ASIA

Sea of Japan

Mediterranean Sea

East China Sea

Tropic of Cancer

AFRICA

Red Sea

Arabian Sea

Bay of Bengal

South China Sea

P A C I F I C

O C E A N

Equator

I N D I A N

O C E A N

Coral Sea

AUSTRALASIA

AND OCEANIA

Tropic of Capricorn

Tasman Sea

S O U T H E R N   O C E A N

Antarctic Circle

A N T A R C T I C A

ARCTIC AND TUNDRA

IN THE FAR NORTH OF THE PLANET, TEMPERATURES CAN BE AS LOW AS −50°C, AND WINTER DAYS ARE JUST A FEW HOURS LONG. FOR THE PLANTS AND ANIMALS THAT LIVE THERE, THE ARCTIC IS A LAND OF OPPORTUNITY, BUT IT TAKES REAL TOUGHNESS TO SURVIVE IN THIS SEA OF ICE AND SNOW.

The heart of the Arctic is a frozen ocean – one that is almost completely surrounded by land. This ocean is the world's smallest, and most of it is covered by a layer of floating ice that is constantly on the move. The land around the Arctic Ocean – known as the tundra – is bleak and treeless, and is frozen for much of the year. But for a few months during spring and summer, the surface thaws, and the tundra suddenly explodes into life.

LIFE IN THE ARCTIC OCEAN
For humans, the Arctic Ocean is dangerously cold. Even in summer, the temperature is close to freezing, and anyone falling in needs to be rescued straight away. In winter, sea-ice stretches as far south as the tip of Greenland, sealing the ocean like a crystalline lid. Icebergs become trapped in the winter ice, but when the ice melts, they can drift south for thousands of kilometres. In 1912, the *Titanic* struck an iceberg that was as far south as Spain, and in 1926, an iceberg was even seen off Bermuda.

◁ *Jellyfish are an important part of the Arctic Ocean's wildlife. This kind swims, but some jellyfish spend most of their time upside down on the seabed.*

▽ *Three young polar bears follow their mother across the ice. Females look after their cubs until they are about two years old – after that they are on their own.*

△ *Every spring, the edge of the Arctic sea-ice starts to break up, forming ice floes that drift with the currents. Here, off the coast of Greenland, floes are beginning to break away from the main ice sheet.*

Compared to air, water is very good at draining away warmth, which is why people cannot last long if they fall into the icy waves. But despite the intense cold, the Arctic Ocean is one of the busiest wildlife habitats on earth. It teems with microscopic plankton, with jellyfish, brittlestars and burrowing worms, and also with fish, seals and whales. How do they manage to survive?

For most Arctic Ocean animals, the cold is simply not a problem, because they do not have any body heat to lose. These 'cold-blooded' animals are quite at home in icy water, as long as it does not actually freeze. Many live on the seabed, where the temperature stays at a steady 4° C all year round. In this dimly lit and not-quite-frozen world, cold-blooded animals move slowly, but they have no trouble staying alive.

DEEP HEAT

For mammals in the Arctic Ocean, the cold is more of a threat. Seals and whales are warm-blooded, and their body temperatures are hardly any different from ours. If they become chilled – even by a few degrees – they risk dying of hypothermia.

Arctic mammals get around this problem by having a wrap-around layer of fat, called blubber, between their internal organs and their skin. Fat is an extremely good insulator, and it makes it hard for body heat to escape. In Arctic seals, this layer is usually about 10 cm thick, but in bowhead whales, it can be 50 cm deep, with a total weight of several tonnes. When these whales were hunted, as long ago as the 1600s, their blubber was highly prized, and it was often cut up into blocks and then floated back to shore.

Blubber alone is enough to keep whales warm, but most seals also have a short coat of dense fur. One Arctic Ocean animal – the polar bear – has much shaggier fur, which is good for keeping warm in air, but not nearly so effective in water. However, thanks to its blubber, the polar bear has no fear of the cold. It is a true sea-going animal, sometimes swimming dozens of kilometres from the nearest ice or land.

△ *Soaking up the summer sunshine, tundra plants bloom among rocks near the Arctic coast. There are hundreds of different flowering plants in the Arctic, but most of them are just a few centimetres tall.*

▽ *Watched by its mother, a harp seal pup takes a feed. Unlike polar bears, female harp seals abandon their young when they are just 12 days old. The pup has to moult its silky coat before it can start feeding at sea.*

◁ *Like passengers waiting for a bus, male narwhals line up in a 'lead', or crack, in the sea-ice. Narwhals sometimes live in family groups, but all these narwhals have long tusks, showing that they are adult males.*

it is designed for attacking large, fast-moving prey. However, walruses actually feed on seabed clams, sucking them up from the chilly mud like gigantic vacuum cleaners.

Polynyas are also a favourite home of two of the Arctic's smallest whales, the white whale, or beluga, and the narwhal – an extraordinary animal with a single tusk that points

GAPS IN THE ICE

Near the North Pole, the Arctic Ocean's surface is almost always frozen, which makes it difficult for air-breathing seals and whales to survive. But in most parts of the Arctic, strong winds and currents jostle the sea-ice, opening up cracks

▽ *Walruses often lounge on ice floes between feeding sessions. Their tusks are mainly a badge of rank, but they also come in handy when a walrus needs to haul itself out of the water and onto the ice.*

of water in some places, crunching the ice together in others. Small stretches of open water, called leads, can appear almost anywhere, but they rarely last for long. Much larger expanses, known by a Russian name – polynya – can last for years or even decades. Today, one of the biggest Arctic polynyas is at the northern end of Baffin Bay. It is almost as big as Switzerland, making it easily visible from space.

For Arctic wildlife, polynyas are like oases in a frozen desert. They are some of the best places to see seals, including the walrus – the biggest Arctic species of all. Weighing up to 1,200 kg, and equipped with impressive tusks, this wrinkly skinned animal looks as if

---

Species Profile

Arctic fox: *Alopex lagopus*

This dainty and inquisitive predator lives right across the Arctic region. In summer, it stays on land, but in winter it may wander hundreds of kilometres onto the sea-ice. Most Arctic foxes have a brown summer coat and a white winter coat for camouflage against the snow. However, in some Arctic foxes the winter coat is bluish-grey. These foxes are not fussy feeders, and they eat anything they can catch or scavenge, from nesting birds to the remains of polar bear kills, such as seals.

hope of escape. This is bad news for the whales, but good news for the Arctic's native inhabitants, which use narwhal meat as a winter food.

TUNDRA TIMES
In the Arctic, winter is a season of darkness, but summer is flooded with light. On the Arctic Circle, the sun dips down to the horizon on midsummer's day, but it starts to rise again before it actually sets. Farther north, summer is even more strange.

△ *In winter, the snowy owl's plumage is perfect camouflage. But in summer, when this picture was taken, this impressive Arctic hunter is much easier to spot.*

forwards. Narwhal tusks look like the horns of legendary unicorns, and in the past were often sold for their supposedly magical powers. Even today, narwhal tusks are mysterious. Found only in males, they are actually highly specialized teeth, up to 3 m long. Males sometimes use them in ritual fights, but their function is still not fully understood.

TRAPPED
Giant polynyas like the one in Baffin Bay make a permanent home for animals that need open water. But with smaller ice-free areas, changing weather and shifting currents can turn a refuge into a prison. As the sea begins to freeze over in late summer, polynyas begin to shrink. Sometimes they can close altogether.

For seabirds, this is only a slight inconvenience, because many species are already moving south to spend the winter in milder climes. But for seals and whales, the ice-up can cause real problems if they linger too long. A fully grown walrus can smash its way up through ice 25 cm thick, but as autumn moves into winter, and the ice keeps growing, keeping a breathing-hole open becomes a really tough task.

Sometimes things go badly wrong. Narwhals live farther north than any other Arctic whales, which means that they are particularly in danger from the late-summer freeze. Occasionally, hundreds of narwhals find themselves trapped in shrinking pools of water, with little

At the world's northernmost town – Ny Ålesund, in Spitsbergen – the sun lifts clear of the horizon in early June, and then does not set again until late July. For nearly eight weeks there is non-stop daylight, making it difficult to know when to get up and when to go to bed.

Arctic animals have no trouble adapting to these conditions, and are up and about round the clock. Ducks and geese feed at midnight on the tundra or along the shore, while snowy owls hunt in broad daylight, relying on surprise to catch their prey. Arctic foxes (see p. 166) are also on the prowl, patrolling nesting sites and coastal rocks in

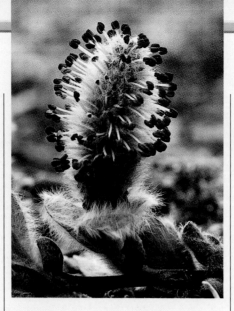

△ *Shown about twice life size, this is a single catkin from the world's shortest 'tree', the Arctic willow. These tough tundra plants are often pollinated by bumblebees, which visit them as soon as spring arrives.*

the hope of finding undefended eggs or chicks. Unlike other foxes, these thickly furred animals breed in underground dens handed down from one generation to the next. The largest can have a dozen entrances and be more than a century old.

THE TUNDRA IN FLOWER

For the plants of the Arctic, the lengthening daylight triggers a race to reproduce. As the snow clears, bright green mounds of sphagnum moss emerge on the waterlogged peat, and bog cotton sprouts around the tundra's ink-black pools. Stony ground is often covered by

Species Profile

Reindeer moss: *Cladonia rangiferina*

Despite its name, reindeer moss is not a moss, but a lichen – a living partnership between an alga and a fungus. It grows throughout the tundra, and is an important food for reindeer, particularly during the harsh winter months when other food can be hard to find in the icy, snow-covered landscape. Reindeer moss is grey in colour, but it grows bright red tips that make its spores.

lichens – particularly kinds that look like grey-green bushes just a few centimetres tall. These are among the toughest plants in the Arctic, and they are an important food for reindeer, which use their hooves to scrape the plants clear of snow. The tundra is also home to the Arctic willow, which grows no more than ankle-high. By sticking close to the ground, this polar 'tree' keeps safely out of the wind – an important survival technique in a habitat where wind chill can kill.

Because the Arctic summer is so short, tundra plants work to a very tight schedule to make their seeds.

▽ Spread out across the snow, reindeer make their way towards their winter quarters. The largest herds, in the Canadian Arctic, can be up to half a million animals strong, and they migrate hundreds of kilometres each year.

Arctic willow grows yellow or rust-coloured catkins, and then keeps them 'on hold' until the ground is clear of snow. As soon as the air temperature reaches about 10°C, they open out, ready to attract any insects that are on the wing. A brightly coloured plant called purple saxifrage is even quicker off the mark. Its flowers sometimes open while the snow is still melting overhead.

ARCTIC INSECTS

For the Arctic's human inhabitants, summer can be a difficult time. This is because the sunshine melts the surface of the soil, turning the tundra soft and boggy, so that it is difficult to move around. To make matters worse, this is the far north's mosquito season. In countless lakes and pools across the Arctic, billions of immature mosquitoes turn into adults, and take to the air on their brand new wings. Male mosquitoes are harmless, because they feed at flowers, but the females need to

drink blood before they can lay their eggs. They normally attack wild animals, but they also cluster over clothes, footwear and even camera lenses, searching for the smallest patch of exposed human skin.

△ For Arctic mosquitoes, humans are an irresistible attraction. The Arctic has some of the largest mosquitoes in the world, with an equally large appetite for blood. Unlike tropical mosquitoes, they rarely carry disease.

△ *By flying in V-formation, geese reduce the amount of energy they use during their long migration flights. Each bird is helped by the slipstream from the one in front, and they take turns to be in the lead.*

The Arctic is also home to blackflies – tiny humpbacked bloodsuckers that have an extremely itchy bite. These troublesome insects can be as little as 2 mm long, but they can attack in clouds that send animals (and people) rushing to escape.

Fortunately, not all tundra insects are as unpleasant as these. Arctic bumblebees perform an essential service pollinating the tundra's flowers, while damselflies feed on blood-sucking insects, catching them in mid-air. And on warm days, when the air is calm, butterflies take to the wing. Some of them are home-grown residents of the tundra, but others are long-distance migrants that arrive when the long days of summer begin. Their journey northward can sometimes be more than a staggering 2,000 km long.

FLYING MIGRANTS

It may seem strange that butterflies travel to such a cold and remote part of the world, but in summer the Arctic's plants are an almost endless source of food. And butterflies are not the only animals that make the journey. Even before the snows have fully melted, flocks of geese arrive from warm lands to the south, ready to raise their young. Each species has its own winter and summer quarters. Snow geese spend the winter in the southern and western USA, and nest mainly in the Canadian Arctic, while the much rarer red-breasted goose

△ *Guillemots are fish-eating birds that use their stubby wings to speed underwater after their prey. These birds are the Arctic's equivalent of penguins, although unlike real penguins they are still able to fly.*

spends its winters near the Black Sea, and nests in the Taymyr Peninsula, in northern Siberia.

Although geese are good swimmers, they do not feed afloat. Instead, they eat grass and other land plants, tearing it off with a sharp tug of their beaks. Throughout the summer, the adults and goslings feed and fatten up, preparing for the long journey south.

▽▷ Musk oxen are the largest full-time land mammals in the Arctic. Their shaggy coats protect them from the cold – especially when they stand with their backs to the wind, like the snow-caked bull below.

HERDS ON THE MOVE

The Arctic's largest grazing animals also travel with the seasons, but their journeys are on the ground. Herds of reindeer move south until they reach the great northern forest, marching across the snow on their unusually broad hooves, and swimming across any rivers or sea inlets in their way.

In Scandinavia, the Sami people once lived as nomadic reindeer-herders, following their animals between tundra and forest, and keeping wolves and other predators at bay. Today, some of the Sami still do this, although these modern reindeer-herders often have motorized sledges, and comfortable houses at the journey's end.

As summer slips into autumn, the Arctic's musk oxen carry out a quite different kind of migration, moving from low-lying tundra to higher ground. These massively horned animals develop an extra-long winter coat, so they are almost unaffected by the cold. But winter snow can be a real problem, because it makes it hard to get at food. In their home in Greenland and northern Canada, moving uphill takes the musk oxen to places where the wind clears the snow from the ground.

HOMES BENEATH THE SNOW

During the Arctic winter, one of the warmest places to be is under the snow. This explains why Arctic plants grow best in snowy areas, and why lemmings prefer them too. There are 12 kinds of lemmings in the Arctic, and all are fast breeders, producing young when they are as little as a fortnight old. One of them, the Norway lemming, is famous for its population explosions about every four years. During a 'lemming year', lemmings outstrip their food supply, and millions of them set off to search for something to eat.

Legend has it that migrating lemmings commit suicide by jumping off cliffs and into the sea. Lemmings are actually good swimmers, but occasionally disaster strikes and huge numbers are drowned.

△ *Even when it is −30° C outside, the tunnels lemmings make are relatively warm and snug. When the snow melts in spring, trails of plant remains often show where they have been feeding and hiding away.*

171

These two photographs show Blomstrandbreen glacier on Svalbard Island, nearly 600 km north of Norway. The main photograph shows the glacier as it was in 1918, while the smaller picture shows it in 2002. Like most of the world's glaciers, Blomstrandbreen is shrinking fast – a change brought about by global warming. In years to come, global warming will have a far-reaching effect on wildlife – particularly near the poles.

ANTARCTICA

HUMANS ARE LATECOMERS TO ANTARCTICA – THE COLDEST AND MOST REMOTE OF THE CONTINENTS ON EARTH. FOR MILLIONS OF YEARS, LIFE HAS FLOURISHED IN THIS FROZEN WORLD, NOURISHED BY THE INCREDIBLE RICHNESS OF THE SURROUNDING SEA.

Unlike the Arctic, Antarctica is a giant landmass almost entirely covered by ice. At its deepest point, the Antarctic ice-cap is over 4 km thick, and its immense weight squashes the bedrock far below. Apart from scientists, hardly anything lives on the ice-cap itself, but Antarctica's coastline – and the stormy Southern Ocean – abounds with life.

△ Photographed by a satellite, a huge iceberg drifts off the coast of Antarctica. It is early autumn, and the sea is already freezing over. The iceberg is surrounded by sea-ice, and will soon be trapped fast until the spring.

▽ Waves crash against a grounded iceberg off Laurie Island, 600 km north of the Antarctic Circle. Laurie Island is covered by glaciers, and is far too cold and desolate to have any full-time human inhabitants. Storm-force winds and jagged rocks make it dangerous even to approach the shore.

THE DEEP SOUTH

Few maps show Antarctica's real frontier with the outside world. It is not the ice-covered coast or the Antarctic Circle, but an invisible boundary far out at sea. Called the Antarctic Convergence, it is the point where cold water flowing northwards from Antarctica meets much warmer water coming south. The Convergence is always on the move, shifting slightly from year to year, but it marks the point where the temperate world stops and the polar world begins.

At this latitude, a ship can sail right around the Southern Ocean without ever meeting land. Because there is no land, there is nothing to block the hurricane-force winds that blow clockwise around the pole. South of the Convergence lies one of the stormiest regions in the world, with mountainous waves and dark, ragged skies. From on board ship, it looks like one of the most hostile habitats on earth, but nothing could be further from the truth.

COMING UP

In the ocean around Antarctica, the currents behave in complicated ways. As well as carrying water from west to east, they also lift it up from below. With this 'upwelling' water comes a rich mixture of seabed nutrients – exactly what planktonic algae need to grow. Thanks to this endless source of natural fertilizer, the Southern Ocean is one of the richest marine habitats in the world.

Every spring, these planktonic plants develop at a rapid rate, just like grassland greening up on land.

In the ocean, there are no herds of grazing mammals to eat the plants, but there are unimaginably vast swarms of krill. These small shrimp-like crustaceans are only finger-sized, but a single swarm of them can weigh over ten million tonnes. During the spring and summer, krill filter out planktonic algae and turn them into protein-packed food. In the autumn and winter, as the algae die out, the krill sink to deeper water where they survive on leftovers that drift down from the waters above.

THE FILTER FEEDERS

For Antarctica's marine life, krill swarms are an almost inexhaustible source of food. Small fish, squid and penguins catch krill one by one, but larger hunters operate on a much bigger scale. One of these larger hunters is the crabeater seal. Despite its name, the crabeater feeds almost entirely on krill, sucking up large mouthfuls and then straining them out with its serrated teeth. In a single feeding session, one

△ *Krill usually swim in the same direction, just like fish do in a shoal. These krill were photographed in a tank at an Antarctic research station. Confused by captivity, they are trying to find their way out.*

crabeater can swallow up to 8 kg of krill – that is about five times as much food as most people eat in a day. Altogether, crabeaters are thought to gulp down at least 60 million tonnes of krill a year, making them the most important krill-eaters in the Southern Ocean.

Antarctic cod: *Trematomus pennelli*

This fish, like its close relatives, is specially adapted for survival in cold water. Its blood contains a chemical antifreeze, and this allows it to live at temperatures close to the freezing point of seawater, which is –1.9° C. It is so well adjusted to these chilly conditions that it dies if the temperature rises by just ten degrees. It lives near the seabed and feeds on smaller fish and animal leftovers, including seal droppings.

Krill are also a favourite food of leopard seals, ferocious and fast-swimming hunters that attack penguins as well. A leopard seal's back teeth have three sharp points, and they can either work like daggers, or they can close to make a krill-trapping sieve. But for individual krill consumption, nothing can beat the Southern Ocean's rorqual whales. Rorquals include the world's largest whales, and they all have deep grooves running lengthwise down their throats. When a rorqual hits a swarm of krill, it swims through it with its mouth open, and the grooves expand to let its throat swell up like a balloon. The whale then closes its mouth and strains out the krill, swallowing up to a tonne of them at a time.

Until the 20th century, blue whales and other rorquals consumed a huge share of the Southern Ocean's krill every year. But when whale stocks began to dwindle in the northern hemisphere, more and more whaling boats started to operate in Antarctic waters. Their catch was processed either on remote islands, such as South Georgia, or on special factory ships designed to spend months at sea. Rorquals were the main whales to be targeted and caught – 29,000 blue whales were killed in one year alone. Today, the entire Southern Ocean is a whale sanctuary, but because whales breed slowly, it will be many years before their numbers reach anything like the level they stood at before.

▽ *Leopard seals can swallow small penguins whole, but with large penguins they have to shake their prey until it falls apart. This seal has caught an Adélie penguin – one of the few kinds that breed on ice.*

△ *Whales migrate south to Antarctica during the southern spring, when the shrinking sea-ice makes it easier for them to get at food. These humpbacks, photographed off Australia, cover 200 km a day.*

A DANGEROUS COAST

Antarctica's coastline is unlike any other on earth. Only about five per cent of it is bare rock – the rest consists of immense ice shelves that inch their way slowly out to sea. These shelves are fed by glaciers, which contain ice that is thousands of years old. As the ice is pushed out to sea, entire sheets up to 200 m high begin to float. Eventually, giant slabs of the ice split away from the leading edge, creating flat-topped islands that are by far the biggest icebergs in the world.

From early autumn on, Antarctica is also surrounded by an expanding belt of floating sea-ice, which grows northwards at up to 4 km a day. Because sea-ice forms in the water itself, it never gets more than a few metres thick. However, by late winter, it covers an area that is three times bigger than Australia, before it shrinks again in the warmth of the Antarctic spring.

For some of Antarctica's animals, floating ice makes a useful place to perch or rest. But for shore animals, ice can be dangerous, particularly when it is on the move. Sea-ice shifts and settles with each tide, scraping animals off shallow rocks and gouging deep furrows in the seabed mud. Icebergs cause even more havoc, particularly when winds or currents drive them back towards the shore. To avoid being scraped or squashed, limpets and other shore animals often move to deeper water in autumn, creeping back to the shallows in spring.

ABSENT PARENTS

Over 40 species of birds live around Antarctica, but very few of them breed on Antarctica itself. Instead, most nest on the Southern Ocean's islands, which include the remotest pieces of land on earth. Bouvet Island, or Bouvetøya, is the loneliest of all – the nearest land to it is the coast of eastern Antarctica, about 1,600 km away.

These storm-lashed islands receive few human visitors, and landing on them is hazardous because of storms and gusting winds. But with so much sea and so little land, they are vital nesting sites for albatrosses – the world's largest seabirds.

△ *Off the coast of Antarctica, animals often grow slowly, but they can live a long time. These feathery sea anemones survive well into their twenties, but some Antarctic limpets can live for a century or more.*

▽ *Four-fifths of Antarctica's icebergs come from ice shelves that slowly feed into the sea. Known as tabular bergs, they have flat tops and sides that look like cliffs. As they drift northwards, cracks start to open up in the ice until they finally break apart.*

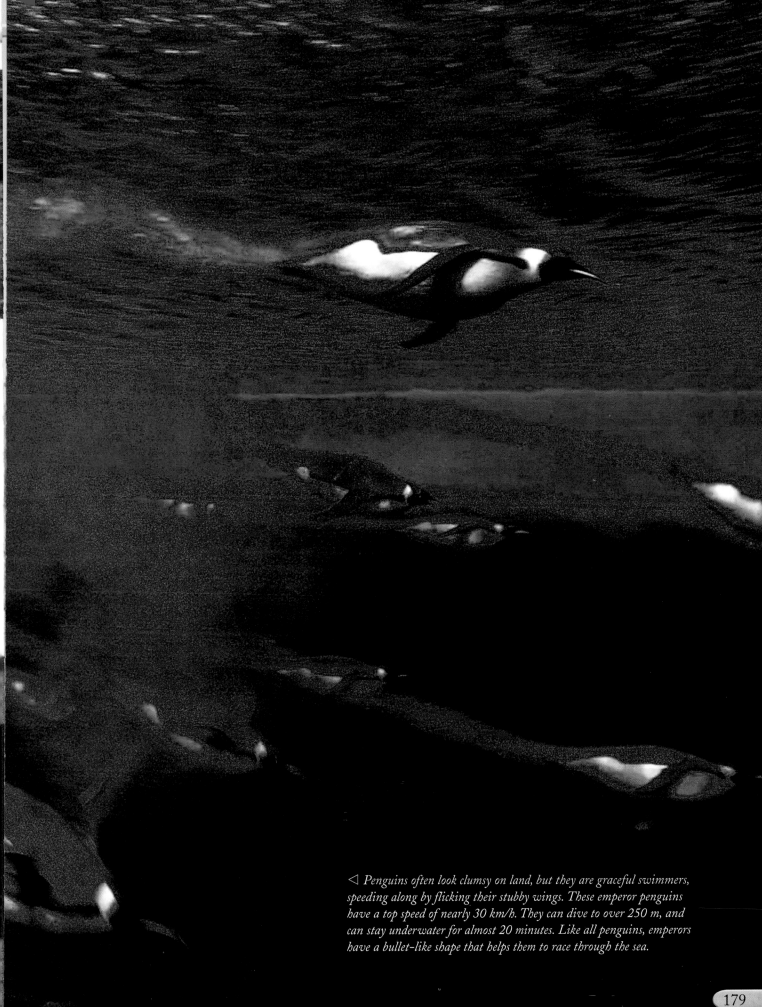

◁ Penguins often look clumsy on land, but they are graceful swimmers, speeding along by flicking their stubby wings. These emperor penguins have a top speed of nearly 30 km/h. They can dive to over 250 m, and can stay underwater for almost 20 minutes. Like all penguins, emperors have a bullet-like shape that helps them to race through the sea.

The boojum tree grows in the part of northwest Mexico, and nowhere else in the world. It has a spongy skeleton, and a trunk that looks like the leg of an elephant rather than a plant.

Because cacti soak up moisture so quickly, they are often surrounded by a 'no-man's-land' where other plants cannot set up home. This space is a good hunting ground for many animals, particularly the roadrunner – a bird that sprints around desert rocks and plants, catching all kinds of small animals, from scorpions to snakes.

BIZARRE BOTANY

Throughout the world's deserts, many plants use the cactus survival technique, storing water in their stems. The plants include some of the world's most bizarre shrubs, such as the Mexican boojum tree, or cirio,

which looks like a bristly telegraph pole. On the island of Socotra, near the Horn of Africa, there is a

Species Profile

Welwitschia: Welwitschia mirabilis

The *Welwitschia* plant grows only in one place – the gravel plains in the heart of the Namib Desert. It has a stubby, flat-topped trunk, and just two leaves, which split and curl as they grow. The plant does not have flowers, and instead it reproduces by growing cones. It grows extremely slowly, but it is one of the world's toughest plants, and can live for a thousand years.

◁ *Penguins often look clumsy on land, but they are graceful swimmers, speeding along by flicking their stubby wings. These emperor penguins have a top speed of nearly 30 km/h. They can dive to over 250 m, and can stay underwater for almost 20 minutes. Like all penguins, emperors have a bullet-like shape that helps them to race through the sea.*

Albatrosses look like giant gulls, but they feed far out to sea, gliding effortlessly for days on end, and snatching jellyfish from the surface of the waves. They can live to a great age, but compared to most other birds, they are very slow at breeding. Parent albatrosses raise just one chick at a time, and they can wander over 3,000 km from their nest before returning with food. Amazingly, their chick waits patiently for them,

and the parents never seem to lose their way home.

BREEDING ON THE ICE

Antarctica's islands are much too windy for trees – instead, their tallest plant is a kind of grass that grows in sturdy clumps that sometimes reach waist-high. These clumps of hairgrass shelter spiders and insects, and also rats that have escaped from ships. On some islands, such as Kerguelen,

▷ Six kinds of albatross breed near Antarctica. This is the black-browed albatross – a species that sometimes wanders as far north as Australia. It snatches food from the sea, without having to settle on the water.

Species Profile

Antarctic skua: *Catharacta antarctica*

Wherever penguins breed, Antarctic skuas are rarely far away. These aggressive birds steal penguin eggs, and eat newly hatched penguin chicks. They also feed on dead remains, using their hooked beaks to tear open the bodies of seals and even whales. Antarctic skuas often breed close to penguin colonies, and will attack anything that gets too close to their nests. They spend the winter throughout the southern seas, returning to Antarctica in spring.

rats have become a real conservation problem because they eat eggs and attack nestlings. Scientists are trying to devise ways of reducing the numbers of these intruders, so that birds have a better chance of raising their young. Hairgrass also grows in the Antarctic Peninsula, which is a part of Antarctica that points towards South America. The tip of the peninsula is like an Antarctic version of Florida, because conditions

are much milder here than in the south. It is where many of Antarctica's scientists are based, and it is also where almost all of Antarctica's land-based animals are found. But compared to the Antarctic's sea-going animals, its land-based animals are extremely small. The largest land predator – a carnivorous mite – is just a few millimetres long.

PETRELS AND PENGUINS

On the Antarctic mainland, two small seabirds share the record as the most southerly breeding birds in the world. Petrels normally feed on the coast, but the snowy petrel and the Antarctic petrel have been found nesting in cliff crevices up to 250 km inland. These hideaways protect the petrels' eggs and chicks from the bitter Antarctic wind, but they still have to be exceptionally cold-proof in order to survive.

In complete contrast, Antarctica's largest birds breed on the windswept ice without any shelter at all. They are emperor penguins, and they are the animal world's unrivalled experts at keeping warm. Throughout the dark winter, male emperors remain on the ice, while their partners are away feeding at sea. By huddling together, they survive temperatures as low as −50° C. When the wind chill is added, this is colder than in any other natural habitat on earth. It is an amazing feat of endurance, but male emperors have more to worry about than just themselves. All winter long, each male protects and incubates its partner's egg, using its feet as a 'nest', and a fold of skin as a warm and feathery pouch.

Most birds lay their eggs in spring, but with emperors, things are the other way around. The females lay their eggs in the autumn, just before they set out to sea. This might seem like a case of extremely bad timing, but emperor eggs take two months to hatch, and their chicks then need four months to grow up. By laying their eggs in the autumn, the females make sure that their young will be leaving home at the best time of year – at the height of the Antarctic spring.

△ *For emperor penguins, huddling together in a large group is the best way of surviving the bitter cold. The chicks take turns at being on the inside, where they get the best protection from the biting wind.*

▽ *Young albatrosses can take up to nine months to leave the nest – a record for any bird. They are brooded for the first few weeks; after that, they sit in the nest alone.*

DESERTS

DESERTS COVER NEARLY A THIRD OF THE
WORLD'S SURFACE, WHICH MAKES THEM THE
MOST EXTENSIVE LAND HABITAT ON EARTH.
DESERT WILDLIFE IS OFTEN THINLY SPREAD,
BUT IT IS GOOD AT COPING WITH EXTREMES
OF TEMPERATURE AND HARSH CONDITIONS.

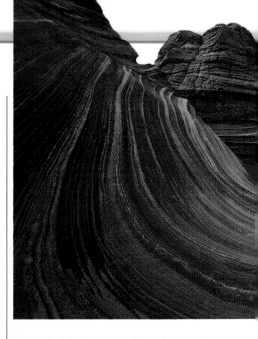

Most of the world's deserts are in the subtropics, where giant swirls of dry air, called anticyclones, sit for months on end. Deserts also exist in other places that moisture cannot reach – either because they are so far inland, or because mountains shield them from rain-bearing winds. Although most deserts are warm and dry, some can be cold and rare storms sometimes drench them with rain.

▽ *These giant sand dunes, in Africa's Namib Desert, are some of the tallest in the world. In the Namib, the coastal wind keeps the sand on the move, and the dunes creep inland like slow-motion waves.*

A FICKLE CLIMATE
In June 1991, one of these storms hit the Chilean port of Antofagasta, where it washed away houses and roads. This storm was all the more remarkable because Antofagasta is in the Atacama Desert, which is normally the driest place on earth. In this strip of land sandwiched between the Pacific Ocean and the Andes mountains, average rainfall can be as low as 0.1 mm a year. Here, filling a coffee mug with rain would take about a century, and every drop of drinking water has to come in by pipeline or by road.

These desert downpours are known as flash floods, and they are one of the reasons why deserts are difficult homes for living things. In deserts, drought is a daily fact

(see p. 204)

◁ *In deserts, exposed rocks are often carved into strange shapes by the wind. It sweeps up pieces of grit and sand, and hurls them against anything that stands in the way.*

plants to take hold. Five centimetres of rain a year is enough for a scattering of low, drought-resistant plants, while 15 cm allows a few taller shrubs to grow as well. By the time rainfall hits 25 cm a year, desert merges into shrubland (see p. 204) – a habitat where many more kinds of plants manage to live.

Plants are the key to desert life, because without them, there is no food for animals to eat. Desert plants are extremely varied, but none can rival cacti for their drought-resisting power. The largest cacti, called saguaros and cardóns, can be over 10 m tall, and their fluted stems work like expandable reservoirs, holding enough water to fill many baths. Like all plants, these giant cacti 'breathe' through microscopic pores, but they do it during the cool desert night – an adaptation that prevents too much

water escaping to the air outside.

Some desert trees and shrubs have incredibly long roots which search out water deep underground. In Arizona, USA, for example, miners have discovered the roots of mesquite trees over 50 m down. But cactus roots are different. Most of them fan out just beneath the surface, where they can intercept the rain as soon as it falls.

△ *Seen from a plane, water pours over Australia's Simpson Desert after a heavy storm. These sudden downpours can flood huge areas of land, but the water is shallow and it soon evaporates.*

of life, but when it does rain the results can be dramatic, as well as dangerous. Another problem is the wind, which can fling sharp-edged grit horizontally across the ground, or blow clouds of sand into the sky. Add blistering sunshine and chilly nights to the equation, and the result is a habitat where almost everything is extreme.

LIVING RESERVOIRS

Parts of the Atacama Desert are so dry that nothing grows there at all. But in most deserts, there is enough moisture to allow some

◁ *In the Mojave Desert in North America, a spectacular flower show follows spring rain. A few weeks later, all these flowers will have disappeared, and the plants that grew them will be dead.*

The boojum tree, growing ... of northwest Mexico, ... in the world. It has pencil-thin twigs and a trunk that looks like ... an elephant rather than on a plant

Because cacti soak up moisture so quickly, they are often surrounded by a 'no-man's-land' where other plants cannot set up home. This space is a good hunting ground for many animals, particularly the roadrunner, a bird that sprints around desert rocks and plants, catching all kinds of small animals, from scorpions to snakes.

BIZARRE BOTANY

Throughout the world's deserts, many plants use the cactus survival technique, storing water in their stems. The plants include some of the world's most bizarre shrubs, such as the Mexican boojum tree, or cirio,

which looks like a bristly telegraph pole. On the island of Socotra, off the Horn of Africa, the ... cucumber tree is another ...

making seeds. When the summer comes, the plants themselves are long dead, but their seeds are scattered across the ground in their millions, waiting for the next burst of life-giving rain.

EPHEMERAL ANIMALS

Plants are not the only things to have evolved this fast-forward lifestyle. Some desert animals have it as well. Most of these breed in water, which means that they depend on rare downpours to survive.

In Australia's Simpson Desert, this kind of rain falls roughly once or twice in every five. The desert is one of the world's flattest, so floodwater takes time to drain away. Shallow pools and lakes spread out in all directions, and within a few days its surface of the water appear tadpole shrimps, which hatch from eggs that lie dormant in the ground.

...they die just at each spring. For a few weeks, patches of the valley floor turn green, and then yellow as the plants run into flower. But the ephemerals have to work against the clock, because as each day passes, the sun rises higher in the sky. By the time summer arrives, the air temperature can reach 55°C, turning Death Valley into one of the hottest places on earth. And the ground temperature can be even higher. In a part of the valley called Furnace

Creek, it once reached a level only 12 degrees short of boiling point.

With this kind of heat just a few months away, there's no time to grow tall and bushy, with long-running roots. Instead, each plant soaks up the moisture around it, and pours all its energy into

Namaqua sandgrouse: *Pterocles namaqua*

There are 16 species of sandgrouse, all specialists in desert life. They can fly long distances to find seeds, and their mottled plumage helps to camouflage them when they are feeding on the ground. They also carry water in their feathers – a remarkable skill that helps their nestlings to survive. The Namaqua sandgrouse is a typical species; it lives in the deserts of southern Africa.

Like ephemeral plants, the shrimps immediately set about reproducing, as if they know that their watery surroundings will not last for long.

Heavy rain also brings frogs and toads scrabbling to the surface, ending a deep sleep underground.

During their long wait, they are wrapped in waterproof cocoons made from thin layers of moulted skin. When rain seeps through the soil, this protective jacket softens, and its owner gulps it down before heading upwards into the light. Soon, the shrimps, frogs and toads are joined by black swans and even pelicans, creating one of the most unlikely-looking collections of desert animals in the world.

WATER MISERS

Burrowing amphibians live in many of the world's deserts, although their part-time lifestyle makes them hard to find. But many desert animals are active throughout the year, which means that they need water all the time. These animals manage their water resources as carefully as an accountant managing money in the bank. They collect water whenever and wherever they can, and make sure that very little goes to waste.

Some desert animals perform an apparently impossible feat – they survive without having to drink at all.

WATER MAKERS

Among these animals are kangaroo rats, which are seed-eating rodents from the deserts of North America. Kangaroo rats are easy to raise in captivity, so scientists have been able to discover the secret behind their survival – they take in some moisture along with their food. This is enough to supply about one-tenth of the water that they need. The remaining nine-tenths comes about in a very different way. Kangaroo rats actually 'manufacture' it through chemical reactions, as they digest and break down their food. Called metabolic water, it is something that many animals allow to go to waste. But kangaroo rats use almost all of it, which explains how they thrive in places where other animals would die of thirst.

WATER STORERS

In deserts, animals get hold of water in some ingenious ways. Desert elephants locate water in dried-up rivers, probably by smell, and dig down several metres to reach it. Sandgrouse fly to distant waterholes, and ferry water back to their chicks. They wade in until they are chest-deep, and use their breastfeathers to soak up water like a sponge. In the Namib Desert and in parts of the Atacama, some insects and lizards survive by drinking fog. They use their bodies to gather droplets of water that form on them like dew.

When desert animals do find water, many of them store it up, so that they can

△ *A kangaroo rat can go through life without drinking a single drop of water. Kangaroo rats need water – just like all other animals – but they can get all of it from their food.*

This is not actually that unusual – wood-boring beetles, for example, do it all the time. But in deserts, non-drinkers also include mammals, which usually need lots of fluid to stay alive.

◁ There are more than 2,000 different kinds of cacti, and the saguaro is the largest, as well as being one of the longest-lived. The water that is held inside a saguaro's stem can weigh more than one tonne.

△ In north Africa, the Middle East and central Asia, camels have been used for milk, meat and muscle-power for at least 4,000 years.

keep going through dry times. These living water storers include desert antelopes such as the gemsbok, and the two kinds of camel. The Arabian or one-humped camel can drink up to 60 litres of water at one time, but the Bactrian or two-humped camel has been reported to swallow 110 litres in a single drinking bout. That is enough to fill two petrol tanks in an average family car.

NIGHT LIFE

In the days when camels were the only kind of desert transport, people often travelled at night. It made good sense, because in deserts the night is usually more comfortable than the day. Once the sun sets, the ground quickly loses its warmth, and the air cools under the cloudless sky. Desert animals also take advantage of this temperature change, and many are active at night rather than during the day. These nocturnal animals include almost all small- and medium-sized mammals, from gerbils to jackrabbits, and also many predators, such as coyotes and the dainty fennec fox. The fennec fox finds its prey mainly by listening with its giant ears, while coyotes track down food by having keen hearing, good eyesight and an acute sense of smell.

△ A fennec fox's ears are so sensitive that they can hear a beetle walking several metres away. Fennec foxes are the smallest members of the dog family, and insects make up an important part of their diet.

Dwarfed by a sand dune, a gemsbok gallops off to rejoin the rest of its herd. Like many desert animals, gemsboks spend most of their lives on the move, searching out places where rain allows plants to grow. In dry times, these African antelope get water by eating gourds – small fruits that look like melons.

△ *For snakes with built-in heat sensors, night is the best time to hunt. Under clear desert skies, the ground quickly cools down. As a result, warm-blooded prey shows up more clearly than during the day.*

Deserts are also the home of rattlesnakes and other pit-vipers, which find their food by sensing body heat. These snakes have a heat-detecting pit between each eye and nostril, and they use them to 'see' anything that is warmer than its surroundings (see p. 127). The pits can detect a temperature difference of just 0.2° C, so to these snakes, warm-blooded birds or mammals must stand out like beacons in the dark.

Because their heat-detectors are paired, snakes can pinpoint their prey and tell exactly where to strike. If a pit-viper is blindfolded, it will even lunge

▷ *For the Gobi Desert's Bactrian camels, moulting is a serious business. The camel on the left still has some of its winter coat, but its partner is ready for spring.*

at a glass of warm water – a demonstration of how heat guides it towards prey.

DESERTS IN WINTER

Only a few of the world's deserts are hot all the year round. Many have a cool season, but in some, winter can be bitterly cold. In the Gobi Desert of central Asia, winter temperatures can fall as low as −30° C, although there is not much snow because this is the driest time of year. Icy winds can make it dangerous to venture outside, and the intense cold means that water is almost impossible to find. North America's Great Basin Desert can get just as chilly, and even Death Valley has frosts – the lowest temperature recorded there is −9° C.

For cold-blooded animals, such as tortoises, lizards and snakes, winter is no time to be on the move. Instead, these animals hide away, often in burrows underground.

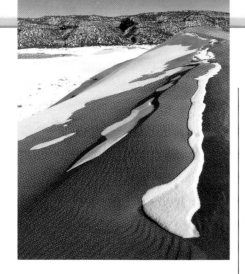

△ *In cold deserts, some of the year's moisture falls as winter snow. But if the air is dry, snow can evaporate without melting, so very little moisture finds its way into the ground.*

Their temperature drops so that their bodies are just ticking over, and they can survive for months without food. Insects behave in the same way, although many of them spend the winter not as adults, but as cold-resistant eggs. Some desert mammals go into hibernation, while others spend much of their time underground, eating food that they have stored. In the Gobi, gerbils are experts at this – a single family can hide away over 50 kg of roots and seeds. Staying above ground calls for different tactics, such as growing warm winter coats. When spring arrives, a Bactrian camel's coat comes off in patches, making the camel look as if it is falling apart.

Desert birds often migrate to warmer places, but one North American species – the common poorwill – has a unique survival technique. It sometimes crawls into rocky crevices, where it becomes dormant for weeks on end. Because dormant poorwills hide so carefully, the first one was not discovered until 1946. Only a handful more have been found since, and they are still the only known hibernators in the entire bird world.

Species Profile

Web-footed gecko: *Palmatogecko rangei*

Geckos are expert climbers. Some can climb up windows, and many run along ceilings upside down. But this gecko lives on desert dunes. Its toes are joined by webs, which work like miniature snow-shoes to stop it sinking into sand. Web-footed geckos live in south-west Africa, and feed mainly on insects and other small animals.

GRASSLANDS AND SAVANNA

WITH THEIR OPEN HORIZONS, SCATTERED TREES AND ISOLATED WATERHOLES, GRASSLANDS AND SAVANNA ARE CLASSIC WILDLIFE TERRITORY. THEY ARE ALSO THE HABITATS WHERE HUMAN LIFE BEGAN.

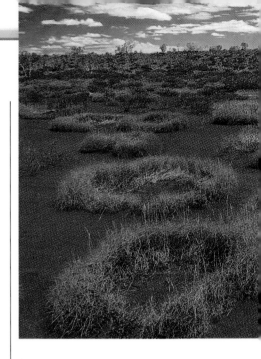

The world's grasslands and savanna are in places that have 'in between' climates – ones that are too dry for forests, but too wet for deserts. Grasslands grow in some cool parts of the world, but tree-studded savanna is found mainly in the tropics. Both these habitats are rich in plant-eating animals, from termites and grasshoppers to the largest land mammals in the world.

SECRET OF SUCCESS
Grasses may not be very eyecatching, but they are some of the most indestructible plants on earth. They can survive being nibbled, chewed and trampled flat, and they even grow back if they are burned. This explains why grasses make good lawns and football pitches, and why they cover the

◁ *Spinifex grass is a common sight in the bone-dry landscape of Australia's Red Centre. As each plant grows outwards, the innermost part dies, creating a grassy ring.*

Most plants have growth zones just at their tips of their stems, which means that they stop growing if the tips are eaten away. But grasses are different, because they can regrow even if they are eaten right down to the ground. As well as growing upwards, grass plants spread outwards too.

GRASSES AND GRAZERS

Scientists do not know exactly when the world's first grasses appeared. Fossil pollen shows that it was at least 60 million years ago, which makes it just possible that the earliest grasses existed when dinosaurs still roamed the earth. In those distant times, there were no grasslands. Instead, grasses probably lived on the edges of tropical forests, where they were

entire landscape in some parts of the world.

The secret of this amazing toughness lies in the way grasses grow. Unlike most plants, grasses branch close to the ground. Their stems are hollow, and they have knobbly joints spaced out from top to bottom. At each joint there is a single leaf, and a growth zone where cells rapidly divide.

△ *Impalas are the most widespread grazing antelopes in Africa. They are also one of the fastest – running at full speed, they can clear 9 m in a single jump.*

△ *Grass flowers are pollinated by the wind. Their feathery flowerheads open to release pollen into the air.*

△ *Surrounded by a sea of grass, a herd of wildebeest moves across the open plains on the border between Tanzania and Kenya. It is shortly after the rainy season, and the grass is still green.*

◁ *Giraffes browse on scattered trees, but the males and females feed in different ways. Male giraffes reach upwards into the treetops, but the females bend their necks to eat leaves closer to the ground.*

scattered among other plants. But after the dinosaurs became extinct, grasses slowly became more widespread, until they were some of the most successful plants on earth.

This remarkable change happened partly because the earth's climate became drier. But a more important reason was that large, plant-eating mammals evolved at the same time. These animals had specialized teeth for chewing their food, and hard hooves that flattened soft-stemmed plants. Many plants could not survive this kind of treatment, but grasses could. Thanks to these grazers, grasses spread out from the tropics, creating the grasslands that exist today.

GRASSLANDS OF THE WORLD

Until 200 years ago, huge stretches of grasslands existed in every continent except Antarctica. Each one had its own grazing mammals. In North America, the prairie grassland was grazed by American bison, or buffalo, and by antelopes called pronghorns, while South America's pampas teemed with

Species Profile

American bison: *Bison bison*

Until 200 years ago, American bison were the commonest large animals in the grasslands of North America. There were almost 100 million of these grazers, and native Plains Indians depended on them for their survival. But with the arrival of European hunters and farms, their numbers collapsed – today, only about 5,000 are left. Most of these survivors live in Yellowstone National Park.

▷ *Nothing can run faster than a cheetah, but speed does not always guarantee success. Gazelles can turn sharply when they are on the run, and a cheetah has trouble following in their tracks.*

grazing rodents and herds of deer. European and Asian grasslands, known as steppes, were grazed by wild horses, which originally came from this part of the world. Australia was unusual, because its grasslands were grazed not by hoofed mammals, but by wallabies and kangaroos.

But the grasslands of Africa were, and still are, home to the largest herds of grazers in the world. In 1888, settlers in South Africa encountered a record-breaking herd of springbok migrating across the treeless grassland, or veldt. It contained at least ten million animals – all of them fuelled by a diet of grass.

MAMMALS ON THE MOVE

Since those times, the world's grasslands have changed a great deal. During the 1800s and early 1900s, buffalo and springbok were hunted so heavily that they almost disappeared. (Fortunately, hunting stopped before they actually became extinct.) In many grasslands, wild mammals were squeezed out by cattle and by sheep, and in others, the land was ploughed up so that it could be used to grow grain. But despite these changes, natural grasslands still exist, and they are the setting for some of the greatest wildlife spectacles on earth.

One of the most impressive can be seen in East Africa's Serengeti and Masai-Mara National Parks. Here, on the edge of the Great Rift Valley, a huge mixed herd of grassland mammals carries out a year-round migration in search of fresh food. These animals include over one million wildebeest, about a quarter of a million gazelles and 200,000 zebras, all moving in step with the seasons. They travel into open grassland at the beginning of the rainy season, and then into wooded savanna as the dry season begins. In this part of the world, no fences stand in their way, so they can go where they like – just as all grassland animals did until a few hundred years ago.

KEEPING TOGETHER

For grazers, grassland is an ideal place to live, because food is all around. But it has one serious minus point – there is almost nowhere to hide. Predators can spot grazers from a long way off, and the only sure defence is to run away. Over millions of years, grazing mammals have evolved powerful legs, which gives them a good chance of making an escape. They have also evolved a lifestyle based around herds, because these make good early warning systems. In a herd, many eyes and ears are on the alert, and a few animals are always watching the horizon while the others feed. If one of these spots possible danger, the entire herd gets ready to run.

◁ *At the end of the rainy season, zebras have no trouble finding food. Life will get harder for them later in the year, when the grass turns brown and dry.*

If grazers actually ran off at the first hint of trouble, they would die of exhaustion in just a few days. Instead, they adjust their behaviour according to the danger that they face. For example, gazelles will often let a lion come to within 200 m,

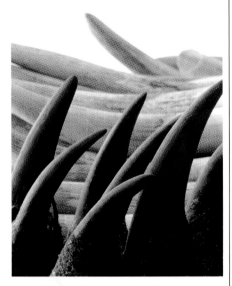

△ *Most people would prefer to see rhino horns and elephant tusks where they belong – on living animals. Sadly, not everyone agrees. These horns and tusks were seized from poachers before they could be sold.*

which looks like a careless way to behave. But gazelles instinctively know that lions hunt by stealth, so if a lion is in the open, it is probably scouting instead of preparing to attack. Cheetahs, on the other hand, are much more dangerous, because they hunt by speed rather than by surprise. If gazelles see one of these, they will break into a run when it is still 500 m away – the minimum needed for a good head start.

ENDANGERED HEAVYWEIGHTS

Giant grazers, such as rhinos and elephants, behave in a different way. They normally move away from danger, but sometimes they stand their ground, or even charge. A charge may be just a warning, or it

▷ *A mother wildebeest looks unconcerned as her calf is born. Compared to many young mammals, wildebeest calves are extremely well developed at birth.*

may be the start of a genuine attack. It can be very difficult to tell the difference, which is why experienced guides and trackers always treat these animals with respect.

Elephants and rhinos are short-sighted creatures, and they detect danger mainly by their keen sense of smell. Unfortunately for them, this is not a good defence against their most serious enemy – humans armed with guns. During the last 30 years, enormous numbers of African elephants and rhinos have been illegally slaughtered for their ivory or their horns.

Today, Africa's white rhinos are making a gradual recovery, thanks to a successful breeding programme in South Africa's national parks. The black rhino, however, is in deep trouble, and may be heading for extinction in the wild. With Africa's elephants, the situation is more complicated. Although there are still thousands of them, their numbers have plunged and their habitat is shrinking year by year. Some conservationists think that the best method of protecting elephants is to crack down even harder on poachers. Others believe that the ivory trade should be legalized, so that elephants pay their way.

FAST START

With fast-running predators on the lookout for an easy meal, grasslands are risky places to give birth, and even more dangerous places to be born. In Africa's grasslands, many antelope improve their chances by moving to the safety of thickets, where they can give birth unseen. After giving birth, the mother leaves her calf hidden away. She visits it up

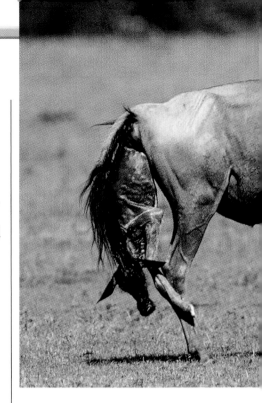

to four times a day, but between meals the calf remains curled up and completely still. Its scent glands are switched off, which makes it harder for predators to sniff it out, and it will not move even if a person walks just a few metres away.

For wildebeest, life starts in a very different way. Instead of wandering off on their own, female wildebeest give birth in the open, and they do it

△ *A young gazelle's hiding place has to stay secret if it is to survive. When the mother arrives to feed her calf, she stops several metres off, to avoid giving it away.*

in record time. The calf is often on its feet within three minutes, and it follows the first moving thing that it sees, which is normally its mother. In under an hour, mother and calf

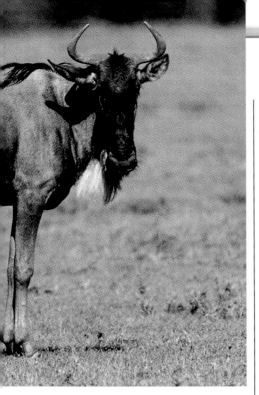

can be trotting along with the rest of the herd. This express delivery means that the herd can keep moving and feeding – the ultimate adaptation to life in the open plains.

However, it is a high-risk strategy, because the mothers and calves are in full view of any predators nearby. To reduce the risk, thousands of females give birth within a two-week period, which makes it harder for any one of them to be singled out.

▽ *While their parents feed, young prairie dogs take the chance to play. For prairie dogs, 'kissing' is a way of identifying close relatives – an important part of life in prairie dog towns.*

Amazingly, if a female is threatened while she is in labour, she can put the birth 'on hold'.

SAFETY UNDERGROUND

Although there are no hiding places on the surface of grassland, there are plenty underground. This is the safe haven used by burrowing animals – ones that use their claws or teeth to excavate a home for themselves. Grassland is a good habitat for burrowing because grass roots hold together the soil, making sure that burrows do not collapse.

Before the world's grasslands were farmed, some of these burrowers worked on a truly incredible scale. In western Texas, a single prairie dog 'town' contained about 400 million animals, scattered over an area almost twice the size of Switzerland. Over countless generations, these industrious rodents dug more than a billion kilometres of tunnels, complete with grass-lined nesting chambers and volcano-shaped entrance mounds. The town's inhabitants were divided up into neighbourhoods, and they lived in small groups, called coteries, which each kept a section of burrows to themselves. On the whole, neighbours maintained good relations – unless an animal strayed into a neighbour's burrow, rather than its own.

With the spread of farming, North America's prairie dogs went into a steep decline. Prairie dog towns still do exist, although none are on this gigantic size. In some places, prairie dogs are still being shot as pests, but in others conservationists are trying to help them to survive. They believe that prairie dogs are actually good for grassland, because their feeding and burrowing helps to fertilize the grass.

One fact is not in doubt – prairie dog burrows are home to lots of animals besides prairie dogs themselves. They include burrowing owls, snakes and spiders, as well as the black-footed ferret – one of North America's rarest predators, only found in prairie dog towns.

Species Profile

Burrowing owl: *Athene cunicularia*

Most of the world's owls nest in trees, but the burrowing owl lives in grassy habitats, where trees are few and far between. It sets up home inside burrows left by other animals, and if it cannot find one, it digs a burrow itself. Burrowing owls spend a lot of their time at their burrow entrances, where they look like sentries standing guard.

Once considered to be a pest, this animal is now being reintroduced into places where it has died out.

THE INSECT-EATERS

Prairie dog burrows are about 15 cm wide, so only slim-bodied hunters can slip their way inside. But in Africa, one of the biggest grassland burrowers makes tunnels that are up to 1 m across. Holes this size are big

During the dry season in Africa's grasslands, waterholes are *magnets for wildlife. Elephants can drink in safety, but antelopes have to be on the alert, because waterholes make perfect places for predators to launch surprise attacks. Faced with this danger, antelopes drink and leave as quickly as they can.*

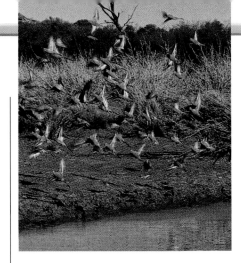

enough for people to crawl into, and they are a serious hazard for tractors and safari jeeps. The animal that excavates these subterranean homes is the aardvark – one of a select band of large grassland mammals that feed on termites and ants. This pig-like creature feeds at night, and rips its way into termite mounds with its scoop-shaped claws. It is one of the world's fastest diggers, and can work faster than a team of people equipped with spades. In South America, the giant anteater is another powerful excavator, although it does not tunnel underground. Its front claws work like pick-axes, hacking open ants' nests made of sunbaked earth.

Both these animals are far too large to survive by eating their prey one by one. Instead, they sweep them up with their amazingly long, sticky tongues. Using this gathering device, a giant anteater can eat 30,000 ants and termites in a day.

△ *Alarmed by a sudden noise, a flock of budgerigars takes to the air. In the wild, budgerigars are just as wary as other birds, and they keep well clear of people.*

Species Profile

Potter wasp: *Sceliphron* and other species

Potter wasps are common in grasslands and dry places, where they hunt for caterpillars. When one of these wasps finds a caterpillar, it paralyses it with a sting, and then drags it back to its pot-shaped nest. It puts the caterpillar inside, and then lays an egg on it before closing up the pot. Once the wasp grub hatches, it uses the caterpillar as its food.

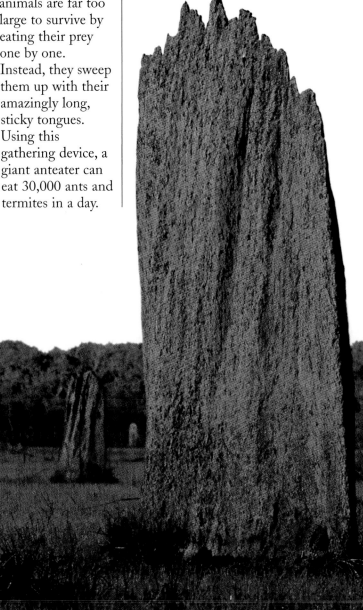

GRASSLAND NOMADS

Grass is easy to find, but it is low in nutrients and difficult to digest. As a result, grazing animals must spend a lot of time eating to stay well fed. Grass seeds, on the other hand, are packed with protein and energy-rich starch, and are much easier to break down. This is why humans eat cultivated grass seeds – or cereals – and why many animals feed on grass seeds in the wild.

In the Australian outback, budgerigars specialize in exactly this kind of diet. As cage birds, 'budgies'

▽ *In Australia, compass termites make flat-sided nests, which are always lined up north-to-south. The nests' flat sides soak up the sun's warmth at dawn and dusk, but they stay cool at midday.*

▷ *Caught by a remote-controlled flashgun, an aardvark takes its own photo as it leaves its burrow to feed.*

are often kept on their own, but wild budgerigars (which are always green and yellow) live in flocks hundreds or thousands of birds strong. They are adapted to life in dry grassland, where good places to feed may be hundreds of kilometres apart. To survive in these conditions, they are nomadic. Once they have finished most of the seeds in a particular area, they soon move on. Budgerigars nest in tree-holes, but they do not have a set breeding season – instead, they lay their eggs only after it has rained.

In Africa, a small finch called the quelea lives in much the same way. However, its flocks can contain a million birds, and they wheel over grassland like clouds of grey smoke. Queleas sometimes descend on farmland, which is bad news for

Species Profile

Baobab: *Adansonia digitata*

With its massive trunk and elephant-grey bark, the baobab is one of Africa's most distinctive trees. It grows in dry savanna, and its trunk works as a water store to enable it to survive droughts. This water sometimes attracts elephants, which gouge into the trunk with their tusks. Baobabs that escape this damage can live to be over a thousand years old.

farmers, because a million-bird flock can swallow 60 tonnes of grain in a single day.

LIFE ON THE GROUND

Budgerigars and queleas are small and fast-flying, which helps to explain their success. But grasslands are also home to much larger birds that never get off the ground. They include two species of rhea from South America, the Australian emu, and the African ostrich, which is the largest of all flightless birds. Like grazing mammals, these birds depend on keen senses and speedy legs to survive. Their main food is seeds, but they sometimes eat insects and other small animals as well.

These giants of the bird world

△ *When rheas breed, the male takes on the job of incubating the eggs and looking after the young. In Africa's grasslands, male ostriches behave in exactly the same way.*

have had mixed fortunes during the last 100 years. Rheas and ostriches are not as common as they once were, and their range is smaller than it was before. But the emu is thriving, and is probably more common now than it was before farming in grasslands began. During the 1930s, emus became so numerous in Western Australia that the army was called in. Despite soldiers being armed with machine guns, they could not keep the emus out, and today emu-proof fences are used instead.

A SHIFTING BALANCE

Even without humans, grassland wildlife would have to adapt to change. Whenever the climate turns slightly wetter, trees get a foothold and turn grassland into savanna, but if it turns drier, fires burn away the trees and give grass a chance to spread. The result is like a slow-running contest between two closely related habitats, with each one

△ *Sometimes it takes an extra special effort to get your favourite food. Standing on its back legs, this bull elephant can reach almost as high as a giraffe.*

trying to get the upper hand.

In Africa, elephants play a part in this contest by knocking down trees as they feed. They use their heads like living bulldozers, so they can

reach the highest and juiciest leaves. After a herd has moved on, the savanna looks as if it has been vandalized, and with the trees gone, the grass soon moves in.

But this is only part of the story, because elephants help to spread trees too. They do this by swallowing the trees' seeds, and then scattering them in piles of dung. These fertile seedbeds give trees the best start in life, and they help the savanna woodlands to spread. Together, elephants and trees form an ever-shifting balance – one of countless thousands that shape the grassland and savanna world.

▽ *Emus stride through the Australian bush. They can run almost as fast as ostriches, and are also good swimmers – an unusual talent for birds that live in grassland and desert.*

SHRUBLANDS

SMALLER THAN TREES, BUT JUST AS TOUGH, SHRUBS MAKE UP A DRYLAND HABITAT THAT IS SCATTERED ACROSS THE GLOBE. IN SHRUBLANDS, LIFE HAS TO SURVIVE LONG SUMMER DROUGHTS, AND THE EVER-PRESENT THREAT OF FIRE.

When the world's land habitats are listed, shrublands often get left out. That is because humans often think of shrublands as waste places, where it is difficult to move about and hard to get anything useful to grow. But for wildlife, shrublands provide lots of places to hide, and plenty of food.

WHAT IS A SHRUB?

Trees are easy to recognize, because they usually have a single trunk. Shrubs are different, because they do not have trunks, and their branches start at or near the ground. Some shrubs can be taller than a one-storey house, but the smallest of them are only ankle-high. They often grow in dense, spiky thickets, which can make travelling through shrublands hard work.

In South America's Gran Chaco, conditions are so uninviting that few people venture far from tracks and into the shrubland itself. Here, to the south of the Amazon rainforest, winters are warm and dry, but summer is extremely hot and humid, with storms that can turn the ground into a sea of mud. This thorny wilderness is tough going for humans, but it is a superb habitat for animal life. Among its natural

▽ *In California, chaparral shrubland is home to cacti and to sagebrush, and also to prickly-leaved oaks. For early settlers on horseback, crossing it could be an uncomfortable experience.*

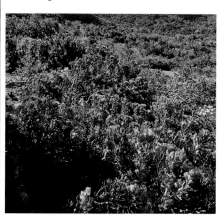

◁ In Kalbarri National Park, in Western Australia, low-growing shrubs provide cover for rock wallabies and grey kangaroos, as well as more than 170 kinds of birds.

in southern California, USA, many cities are surrounded by a kind of shrubland called chaparral.

SHRUBLAND CLIMATE

Most of the world's shrublands are found in places where it is dry for several months each year. This kind of climate makes life difficult for trees, but it allows smaller woody plants to thrive. In fact, the shrubland climate seems to encourage plants to evolve, so an astonishing number of different plants may end up living side by side.

For sheer plant variety, one kind of shrubland breaks all records for a habitat of its size. This is South Africa's fynbos (pronounced 'fine-boss'), which grows on the

mountains around the Cape of Good Hope. Fynbos is like an evergreen carpet across the ground. Although the fynbos region is less than 500 km across, it contains 8,500 species of shrubs and other

△ South Africa's fynbos starts flowering in August – the start of the southern spring. By December, most of the flowers are over, as the summertime heat sets in.

residents are colourful birds and biting insects, and also some of the most poisonous snakes in the world.

But not all shrublands are this inhospitable, or this little known. In southern Europe, for example, shrubland grows along the coast of the Mediterranean Sea, while plants – almost as many as in all the countries of Europe combined.

Thousands of kilometres to the east, across the Indian Ocean, the shrublands of Western Australia are another of the biological hotspots of the world. Unlike South Africa, this region is almost flat, and shrubland grows on a deep layer of peaty sand. But despite this poor ground, Western Australia has over 7,000 different kinds of plants, and is famous for its incredibly varied spring flowers. This part of Australia is surrounded by desert, so it is like a biological island in the corner of a continent. In some places, over four-fifths of its plants are ones that live nowhere else in the world.

SHRUBS AND POLLINATORS

Most flowers are pollinated by insects or by the wind, but in shrublands, birds often visit flowers as well. In South Africa and Australia, some of these birds have become very close partners with shrubs – without them, they would find it difficult to survive.

In the fynbos, the Cape sugarbird visits shrubs called proteas, and uses their nectar as food. Proteas grow in shrublands throughout southern

◁ *With its long tail feathers fluttering in the breeze, a male Cape sugarbird looks out from its perch on a protea bush. At the beginning of the breeding season, the males call loudly from their own private patch of flowers.*

Africa, but the fynbos is their most important home. The largest kinds grow into head-high bushes, and they have red or yellow flowerheads, packed with dozens or hundreds of blooms. Each flowerhead is shaped like an ice-cream cone, and it produces nectar for weeks at a time.

Sugarbirds often feed on insects, but they switch to nectar when the proteas start to bloom. Their slender bills are ideally shaped for probing deep into the flowers, which is important as they may visit up to 250 in a day. As the birds feed, they collect pollen on their foreheads

△ *Australian blackboy trees have spires of flowers that look like poles pointing towards the sky. These plants nearly always flower after there has been a fire.*

and carry it from plant to plant, which enables the proteas to form their seeds. Later in the season, the birds collect some of the seeds, because their fluffy down makes a snug lining for sugarbird nests.

MAMMALS THAT FEED AT FLOWERS
Bird-pollinated shrubs are not hard to recognize, even when birds themselves are not around. Their flowers are often bright red, orange or yellow, and they grow on long stalks, which makes it easier for birds to come and go. The flowers are also extra tough, because birds can do much more damage than insects as they set about finding a meal. But in the fynbos, one kind of protea has dull-coloured flowerheads that open at night, and that are hidden away near the ground. Flowers like this do not attract birds at all – small mammals visit them instead. These mammalian visitors include at least two kinds of rodents, and an elephant shrew (*Elephantulus edwardii*) from

Africa. All these animals are nocturnal, and all of them track down protea flowers by smell rather than by sight. The flowers have a musky scent, and they produce an extra-syrupy nectar, which suits mammals best. The nectar is a useful food, particularly as it is produced during the winter, which can be a hungry time of year.

Australia also has mammalian pollinators, although these are small marsupials. They include several species that feed high up in eucalyptus trees, and that glide between them using flaps of skin as wings. But one non-gliding species, the honey possum, depends entirely on shrubland flowers. This mouse-sized marsupial lives in the shrublands of Western Australia, and it gives birth to the tiniest

△ *The pygmy glider lives in eastern Australia, in forests and in shrublands. It feeds at night, jumping fearlessly into the dark so that it can glide from tree to tree.*

young mammals on earth. Each one weighs about 0.005 g – less than a postage stamp.

FIRE!
Fires are a normal part of shrubland life, particularly after weeks or months without rain. Dead leaves and wood are easily set alight, and within a few hours, thousands of hectares of shrubland can go up in flames. These fires are a threat to

---

Species Profile

Honey possum: *Tarsipes rostratus*

This tiny Western Australian marsupial is not much bigger than a mouse. It is active at night, when it climbs up banksias and other shrubs, feeding on nectar and pollen from their flowers. It finds the flowers by its keen sense of smell, and it pollinates them as it feeds. Honey possums have feet that are good at gripping, and non-slip pads on their toes.

Fanned by strong winds, a wildfire sweeps through a clump of Joshua trees on the edge of the Mojave Desert, California, USA. In this dry shrubland, dead vegetation burns away quickly, but living plants are much tougher. The Joshua trees will lose some of their leaves, but otherwise the fire will do them little harm.

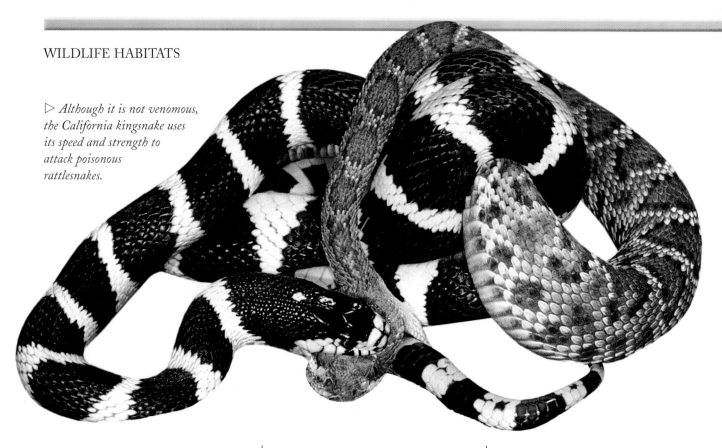

▷ *Although it is not venomous, the California kingsnake uses its speed and strength to attack poisonous rattlesnakes.*

people and their homes, but for shrubs themselves they are not as harmful as they seem.

In California, USA, these summer fires often hit the headlines, because of the speed with which they spread. But once a fire has burned out, nature soon starts carrying out repairs. Within a few weeks, many of the shrubs are sprouting leaves, and within two or three years, the

△ *Two months after a heathland fire, a pine seedling sprouts a tuft of brand-new leaves. The ash on the ground contains minerals that will help it grow.*

burned chaparral starts to look like it did before.

Chaparral can recover like this because many of its shrubs have evolved their own fire defences. For example, one common shrub called chamise, or greasewood, has tough woody stems, and roots that run deep underground. Fire often burns away its smaller branches, but usually the core of the plant is left alive. Once the damage has been done, chamise produces new buds, and then a new set of branches starts to grow.

SHRUBS AND FIRE

After a plant has been pollinated, it sets about making and scattering its seeds. But in shrublands, plants like proteas and chamise behave in an unusual way. Instead of shedding their seeds as soon as they are ripe, they can hold on to them for years, waiting for a fire to come their way. When a fire does sweep past, their seed-cases open and the seeds inside drop to the ground. Some conifers behave in a similar way, because the heat from a fire opens

up their cones to release seeds.

Shrubs do this because the days after a fire are the ideal planting time. The ground is covered with fertile ash, and all the dead leaves have been cleared away. This gives the seedlings a good start in life, and it also makes sure that they will have

Species Profile

California quail: *Lophortyx californica*

This attractive ground-feeding bird sometimes lives in fields, but its natural home is shrubland on mountains and hills. California quails live in flocks called coveys – in winter these can contain as many as 200 birds. They feed mainly on seeds, and they only take to the air if they are alarmed. Like many ground-feeding birds, they spend the night roosting in trees.

several years to grow before they have to face a fire themselves.

GROUND PATROL

In shrublands, wildlife can be difficult to spot, but sounds often give animals away. The snapping of twigs may be a sign that antelope or deer are feeding, while a rustle of dry leaves, followed by silence, often shows that lizards are on the move. For lizards, shrubland is close to an ideal habitat. There is plenty of cover, but there are also patches of open ground that allow them to warm themselves in the sun.

For most shrubland lizards, insects top the menu – particularly the fat-bodied crickets and katydids that feed among the leaves. Lizards hunt insects mainly by sight, and they

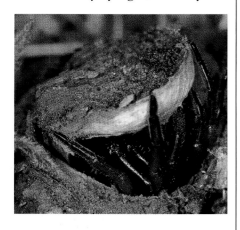

△ *Trapdoor spiders are common in shrublands. They live in silk-lined burrows that have a hinged lid, or trapdoor. If anything edible comes close by, the spider rushes out and grabs it with its fangs.*

are easily tricked by camouflage. The moment an insect moves, however, it risks being spotted and then snapped up by the quick-moving jaws of a predator. But the insect-eaters themselves also have to keep on the alert, because many birds and snakes like to feed on lizard flesh. Worse still, many lizards like to as well.

For reptiles, this kind of behaviour is not at all unusual. Large lizards often eat smaller species, and some kinds have a cannibalistic streak, even attacking their own young.

△ *Shrikes catch insects and lizards, spearing any surplus food on thorns. They use this 'larder' if food becomes hard to find.*

As a result, young lizards have to be very wary of adults if they are to avoid ending up as their prey.

SNAKES THAT EAT SNAKES

Just as lizards eat other lizards, some shrubland snakes use other snakes as food. For snakes, this makes good sense, because a smaller snake makes a perfectly shaped meal. Once the unfortunate victim has been swallowed and digested, it can provide the predator with enough food

▷ *Madagascar's Spiny Forest is one of the strangest habitats in the world. Here, shrubs and trees have adapted to the harsh climate by evolving bizarre shapes, sharp spines, and tiny leaves.*

for several weeks. Surprisingly, poisonous snakes are often eaten by ones that have no venom at all. For example, in Mediterranean scrubland non-poisonous whipsnakes sometimes eat venomous adders, while in the Californian chaparral non-poisonous kingsnakes feed on highly poisonous rattlesnakes. In both cases, the hunter relies on the fact that its prey is comparatively slow. It makes a lightning-fast lunge, grips its prey's neck with its teeth, and then coils itself tightly around it. Once the victim is dead it can then be swallowed – a task that may take over an hour.

TEMPERATE FORESTS

MANY HABITATS CHANGE WITH THE SEASONS, BUT IN TEMPERATE FORESTS THESE CHANGES ARE MORE IMPRESSIVE AND MORE COLOURFUL THAN ANYWHERE ELSE ON EARTH.

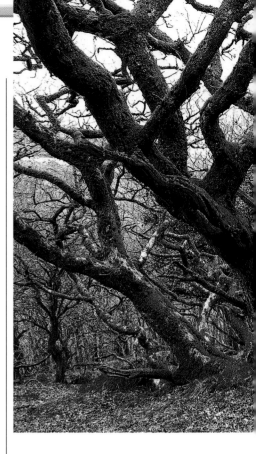

Temperate forests originally covered large parts of Europe and North America. Despite centuries of clearance, a lot of these forests still remain. In this habitat, animal life has to cope with very different seasons, and some wild swings in the forest's food supply. There is plenty to eat in summer, but in winter food can be hard to find.

TREES AT THE END OF THE WORLD
Because the continents are unevenly spread out, the world's temperate forests are uneven too. The southern hemisphere has by far the smallest share, concentrated mainly in New Zealand and the tip of South America. In both these places, the most important trees are southern beeches. Some of these trees are evergreen, but one South American species, called the nire or Antarctic beech, turns a brilliant red every autumn, just before losing its leaves. The nire grows on the stormy coast around Cape Horn, which is closer to Antarctica than any other kind of tree in the world.

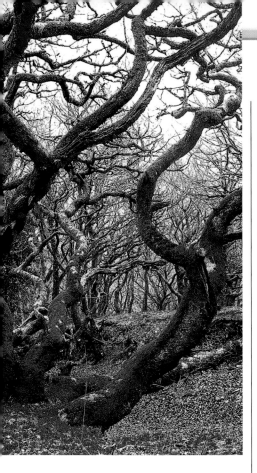

These southern forests are home to some unusual animals, including the world's southernmost parrots and one of its strangest amphibians. Called Darwin's frog, this South American oddity has a sharply

◁ In midwinter, the bare branches of this ancient oak snake against the sky. The tree's shape shows that it was coppiced – cut down to ground level – long ago.

pointed snout, and lives in forest streams. Its breeding system is unique – the male guards the eggs until they hatch, and then promptly swallows them. Instead of ending up in his stomach, the tadpoles lodge in a pouch in his throat, where they stay for several weeks. When the tadpoles have turned into froglets, the male coughs them up and they swim away.

WORKING WOODLANDS

In South America and New Zealand, some parts of the beech forest are very much like they were before humans arrived on the scene. But in Europe and North America, temperate forests have had a very different history. Here, many forests have been managed for their timber, while others have been cleared to make way for farms. As a result, the original forest has become

a patchwork of woodland, scattered among fields and towns.

In these woodlands, old trees often have a story to tell. For example, in England, it is not unusual to find ancient trees that have been cut through at ground level long ago.

△ With its bright green skin and sharply pointed nose, Darwin's frog looks like a freshly fallen leaf. This male is guarding one of his froglets.

▽ In Chile's Huerquehue National Park, southern beech trees show off their beautiful autumn colours. Southern beeches grow in South America, and also in New Zealand and Australia.

◁ In English woodlands, bluebells turn the ground into a carpet of blue in spring. Bluebells finish flowering by the time the trees are fully in leaf.

This operation, called coppicing, created lots of fast-growing shoots which could be used for making charcoal and all kinds of useful objects, from fence poles to wooden clogs. The shoots were harvested every few years and, after each cut, another batch would grow in their place. Today, coppicing is not so common, but old coppiced trees are still easy to spot. That is because they have lots of trunks, growing from a massive stump just a few centimetres high.

Coppicing sounds drastic, but it can actually lengthen a tree's life. In English woodlands, some coppiced hazel trees are thought to be 1,500 years old – ten times the age that they normally reach in the wild.

THE FOREST YEAR

On a cold day in late winter, temperate forest can seem like a habitat whose wildlife has disappeared. There are no leaves on the trees, no flowers, no insects, and only a few mammals and birds on the move. The forest floor is silent – particularly when it is covered by snow. Looking at such a scene, it is hard to imagine how quickly it can change. But by the time spring arrives, this kind of forest is completely transformed. With the lengthening days and increasing warmth, woodland wildflowers quickly come into bloom. Soon afterwards, buds burst overhead as the trees start to grow. During three hectic months, some of these trees can outgrow ones in the tropics, as their branches lengthen and their leaves soak up the strengthening sunshine. At the same time, animal life also takes off. The air is full of flying insects, and newly hatched caterpillars nibble through the fresh young leaves. Migratory birds flood in to eat them, and their songs resonate through the treetops, showing that spring is fully under way.

CLOSING DOWN

This burst of growth is so fast that it cannot continue for long. And by the time midsummer is over, life changes gear. Animals are still everywhere, although the forest birds are much quieter now that their breeding season is near its end. But by now most of the trees have finished growing, and are concentrating on producing seeds. Their leaves have lost their brand-new look, and some have even started to yellow – an early hint of some major changes that are still to come.

By the time the clock has ticked onward another three months, autumn is well advanced. The forest's animals are preparing for harder times, and most of the migratory birds have gone. But the biggest difference is

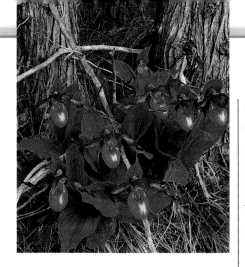

△ *Lady's slippers are woodland orchids that grow across the northern hemisphere. In many places they have become rare, because their flowers are often picked.*

WHY LEAVES CHANGE COLOUR

This annual blizzard of leaves is one of the most beautiful spectacles in the natural world. It happens in places as far apart as Europe and Japan, but nowhere quite matches the display in the northeastern corner of the USA. Here, in New England, the forest's birches, maples and beeches blaze into colour after the first sharp frosts, before their leaves slowly melt away.

Leaves suffer a lot of wear and tear, which means that they have to be shed and replaced. Evergreen trees do this all the time, so their branches are never left bare. But in the temperate world, most broadleaved trees shed all their leaves at once, and grow a whole new set the following spring.

overhead, where the deep greens of summer have given way to a rainbow of autumn hues. After a working life of just six months, billions of leaves are starting to fall, marking the end of the forest year.

Species Profile

White trillium: *Trillium grandiflorum*

Trilliums are common forest floor plants across North America. This species – also known as the wake robin – is often one of the first flowers to appear in spring. Like many woodland wildflowers, trilliums store food in underground stems, so they can start growing quickly as soon as spring arrives. Trillium seeds have a stick-on package of food which attracts ants. The ants carry off the seeds, eat the food package and then drop the seeds on the ground.

◁ *Eurasian badgers spend much of the winter asleep. As soon as spring starts, they become much more lively, emerging from their burrows every evening to look for food.*

millions of microscopic fungi and several billion bacteria. For all of them, leaf litter is a complete habitat, just as mud and ooze is for animals that live at the bottom of the sea.

Most of the inhabitants of this hidden world live by breaking down dead remains. These natural recyclers include woodlice and millipedes, as well as much smaller animals that can only just be seen with the naked eye. With the help of the leaf-litter microbes, they process every scrap of dead matter, using up its energy and returning its nutrients to the soil. Like all habitats, leaf litter contains predators too. They include centipedes armed with poisonous claws, and minute animals called pseudoscorpions, which look like miniature versions of real scorpions, with poisonous pincers instead of a sting. Pseudoscorpions use their pincers to paralyze prey, and also to communicate with their own kind.

△ *Woodlice eat all kinds of plant remains, including rotting wood and fallen leaves. They have to stay damp to survive – if they dry out, they cannot breathe.*

▷ *Pseudoscorpions have pear-shaped bodies and tiny mouths. They are often less than 2 mm long.*

LIFE IN LEAF LITTER
In the steamy climate of tropical rainforests, fallen leaves rot away within a few weeks. But in the broadleaved forests of the temperate world, leaves take much longer to break down. As a result, the forest

This stop-start lifestyle means that broadleaved trees do not need leaves that can cope with winter. But throwing away an entire set of leaves is still an expensive business, so the trees recycle any useful substances that they contain. One of these is chlorophyll – the green chemical that plants use to grow. The tree breaks this down and removes it, and the leaf's green colour slowly fades. This often reveals other coloured chemicals in the leaf, which are broken down in turn. Many leaves turn yellow, but some become orange, scarlet or several shades at once. The warmer the summer has been, the more colourful the display.

Once everything useful has been extracted, the tree shuts off the leaf stalk. This disconnects the leaf's water supply, and a few days later it flutters to the ground.

floor is covered by leaf litter – a fertile layer of leafy remains that gives the forest its earthy smell. A teaspoonful of leaf litter can contain hundreds of tiny animals,

△ *For a fire salamander, an earthworm makes a filling meal. Like many salamanders, this European species has bright colours to warn predators that its skin is poisonous.*

▷ *A nutcracker fluffs out its feathers to keep warm. Nutcrackers live in Europe and Siberia.*

They live in forests all over the world but, as they are so small, few people ever see a single one.

With so much life underfoot, other predators also search the leaf litter for food. Shrews push their way through it like miniature moles, rustling the leaves as they sniff out their prey. Although shrews are tiny, they are always hungry, because their high-speed lifestyle uses energy at a rapid rate. Toads and salamanders are very different – they move slowly, and can survive for several weeks between meals. They hide under logs and leaves during dry weather, but come out to feed when the forest floor has been dampened by rain.

OAKS AND ACORNS

In broadleaved forests, animals often need particular trees to make them feel at home. For example, the common dormouse is often found in hazel woods, because hazelnuts are one of its favourite foods. But of all deciduous trees, oaks hold the record for animal life. Oak leaves and acorns provide food for dozens of mammals and birds, and hundreds of species of insects, from moths to tiny flies. Some of these animals are occasional visitors, but many live on or near oak trees for the whole of their lives.

For the Eurasian jay, a bountiful acorn crop makes the winter a much

easier time. Unlike many birds, jays stay in deciduous forests all year round, and their diet changes as the seasons pass. In spring and summer, they eat insects, and they also have a liking for other birds' eggs and young. But in autumn, when these are off the menu, acorns are their most important food.

Jays do not only eat the acorns – they also bury them in the ground. They have an amazing memory for these food stores, and in winter they dig up the acorns and eat them. A few always get overlooked, and they take root, helping oak trees to spread.

SECRET STORES

This food-storing behaviour is called 'caching', from a French word that means to hide. Eurasian jays cache food on their own, and so do nutcrackers, which live in coniferous woodland and bury seeds from pines. But in North America, acorn woodpeckers work in family groups. They store acorns in the trunks of dead trees, wedging each one into a pre-pecked hole. A single storage tree can contain up to 50,000

acorns, enough to keep a group of woodpeckers well fed until spring. This food hoard often attracts other birds, so the woodpeckers keep watch like a team of security guards.

Foxes and squirrels make food stores as well. None of these animals can actually plan ahead, and none of them knows that winter is a difficult time. Instead, their behaviour is controlled by instinct, which enables them to survive.

◁ *Some squirrels nest in trees, but chipmunks make their nests in burrows underground.*

DIGGING FOR FOOD

During the Middle Ages, many of Europe's forests were owned by feudal landlords, who kept them as parks for hunting wild boar and deer. A hunting forest was a status symbol, designed to impress visitors just as much as to provide food. Most of these private forests disappeared long ago, but wild boar and deer still thrive, even in woodland close to cities and towns. The success of these animals is mainly due to their wariness – they keep well clear of people, and in busy areas they feed only after dark.

Wild boar are the original ancestors of domestic pigs, and they have the same powerful jaws and flat-ended snouts designed for shovelling through the ground.

The tip of the snout can swivel upwards, quickly turning it from a bulldozer into a spade. Using this implement a wild boar can dig through the ground to reach nutritious roots, or it can unearth moles and earthworms. In fact, there are very few things that these animals will not eat – they prefer fresh food (including crops), but they also dine on dead remains. Wild boar find most of their food by using their sense of smell. It is so keen that a boar can tell the difference between kinds of potatoes when they are still underground.

Like many of their relatives in the pig family, wild boar have stripy young, and they give birth to litters of up to ten piglets in a leafy 'nest' on the forest floor. Females, or sows,

Species Profile

White-tailed deer: *Odocoileus virginianus*

This adaptable deer is found in forests from Canada to South America. In the far north, males can weigh up to 180 kg, but further south the deer are often smaller, and their antlers have fewer points. When a white-tailed deer is frightened, it runs for cover with its tail raised, showing its white underside. These deer are fast runners, and can clear 9 m in a single leap.

FEEDING ON BARK

Wild boar live in Europe and Asia, but deer live in almost all the broadleaved forests of the world.

White-tailed deer live only in the Americas, but the red deer is found across the northern hemisphere, from Canada to China. It has also been introduced to other parts of the world, including Argentina, Australia and New Zealand, where it arrived in 1851. Here, red deer have become so common that they are now a problem for New Zealand's own wildlife.

For most of the year, deer feed mainly on the leaves of forest floor plants and trees. But when the leaves disappear in autumn, they have to switch to tougher food. They bite the tops off small saplings, and they also feed on bark. During the winter, a tree's bark is firmly fastened to its wood, so deer can only gouge out small pieces at a time. But in early spring, when a tree's sap starts to rise, the outer wood turns slippery,

△ *Moving as quietly as a cat, the red fox is good at pinpointing small animals beneath the snow. Like a cat, it catches them with a well-aimed pounce.*

have a strong nest-building instinct, which is why thoughtful farmers give their domestic pigs nesting material too.

▷ Wild boar piglets start life with a stripy coat that is very different to their mother's bristly fur. Their markings help to camouflage them on the sun-dappled forest floor.

which makes the bark more loose. When a deer bites on the bark and then pulls, it comes away in long strips, sometimes killing the tree.

These eating habits do not do too much harm in a natural forest, but they can cause havoc in plantations. That is why young trees have to be protected by fences, or by plastic guards around their trunks.

Unlike wild boar, most deer give birth to just one young, called a fawn. At first, the fawn stays curled up in the undergrowth, and its mother returns every few hours to give it a meal of milk. Red deer fawns follow their mother after about three or four days, but young white-tailed deer can stay in hiding for a month. Fawns look as if they have been abandoned, and they are sometimes taken to animal rescue centres by people wanting to help. But they do not need a hand from humans, because their mothers are never far away.

ANTLERS

Most animals look their best during the breeding season. Some birds grow extra-colourful plumage, while woodland butterflies show off their brightly patterned wings. But male deer grow antlers – some of the biggest and most eyecatching

▷ The size of a deer's antlers depends partly on its age and partly on its food. This red deer has six points on each of its antlers, but some of the biggest red deer stags can have twelve.

accessories in the animal world. Unlike horns, a deer's antlers are made of solid bone. Red deer antlers can be 70 cm long, and weigh up to 3 kg. Moose antlers are even larger – theirs can weigh 30 kg, and may measure 2 m from tip to tip.

Antlers grow from the top of a deer's forehead, and at first they are covered by a layer of velvety skin. They often branch as they grow, and after about 15 to 20 weeks, the new antlers are complete. Once they have finished growing, the velvety skin dries up and starts to fall off. This is an uncomfortable time for the

deer, and they scrape their antlers against trees and shrubs to clean away the remaining skin.

In autumn, the rutting season begins, and rival males use their antlers in the annual contest for the right to mate. Sometimes, two males simply show off to each other, until one decides that it is safer to beat a retreat. If neither male backs down, the contestants clash head-on, and serious injuries can occur. Winners gather a group of females, while losers keep a low profile, nursing their bruises and saving their energy for the following year.

△ *Unlike other woodland birds, woodpeckers usually feed with their bodies upright. They cling on with their claws, and their strong tail feathers work like a prop, stabilizing them while they peck into the wood.*

STARTING AGAIN

Antlers take a lot of time and energy to grow, but once the rutting season is at an end they start to weaken at the point where they are fixed to the skull. For several weeks, each antler stays in place, like a dead branch on a tree. Finally, a sudden movement by the deer makes the antler snap off and drop to the ground.

Why do deer go to all the trouble of growing new antlers each year? The answer is probably that it helps them to impress females just as much as males. Large antlers are a sign that a deer is strong and well fed, and these are features that he is likely to pass on to his young. When females decide which males to mate with, antlers help them to make their choice.

PREDATORY FUNGI

For broadleaved trees, deer are a problem, but much more serious enemies are all around. These are fungi, an ever-present and sometimes deadly feature of forest life. For fungi, every tree – no matter how young or old – is a potential source of food. With their microscopic feeding threads, they grow through leaf litter and wood, digesting living matter and dead remains.

Species Profile

Tawny owl: *Strix aluco*

One of Europe's commonest owls, this nocturnal hunter often roosts in parks and gardens, but it is so well camouflaged that it is rarely seen. Its call is easier to pinpoint – during the breeding season, males make a far-carrying hooting sound, while females reply with a sharp 'kee-wick'. Tawny owls feed mainly on small rodents, but their diet also includes frogs, beetles, earthworms, moths and other birds.

Some woodland fungi behave like roving predators that spread unseen through the forest floor. One of these is the voracious honey fungus, which lives throughout the northern world. Honey fungus grows average-sized toadstools, but its underground threads can reach incredible lengths. One network, found in an oak forest in Michigan, USA, covered 15 hectares and probably weighed ten tonnes. The clump was almost certainly started by a single spore, and had been feeding in the forest for over a thousand years. Some fungal networks can be bigger still – they include the largest living things ever found by scientists (see p. 75).

When honey fungus finds a suitable victim, it grows upwards beneath a tree's bark, stealing nutrients from its new wood. During the first stage of the attack the tree still looks healthy, but as time goes by the damage starts to show. Its leaves turn yellow, its growth slows down, and whole branches start to sicken. By the time honey-coloured toadstools sprout around its trunk, the tree's fate is sealed.

STAYING ALIVE

Unlike animals, trees can take many years to die. English oaks are particularly stubborn, and can be 'on their last legs' for more than 200 years. Even when the inside of its trunk has rotted away, a tree can keep going. In the 1800s, one famous hollow oak, at Bowthorpe in England, was carved out even further to make a large room. The local squire and up to 20 guests were able to dine inside. During the last century, in California, several giant redwoods were hollowed out so that cars could drive through them. The tallest of these living drive-throughs is doing well, and is more than 90 m high. Trees can also recover after being struck by lightning, or after having their trunks snapped in half by storms. Some kinds, including oaks, sweet chestnuts and hazels, can even survive being coppiced (see p. 214) – not just once, but many times over hundreds of years.

Trees can put up with all this because the only wood that really matters is the living layer just beneath the bark. As long as enough of this is left, it can carry out the vital task of carrying water and sap. But if a tree is attacked by fungi, the sapwood finds it harder to do its work. Eventually, its pipelines become blocked and the tree dies slowly.

◁ *Honey fungus toadstools grow in clumps around dying trees. This fungus is dreaded by gardeners, because it attacks all kinds of trees and is very hard to get rid of.*

their eggs on the bare floor of their homes, but many smaller birds make their nest holes snug by lining them with moss and leaves.

In some woodlands – particularly ones that are managed for timber – dead trees are few and far between. Here, there is strong competition for homes, and if a bird is lucky enough to find a hole, it may have to fight off others that want it for themselves. Nuthatches have an ingenious way to stop larger birds moving into their nests. They plaster mud around the entrance until there is only just enough room for a nuthatch to squeeze inside. If a bigger bird examines the hole, it mistakes the mud for wood, and decides that there is not enough room to move in.

Hollow trees are also favourite roosting places for bats, because they shelter them from the weather and hide them from prying eyes. In temperate woodlands, most bats are insect-eating species that catch their prey in mid-air. But woodland bats are very varied, and not all of them behave in this way. One of the exceptions is the greater mouse-eared bat, which lives in western Europe. It emerges late at night, and grabs beetles and spiders on the ground, as well as hunting in the air. It does not use its sonar to do this – instead, it simply listens for the sounds of moving insects as they crawl across the ground. But the short-tailed bat, from New Zealand, is the real expert at this way of life. It folds its wings up tightly, and catches food by scuttling across the forest floor or even up the trunks of trees. Short-tailed bats feed mainly on insects, but they also eat fruit, as well as nectar and pollen from flowers.

△ *The greater mouse-eared bat hunts in fields, gardens and woodland. Compared to other small mammals, bats live a long time – the record for this species is 28 years.*

AT HOME IN DEAD WOOD

Once a tree is dead, its useful existence is far from over. Dead tree trunks make high-rise homes for woodpeckers, and for birds that nest in these holes after their original owners have moved on. These hole-nesters include dozens of different woodland species, from tits and chickadees to predators such as owls. Woodpeckers and owls lay

▷ *Burying beetles search for dead animals, and then bury them under loose earth. These beetles have found a dead mouse – once it is underground, they will use it as food for their grubs.*

For a few weeks each autumn, the woodlands of New England, in the USA, attract admiring visitors from all over the world. In this part of North America, autumn colours are particularly vivid – a result of the sudden drop in temperature as cold air sweeps down from the north. This woodland walk is flanked by maple and birch trees. Soon, all the trees will have lost their leaves and the forest will be quiet and bare until spring.

CONIFEROUS FORESTS

CONIFERS ARE SUPERBLY PROTECTED AGAINST DROUGHT, WIND AND COLD, AND THEY THRIVE IN PLACES WHERE OTHER TREES STRUGGLE TO SURVIVE.

Coniferous trees are experts at coping with extreme conditions. Thanks to their needle-like leaves, they can grow high up in mountains and on dry, rocky hillsides. Some conifers also grow in tropical forests and waterlogged swamps, although they are greatly outnumbered by broadleaved trees. But the real stronghold of conifers is in the far north. Here, they form the boreal forest – a vast and often remote habitat that almost encircles the earth.

CROSSING CONTINENTS
The boreal forest is often known as the taiga, which is its Russian name. In Russia itself, the taiga stretches across 11 separate time zones, and in some places it is over 1,500 km wide. By train, travelling right across it can take over a week,

◁ *With their straight trunks and sloping branches, coniferous trees are good at coping with snow. Frost is more of a problem, as it can kill buds when they start to grow.*

figure is not much higher. By comparison, tropical forests can have hundreds of different trees in an area as small as a football pitch.

For wildlife, fewer species mean fewer opportunities to find food. But there is another side to the coin. If an animal can make a living here, its home is the largest land habitat on earth.

WINTER FUR

For animals in boreal forest, surviving the winter is the most serious challenge in life. Where Canada's forest meets the tundra, winter temperatures can often drop to −40° C, but in eastern Siberia, the climate is even more severe. Here, a temperature of −68° C was once recorded in the mining town of

Verkhoyansk, making this region colder even than the North Pole. During the winter, the ground freezes solid for months on end, making liquid water hard to find.

△ *Tits and chickadees are common birds in coniferous forests. This is the crested tit, a European species that lives in forests that contain mature trees.*

▽ *Reindeer run through the forest near Oymyakon, in eastern Siberia. The open spaces between the trees are a sign of the cold winter climate.*

but it is a journey that sees very few changes in the outer appearance of the forest. Sameness is a trademark of boreal forest, because the forest contains a remarkably small variety of trees. In the entire Russian taiga, for example, the forest is dominated by just ten different kinds, while in North America's boreal forest, the

Protected by its thick winter coat, a Siberian tiger looks completely at home in a winter landscape. Weighing up to 300 kg, Siberian tigers live in the Russian Far East – a part of the world where summers are warm but winters are cold, with lots of snow. One of five surviving subspecies of tiger, they are among the largest and the rarest, with just a few hundred animals left.

One way to deal with the cold is to leave it behind – a solution used by the forest's migratory birds. Mammals do not have this option, however, because they cannot travel

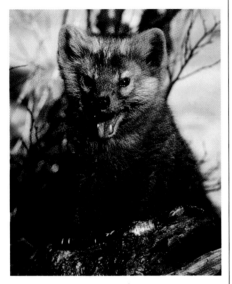

△ *The Russian sable has a fox-like face, but it is a close relative of the American mink. It lives alone, except in the breeding season, and fiercely defends its territory against any rivals on the lookout for food.*

nearly so far. Instead, they rely on one of the natural world's best insulators – a coat of fur. The outer part of the coat is made of long guard hairs, while the inner part consists of fluffier underfur. The underfur becomes thicker in autumn, adding extra warmth for the winter ahead.

Many of the boreal forest's carnivorous mammals are renowned for their luxurious coats. One of the best known is the American mink, an agile and aggressive hunter that normally feeds in or near water. Another is the fisher – an animal that looks very much like the mink,

▷ *Grey wolves live in a wide variety of habitats, from coniferous forests to Arctic tundra. In each pack, all the adults hunt, but only the senior male and female breed.*

but which actually hunts in trees. But as a fur-bearer, the most famous by far is the Russian sable, a fox-sized animal that lives in eastern Siberia, where it has to face the record-breaking cold. The sable eats small animals and fruit, and thanks to its sumptuous fur it keeps active even in temperatures of −50° C.

Unfortunately for all these mammals, humans value their fur, and they have been trapped and hunted for hundreds of years. Many of them are now raised in captivity – sometimes in grim conditions – but every year hundreds of thousands are still caught in the wild.

THE VANISHING WOLF

In folklore, the coniferous forest is a menacing place, full of dangers for the unwary. Most of these dangers are make-believe, but at one time, people did have reason to fear the forest's wolves. Until about 400 years ago, the grey wolf was widespread across the entire northern world, and the forest was where it was most at home.

There are very few records of wolves attacking people, but they can be a major threat to farm

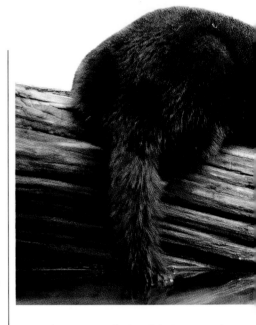

animals – particularly if their natural prey starts to disappear. As a result, wolves have been widely persecuted. Over the centuries, they have been driven back to uninhabited regions, or wiped out altogether. In the British Isles, for example, the last wild wolf died in about 1770. There are still plenty of wolves in Russia, and also in Canada and Alaska, but in the rest of the USA, wild wolves have almost disappeared.

STAGING A COMEBACK

America's wolves might have vanished entirely were it not for

◁ *The American mink hunts mainly at night, stalking animals on riverbanks and in the water. Like the Russian sable, it usually kills its victims with a bite to the back of the neck.*

human help. During the 1990s, conservationists began a programme of wolf reintroductions, with the aim of putting wolves back in territory that was once their own. Canadian

Species Profile

Fly agaric: *Amanita muscaria*

Many fungi grow in coniferous forests, because they thrive in dim, damp conditions on the forest floor. Fly agaric is one of the easiest to recognize, because its toadstools are so brightly coloured. It nearly always grows near spruce or birch trees, and its toadstools appear in late summer and early autumn, after it has rained. Fly agaric is very poisonous to humans, but some forest animals eat it.

wolves were flown to the mountains of Montana, Idaho and Wyoming, and gradually released. These reintroductions proved very successful, and there are now over two dozen wolf packs in this part of the USA alone.

Not everyone is pleased at the wolf's return, however. Most ranchers think that the wolves will attack their cattle, and in some places, suspect wolves have been caught and killed. For this reason, the introduced wolves are being carefully monitored and controlled, in the hope that people and wolves will be able to live side by side.

THE LONG SLEEP

Wolves may not deserve their dangerous reputation, but there is no doubt at all about the brown bear. After the polar bear, brown bears are the world's largest land-dwelling carnivores, and their strength is awesome and legendary. They feed on an amazing variety of food, from roots and insects to fish and deer, and they are capable of dragging an adult moose or horse hundreds of metres with their jaws. For these short-sighted but immensely powerful animals, a human can be a threat or, just occasionally, a meal.

Like wolves, brown bears once lived right across the northern hemisphere, and they have seen the same steep decline in their natural range. But brown bears have a very different way of coping with the ups and downs of life in the forest habitat. Instead of keeping on the move throughout the year, they hibernate for up to six months – a survival technique that saves energy when food is hard to find. Their winter quarters are usually dug into a north-facing slope, and they are lined with branches and leaves. The den is usually not more than 1.5 m wide, making it a tight fit for an animal that can weigh half a tonne.

In the autumn, up to a half of a bear's weight consists of fat – its equivalent of winter fuel. Fat is the richest source of energy in an animal's body, and a bear builds this up by gorging

△ *Despite their huge size, brown bears – or grizzlies – are good runners and climbers. They can easily overtake a human running at top speed, and have been known to chase people up trees.*

itself on whatever food it can find. When the bear enters hibernation, its body temperature drops by about 5° C, its heartbeat slows, and the fat is gradually used up to keep it alive.

△ These pine shoots are just starting their burst of growth. The yellow objects are male cones, which will soon scatter pollen into the air. The female cones are bigger – their woody scales protect developing seeds.

that they spin at the tip of a branch. The silk is strong but elastic, which makes it hard for animals to rip apart, and difficult to cut even with a knife. From the nest, silk trails lead down the tree, towards other shoots with fresh leaves. At night, the caterpillars file out to feed in a single line – a feature that gives them their name.

LIVING IN WOOD

For some coniferous forest insects, wood is much more appetizing than leaves. In boreal forest, one of the most impressive of these animals is

Species Profile

Black woodpecker: *Dryocopus martius*

This woodpecker lives in coniferous forests from western Europe through Siberia to the Far East. It feeds on insect grubs, hacking out wood chips up to 20 cm long as it digs out prey. It also eats the chicks of hole-nesting birds, by smashing into their nests. Woodpeckers usually dig nest holes in rotting wood, but this species uses healthy tree trunks too.

But compared to many other hibernators, such as marmots (see p. 263), bears sleep lightly and their temperature drop is relatively small. They remain dimly aware of their surroundings, and they can wake instantly if they are disturbed. This rapid response means that, even in the depths of winter, bears' dens are not good places to explore.

△ *Pine sawfly grubs can kill trees by eating their leaves. The adults look like small wasps – females can live for several weeks, but the males often die a few hours after they have mated.*

THE LEAF-EATERS

Bears will eat almost anything, but even they avoid conifer leaves. Compared to most leaves, these ones are tough and waxy, and they contain strong-smelling resins which make them hard to digest. They are left to the forest's professional leaf-eaters: moth caterpillars and sawfly grubs. The pine beauty moth is one European species that grows up on this unpromising food. The adult moth is brown and grey, but the caterpillars have green and white stripes that exactly match a pine needle's waxy shine. They feed voraciously on young pine needles, staying stretched out on their food, which makes them even harder to see. A single adult female can lay hundreds of eggs, so moths like these can spread quickly.

Pine beauty caterpillars feed around the clock, but another species – the pine processionary moth – organizes its time in a different way. During the day, processionary moth caterpillars live in a silk tent

the horntail, or giant wood wasp, which buzzes noisily among the trees. The adults are black and yellow, and the females are equipped with what looks like a menacing sting. This 'sting' is harmless, however,

◁ *Using her ovipositor, a female horntail drills deep into wood to lay her eggs. When not in use, her ovipositor is stowed inside a yellow sheath – seen here on the left.*

because it is actually an egg-laying tube, or ovipositor, which is designed for drilling through wood.

Female horntails search for weakened or fallen trees, and they inject their eggs one by one into the wood just beneath the bark. When the grubs hatch, they spend up to three years burrowing through their home. But instead of eating the wood itself, they are thought to feed on a fungus that grows on the inside of their tunnels. Fungi are good at breaking down the tough substances in wood, and horntails turn this to their own advantage, by 'farming' the fungus and helping it to spread.

ATTACK FROM OUTSIDE

Unhappily for horntail grubs, their homes are not quite as safe as they seem. That is because another insect, the giant ichneumon wasp, uses horntail grubs as food for its young. Using its incredibly acute sense of smell, the wasp can detect horntail grubs feeding in the wood. It drills down towards them with its own ovipositor, and lays a single egg next to each grub. When the egg hatches, the ichneumon feeds on the horntail grub, eating it alive.

If a grub escapes this fate, another kind of danger can strike at any time. Woodpeckers hammer their way into trees, and flick their tongues up and down any tunnels that they find. Their tongues have barbed tips to haul out the grubs.

THE CONE-CUTTERS

Conifers do not grow flowers or fruit, but they do produce nutritious seeds tucked away inside cones. Most cones are small enough to fit in your hand, but the ones grown by North American sugar pines can be 50 cm long. The heaviest cones are produced by the Australian bunya pine. Shaped like a prickly melon, they are hard, and weigh up to 5 kg.

Bunya pine cones break up when they are ripe, which makes it easy for animals to get at their seeds. But most other cones stay in one piece, and release their seeds before they drop onto the forest floor. Jays and nutcrackers collect the seeds once they have fluttered to the ground, but some birds intercept them even before they have left the tree. In the boreal forest, first in the queue are birds called crossbills – finches with beaks that cross over at their tips. Using this handy device, a crossbill levers apart the scales on a cone, and removes the seeds with its tongue.

Crossbills rely on the seed crop, and their numbers boom if the harvest is good. But if a bad year follows a good one, many birds find that they have too little to eat. When this happens, crossbills fly far south of their usual range, turning up in places well outside the boreal forest zone. This kind of migration, called an irruption, happens with other seed-eating finches as well.

FLYING PREDATORS

With its long winter nights and dense cover, coniferous forest seems almost purpose-made for owls. Some of the world's largest species live here, including the northern eagle owl from Europe and Asia.

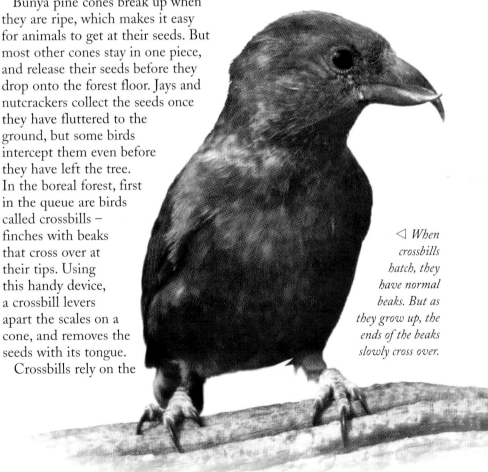

◁ *When crossbills hatch, they have normal beaks. But as they grow up, the ends of the beaks slowly cross over.*

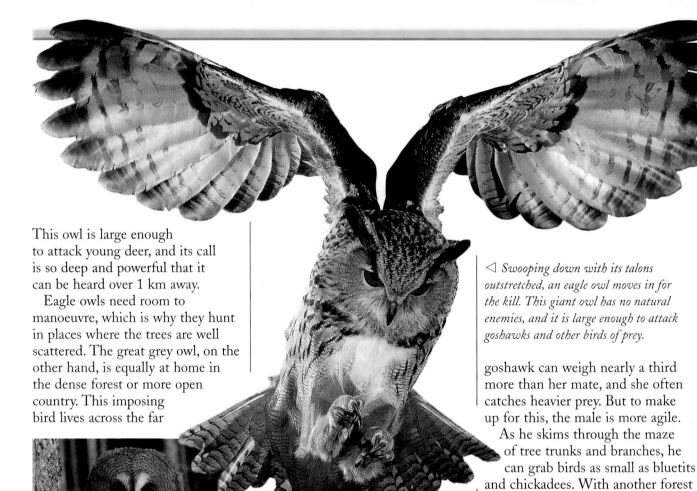

This owl is large enough to attack young deer, and its call is so deep and powerful that it can be heard over 1 km away.

Eagle owls need room to manoeuvre, which is why they hunt in places where the trees are well scattered. The great grey owl, on the other hand, is equally at home in the dense forest or more open country. This imposing bird lives across the far

△ *The great grey owl's round face works like a feathery satellite dish. It funnels sound towards its ears, which are hidden beneath its plumage. Using sound alone, this owl can find rodents under the snow.*

north, where it perches in living trees and on dead trunks, looking at the world through staring yellow eyes. Despite its great size, it feeds almost entirely on small rodents, using its hearing to pinpoint them beneath winter snow. In coniferous forests, most birds steer well clear

◁ *Swooping down with its talons outstretched, an eagle owl moves in for the kill. This giant owl has no natural enemies, and it is large enough to attack goshawks and other birds of prey.*

of humans, but the great grey owl does not hesitate to attack if its nest is under threat. With a wingspan of 1.5 m, it can make even the most determined intruder run away.

UNEQUAL PARTNERS
During the daytime, most owls roost in trees, but birds of prey come out to hunt. Eagles and buzzards find it hard to steer between the trees, but the northern goshawk is specially built for this kind of terrain. Using its tail and wings like a rudder and a brake, it twists and swerves through the forest, attacking prey in trees, and also on the ground. This high-speed hunter feeds mainly on other birds, but it also snatches squirrels or young porcupines from branches, where they are easy to pick off.

With mammals, males are often larger than females, but with birds of prey, things are often the other way around. The female northern

goshawk can weigh nearly a third more than her mate, and she often catches heavier prey. But to make up for this, the male is more agile.

As he skims through the maze of tree trunks and branches, he can grab birds as small as bluetits and chickadees. With another forest hunter, the sparrowhawk, the difference between male and female is even greater – female sparrowhawks sometimes weigh twice as much as their mates.

Species Profile

North American porcupine:
Erethizon dorsatum

Porcupines are common in the tropics, but this is the only species that lives in the northern coniferous forest. If the porcupine is attacked, its sharp quills come loose and work their way into its enemy's skin. North American porcupines eat leaves, bark and buds. They gnaw wooden tools and even window-catches, because they like the salty taste of human sweat.

CHANGING FORESTS

Wild animals are not alone in finding coniferous forests useful. For hundreds of years, people have harvested conifers for their timber, because it is often dead straight and easy to work. During the 1800s, millions of conifers were used for making sleepers for railways, and millions more ended up as pit props in mines. Today, conifer wood is used in construction and for making paper, and conifer resin is used for making all kinds of products, from ink and solvents to glue.

Despite this, the world's coniferous forests are not shrinking, so they are in no danger of dying out. But they are changing. Every year, large areas of forest are cut

▷ *After coniferous forests have been cut, they are often replanted with saplings grown in nurseries. Unlike wild trees, the saplings are bred to grow rapidly, and to produce straight-grained wood.*

down for their timber, and are then replanted or allowed to regrow. These planted forests are quite different from natural ones, because they often contain just one kind of tree. All the trees are the same age, and the forest is often cut down long before the trees mature. For most animals, these planted forests are difficult places to make a living.

PRESERVING OLD FORESTS

Alarmed by the spread of plantations, conservationists have been working hard to protect the remaining truly wild forests. One of the most important battlefronts has been in North America's Pacific northwest, which straddles the border between the USA and Canada. This region is one of the world's leading producers of timber, and most of the 'old growth' forest has already been cut down.

On the American side, the Olympic National Park protects one of the world's few coniferous rainforests – an extraordinary habitat where ancient trees grow over 100 m high. Further north, in Canada's Clayoquot Sound, a new biosphere reserve has been set up to safeguard ancient forest on Vancouver Island. Compared to the forest that has already been cut down, these reserves are small, but they show that ancient forests can be saved.

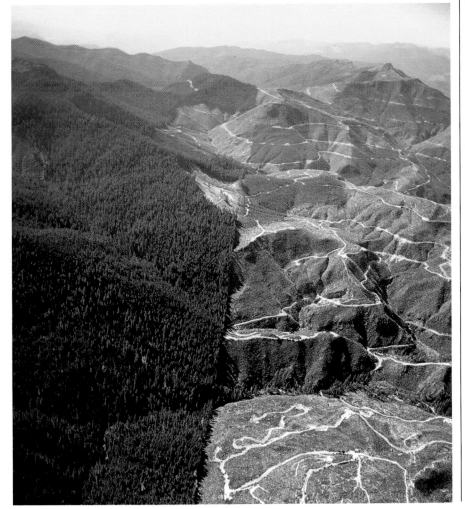

◁ *Running as straight as a ruler, a boundary line marks the edge of a recently cut block of forest. This view was taken in the Cascade Mountains, in North America's Pacific northwest.*

TROPICAL FORESTS

TROPICAL FORESTS TEEM WITH WILDLIFE, FROM
APES AND MONKEYS TO THE WORLD'S LARGEST
INSECTS. BUT MUCH OF THIS WILDLIFE IS
THREATENED, BECAUSE TROPICAL FORESTS
ARE DISAPPEARING FAST.

There are two main types of forest in the tropics. The kind
that most people have heard of − called tropical rainforest −
grows near the equator, where the climate is wet and warm
all year round. These steamy conditions can be really uncomfortable
for humans, but they are perfect for trees and other plants. The
other kind − called seasonal or monsoon forest − grows near the
edges of the tropics. Here, there is a long dry season each year.
In this habitat, plants and animals have to cope with torrential
rain followed by months of drought.

A SEE-SAW CLIMATE
In seasonal forest, the rainy season
begins in a spectacular way, when
electric storms light up the night
sky. At first, these storms are dry,
but a few days later the rain begins
to fall. As the heavy clouds roll in,
grape-sized raindrops crash their

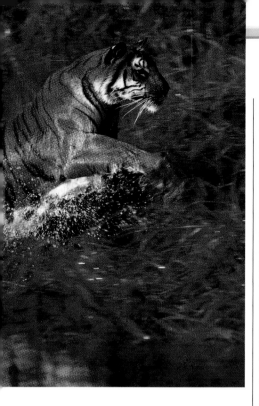

△ *Asia's tropical forests are home to three-quarters of the world's tigers – some of the most endangered predators in the world.*

▽ *Early morning mist snakes over the forest-covered hillsides of central Africa. These forests are the habitat of the rare mountain gorilla.*

way through the foliage and pound the forest floor. The forest often floods, but trees need this water, because this is the time when they start to grow.

Six months later, during the height of the dry season, the forest looks completely different. The floods have been replaced by drought, and most of the trees have shed their leaves. The air shimmers in the heat, and fallen leaves crunch underfoot. With so many bare branches, the forest looks like a winter landscape, but not all the trees are asleep. Instead, some of them choose this time of year to flower. One of the most famous of these dry-season flowerers is the jacaranda, which is covered with lilac blooms. This colourful tree has been planted in parks and gardens, and along roadsides, all over the tropical world.

TOP CATS
Seasonal forests grow right across the tropics, from Central and South

△ *Jacaranda trees grow wild in the forests of Bolivia and northern Argentina.*

America to Southeast Asia and northern Australia. In Asia, they are home to rhinos and elephants, as well as three of the world's biggest cats. The tiger is the largest, and also the one that is causing most concern to conservationists. A century ago, tigers were widespread across southern Asia. Today, they are dwindling fast, almost entirely because of hunting.

Tigers are dangerous animals, so it is not surprising that people do not want them living too close to home.

Reaching out with its arm, a baby orang utan plays with its older sister while its mother chews some food. Young orangs stay close to their mother until they are four years old, and after that they keep in touch by visiting her regularly. These gentle plant-eaters live in the forests of Southeast Asia – a part of the world that has been badly affected by deforestation in recent years.

237

But safety is not the main reason why tigers are killed – a more important factor is money. Tiger body parts are sold for use in traditional eastern medicines, and they fetch astronomical prices. A leg bone, for example, can be sold for around $5,000. It is illegal to sell tiger body parts, but with such huge profits at stake, the trade still goes on.

The second of the big three cats – the Asiatic lion – is a close relative of the lions that live in Africa. Asiatic lions once ranged across the Indian subcontinent, but today they live only in the Gir Forest Sanctuary in northeast India. There are only about 400 of these lions left, but their forest refuge is carefully guarded, so their future seems secure. From a distance, Asiatic lions look very similar to their African cousins, but two features tell them apart – their manes are smaller, and they have an unusual fold of skin

▽ *The jaguar is the largest cat in Central and South America. It looks very much like a leopard, but it behaves more like a tiger, hunting in thick forest and swamps. Jaguars like water and are good swimmers.*

running along their undersides.

Compared to tigers and lions, leopards have proved surprisingly good at coping with humans and habitat change. Like most cats, they are chiefly nocturnal, but they are not at all choosy about what they eat. Leopards can kill adult deer, but if this kind of food is hard to find, they will target much smaller prey, including rodents and even large insects. This adaptability helps them to get through hungry times.

FIGHTING FOR LIGHT

In seasonal forest, plants and animals have to fit in with the calendar, and they breed at particular times of the year. But in tropical rainforests, there are no real seasons, and life continues at the same hectic pace all year round. For rainforest plants, the most urgent priority is to get enough light – a tricky task in a habitat where so many plants live side by side. The forest's tallest trees grab their share by towering over smaller ones. Called emergents, they can be as tall as 12-storey buildings, and their crowns look like leafy islands floating on a deep green sea.

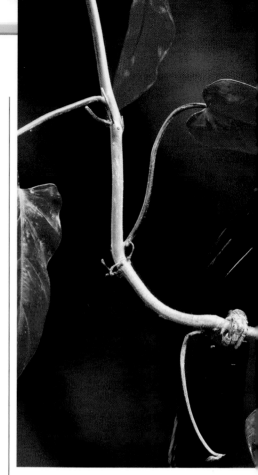

△ *Perched on a climbing plant, a fruit-eating toucan shows off its gigantic and brightly coloured beak. The beak is filled with air spaces, so it is not nearly as heavy or cumbersome as it looks.*

Before an emergent can reach this gigantic size, it has to fight its way upwards through the gloomy depths near the forest floor. To do this, many trees play a waiting game. They grow upwards, but stay thin, so they need only a small amount of energy to stay alive. Some never get past this stage, and they die before they reach a place in the sun. But others are luckier. If an old tree falls, light suddenly floods in from above, giving saplings the break that they need. They rush to fill the gap, and the winners stand a chance of becoming emergents themselves.

PRIVATE PERCHES

Some rainforest plants have a very different way of getting the daylight that they need. Instead of growing upwards, they spend their entire

△ *This bromeliad uses brilliant red leaves instead of flowers to attract pollinating animals.*

lives on branches and tree trunks high above the ground. These plants are called epiphytes, and they include thousands of kinds of orchids, as well as spiky-leaved bromeliads and ferns. Many

Species Profile

Oncidium orchid: *Oncidium* species

Oncidium orchids have amazingly showy flowers, but most of them live high in the forest canopy, so they are difficult to see. These orchids are usually pollinated by bees. Instead of visiting the flowers for nectar, male bees sometimes attack them – perhaps because the flowers smell like rival males. The male bee head-butts a flower and picks up its pollen, transferring it to the next flower that it attacks.

epiphytes could easily fit into a matchbox, but some are bigger than a dustbin, and can weigh more than a quarter of a tonne.

Unlike parasitic plants, epiphytes do not steal anything from their hosts. Instead, they get water from rain, and nutrients from dust and fallen leaves. Some bromeliads have their own water tanks, made of a circle of leaves, while others soak up water through special scales that are as absorbent as cotton wool. Staghorn ferns, from Australasia, even make their own private compost heaps, by trapping dead leaves that fall from above. Using this compost they can grow up to 2 m across.

DEADLY PASSENGERS

Epiphytes do not harm trees, although their combined weight can send branches crashing to the ground. But some perching plants have much more sinister ways of life. For rainforest trees, the most dangerous is the strangler fig.

This plant is a parasite, and it slowly smothers its host to death.

A strangler fig starts life high above the ground, from a seed that is lodged in a branch. When the seed germinates, it develops into a bush. The bush sprouts a handful of slender roots, and it is then that the trouble begins. These roots are as thin as a pencil, but they snake their way right down the tree's trunk, until they touch the ground. Once they reach it, the strangler starts to grow much faster than its host. Its roots become thicker and stronger, until they form a living straitjacket around the trunk. As the years go by, the strangler's grip tightens and the host tree is slowly choked and smothered to death.

After the host tree dies, its trunk often rots away completely, leaving the strangler standing on its own. Inside the strangler's trunk is a hollow space – a ghostly relic of the tree that it killed.

PARTNERSHIPS IN THE FOREST

Strangler figs depend on birds, because birds spread their seeds. They feed on the strangler's fruit, but the seeds pass through their bodies unharmed. When a bird lands on a branch, it often leaves

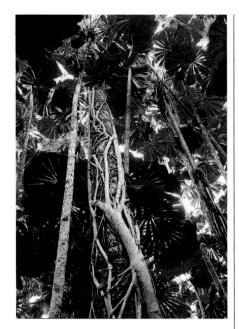

△ *This strangler fig is starting to tighten its hold around its host. The strangler's roots merge together wherever they cross.*

droppings containing some strangler seeds. In this convenient arrangement, both the bird and the strangler gain.

Partnerships like this are very common in tropical rainforests, because so many different kinds of plants and animals live close together. Animals not only spread seeds – they also pollinate rainforest flowers. In temperate forests, pollinating animals are almost always insects, but in the tropics very different animals perform this service as well. They include nectar-eating birds, such as hummingbirds and parrots, as well as hundreds of kinds of bats. Compared to insects, birds and bats are big and clumsy, so flowers that attract them have to be large and very tough. Bat-pollinated flowers are often creamy white, and they have a powerful musky smell after sunset that guides bats towards them in the dark.

Many pollinating animals visit a wide range of flowers, but some concentrate on one kind. One of the most remarkable of these pollinators is a hawkmoth from Madagascar. Its tongue measures up to 30 cm long, and it works like an extra-large drinking straw that can reach deep into orchid flowers. Once the

◁ *With their tapering wings and streamlined bodies, hawkmoths are designed for travelling at speed. They can fly long distances to find food.*

Species Profile

White-tipped sicklebill: *Eutoxeres aquila*

Most hummingbirds hover in front of flowers to feed, but the white-tipped sicklebill often clings to them with its claws. Its curved beak is the perfect shape to probe into flowers with a built-in bend, such as heliconias. Other hummingbirds have difficulty feeding on these, so the sicklebill has them more or less to itself. It lives in the forests of Central and South America.

moth has finished feeding, it rolls up its tongue and flies off to find its next meal.

A BUG-HUNTER'S PARADISE

Scientists do not know exactly how many insects live in rainforests, but they include at least 5,000 kinds of crickets, 40,000 species of butterflies and moths (and their hungry caterpillars) and over 100,000 types of beetles. Among them are some giants of the insect world. The goliath beetle, from central Africa, is the world's heaviest insect, weighing three times as much as a mouse. The harlequin longhorn beetle, from South America, has some of the longest antennae. Stretched out straight, they would reach most of the way across this page.

It takes patience to track down these monsters, as they are mainly active after dark. But ants are much easier to find, because most of them work during the day. At sunrise in the forests of Central and South America, leafcutter ants pour out of their subterranean nests and climb up into the trees. Walking out onto the thinnest twigs, they neatly snip off pieces of leaf, and then carry them underground. They use the leaves to grow a fungus that provides them with their food. Leafcutters are amazingly industrious, but they do not work when it rains. At the first sign of a downpour, they drop their loads, leaving a trail of leaf fragments leading to their nest.

THE NEST RAIDERS
Leafcutters are relatively harmless, but many tropical forest ants have powerful bites or stings. Weaver ants live in bushes and trees, and although they are small, they ferociously attack anything that comes within reach. These tiny ants make pouch-shaped homes out of leaves, sewing them together with sticky silk. Army and driver ants are even more dangerous. These nomadic insects live in roving swarms, which can be up to 100,000 strong. They surge across the forest floor, overpowering anything that is too small or too slow to escape. As dusk falls, the worker ants stop moving and link up their bodies to make a temporary camp on the forest floor. Called bivouacs, these camps can be as big as footballs, with the queen ant hidden inside.

▽ *These leafcutter ants are carrying pieces of leaf back to their nest. The ant taking a free ride is a 'minima' worker – it will process the leaf once it is stored underground.*

△ *Many forest insects use bright colours to warn that they are dangerous, but this longhorn beetle is bluffing, because it is quite harmless.*

Few animals dare to feed on army ants, although some birds flutter around their swarms. Called antbirds, they do this to pick off insects and other animals trying to get away. But some forest mammals specialize in breaking into ant and termite nests. They include the lesser anteater, or tamandua, from South America, and scale-covered pangolins from Africa and Asia. They are all good climbers, and they have long, sticky tongues to lick up their food.

EIGHT-LEGGED HUNTERS
Some rainforest spiders protect themselves by looking like ants, even though they do not have stings. Rainforests are also home to giant

◁ *Green tree pythons are born brown, red or yellow. This young python has caught a mouse. Like all tree snakes, it has no difficulty swallowing upside down.*

lizards, because low temperatures make it hard for them to move about. But in tropical forests, conditions could hardly be better. It is always warm, and there are plenty of places to hide. Snakes and lizards are experts in the art of camouflage, and many of them are agile climbers. Tree pythons and boas lie in wait with their tails wrapped tightly around a branch. If a bird or monkey comes within range, the snake suddenly lunges forwards with the front of its body, grabbing the prey in its jaws. In the forests of Central America, the slender eyelash pit-viper uses a similar technique, but it often lurks close to flowers. It waits for hummingbirds, snatching them out of the air as they feed.

Rainforest lizards do not have fangs or venom, so they need camouflage to hide away from birds. Many of them are green, but Australian leaf-tailed geckos have an intricate pattern of grey and brown markings, which makes them almost invisible when they rest on bark. To make their camouflage even more effective, their bodies are almost flat, so they do not cast any tell-tale shadows that might give them away.

orb-weaving spiders, which make webs up to 1.5 m across. But the largest webs of all are made by social spiders. These live in groups of several thousand animals, and they work together to spin enormous networks of silk up to 500 m long. Together, they can catch much larger prey than if they lived on their own. But the rainforest's most famous spiders do not build webs at all. They spend the day underground

emerging to hunt after dark. Although they are called bird-eating spiders, or tarantulas, these predators have a very varied menu. They hunt by touch, feeling for their prey with hairy legs that can measure up to 28 cm from tip to tip. Once the spider has pinned down its victim, its poisonous fangs set to work. Birds often manage to escape, but insects, frogs and other small animals are not so lucky. The spider usually feeds on the spot, before returning to its burrow at dawn.

TREE-CLIMBING SNAKES
In cold parts of the world, forests are not good places for snakes and

LIFE ON THE FOREST FLOOR
Like the bird-eating spider, most forest floor animals hide away when the sun is up. Butterflies are a big exception, however. Although they usually live high in the treetops, many of them flutter down to the ground at least once a day. They make these journeys to feed on salts and other substances that are essential for their diet. Butterflies find these in wet soil, in rotting fruit and also in droppings left behind by animals. At good feeding sites, hundreds

of them push and jostle as they try to get their share.

At the first sign of trouble, butterflies quickly flutter into the air. But even in broad daylight, tiny poison-arrow frogs show no signs of fear. Small enough to fit in a thimble, these brilliantly coloured amphibians hop over leaves and fallen logs, searching for small insects and worms. Poison-arrow frogs can afford to be confident, because their bodies contain some of the most powerful poisons in the animal world. Their gaudy colours warn other animals to leave them well alone.

Poison-arrow frogs are found only in Central and South America. At one time, several kinds were used to make poison-tipped arrows, which is how they got their name.

TREETOP CHORUS

Compared to rainforest insects, few large animals manage to live entirely on leaves. This is because rainforest leaves are tough, and they often contain substances that make them taste unpleasant, or difficult to digest. Insects have evolved ways around these chemical defences, but only a handful of mammals eat leaves full-time. Howler monkeys are some of the most successful. They live in tropical forests from Mexico to northern Argentina, and they are famous for their extremely loud calls. The calls are made by the males, which have a throat chamber that works like an amplifier, built in just below the chin. Howlers live in small troops, and they use their calls to mark their feeding territories high up in the trees.

◁ *Threatened by a predator, a tamandua uses its prehensile tail like a prop, allowing it to rear up on this termite nest and slash with its front claws.*

▷ *This bug-eyed horned katydid lives in the Amazon rainforest. Katydids usually eat leaves and fruit, but their powerful jaws can deliver a painful bite.*

△ *A woolly spider monkey's tail works like an extra leg, leaving its hands free to collect food. This female is hanging from a branch, with a baby clinging to her fur.*

Monkeys live throughout the tropics, but only New World monkeys – including howlers – have fully prehensile tails. These tails can wrap around branches, and they have a patch of bare skin on the underside that gives them

a good grip. Howler monkeys have heavy bodies, and they usually hang on with their hands and feet as well. But spider monkeys are more lightly built, and they often dangle from branches using their tails and nothing else.

PRIMATES IN MINIATURE

Tropical forests are home to over half the world's primates – the group of animals that includes apes, monkeys and their relatives. Gorillas are the largest, while the smallest are mouse lemurs, which live in the forests of Madagascar. The rufous mouse lemur weighs about 40 g, which is roughly the same as a chicken's egg. These tiny creatures feed on fruit, nectar and insects, using their sharp hearing and eyesight to find food after dark. Madagascar is famous for its bizarre primates, but other parts of the

▽ *Male morpho butterflies can be as big as a human hand, with beautiful metallic-blue wings. These butterflies often glide through the forest a few metres above the ground, searching for their favourite food – rotting fruit.*

Species Profile

Tarsier: *Tarsius* species

Tarsiers are related to monkeys, but they behave more like tree frogs, using their strong back legs to jump from branch to branch. They can leap more than 40 times their own length, and move about almost entirely after dark. There are five species of tarsier, and they all live in the forests of Southeast Asia.

world have theirs too. One of the most agile is the tarsier, from the forests of Southeast Asia, which leaps on insects after dark. This pocket-sized primate hunts by sight, using enormous eyes that are bigger than its brain.

Despite the huge difference in their sizes, primates share many features. Most of them have nails rather than claws, and fingers and toes that are good at gripping. Their eyes face forwards, which helps them to judge distances when they jump. Compared to other rainforest mammals, primates are often slow to reproduce. Tarsiers, for example, have just one baby at a time, and it takes nearly six months before it is ready to be born.

FORESTS AND THE FUTURE

Sadly for primates – and for many other animals – tropical forests are disappearing fast. Already, more than one third of the world's primates are threatened with extinction, together

> There are more
than 100 kinds of
poison-arrow frogs.
They usually feed on
the ground, but they
can also climb well,
because their toes end
in sticky pads. These
strawberry poison-arrow
frogs, from Costa Rica,
are only 2.5 cm long.

with hundreds of
tropical forest birds,
from parrots to toucans,
and thousands of plants.
Some of these species
are rare because they are
hunted or collected, but
many are in trouble because
they live in a shrinking
world, where bulldozers and
chainsaws move closer every
day. Once the timber has been
removed, people move in and
the forest is replaced by farms.
    Humans have cut down
forests for thousands of years,
and people depend on farmland
for food. But tropical forests are
being cleared at a record rate,
destroying some of the richest
wildlife habitats in the world.
Endangered species – such as
orang utans – can be helped by
keeping them in reserves, but
this rescue work is expensive, and
it can only protect a tiny fraction
of the forest species. Because
tropical forests are so rich and
complicated, we cannot save their
wildlife without saving forests too.

RIVERS, LAKES AND WETLANDS

FOR PLANTS, ANIMALS AND MICROLIFE,
FRESHWATER IS ONE OF THE MOST POPULAR
HABITATS ON EARTH. SOME SURVIVE IN THE
TINIEST PUDDLES, BUT OTHERS TRAVEL LONG
DISTANCES BETWEEN FRESHWATER AND THE SEA.

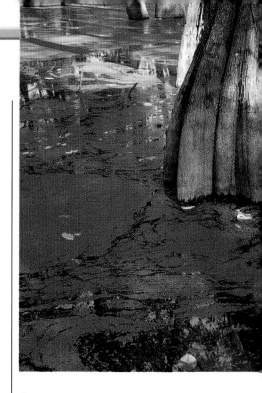

If all the world's water was shrunk so that it filled a bucket, the amount contained in rivers, lakes and wetlands would not even fill a thimble. But because the planet is so large, freshwater habitats can be immense. Russia's Lake Baikal, for example, is nearly 2 km deep, while the River Amazon is over 6,500 km long. Every year, it empties 50 billion tonnes of rainwater back into the sea. Compared to seawater, freshwater is often full of nutrients, which makes it a good habitat for living things. But freshwater habitats can dry up in summer or freeze in winter, and in rivers, there is the risk of being swept away.

SMALL BEGINNINGS
Lakes and ponds are great places for studying nature, because they are home to an incredible variety of living things. These watery worlds contain lots of animals, but, just as on land, life ultimately depends on plants. This is because plants make the food that animals need to survive. In freshwater, the smallest 'plants' are microscopic algae which drift near the surface of the water.

▽ *The glass-like surface of this South American river conceals a world that is teeming with life. This is the home of giant freshwater fish, and also of the Amazonian river dolphin, or bôto.*

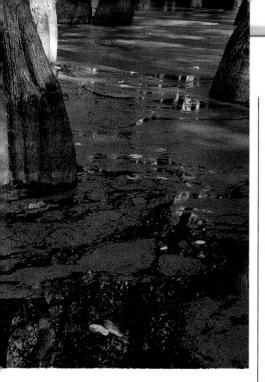

△ *North American bald cypresses are some of the few conifers that can grow in swamps.*

Although they are tiny, algae can reproduce at an amazing rate, sometimes turning the water bright green. These minute specks are devoured by microanimals, which provide food for larger hunters, such as newly hatched fish. One common pond animal, called a hydra, gets the best of both worlds. Its body contains thousands of single-celled algae, which it shelters in return for food. But the hydra also has stinging tentacles, and it uses these to grab smaller animals passing by. Hydras can move, but only slowly, so they have to be alert for predators. If anything threatening comes too close, they quickly pull in their tentacles until the danger has passed.

REEDS AND REEDBEDS

Most waterplants have roots, so they can anchor themselves on the bottom. Some stay underwater all their lives, but most grow upwards so they can flower in the open air. One of the most successful of these plants is the common reed – an extra-tall grass that is probably the most widespread flowering plant in the world. Common reed grows from the Arctic as far south as Australia, and it lives in ponds and ditches, and also in shallow lakes and lagoons. Where there is enough space, it forms waterlogged reedbeds that stretch as far as the eye can see.

Reedbeds are bad places for taking

▷ *Hydras reproduce by growing tiny buds, which break off to start life on their own. This adult hydra has grown a two-day-old 'baby', which is still fastened to its side.*

△ *Reedbeds often look deserted in winter, but closely packed reed stems make good hiding places for moorhens and other birds.*

Species Profile

Giant waterlily: *Victoria amazonica*

This South American waterlily grows the largest floating leaves in the world. Each leaf can be up to 2 m across, and contains hundreds of air spaces that make it float. Its raised rim has a single notch to let rain drain away, and the underside is reinforced by prickly struts. A large leaf can hold a child's weight – as long as he or she is lying down.

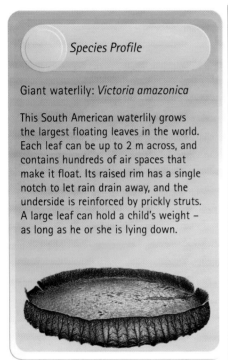

a walk, but they make perfect hideaways for birds. Starlings and swallows use them as night-time roosts, but other birds feed in them and use them as places for raising their young. Herons and bitterns nest on the ground, but the reed warbler stays high and dry. This skilful builder weaves a cup-shaped nest out of dead leaves, using reed stems as props.

FLOATING ON THE SURFACE

Waterlilies have a very different way of growing. Unlike reeds, their stems are floppy, and their leaves are designed to float. Waterlilies can live in water several metres deep, and they grow up from the bottom each spring. When their leaves reach the surface, they unroll and lay flat like plates. Some are only the size of a coin, but the largest leaves – grown by giant waterlilies from South America – are as big as a paddling pool, and have 15 cm-high rims. Waterlily leaves contain air cells, just like sheets of bubblewrap, and they have a waxy upper surface that makes rain roll off. These features mean that 'lilypads' are practically unsinkable. They make ideal perches for dragonflies, and also useful stepping stones for jacanas – small birds with outsize feet. Fish also use them as a security screen, to hide from hungry birds.

◁ *Watched by their nestlings, parent herons greet each other at their treetop nest. Many other wetland birds build their nests on the ground.*

△ *Waterlilies are pollinated by insects, and they flower at different times. Some close up at sunset to keep insects 'on board' overnight.*

Waterlily flowers attract lots of different insects, but beetles are their most frequent visitors. Some waterlily flowers close up at sunset, trapping their visitors inside. During the night, the insects become thoroughly dusted with pollen, and they carry it off when the flower opens the following day.

THE DRIFTERS

Some freshwater plants have cut adrift from the bottom, and spend their lives afloat. The commonest by far are duckweeds, which look like tiny green pills. Duckweeds are the world's smallest and simplest flowering plants. The tiniest species of all, from Australia, is no bigger than a grain of salt. Instead of leaves and stems, they have a rounded plant 'body' and, in most cases, just a single trailing root. Stagnant ponds and shady ditches are ideal duckweed habitats. Here, they cover the surface in floating lawns which can contain tens of thousands of duckweed plants. When autumn arrives, the plants sink to avoid being frozen, and the duckweed disappears until the following year.

In warm parts of the world, stagnant pools are often covered with floating ferns. Unlike land ferns, these ferns are small and flat, and many of them have leaves that are covered with water-repellent 'hair'. When it rains, the water rolls off, so the fern does not sink. One kind of water fern often lives in flooded paddy fields that are used for growing rice. It is a useful plant, because it contains bacteria that help to fertilize the soil.

△ *Covered with duckweed, a bullfrog looks out across a pond. In many parts of the world, duckweed does not flower – it relies on animals to spread it from pond to pond.*

A much bigger plant, called water hyacinth, is even better at spreading. Water hyacinth originally came from slow-flowing waters in South America, but it was carried around the world by plant collectors because it has beautiful flowers. Unfortunately, this attractive emigrant proved much too successful, and in some parts of the world it is now a serious pest. In Africa's Lake Victoria, water hyacinth covers hundreds of square kilometres of shallow water, and it smothers wildlife and clogs up boats. Scientists are working on ways to control it, but they face a long struggle because it is so widespread.

The largest drifter of all is a plant called papyrus, which can be over 4 m tall. Papyrus comes from Africa, and the ancient Egyptians discovered how to flatten it to make paper over 4,000 years ago. Normally, papyrus grows at the water's edge, but it sometimes breaks away in drifting islands many metres across. In the Sudd – a swamp in the upper reaches of the Nile – some of these islands are inhabited by people,

◁ *With its amazingly long toes, a jacana uses waterlily leaves as floating platforms. There are eight kinds of jacana, and most live in warm parts of the world. This one is common in Southeast Asia and Australia.*

while others make handy pens for farm animals.

PART-TIMERS

Freshwater animals include permanent residents and part-timers. Some of the part-timers, such as otters, shuttle between the water and land every day. Others spend their early lives in water, and then leave it when they grow up. Most of these animals emerge on their own, but mayflies burst out in fluttering swarms, creating one of the most impressive spectacles in the freshwater world.

The best time to see these swarms is on calm summer evenings, along

△ *The hippo is the largest and most dangerous freshwater mammal. Male hippos are unpredictable, and their huge tusks can bite metre-wide holes in wooden boats.*

the banks of slow-flowing rivers. If conditions are right, immature mayflies crawl out of the water in their thousands, before shedding their skins and taking to the air. These insects take up to four years to develop, but the adults do not have working mouthparts and live for just a single day. After mating, the females scatter their eggs on the water in a final flight, and once this task is over, all the adults die.

CHANGING DIETS

For most other freshwater insects, adult life lasts much longer than this. Adult mosquitoes can survive for several weeks, while adult damselflies and dragonflies last for several months. To live this long they need food, and the young eat quite different things to the adults. Young damselflies and dragonflies feed on all kinds of water animals, and they snatch them with a lethal weapon called a mask, which is like a set of telescopic jaws. The adults are also predatory, but they use their legs to snatch other flying insects in mid-air. But for mosquitoes, growing up means a much bigger

▽ *Papyrus is one of the world's most useful waterplants. In ancient Egypt, it was used not only for making paper, but also for mats, cloth and even sails.*

change in diet. Young mosquitoes feed on microscopic organisms that they filter out of the water, and they can survive in the smallest imaginable habitats, including the water that collects in abandoned tyres. Once they become adult, they switch to liquids – nectar for males, and for females, blood.

RETURNING TO WATER
Because freshwater habitats are often scattered, animals have to be in the right place at the right time to breed. Flying insects are well equipped to do this, because they can easily move from place to place. Mosquitoes can find

Species Profile

Eurasian river otter: *Lutra lutra*

Sleek, lithe and agile, otters divide their time between land and water. Like other freshwater otters, this species has webbed feet, a streamlined body and extremely thick fur. When it dives to catch fish, the surface of its coat gets wet, but its underfur stays dry. It breeds in riverbank dens, and it is a remarkably playful animal, sometimes sliding into the water just for fun.

△ *Mosquito larvae have to come up for air. Hanging beneath the surface, they breathe through a 'snorkel' that has a water-repellent tip.*

water by sensing the humidity of the air, but many other insects – including dragonflies – find it by sight. Occasionally, they make mistakes: diving beetles, for example, sometimes crash into greenhouses on moonlit nights, because they mistake the shiny glass for the surface of a pond.

For frogs and toads, the breeding season starts with a journey back to the particular pond or lake where they started life as tadpoles. In many species, the males arrive first, and begin a loud chorus of croaking that attracts the females towards them. When the females arrive, the males compete with each other in a furious scramble for the chance to mate. Once mating is over, they often abandon the water, leaving the tadpoles to grow up on their own.

Frogs and toads find their way by building up a memory map of their surroundings, which guides them towards their goal. Because frogs and toads do not have good eyesight, this map works by smell. If a frog or toad is moved a few kilometres from its own home area, it will often discover a new place to breed. But it seems that amphibians have good memories, because after three or four years, many of them return to their original homes.

LONG-DISTANCE MIGRANTS

Amphibians are not the world's fastest movers, so their annual journeys are quite short. But rivers and lakes are also home to some of the greatest travellers in the animal kingdom. These are fish that divide their lives between freshwater and the open sea. Fish do this to get the best of two different worlds.

For most of them, freshwater is a safer place to breed, while the sea is a better place to find food. But strangely, this rule does not always hold true, because some migratory fish do the reverse. The Atlantic salmon returns to freshwater to lay its eggs.

△ *Damselflies are graceful predators that flutter over pools and streams. They live all over the world, from the steamy tropics to Arctic tundra.*

Adults make their first return journey at the age of three or four years, and they navigate by taste, finding their way back across the ocean to exactly the same river

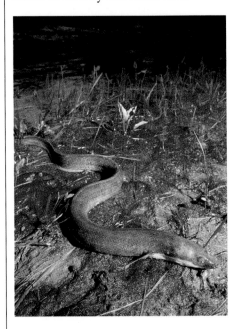

△ *Slithering over the ground, a European eel makes its way towards a pond. Eels are covered in slimy mucus that stops them drying out.*

where they grew up. The upriver journey is exhausting, but they eat nothing on the way. Once the fish have laid their eggs, some are so weak that they die, but most manage to return to the sea.

MYSTERIOUS TRAVELS
Atlantic salmon can migrate over 1,000 km, but the European eel's migration is longer still. Unlike the salmon, this snake-like fish starts life in the open ocean, in a part of the west Atlantic known as the Sargasso Sea. From here, young eels travel northeast with the ocean currents until they arrive at the coast of Europe after a journey lasting over two years. Once here, they make their way upstream, to the rivers and wetlands where they slowly grow up. After a 'childhood' lasting up to 30 years, the eels

△ When frogs and toads breed, the male holds on to the female for several days. Males often have special pads on their thumbs to stop them slipping off.

▽ For migrating salmon, waterfalls are a major obstacle on the way to their breeding grounds. These muscle-packed fish can make vertical leaps of over 3 m at a time.

With their elegant shape and pink plumage, flamingos are among the world's most beautiful wetland birds. They can be up to 1.5 m tall, but despite their size, they feed entirely on microscopic water plants and animals. To collect this food, they use their strangely shaped beaks as sieves. Flamingos often feed in huge flocks, and they live in some of the toughest wetland habitats on earth. In East Africa and South America, they feed in barren, salt-encrusted lakes where daytime temperatures can reach over 40° C

△ *American alligators prey on anything that moves. Young ones eat small fish, crabs and even snails, but the adults tackle much larger animals. They have even been known to attack cattle.*

become adult and are ready to breed.

This is the time when eels move downriver, on a one-way journey that takes them to their distant spawning grounds. These adult eels have silvery skin and large eyes, which suggests that they travel in deep water as they cross the ocean. But no one knows for certain how deep they swim or which route they take because, amazingly, not a single adult European eel has ever been caught at sea.

FRESHWATER WETLANDS
In rivers and lakes, there is plenty of open water, making it easy to spot any animals on the move.

▽ *The gharial is a large Asian crocodile with an amazingly long and slender snout. In the mid-1970s, gharials almost became extinct, but a conservation programme is now helping the species to survive.*

But wetlands are a different matter. Here, the water is often hidden by plants, providing lots of places for wildlife to hide away. Marshes are one example of a wetland, but they also include dozens of other soggy habitats, from peat bogs in the Arctic to sticky tropical swamps.

Wetlands can be hostile places for humans, because they are full of hazards, from poisonous snakes to treacherous mud. But for animals and plants, these waterlogged worlds can be ideal places to live. One of the world's largest wetlands – Florida's Everglades – is home to over 250 species of birds, as well as the American alligator, one of the largest reptiles in the world. In southern Africa, the Okavango Delta is even richer. This wetland is formed by a river that empties inland, instead of flowing out to sea. Its inhabitants include hippos, elephants and antelope, as well as some of the largest and noisiest frogs and toads in the world. It is also a favourite haunt of the black heron – the only bird that fishes under the shade of an umbrella, made by its outstretched wings.

DROUGHT
In cool parts of the world, wetlands stay wet all year round. But in the tropics, some of them dry out for several months every year. As the water level begins to drop, plants die back and animals find

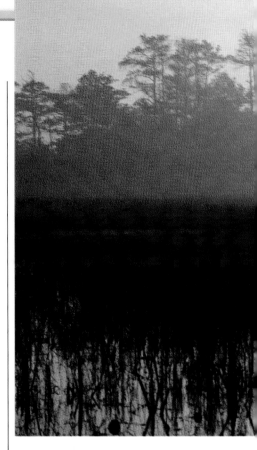

△ *Perched on an airboat, park rangers skim through Florida's Everglades. Wildlife here faces many problems, such as hurricanes, falling water levels and expanding cities.*

themselves crowded into a smaller and smaller space. When life gets really difficult, birds can always fly off, but water animals need other ways of surviving.

In the Everglades, alligators get around this problem by excavating private ponds, called 'gator holes'. While the rest of the ground dries out, gator holes stay full of water. These holes are scattered across the landscape, and they are not only used by alligators – fish, turtles and frogs take refuge in them as well. In other parts of the world, crocodiles and caimans often bury themselves in the mud. Like alligators, they can survive without eating for several months, and often a pair of nostrils surrounded by mud is the only sign that gives them away.

Wetland fish are good at surviving

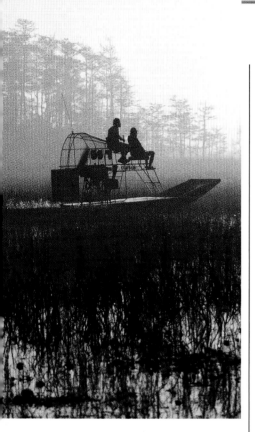

in shallow water, but when a drought really begins to bite, they take emergency action too. Catfish can crawl from pond to pond, while lungfish bury themselves in the mud and surround themselves with slimy cocoons. As long as they stay moist, they can keep alive by breathing air. Other fish are not so lucky. They die in their thousands, but they leave behind their eggs, which hatch when the rains return.

LOOKING AHEAD

Natural droughts are not the only challenge that freshwater plants and animals have to face. In many countries, humans are using so much freshwater that wetlands are drying out permanently. Water pollution is another problem, because humans have used rivers and lakes as a free way of getting rid of waste.

In Florida, water that once flowed through the Everglades is now diverted to farmland and to cities. As a result, half the state's wetlands have disappeared. This change has hit many of the Everglades' natural

inhabitants. In Europe, many former wetland areas have been drained and used to grow crops. Today, only a tiny fraction of Europe's original wetlands remain.

Water pollution harms river life, but it is particularly damaging when it affects lakes. This is because lakes are dead ends – once polluting chemicals flow into them, they can stay there for years. During the 1970s, pollution in North America's Great Lakes became so bad that most of their fish disappeared. In Russia, it threatens the unique wildlife of Lake Baikal, while in East Africa, it threatens the flamingos that feed in the Rift Valley's salt lakes.

It is too late to bring back most of the wetlands that have disappeared, but thanks to anti-pollution laws, many rivers in industrialized countries are now cleaner than they were a

▽ *A green anaconda is lifted out of a swamp. This South American snake is the world's heaviest, weighing up to 250 kg. It spends most of its life in or near water.*

hundred years ago. But as the world's population grows, more freshwater will be needed, and more waterborne waste will be produced. The battle to save freshwater habitats will be fought all over the world.

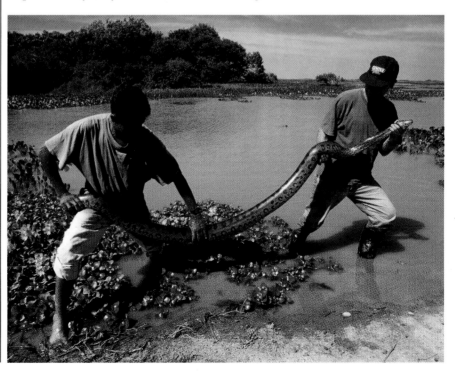

MOUNTAINS AND CAVES

LIFE IS TOUGH AT THE TOP – PARTICULARLY IF YOUR HOME IS SWEPT BY ICY WINDS, BURIED BY SNOW OR SCORCHED BY THE GLARE OF THE MIDDAY SUN. BUT NATURE'S MOUNTAIN-DWELLERS ARE WELL ADAPTED TO THESE CONDITIONS, AND THEY TAKE THEM IN THEIR STRIDE.

Mountains are an important habitat for wildlife, because they exist in every continent on earth. But living in mountains is no easy matter. For every 1,000 m that an animal climbs, the temperature drops by 5° C. To make matters worse, the air gets thinner, so it becomes harder to breathe. Plants also face problems, because mountain soil is thin, and there is very little shelter. Caves are a completely different habitat. Here, there is no weather, but there is also no light and very little food.

▽ *High up on the slopes of Mount Kenya, giant lobelias are the tallest plants. As the sun sets, their leaves fold inwards to keep out the cold.*

HIGH-ALTITUDE PLANTS
In 1887, a Hungarian explorer named Samuel Teleki climbed Mount Kenya in East Africa. As he neared the summit, he travelled through some of the most unusual vegetation in the world.

On its lower slopes, Mount Kenya is covered by evergreen tropical forest, which then gives way to bamboo. But at an altitude of about 3,500 m, the bamboo is replaced by alpine moorland, which is home to giant lobelias and groundsels, enormous heathers and many other remarkable plants. At nearly 4,500 m, this strange landscape is replaced by fields of ice and snow, which lead to the mountain's triple summit.

Since Teleki's pioneering expedition, scientists have discovered equally strange mountain plants in other parts of the world. Mauna Kea – an immense volcano in

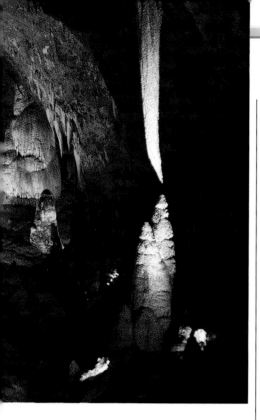

△ Unlike mountainsides, caves do not have any natural light, so plants cannot grow inside them. Animals survive by eating food from outside, or each other.

Hawaii – is the only habitat of the silversword, a spectacular plant that grows on lava fields close to the summit. In Venezuela, flat-topped mountains called *tepuis* are like gardens floating in the clouds. Here, the plants are small and stunted, but they include hundreds of species that are found nowhere else in the world.

DOUBLE PROTECTION

Mount Kenya and Mauna Kea owe their strange plant life to the fact that they are completely alone. These mountains are like ecological islands, and their plants have evolved in isolation, with hardly any contact with the outside world. Mount Kenya lies exactly on the equator, so the sunshine here is fierce. Plants like the giant lobelia are protected by a layer of felt-like hair, which stops the intense ultraviolet light from burning up their leaves. This covering also comes in handy at night, because temperatures can drop well below freezing on the upper slopes. Mauna Kea's silverswords have evolved exactly the same adaptation, although they live on the other side of the planet.

In most other parts of the world, mountains are linked together in ranges, so plants can spread from one mountain to another. Conifers are particularly good at coping with sunshine and cold, which explains why they grow on mountains all over the globe. In the Rocky Mountains, these extra-tough trees include some of the oldest living things in the world – bristlecone pines. For a bristlecone, 1,000 years old is young, while 3,000 is only middle-aged.

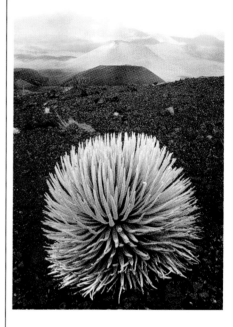

△ With its felt-covered leaves, the silversword plant is well protected from the sun. After growing for about 20 years, it produces a giant flowerhead and then dies.

Running from Canada to New Mexico, the Rocky Mountains reach a height of over 4,000 m. With their jagged peaks and year-round snow, these mountains are home to the bighorn sheep – one of the animal world's greatest climbers. Bighorns can scale near-vertical slopes using their non-slip hooves.

SURVIVAL ABOVE THE TREE LINE

On high mountains, trees stop growing at the point where frost kills their buds. This altitude is marked by the tree line – a ragged frontier that separates forested slopes from much tougher terrain. On tropical mountains like Mount Kenya, the tree line is high up, but in colder places, such as Alaska, it can be as little as 750 m above sea level.

Plants that live above the tree line have to face the worst of the

△ *Like many mountain plants, moss campion has long roots, so that it can grow on slopes of loose rock. When it dies, it helps to create soil that other plants can use.*

△ *In the White Mountains of California, bristlecone pines live for more than 5,000 years. On the highest slopes, they are twisted and gnarled by the mountain climate.*

weather, and most of them survive by having tough stems, small leaves and a cushion-like shape. This gives them maximum protection from the wind, and helps to stop them drying out. During the winter, they are often covered by snow. This actually helps them, because it keeps them much warmer than they would be in the open air. These plants are known as alpines. Many of them – such as moss campion – start growing before the snow has fully thawed. As soon as it starts to clear, their flowers burst open, giving them an early start in the race to produce their seeds.

STRANDED ON THE SLOPES

Spring is also the time when mountain insects begin to stir. Many of these animals spend the winter as eggs or chrysalises, which can be frozen solid for several months without being harmed. As the days

lengthen in spring, they thaw and start to develop, and insects appear as if by magic, crawling or fluttering across the slopes. On mountains, flying insects include midges, bees and butterflies, all of which stay low to keep out of the wind. Butterflies usually avoid cold places, but apollos specialize in life high up. These butterflies fly slowly, and their bodies are covered with furry scales, helping to keep them warm.

Butterflies need plants, and they normally steer clear of ice and snow. But ice bugs, or grylloblattids, survive under rocks near the snow line, and sometimes even higher. These primitive insects do not have wings, and some of them do not have eyes. They feed on other animals – including insects that have been blown uphill by the wind, leaving them stranded in the cold. In the Rocky Mountains, grasshoppers sometimes become stranded like

△ *Apollo butterflies live on mountains in Asia, Europe and North America. They make chrysalises that are hidden in low-growing plants, wrapped in silken webs.*

this when they migrate. Grasshopper Glacier, in Montana, contains millions of dead grasshoppers. The ones deepest down are thought to be several centuries old.

MOUNTAIN MAMMALS

Unlike insects, mammals are warm-blooded, so they can stay active no matter how cold it gets. But mammals need more oxygen than insects, which can be a problem where the air is thin. Mountain species make up for this by having larger lungs, bigger hearts, and more oxygen-carrying cells in their blood. Vicunas, from South America, spend their lives in mountain grassland up to 5,000 m high. At this altitude, the air is so thin that engines have

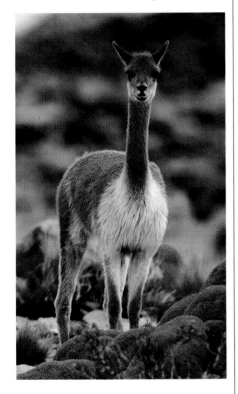

△ *Despite its dainty appearance, the vicuna is one of the toughest animals on four hooves. It lives on the Altiplano – a high-altitude plateau in the central Andes.*

trouble starting, and planes need extra-long runways to take off. But thanks to their special adaptations, vicunas can run up steep slopes without even getting out of breath.

The snow leopard, a beautiful predator from central Asia, hunts well above the tree line, reaching an altitude of 5,500 m, and perhaps more. But the altitude record for large mammals belongs to the yak, a grazing animal related to farmyard cattle. Yaks live in the dry and windswept slopes of the Himalayas, and in summer, they roam as high as 6,100 m. In the Himalayas, yaks are often kept as domesticated animals, because they are useful for milk and for carrying loads. Wild yaks, on the other hand, have become very rare.

WINTER RETREAT

Snow leopards can usually find prey all year round, but for grazers, winter is a difficult time. Vicunas and yaks move to lower ground, and so do ground-feeding birds, such as grouse and ptarmigan. Even here, however, food can be difficult to find and the threat of starvation is never far away. To get around this problem, many smaller mammals use a different way of surviving: they hide away in underground burrows, and hibernate until winter has passed.

The champion hibernators are rodents, and some of them sleep for amazing periods of time. Marmots can hibernate for eight months of

Species Profile

Alpine marmot: *Marmota marmota*

Marmots are ground squirrels that live in open grassland and mountain pastures. The only kind found in western Europe is the Alpine marmot. It weighs up to 4.5 kg – over ten times as much as most tree squirrels – and it has a plump body, short legs, and walks with a rolling gait. The Alpine marmot often sits upright near its burrow, and it communicates with a high-pitched whistle.

the year, but some other ground squirrels manage even longer than this. Scientists studying one North American species, called the uinta ground squirrel, found that it was active for only 12 weeks a year. It sleeps through the whole of the winter, and also the autumn and much of the spring. During the summer, ground squirrels feed almost non-stop, because they need lots of body fat to keep them alive during their long sleep.

▽ *A sprinting snow leopard shows off its beautiful coat. This graceful predator is endangered because it is hunted for its fur.*

△ *Gathering on a rocky ledge, feathered scavengers arrive for a meal. The bird in the centre is a lammergeier – a specialist at making a meal from bones.*

GIANT SCAVENGERS

Compared to mammals, birds make light work of travelling over mountains. Geese have been seen flying over the highest peaks of the Himalayas, and radar echoes show that some birds fly higher still. In 1973, a plane hit a vulture at over 11 km – the highest altitude ever recorded for a bird. Birds can survive at this height because their lungs are extremely efficient at gathering oxygen, and because their plumage keeps out the intense cold.

Many birds migrate over mountains, but lots also use them as their homes. Vultures and birds of prey are tailor-made for this kind of habitat, because they need open spaces to search for food. The world's largest vulture is the Andean condor, with a wingspan of nearly 3 m. It soars on strong updraughts along mountain ridges, staying airborne for hours at a time. The condor nests on remote ledges, returning to the same one all its life. These nesting sites become splashed with white droppings, which are often easier to spot than the condors themselves.

In Africa, Asia and southern Europe, another mountain vulture has an extraordinary way of getting food. After it has stripped a carcass clean of meat, the lammergeier carries large bones into the air. It drops the bones onto rocks to break them open, then glides down to feed on the marrow inside.

BIRD MOUNTAINEERS

Mountain birds also include species that search for food on the ground.

▽ *The California condor is the rarest mountain vulture. In the 1980s, only three wild birds were left. Thanks to a breeding programme, there are now more than 170.*

Choughs probe mountain grassland for insects and worms, while wrens hop in and out of crevices, looking for spiders living among the rocks. But in the Alps and the Himalayas, the wallcreeper behaves much more like a true mountaineer. This small, grey bird has extra-sharp claws, and its uses them like crampons to get a grip on rock. Using its tail as a brace, it climbs up sheer walls and overhangs, inspecting the surface for any signs of food. Unlike a human mountaineer, however, the wallcreeper does not have to worry about falling off – it can abandon a climb at any moment by fluttering into the air.

LIFE UNDERGROUND

Before humans learned how to build, they often used caves as shelters. In one cave in France, footprints show that Ice Age humans reached at least 2 km underground. These people would have found their way with candles made of animal fat, although why they went this far, no one knows. But animals have lived in caves for far longer than humans. Unlike us, they can navigate in total darkness, and one of the ways they do this is by sound.

Bats use sound to hunt flying insects and to find their way to and from their homes. In one cave system, near San Antonio in Texas, USA, up to 50 million bats pour into the air every evening. After feasting on insects high in the sky, they make their way back into the caves to feed their young. Amazingly, the bats' echolocation system works even when such huge numbers are on the move. The bats do not only avoid hitting the cave's walls – they also avoid hitting each other.

In northern South America, Trinidad and Panama, the oilbird performs a very similar feat. It feeds

△ *Most fruit bats roost in trees, but these African fruit bats prefer rock crevices and caves. Each night, they take off in a group, flying up to 25 km to find food.*

on oily fruit, but it nests on rocky ledges up to 500 m underground. Oilbirds have good eyesight, but once they enter a cave they rely on bursts of sound to find their way to their chicks.

PERMANENT CAVE-DWELLERS

Bats and oilbirds are part-time cave-dwellers, but some animals spend their whole lives underground. For them, darkness is a minor problem – a much more important one is finding food. Caves do not have any plant life, so they do not produce any food of their own. Instead, their full-time inhabitants depend on food that comes from outside.

The menu in caves is based on waste and dead remains. At the top of the list are bat droppings, which can build up into knee-deep layers over hundreds of years. This rich refuse is mined by primitive animals called springtails, and by cave-dwelling millipedes and crickets. From time to time, dead bats drop onto the heap – a welcome extra dish that is packed with useful protein. While these animals feed, spiders and harvestmen prowl nearby, waiting to pick off any

scavenger that comes within reach.

In many caves, flowing water brings in particles of food from the world outside. This food nourishes a completely different collection of animals, including cave fish, cave salamanders and cave shrimps. Many of these animals have very small eyes and cannot see, but they are incredibly sensitive to movement, and to any smell that might lead to a meal.

△ *Deep in a cave, an oilbird stares at the camera. Oilbirds can navigate using vision or echolocation, no matter how dark it is.*

OCEANS

SEAWATER COVERS NEARLY THREE-QUARTERS OF THE WORLD'S SURFACE, BUT BECAUSE IT IS SO DEEP, IT MAKES UP OVER 95 PER CENT OF ALL THE LIVING SPACE ON EARTH. THE OCEANS ARE WHERE LIFE FIRST APPEARED, NEARLY FOUR BILLION YEARS AGO, AND THEY ARE STILL HOME TO MOST OF THE WORLD'S LIVING THINGS.

The oceans are so vast that they are like many habitats rolled into one. These habitats range from the sunlit shallows near tropical coasts to icy-cold sediment on the deep ocean floor. Oceans have their own mountains, valleys and plains, and they even have their own deserts – huge spaces of almost empty water, where a shortage of nutrients makes it difficult for living things to survive. Unlike life on land, ocean life does not have to face sudden changes in temperature, or natural disasters such as drought and fire. But living in the oceans is dangerous. No matter how carefully things protect themselves, or how fast they move, predators are always waiting to strike.

◁ *Giant spider crabs are the world's largest crustaceans, with a legspan of over 3.5 m. They are found in the north Pacific.*

LIFE AT THE SURFACE

If seawater was as transparent as air, the oceans would still be easy to see. The surface would look like a layer of mist, floating high above the

◁ Drifting close to the coast, a swarm of plankton looks like a blue-green stain. Plankton is normally invisible to the naked eye, but it can be detected by satellites orbiting above the oceans.

by collecting the energy in sunlight. Drifting among the algae are single-celled protozoans, and also a whole galaxy of planktonic animals, from newly hatched fish to the larvae of lobsters and crabs. These animals are eaten by larger hunters, which are swallowed by other predators in their turn. In the plankton, food is the most important thing in life, and everything – no matter how small – is on the menu of something else.

ATTACK FROM ABOVE

The busiest part of the plankton is nearest the surface, where there is maximum daylight for algae to use. This is also where most planktonic animals live, because it is the best place for them to find food. But the ocean's surface is a hazardous place, particularly for creatures that are big enough to be spotted from the air. Planktonic animals are the oceans' equivalent of insects,

and plenty of birds watch out for them, eager to get their share.

Terns splash headfirst into the water, and the same technique – dive-bombing larger prey – is used

△ Jellyfish live in all the world's oceans. These simple animals use stinging tentacles like fishing lines – most are harmless to humans, but a few can be deadly.

▽ Skimming over the waves, gulls keep a sharp eye open for food. Gulls usually stay close to the shore, but many other seabirds roam far out to sea, returning only to breed. For these birds, land is a strange and dangerous place.

seabed. In some parts of the oceans, the mist would be thin, but in others it would be more like fog on a winter's day.

This mysterious 'mist' really does exist, but water prevents us seeing it. It is formed by plankton – a floating mixture that teems with small and microscopic living things. Its most numerous inhabitants are single-celled algae, which live like plants

Species Profile

Storm petrel: *Hydrobates* species

Storm petrels are some of the world's most common seabirds, roving far out across the oceans. They feed mainly on shrimps, but they hardly ever settle on the water, despite spending most of their lives at sea. Storm petrels nest in burrows and crevices, but because they are clumsy on land, they come ashore at night, when there is less risk of being attacked by gulls. There are 24 species of these birds, but at sea they are very difficult to tell apart.

by gannets and boobies. Albatrosses do their fishing from the air, snapping up food as they glide close to the surface of the waves. Thanks to this in-flight refuelling, they can stay airborne for days at a time. But the world's smallest ocean-going birds, called storm petrels, feed in a quite different way. They look as if they are walking on water, because they patter their feet on the surface. Although they can be smaller than blackbirds, they sometimes roam thousands of kilometres from land.

MAKING AN ESCAPE

When Christopher Columbus sailed to the Americas, he became the first person to cross the Sargasso Sea, in the west Atlantic Ocean. Unlike all other seas, this one is an enormous swirl of calm water, famous for its drifts of floating weed. In Columbus's time, it developed a sinister reputation as a place where ships could become tangled up and sink.

The Sargasso Sea is not really this dangerous, but it is one of the few parts of the open ocean where animals have somewhere to hide. One local inhabitant, called the sargassum fish, is almost perfectly camouflaged for life among the floating weed. About the size of a thumb, it lurks completely motionless until something edible swims by. When this happens, its mouth opens in less than a fiftieth

▽ *Lurking under a tangle of floating weed, a sargassum fish is very difficult for other animals to spot. Its body has fleshy frills that look just like pieces of weed.*

◁ *Atlantic spotted dolphins' beak-shaped jaws contain over 120 small but sharply pointed teeth. They are often plain when young – they become spottier as they age.*

enemies are on their tails. One of the most dangerous is the needlefish. Up to 1.5 m long, and armed with spike-shaped jaws, it has been known to crash-land in boats, spearing people on board.

▽ *Needlefish have amazingly slender bodies, with snouts that taper to a narrow point. All their internal organs are stretched lengthways to fit inside.*

of a second, sucking the unfortunate victim inside. Across other parts of the oceans, there are no hiding places, and animals use different ways of concealing themselves. One common method is countershading – a two-tone colour scheme that works as camouflage in open water. Countershaded fish have dark backs, which makes them blend in against the water when seen from above. Their undersides are much paler, so they blend in against the light when seen from below. The same colour scheme can be seen in dolphins and also some of the largest whales.

SHOALS

In open water, sticking together is another tactic for avoiding attack, because it is more difficult for a predator to pick out a single animal from a shoal. Over half the world's

fish stay together in shoals when they are young, and a quarter stay together throughout their lives. In a shoal, fish often move with amazing precision. They twist and turn as if they are following secret commands, and if attacked they can form a living tunnel, so that predators swim right through the shoal. Shoals can react like this because fish have built-in pressure sensors, called lateral lines. Even without looking, each fish can tell how its neighbours are moving, so it can behave in a similar way. In extreme circumstances, open-water fish sometimes use other ways of making an escape. One of the most drastic is jumping right out of the water – a trick that can throw a predator off the trail. Flying fish can 'jump' up to 300 m, by gliding on their outstretched fins, and many other species make shorter leaps when

FILTER FEEDERS

Occasionally, sticking together can backfire, and lead fish into a trap. This is what happens when shoals of fish are hunted by humpback whales. Humpbacks circle around a shoal, and blow curtains of rising bubbles which surround the fish like a wall. Panicking, the fish form a tighter and tighter mass, until the whales suddenly burst up from below, swallowing thousands of fish at a time.

Humpbacks have unusually varied feeding techniques, and most of their relatives – including the blue whale – hunt smaller prey. These whales, which are known as rorquals, have deep grooves along their throats. The grooves stretch when the whales open their mouths, allowing them to take up several tonnes of water at a time. A rorqual then closes its

△ *Salps are some of the commonest animals in the sea, but because they are transparent, they often go unnoticed. These ones are fastened together in a chain.*

Species Profile

Basket star: *Gorgonocephalus* species

With its highly branched, writhing arms, the basket star is one of the strangest inhabitants of the seabed, measuring up to 50 cm across. It hides away during the day, but at night it creeps out and extends its arms to catch planktonic animals drifting past. The arms have tiny hooks that help trap food.

mouth, forcing the water through the bristly baleen plates that hang from its upper jaw. As the water is pumped out of the whale's mouth, almost all the plankton is left behind. It is the world's largest example of filter feeding – a highly efficient way of getting food which has made whales the largest mammals on earth.

Whales are well-known animals, but many smaller and less familiar creatures filter their food from the sea. Some of the most numerous are animals called salps, which look like tiny transparent barrels open at both ends. Salps take in water through their front opening and, after filtering it, they pump it out through the rear. This 'exhaust' works like a tiny jet engine, pushing the salp

along. Salps' filters are extremely fine, allowing them to collect bacteria and other kinds of microscopic food. They are very successful, and in some parts of the world's oceans, salps form invisible swarms hundreds of kilometres across.

OASES AND DESERTS

For centuries, fishermen have known that ocean life is not evenly spread. Some of the best fishing grounds are on continental shelves, where shallow water stretches a long way from the coast. Here, nets can reach down to the bottom, bringing up fish that live on or near the seabed. Continental shelves are important breeding grounds for fish, but many have been badly affected by fishing fleets. For example, the Grand Banks off Newfoundland once produced the biggest catches of cod in the world, but after decades of overfishing, the great shoals of cod have disappeared.

◁ *During the last 40 years, fishing has had a growing impact on ocean life. Modern boats can fish in water over 1,000 m deep, using sonar to track shoals.*

THE OCEAN DEEPS

Between the surface of the oceans and the seafloor below, there is a lot of water and an almost unbelievable amount of space. Just one cubic kilometre of ocean contains as much water as 500,000 Olympic swimming pools, but there are over one billion cubic kilometres of water in the oceans as a whole. Daylight quickly fades away with increasing depth, and below about 250 m, the oceans are permanently dark.

It is hard for any of us to imagine what this hidden world is really like. There is nothing to distinguish up from down, and no solid surfaces of any kind. The water is under intense pressure and its temperature is bone-chillingly cold. Sometimes there is a gentle current, but because everything is nudged along with it, the water seems perfectly still. But here and there, in this cavernous

No one knows for certain if – or when – they will come back.

Other prime fishing grounds are found where currents flow upwards towards the surface, bringing nutrients from far below. These nutrients work like fertilizer for plankton, creating food for enormous shoals of fish and squid. One of these upwelling zones is off the coast of northwest Africa, while an even richer one lies off Peru. But there are some parts of the oceans where fish are few and far between.

▽ *Hurling its 30-tonne body out of the water, a humpback whale 'breaches' during the breeding season.*

These are the oceans' great deserts, where the water contains so few nutrients that plankton finds it difficult to grow. Most of them are in the tropics, far from the nearest coasts. Without plankton, very little stirs in the water and hardly any birds cross the sky. Apart from the polar icecaps, these watery deserts are some of the emptiest places on earth.

△ *Most shark attacks on people happen near coasts. The great white has caused at least 300 human deaths, but it is rapidly becoming endangered itself.*

identify each other. In the abyssal zone, the water also reverberates with some strange sounds. Most of these eerie clicks and creakings are made by fish, intent on finding each other in the dark.

PERMANENT PARTNERS
In the vast emptiness of the abyssal zone, fish cannot afford to miss a meal. Thanks to their huge mouths, and to stomachs that can stretch out like balloons, many of them can eat fish as large as themselves. Once a fish has swallowed this much food, it does not need to make another catch for weeks. For marine biologists, these deep-sea predators work like living collection devices. Some of the species found in the stomachs of these fish have never been found in the open sea.

Finding a suitable partner can be even harder than finding food, so if a male and female do meet, they must not waste the opportunity to mate. Deep-sea anglerfish have evolved a unique way of making sure that this happens. The males are far

smaller than the females, and they are unable to hunt, so they cannot survive for long on their own. Instead, each male seeks out a female, and latches on to her with his jaws. The two fishes' bloodstreams join together, which means that the male is kept alive by his mate.

△ *Drop-down jaws and outsize teeth give the viperfish a fearsome appearance. Its fangs are so big they protrude outside when its mouth is shut.*

blackness, there are signs of life.

In the oceans' depths – known as the abyssal zone – many animals use light to lure their prey. The bearded anglerfish has a luminous lure that dangles in front of its mouth, and a light-up 'beard' trailing beneath its jaws. It is a distant relative of the sargassum fish, and it has the same kind of trapdoor mouth that sucks its food aboard. The viperfish also has a light-up lure, as well as light organs, or photophores, in a line along its sides. Some of these are constantly alight, while others can flash on and off. If threatened, a few deep-sea fish can squirt out clouds of luminous fluid – a startling trick that may help them to escape attack.

As well as for catching food, fish use these lights to attract mates. Often, males and females have different patterns to help them

▷ *With her mate dangling beneath her, a female anglerfish hunts for prey. She feeds for two, because the food that she eats also keeps the male alive.*

the oceans also contain animals that travel down into the darkness and back again several times a day. These are the sea's deep divers, and all of them are mammals – animals that breathe air.

Using satellite transmitters, scientists have discovered that elephant seals can dive to at least 1,300 m, and they can hold their breath for over an hour. They feed on squid and deep-sea fish, although exactly how they find their prey is not known. Sperm whales dive even further. These blunt-headed monsters feed on fish and giant squid, and they can hunt at depths of 2,000 m, or even 3,000 m if food is hard to find. Dives like this can last almost two hours – an amazing endurance test for an animal that needs to come to the surface to breathe.

Although experts know what the sperm whale eats, they are not at all sure how it dives or how it finds its prey. In answering these questions, the spermaceti organ may provide some clues. This gigantic reservoir of waxy fluid fills most of the sperm

◁ *Unlike other starfish, feather stars are good swimmers. This one has settled on a rock, and is gripping it with its cirri, which work like tiny feet.*

△ *The goosefish uses the same hunting technique as deep-sea anglerfish, but it lies in wait on the seabed. Its camouflage hides an enormous mouth, up to 30 cm across.*

He stays permanently attached to his partner, fertilizing her eggs whenever she is ready to breed.

DEEP DIVERS

Many deep-sea fish start life in the plankton near the water's surface, and then sink down into the depths as they grow up. But

▷ *Drifting near the surface, a sperm whale gets ready for its next dive. It can dive for over an hour, but needs only five minutes to get its breath back at the surface.*

Species Profile

Vampire squid: *Vampyroteuthis* species

Despite its name, this tiny deep-sea squid does not suck blood. Instead, it catches small animals, using arms that are joined together with a web of skin. It can swim by rippling a pair of fins, but like many deep-sea animals, it spends most of its time motionless, waiting for food to come within reach. The vampire squid has an unusual way of defending itself: if it is attacked, it ejects a cloud of luminous mucus while it makes its escape.

whale's head, and it contains passageways that can carry water or air. Some scientists think that it works like an adjustable ballast tank, because spermaceti contracts and turns solid when it cools. According to this theory, a sperm whale cools its spermaceti to make itself sink, and then warms it up when it needs to rise. But not everyone is convinced. Some whale experts

Holding its arms out like a parachute, a day octopus swims over the seabed off Hawaii. It feeds on shrimps and crabs, and often surrounds its lair with their discarded remains. The day octopus can grow up to 1 m long, but the world's largest species – the giant Pacific octopus – has an armspan of up to 8 m, and can weigh more than a quarter of a tonne.

△ *Hydrothermal vents – or black smokers – are the strangest habitats on earth. Here, life is fuelled by dissolved minerals which gush upwards in clouds of superheated water.*

think that the spermaceti organ is really a sound focusing device, which the whale uses to 'see' its prey in the dark.

MYSTERIOUS GIANTS

No one has ever seen a sperm whale hunting, but scientists have found some signs of their prey. Sperm whales often have circular scars on their skins, and pincer-like beaks have been found in their stomachs.

These beaks are all that remains of giant squids, because they are too tough to be digested. The circular scars are made by the squids' suckers, as they make a desperate attempt to fight back.

Giant squids are shrouded in mystery, because scientists have yet to find one that is still alive. Despite reports of boats being attacked by these animals, nearly all of our knowledge of them comes from dead ones caught in nets or washed up on the shore. Atlantic giant squids can be 17 m long, and until recently they were thought to be the largest invertebrates in the world. But in 2003, a giant squid was found off Antarctica which belonged to a species that is bigger still. When fully grown, this mega-invertebrate could be 25 m long, or possibly more.

LIFE IN THE DEPTHS

Until the middle of the 19th century, biologists thought that the deep seabed was too hostile for living things. The cold, the darkness and the extreme pressure made it seem very unlikely that anything could survive. But in 1871, a ship called *Challenger* collected animals from several kilometres down,

▷ *Glass sponges have fragile skeletons made of silica – the same material used to make glass. These seabed sponges are most common in the tropics.*

showing that this was not true. Nearly a century later, in 1960, the two-man crew of the *Trieste*, a deep-sea submersible, reached the bottom of the Marianas Trench. Here, at the oceans' deepest point – nearly 11 km down – they found animal life.

△ *The bathyscape* Trieste *was the first submersible to reach the oceans' deepest point. The crew's quarters were underneath the vessel, inside a steel sphere designed to withstand extreme pressure.*

In the oceans' greatest depths, the lack of light means that algae cannot survive. Without them, there is no home-grown food. Instead, life is fuelled almost entirely by dead remains that drift down from above. Just occasionally, a really massive meal makes its way down to the depths. The dead body of a whale, for example, is a gigantic banquet, and the scent of rotting flesh attracts scavenging animals. They include deep-sea crustaceans that resemble

◁ *Although it is covered by water, the seabed is just as rugged as dry land. This sonar picture shows the seabed off the coast of California. The shallow continental shelf, coloured orange and yellow, ends in a sudden drop where deep water begins.*

giant woodlice, and the hagfish – an animal that looks more like a snake than a fish, with a mouth that does not have jaws. Together, these animals pick the flesh from the carcass, until nothing is left but bones.

SURVIVING ON SEDIMENT

Feasts like this are extremely rare, and most seabed animals live on a very different kind of food. They

> Coiled up on the seabed, a hagfish takes a break between meals. Hagfish find their food by smell.

collect tiny particles of dead matter, which drift down towards the seabed like snow. Most of these particles are the remains of plankton, including cases and tiny shells. They can be smaller than grains of salt, and it can take them weeks to complete their journey from the sunlit surface to the ocean floor.

Some deep-sea worms collect this food using fan-shaped tentacles, while brittlestars use their slender arms. These deep-water relatives of starfish can be incredibly common – in some places they cover the seabed in writhing masses many millions strong. Glass sponges use a different

technique – they pump water through their bodies, sieving out anything that they can eat. When the sediment has finally settled, another group of animals takes over – ones that bulldoze or burrow their way through it, extracting anything that can be used as food. Hidden away beneath kilometres of seawater, these scavengers and recyclers are the deepest animals on earth.

HEAT IN THE DARK

The temperature on the deep seabed is just 4° C – only a few degrees warmer than seawater around the poles. But in a few places, underground water heated by volcanic rock pours upwards into the sea. Here, the temperature of the water can be as high as 360° C, and only the crushing pressure of the ocean above stops it boiling away. These springs are known as hydrothermal vents. The first one was found in 1977. Since then, many more have been discovered.

The water in hydrothermal vents is laden with dissolved minerals, which makes it look like black smoke. As the water gushes out, the minerals are deposited, forming chimneys up to 10 m high. But the most remarkable feature

▷ The seabed is an important habitat for worms. This species collects particles of food with its slender tentacles

of vents is found on the rocks below, which teem with life. Giant tubeworms grow in tangled clusters, while clams are fastened to the seabed. Ghostly white crabs and lobsters clamber among them. These animals depend on bacteria that use minerals to get energy. If the sun

Species Profile

Open-water amphipod: *Cystisoma* species

Amphipods are shrimp-like animals that live in many habitats, including beaches and the deep seabed. Measuring 15 cm long, this species is one of the largest. It is unusual because it is a good swimmer, and it lives in the open sea. It has huge, upward-facing eyes, and it probably feeds on soft-bodied animals such as salps, spotting them against the light shining down from above. When the open-water amphipod breeds, it carries its young until they are ready to look after themselves.

stopped shining tomorrow, most life on earth would soon die, but vent life would carry on – exactly as it has done for millions of years.

COASTS

If the world's coasts could be straightened out and joined together, they would circle the globe many times. Coasts are a very important habitat for wildlife, because they bring together species that live on land, and ones that spend most or all of their time in the sea.

Habitats are always changing, but on coasts, nature really shows its power. In stormy weather, waves smash against rocks and undermine cliffs, while powerful currents shift millions of tonnes of sand and mud. All this energy turns the shore into a constantly moving battlefront – a place where buildings topple into the sea and where ports silt up and become stranded inland. Coastal animals and plants have to cope with all these changes without being smothered or swept away. They also have to fit in with something much more predictable – the twice-daily rise and fall of the tide.

WATER ON THE MOVE

Tides are caused by the moon and the sun as they move in relation to the earth. Their gravity tugs on seawater, making oceans bulge towards them as they travel across the sky. In the open sea, these bulges are barely noticeable, but when they approach land the water piles up, creating a tide. The height of the tide depends on the shape of the tidal funnels is the Bay of Fundy, a long inlet on the east coast of Canada. Here, the highest tides reach 21 m, and when the tide is coming in, it can rise by an adult's height in as little as half an hour. But in landlocked seas such as the Mediterranean, there is hardly any tide at all. Tides can also travel up rivers – in the Amazon, they reach more than 400 km inland.

On coasts, the tide is very important in deciding what lives where. Most coastal plants cannot survive in seawater, so they grow far enough up the shore to miss the highest tides. Seaweeds are exactly the opposite, because they need to be submerged. Some brown seaweeds can cope with several hours in the air, as their fronds are extra-tough. But red seaweeds are much more fragile, which explains why they live below the level of the lowest tides.

▽ *Limestone cliffs make good homes for plants and seabirds, because they have lots of rocky ledges. These cliffs are in the Algarve, in southern Portugal.*

△ *Starfish creep over submerged rocks, searching for mussels and other molluscs. Their top speed is only about 2 m per hour.*

LIVING CLOCKS
For coastal animals, the tide is like a timer that resets itself twice a day. As the tide rises and the shore is flooded, many of these animals start to feed. Mussels open their shells and start up their on-board pumps, while barnacles beat their feathery legs. In their different ways, both feed by trapping tiny particles of floating food.

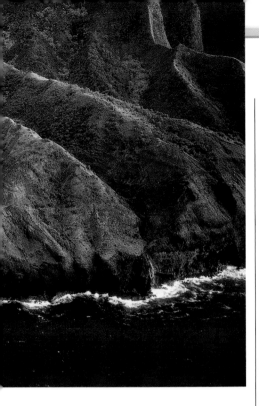

△ *Hawaii's northern coast is made of volcanic lava, which is easily broken up by the sea. Strong waves and jagged rocks make it dangerous for boats to put ashore.*

coastline, and also the amount of water on the move. If the coast is shaped like a funnel, the water is squeezed into a smaller and smaller space, leaving it nowhere else to go but up. One of the world's biggest

△ *Mussels anchor themselves to rocks with extra-tough threads, but sometimes they get torn off during storms, and thrown ashore.*

Limpets eat on the move, and for them the rising tide is the signal to set off. For three or four hours they crawl over the rocks, scraping up algae with their microscopic teeth. But as soon as the tide begins to fall, everything goes into reverse. Mussels and barnacles shut up their shells, while limpets make their way back home. They cannot afford to be late, because home is the only place where their shells fit exactly against the rock.

Many of these small animals can sense the tide's ebb and flow. But some also have a 'clock' in their nervous system that tells them when to start feeding and when to stop. Scientists have tested this clock by collecting crabs and oysters, and carrying them inland. Even when these animals are far away from

their original home, they keep in step with the tides.

TIDELINE BIRDS

Coastal birds also fit in with the tides, but they work the other way around. For gulls and waders, the busiest time is when the tide is falling, because the retreating water uncovers plenty of food. Gulls are the great scavengers of the seashore world, and they glide along the water's edge, looking out for live animals and dead remains. They are quarrelsome feeders, but they are also quick to spot any chance of a meal. If the weather turns bad or they run out of food, they often abandon the coast and head inland.

Compared to gulls, waders – also called shorebirds – are more fussy

△ *Many birds nest above the high-tide mark, but they have trouble finding a spot when the coastline is backed by houses and hotels.*

Species Profile

Ragworm: *Nereis* species

Ragworms are distant relatives of earthworms, but they live on the seabed and move by using dozens of fleshy flaps that work like miniature feet. Each flap ends in a set of bristles that help the worm to get a good grip. Ragworms catch other animals with a pair of strong, pincer-like jaws. They are an important food for wading birds, which search for them at low tide in mud or sand.

about what they eat. Oystercatchers feed mainly on mussels and cockles, and have chisel-shaped beaks that can smash open shells or prise them apart. Turnstones have much shorter beaks, and they feed by flipping over pieces of seaweed and snapping up small animals hiding underneath. The sanderling is one of the smallest waders, but one of the fastest on its feet. It scoots along the surf like a clockwork toy, pecking up any

▽ *With their brightly coloured beaks and noisy calls, oystercatchers are easy to recognize on muddy and rocky shores.*

△ *Peering out of its burrow, a mantis shrimp waits for victims to come within range. Its barbed front legs can grab prey in four-thousandths of a second – one of the fastest movements in the animal world.*

shrimps and sandhoppers that are stranded by the waves.

These three waders hunt by sight, but many others hunt by touch. One of the largest is the curlew – a long-legged bird with a curved beak over 15 cm long. Curlews feed on muddy shores, and they specialize in finding buried animals that other shorebirds cannot reach. Their beaks are as slender as pencils, and have sensitive tips that can feel animals that are hidden away. The tip can open while the rest of the beak stays shut, allowing a curlew to grip its food and pull it up out of the mud.

THE BURROWERS

Humans and wild animals have different ideas about what makes the perfect beach. For us, the ideal beach has golden sand, with no seaweed, and definitely no flies. But for wildlife, clean sand is not a good habitat, because it is a sign that not much food comes in with the tide. Shingle is even worse. It can be uncomfortable for people to lie on, but for small animals it can be a killer. At high tide, small stones are smashed together by the waves, crushing anything among them.

For many animals, the ideal beach is one that has mud or sediment mixed up with the sand. Sediment contains particles of food and, because it is sticky, it helps to keep the sand in place. This kind of gooey mixture is ideal for cockles and

burrowing shrimps, and incredible numbers of them can be hidden away. In muddy coasts, particularly near river mouths, more than 5,000 shrimps can live in a piece of shore no bigger than a handkerchief. Together, these animals are a huge store of food – one that attracts birds like a magnet.

SALTMARSHES AND SWAMPS

Life gets even stickier on really flat shores, where the tide travels a long way inland. Here, land and sea meet in mudflats and saltmarshes, well beyond the reach of the waves.

△ *This muddy sand looks deserted, but thousands of animals are hidden beneath the surface, waiting for the tide to return.*

△ *Lobsters feed on crabs and molluscs, but they also scavenge on dead remains. They have a very good sense of smell, and are easily lured into lobster pots by pieces of dead fish.*

When the tide comes in, the water winds its way through creeks and channels. When it goes out, it leaves behind a landscape of glistening mud.

For humans, this kind of habitat is tough going, because the ground is treacherous and the creeks are like a maze. But for plants that can cope with salt, it is a perfect place to live. Most of these plants are low growing, and their leaves often have a crunchy feel. This crunchiness is produced by surplus salt, which the plants get rid of as they grow. Some saltmarsh plants even spread along roadsides, because road salt makes them feel quite at home.

In the tropics, saltmarshes look completely different. Instead of being empty and open, they are covered with a tangle of trees. These trees are mangroves, and they are the only ones in the world that can survive in the zone between the tides. Many of them have stilt-like roots that anchor them in place. Some also have 'breathing' roots which poke upwards like miniature snorkels from the mud.

Mangrove swamps are like tropical forests in miniature, and they are home to all kinds of animals, from monkeys and snakes to biting ants. But their most interesting inhabitants live further down, on the mud itself. They include hordes of tiny fiddler crabs and also mudskippers – finger-sized fish that use their pectoral fins to hop and climb, and which survive out of the water by breathing air.

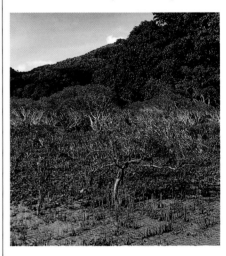

△ *Perched above the sticky mud, mangrove trees spread out from the shore. They stop where the water at high tide is deep enough to reach their leaves.*

ROCKY COASTS

Compared to sandy and muddy shores, the wildlife of rocky shores is easier to find. This is because animals have to live in the open, unless there are crevices where they can hide. Sea urchins are armed with spines, but most other rock-dwellers use hard shells or body cases to keep themselves out of trouble. A shell does several jobs at once – it protects the owner from the waves and it stops the animal drying out at

◁ *Sea urchins use their brittle spines as a defence against attack. Hidden among the spines are small pincers that keep the urchin's surface clean.*

Great scallop: *Pecten maximus*

This mollusc is one of the few that can swim by opening and shutting its shell. It normally rests on the seabed, but if it is touched by a starfish, it activates an emergency escape system. The two halves of its shell snap shut, squirting out a jet of water and making the scallop jump in the opposite direction. Scallops sense danger with their eyes – they have over a hundred, arranged around the edges of their shell.

△ *Terns' eggs are so well camouflaged that they are almost impossible to see when the parents are away from their nest.*

low tide. Even more importantly, it keeps predators at bay.

Unfortunately for shell-owning animals, no shell is guaranteed to withstand a determined attack. Oystercatchers can smash some shells open in seconds, but other predators go about opening them in much more stealthy ways. Starfish wrap themselves around mussels and clams, and then use their tiny sucker-tipped feet to lever the two halves of the shell apart. Once a

paper-thin gap has opened up, the starfish slips its stomach through it, and digests the soft body of the luckless victim inside.

Lobsters can crack open shells with their claws, but shelled animals are also attacked by predators that have shells themselves. One of the most common is the dog whelk, which often lives in mussel beds. It bores its way into its victims, using drill-like mouthparts backed up by a shell-dissolving acid. It is a long job, but once the dog whelk starts work, there is nothing that a mussel can do to escape.

For thousands of years, humans have also collected shellfish from rocky shores, and on some coastlines, archaeologists have found mounds of empty shells that early humans left behind. These piles of ancient leftovers are known as shell middens. Some of them are many metres across, and they are among the earliest and most unusual rubbish dumps in the world.

▽ *Most seabirds return to the same nesting site year after year. Gannets like steep, rocky islands, where there are no predatory mammals on the prowl.*

This bird's-eye view shows the coast of Whitsunday Island, off the northeast coast of Australia. Sandwiched between the mainland and the Great Barrier Reef, this tropical island is used as a nesting ground by turtles, and by birds that breed along the shore. Each year between June and September, the shallows are visited by humpback whales, which travel here from the Southern Ocean to give birth to their calves.

△ *Stretching its wings, an Atlantic puffin stands by its clifftop burrow. During the breeding season, both males and females have brilliantly coloured beaks and feet.*

CLIFFS AND ISLANDS

No matter how far they roam, seabirds have to come back to land to breed. Terns lay camouflaged eggs directly on the shingle or sand, and they fearlessly dive-bomb any animal – or human – that comes nearby. But at nesting time, most seabirds steer clear of the hazardous world

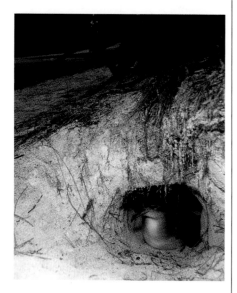

△ *Shearwaters dig their own burrows, or take over ones that have been dug by rabbits. Where there are lots of shearwaters, the ground becomes riddled with holes.*

of the open shore. Instead, they breed on steep cliffs or on inaccessible islands, where they are much safer from attack.

At the height of the breeding season, these nesting sites become some of the busiest, noisiest and smelliest wildlife shows on earth. On Scotland's Bass Rock, for example, nearly 100,000 gannets crowd onto a tiny island only a few hundred metres across. On Babel Island, between Australia and New

△ *Seals use the coast as resting places, but they can also sleep in the sea. A sleeping seal floats like a bottle, with just its face and muzzle out of the water.*

Zealand, over two million slender-billed shearwaters arrive every year to raise their young. They reach the island after a migration that takes them around the entire Pacific Ocean, a distance of more than 30,000 km.

SEABIRD COLONIES

With so many birds nesting side by side, space is short and tempers often fray. Gannets defend their nests fiercely, pecking at any neighbour who strays within reach. When an adult gannet comes back from a fishing trip, it has to locate its mate before it lands, to avoid painful mistakes. It does this by making a landing call, which its

partner picks out from the noise created by the other birds. The bird on the ground is instantly on the alert, and calls back to its mate to guide it towards the nest. Shearwaters nest in clifftop burrows, and they come and go after dark. But amazingly, they also recognize their partners by sound. At the dead of night, the air is filled with unearthly screeches and wails, as birds hidden underground call to ones flying overhead.

Some seabirds, such as pelicans and cormorants, are natural 'landlubbers', and stay near the coast all year round. Others are more adventurous, and head out to sea as soon as their young are ready to follow. But shearwaters and puffins don't even wait that long. Once their chick has had enough food, the parents abandon it in its underground burrow. The chick waits until its feathers have grown, and then heads out to sea alone.

△ *Seagrasses live in shallow water close to the shore. Although they look like seaweeds, they are flowering plants, with tough stems and strap-shaped leaves.*

▽ *Walruses use their sensitive whiskers to find clams and cockles on the seabed. They suck these animals out of their shells.*

Species Profile

Magnificent frigatebird:
Fregata magnificens

Soaring high over the sea, the magnificent frigatebird hardly ever lands on water. Instead, it steals food from other birds, chasing them so that they drop their catch. The frigatebird goes into a sharp dive, intercepting the food before it hits the waves. There are five species of frigatebird – this one lives on the coasts of the American tropics. Male frigatebirds inflate their bright-red throats to attract a mate.

BORN ON THE BEACH

Compared to most seabirds, seals are fully at home in water, and can stay in it for weeks at a time. But even seals have to come to land to breed. Like seabirds, most of them are faithful to their breeding sites, and they return to the same piece of coastline year after year.

True seals are not very nimble out of the water, because they move by shuffling along on their undersides. They usually breed on flat coasts or on ice floes, where they find it easiest to get around. But fur seals and sea lions are much more agile, because they use their flippers like feet. They can climb rocks to bask in the sun, and some of them can 'gallop' almost as fast as a person can run.

Seals choose their breeding sites carefully, because they need to be in places where their young are safe from attack. Compared to birds, their young grow up incredibly quickly, nourished by some of the richest milk in the mammal world. Young grey seals, for example, often finish feeding on milk when they are

just 16 days old. Their speedy growth is vital, because it means they can soon leave the land and move into the relative safety of the sea.

Unfortunately for seals, many of their breeding sites can be reached by human hunters. In the early 1800s, seals were hunted even more relentlessly than whales, and by the early 1900s, many species were in serious danger of becoming extinct. This steep decline forced countries to bring in conservation measures, and since then, some species have staged a spectacular recovery. One of the biggest success stories is the Antarctic fur seal. In the 1930s, there were only a few thousand left, but today there are several million.

MEADOWS UNDER THE SEA

Lots of flowering plants live along coasts, but hardly any manage to survive full-time in the sea. The rare

△ *Dugongs and manatees eat up to 100 kg of seagrass a day. Between meals, they spend most of their time resting at the surface.*

exceptions are plants called eelgrasses or seagrasses, which form underwater 'meadows' in many parts of the world. These meadows are invisible from the shore, but they look like large dark patches when seen from a boat or from the air. Seagrass usually grows in water at least 5 m deep, which means that it is safely below the waves. But if it gets churned up by storms, banks of dead leaves are often washed ashore.

Seagrass meadows are an important habitat for many inshore animals. Fish shelter among the leaves and turtles graze on them with their sharp-edged beaks. In the tropics, barrel-shaped dugongs and manatees feed on leaves, and also on seagrass roots. These large but harmless creatures look like seals, but they do not have to come to land to breed. They are the only marine mammals that feed entirely on plants – one reason why they used to be called 'sea cows'.

KELP FORESTS

Seagrasses grow by creeping sideways, and they spread out to form a mat. But in some parts of the world, where the water is cool and the seabed is rocky, giant seaweeds grow upwards like trees. The largest

▽ *On the coast of southern California, a lone heron stalks a seagrass meadow for food. At low tide the water is calm, making fish and crabs easier to spot.*

Species Profile

Leafy seadragon: *Phycodurus eques*

This extraordinary fish lives among kelp-covered rocks off southern Australia. It is a slow swimmer, but it is protected by amazing camouflage – the leafy flaps that sprout from its body make it look like a piece of drifting weed. Seadragons are close relatives of seahorses. They feed on tiny animals, sucking them up with their tube-shaped mouths.

of these seaweeds, called kelps, are the fastest-growing living things in the seas. One North American species, bull kelp, can reach a length of 35 m in one year. But the record goes to the giant kelp – it grows up to 65 m long, and at top speed, it can put on an extra 60 cm each day.

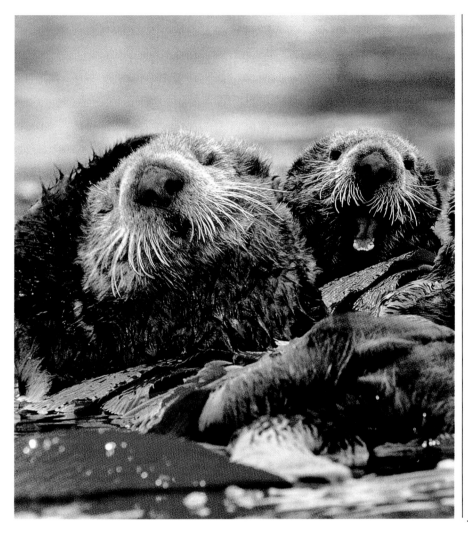

These giant seaweeds create underwater forests that teem with all kinds of life. On the rocky forest floor, octopuses search for shrimps and crabs, while moray eels peer out of hidden lairs, waiting for prey. Above them, fish and squid swim among the fronds, while sea otters dive down from the surface to collect abalones and clams. Sea otters are the only mammals apart from apes and monkeys that use tools to get at food. They hit abalones with stones to loosen them from rocks, and smash open clam shells while floating on their backs.

More than 750 different kinds of animals live in the kelp forest itself, but over half a million individual animals may crowd together on the surface of a single kelp plant. These forests are the coast's furthest-flung outposts – beyond them lies the very different world of the open sea.

◁ *Sea otters spend nearly all their lives in water, but their fur is so thick that it keeps them dry and warm. Young sea otter pups use their mothers as rafts – the mother floats on her back, with the pups on top.*

CORAL REEFS

CORAL REEFS ARE BY FAR THE RICHEST WILDLIFE HABITATS IN THE SEAS. WITH THEIR COLOURED CORALS, DEEP CREVICES AND SHADOWY CAVES, THEY ARE HOME TO A THIRD OF THE WORLD'S FISH SPECIES – AND MANY OTHER ANIMALS BESIDES.

Just like forests on land, coral reefs are habitats that are entirely created by living things. They are built by coral polyps – soft-bodied animals that collect chalky minerals from the sea. Corals use these minerals to make cup-shaped skeletons, which protect them and keep them in place. Coral skeletons are tough, and they survive long after their makers are dead. As they pile up, they form rock-like outcrops and reefs. Today's reefs have taken thousands of years to develop. They are the largest objects ever built by living things, and many of them are clearly visible from space.

△ *A helicopter speeds over the Great Barrier Reef. This coral reef – the world's largest – runs parallel to the east coast of Australia for more than 2,000 km.*

HOW CORALS LIVE
Seen through a pair of goggles, a coral reef is like a fantastic and intricate landscape hidden just

This dazzling world is the work of coral polyps. Polyps are individual coral animals, and they spend their adult lives fastened firmly in place. Each one has a short, hollow body, topped by a ring of stinging tentacles that surrounds a tiny mouth. To feed, the polyp spreads its tentacles in the water to catch anything edible that comes its way. But reef-building polyps do not live just by catching food. They also use energy from sunlight, thanks to millions of microscopic algae that live on each polyp. The algae make food by photosynthesis (see pp. 84–85). In return for a share of the food, the polyp provides its guests with a home. Corals are not the only reef animals that harbour algae – giant clams, sea anemones and flatworms do as well.

Most coral polyps feed at night, while their algae are busy by day. It is a neat arrangement, but it only works in places where the water is warm, clean and clear. This is why

beneath the waves. Some of the corals spread out in delicate folds or sheets. Others look more like jagged antlers or the coiled, twisting surface of a brain. In bright sunshine, the entire reef overflows with colour, and many of the fish that dart among the coral are so vivid that it is hard to believe they are real.

△ *Not all corals build reefs. These soft corals, from the Red Sea, grow in flexible colonies that bend as the sea washes past.*

most reefs are in the tropics, in places where the water temperature never falls below 18° C. On muddy coasts, reefs are very rare.

REEF SHAPES

In the days when ships were made of wood, coral reefs were a major hazard. If a boat so much as grazed a reef, its hull was likely to be ripped apart. This is one of the reasons why reefs were carefully charted, and why scientists noticed that there are three

▽ *Sheltering among the tentacles of a sea anemone, a clownfish is well protected from danger. The tentacles have powerful stings, but the fish does not set them off.*

△ *From the air, an atoll's ring-shaped reef is easy to see. This atoll is near the Palau Islands, in the western Pacific Ocean.*

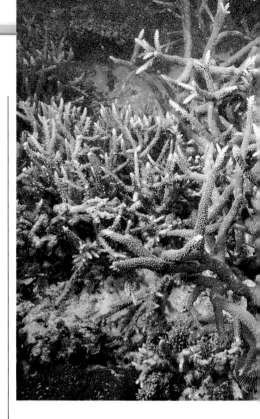

main types of reef. The first type, called a fringing reef, spreads out from the shore. Fringing reefs are the easiest to investigate, because they are usually just a short swim away.

The second type, called a barrier reef, runs parallel to the coast, but is often much farther out to sea. Australia's Great Barrier Reef is the most impressive example – actually several reefs in succession, it lies up to 250 km offshore.

The third kind of reef is very different. Instead of being open-ended, it is ring-shaped, and surrounds a shallow lagoon. Reefs like these are called atolls, and they form on the slopes of ancient

volcanoes that have subsided into the sea. Most of the world's atolls are in the Indian and Pacific Oceans, and they include the thinnest, lowest and remotest islands in the world. Some of them are vast: the world's largest atoll – Kwajalein in the Marshall Islands – would fit around the whole of London with plenty of room to spare.

CORAL SHAPES
Because coral polyps and their algae need food and light, they grow on the surface of the reef like a living skin. Some polyps live on their own, but most grow in clusters called colonies, which have all kinds of different shapes. Staghorn corals are the fastest growers – their spiky branches can put on up to 15 cm of new growth a year. This kind of shape is good for collecting food and gathering light, but it has one disadvantage – the branches are easily broken by storms. As a result, staghorn coral has to grow in the middle of the reef, where the water is shallow and fairly calm.

Finger-shaped corals are not quite as fragile, but brain corals are the toughest of all. These solid domes

grow more slowly than other corals, but after two or three hundred years they can be bigger than a car. They live on the seaward edge of the reef, and also in the middle of lagoons. Here, ancient brain corals look like giant boulders rising up from the seabed sand.

HOW CORALS REPRODUCE
Coral colonies start life when a single polyp sets up home on the surface of the reef. As the polyp grows, it divides, producing many copies of itself. These copies divide in turn, creating a community of polyps that live separately, but which are also joined together. If one polyp is touched, its neighbours 'feel' it too. Polyps are close in more ways than one, because each colony is a genetic clone. This means that they are all exactly alike, like a giant set of identical twins.

On a few nights each year – usually at full moon – mature coral colonies spawn. Some shed clouds

◁ *A giant clam's rubbery 'lips' contain microscopic algae that soak up the energy in sunlight. These molluscs grow the world's heaviest shells, weighing up to 300 kg.*

△ *Staghorn corals grow quickly, shading out other corals with a tangle of spiky branches. The branches are sharp, and they break easily if trodden on at low tide.*

of egg and sperm cells, while others give birth to developing eggs, which have been fertilized before they are released. This burst of reproduction produces tiny coral larvae, called planulae, which drift in the open sea. After a few days or weeks, each planula sinks to the surface of the reef and searches for somewhere to set up home. If it succeeds, it turns into a polyp and a completely new colony is formed.

△ *These spawning corals are releasing packets of egg and sperm cells into the sea. The packets break open as they near the surface, so that the egg cells can be fertilized.*

HIDING IN THE REEF

Compared to the open seabed, coral reefs are full of places to hide. This is one of the main reasons why so many animals use coral reefs as their home. Young fish swim close to the coral, ready to dart into holes and crannies at the first sign of trouble. Mantis shrimps lurk in coral crevices, while octopuses hide in the reef by day and emerge to feed after dark. Holes in the reef are always in demand, so animals that 'own' them have to be careful when returning home – just in case something else has moved in.

Some of the most aggressive reef predators venture into open water, but very rarely. Usually, they remain in their lairs and lunge at passers-by.

△ *Moray eels are short-sighted, but they can inflict serious injuries to divers who venture too close to their lairs.*

These reef ambushers are moray eels – snake-like fish equipped with dozens of teeth and extremely powerful jaws. There are over 200 kinds of moray eels, and the largest of them is more than 3.5 m long, and as thick as a human thigh. Morays are often vividly coloured, with fleshy skin and glaring eyes. They hold their mouths open to

get oxygen, a habit that makes them look more menacing still.

SCRAPING THE SURFACE

Not all reef animals are this big or this dangerous. Coral reefs are also home to thousands of smaller animals that nip and nibble at plants and animals which carpet the coral surface. This food includes algae, sponges, sea anemones and sea squirts, as well as bryozoans, or moss animals – tiny creatures that live in cases with tightly-fitting lids.

△ *Adult sea squirts have bag-like bodies, and they live by filtering food from water. Their larvae are very different – they are shaped like small tadpoles, and can swim.*

In the warm waters of the Red Sea, corals soak up the energy
in sunshine. Corals get their amazing colours from chemical
pigments called carotenoids, which are often found in plants.
Pure carotenoids are normally orange, yellow or red, but corals
can mix them with other substances to produce eyecatching blues,
purples and violets. Many corals also fluoresce, which means that
they give off bright colours when seen under ultraviolet light.

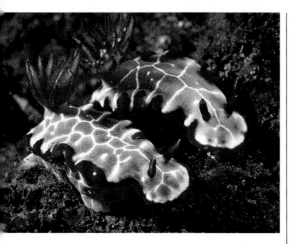

△ *These two sea slugs are feeding on a reef off the island of Sulawesi, in Indonesia. Each one has a pair of tentacles on its head, and a tuft of feathery gills near its tail.*

Many of these animals are stuck in place, so they cannot get away.

Sea slugs specialize in this kind of food, and they crawl slowly over the reef surface, scraping it away with rows of microscopic teeth. Compared to molluscs that live on land, many sea slugs are brilliantly coloured and quite easy to spot. But even so, very few animals attack them, because sea slugs have an unusual and very effective system of self-defence – they steal sea anemones' stings. When a sea slug eats a sea anemone, it digests most of the animal but leaves its stinging cells unharmed. The stinging cells then migrate through the sea slug's body and end up in its skin. Once in place, they protect their new owner, just as if they were in their original home.

PARTNERS ON THE REEF

With so many species living side by side, it is not surprising that some join forces to improve their chances of survival. For small fish called gobies, teaming up is a way of finding a home. These fish often move into burrows dug by blind shrimps, which live in coral sand. While the shrimp dutifully maintains the burrow, the goby acts as a lookout, alerting the shrimp if it spots danger on the way.

Clownfish have an even stranger partnership, because they live among the stinging tentacles of some of the world's biggest sea anemones. These tentacles can kill other fish on contact, but the clownfish darts among them without coming to any harm. It can do this because it is covered with a special coat of mucus – one that contains the same chemicals that anemones use to prevent their tentacles stinging each other. This remarkable trick provides the clownfish with a perfect place to live, and it never wanders more than a few centimetres from its home. For the fish, the advantages are obvious, but for its host, they are not so clear. The clownfish may work as a decoy, luring other animals towards the anemone, or it may keep the anemone clean. But some scientists suspect that it does not help the anemone at all.

The partnership between cleaners and their 'clients' is much easier to

△ *Holding its mouth wide open, a spotted coral grouper lets a cleaner fish get to work. In coral reefs, cleaning services are also provided by brightly coloured shrimps.*

understand. Fish often become infested with parasites, but they cannot pick them off. Instead, they use a cleaner fish or a cleaner shrimp to do this work for them. While the client fish patiently waits, the cleaner swims over the surface of its body, swallowing any parasites and also eating any damaged scales. Towards the end of the session, the client fish often opens its mouth, so that the cleaner can tidy up inside. Cleaners seem to be very important for reef fish. When scientists temporarily removed the cleaners from one section of reef, many of the client fish swam away.

CRUNCHERS AND BORERS

Coral reefs are not only extremely colourful – they can be surprisingly noisy as well. Some of the noise is produced by parrotfish, which feed on algae and living coral – the reef's crunchiest food. Parrotfish bite off mouthfuls of coral polyps, using flat teeth that are joined together to make a beak. Once they have digested the soft parts of the coral, the remainder travels through their bodies and emerges as a shower of gritty sand. A parrotfish can eat more than a tonne of coral a year, so if corals did not keep on growing, reefs would soon start to shrink.

Other tough-jawed animals also eat this difficult but plentiful food. One of the most notorious is the crown-of-thorns starfish, which lives in parts of the western Pacific Ocean.

Measuring up to 40 cm across, the crown-of-thorns can have over 20 arms, each covered with poisonous spines. Crawling over the reef, it eats the soft parts of corals, but leaves their hard parts behind. In recent years, periodic starfish plagues have swept over Australia's Great Barrier Reef, raising fears for the reef's survival. Today, scientists believe that the plagues are not such a major threat, because the starfish eventually die down and the reef slowly recovers.

PEOPLE AND REEFS

Over the last 50 years, there has been an explosion of interest in coral reefs. Millions of people visit them each year, so that they can see their incredible wildlife at first hand. Internet sites give daily updates of diving conditions, as well as profiles of the animals that can be seen.

At the same time, the world's reefs are in trouble. In some regions, fish numbers have fallen by up to a half, because they are caught by divers using spear-guns or poisons. Reef sharks have been particularly badly hit, as have sea cucumbers, because both are valued in the Far East as food. Scientists have found that if overfishing stops, reefs soon recover. But in poor regions, few people fish for fun – instead, they depend on it to make a living.

Reefs also face problems that are much harder to put right. On coasts, deforestation and construction work create water pollution, which makes it harder for corals to grow. Coral is also damaged by boats, and sometimes collected to make building materials. But the greatest threat of all comes from global warming, which is raising sea temperatures worldwide. Corals need warmth, but too much warmth can kill them. Some stretches of reef have already been affected, and scientists are anxiously waiting to see how others fare in years to come.

$\triangledown$ *A grey reef shark searches for prey above the coral. Found in the Indian and Pacific Oceans, this medium-sized shark has been known to attack divers, but it often bites just once before swimming away.*

Species Profile

Sea krait: *Laticauda colubrina*

Most snakes are good swimmers, but some species are specially adapted for life at sea. Sea kraits have paddle-shaped tails, and nostrils that can be closed off when they dive. They live among the coral reefs and mangrove swamps of Southeast Asia, feeding on fish and other animals. Although sea kraits have small fangs, their venom is extremely strong – fortunately, they rarely bite humans. Some sea snakes give birth to live young, so they can spend their whole lives at sea. But sea kraits lay eggs, so they have to come ashore to breed.

TOWNS AND CITIES

WITH THEIR BUILDINGS, NOISE AND BUSY TRAFFIC, TOWNS AND CITIES ARE VERY DIFFERENT TO HABITATS IN THE WILD. DESPITE THIS, THOUSANDS OF DIFFERENT PLANTS AND ANIMALS MANAGE TO USE BUILT-UP AREAS AS THEIR HOME.

The world's first towns were built about 10,000 years ago, when people started farming and took up a settled way of life. Compared to today's cities, these towns were tiny and primitive, but they attracted wildlife right from the start. Weeds sprang up around the mud-brick houses, and birds nested in crevices in their walls. Today, urban wildlife is still with us, but towns and cities are vastly bigger than they were before. Together, they make up the fastest-growing wildlife habitat in the world.

AT HOME WITH US
People have no difficulty telling the difference between towns and open countryside. But for animals there is no real difference at all. Instinct drives them to look for food and shelter, and wherever they find it, that becomes their home. This is exactly what happened with the

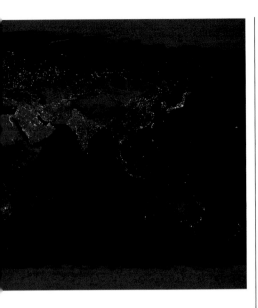

△ *Seen from space, the light from billions of buildings and streetlamps floods into the sky. The far north, the Sahara and Antarctica are some of the few completely dark areas.*

▽ *In cities like Hong Kong, buildings seem to be everywhere and open space is hard to find. But on the steep slopes behind the tower blocks, wild plants and animals still survive.*

house sparrow, a small brown bird that originally lived in Africa. In the wild, house sparrows nest in trees, and they feed mainly on seeds. But when humans started to grow crops and build houses, house sparrows moved in. Towns gave them a safe haven from many of their enemies, and a reliable supply of food.

Since those early days, the house sparrow's spread has been phenomenal. It now lives across most of the world, except in the far north and parts of the tropics. Sparrows have been seen feeding on the 80th floor of the Empire State Building, in New York, and they are also a common sight in supermarkets, warehouses, subways and multistorey car parks. One group of sparrows even lived and bred over 600 m deep in an English coalmine, where they fed on scraps that the miners gave them. With this kind of adaptability, it is no surprise that the house sparrow is such a success.

△ *The sparrow may not be the world's most colourful bird, but it is one of the most successful. This bird's black bib shows that it is a male.*

LIVING ON LEFTOVERS
For most urban animals, the number one attraction of towns is food. Compared to wild animals, humans are amazingly wasteful eaters, and a lot of food is thrown away. In the days before organized rubbish collection, most of this waste ended up on the streets, where animals would be waiting to turn it into a meal. In Europe and Asia, these

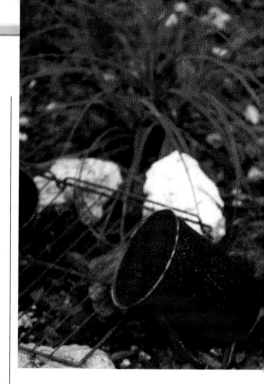

Black rat: *Rattus rattus*

An expert climber and jumper, the black rat is almost purpose-made for living in buildings. Originally from Southeast Asia, it managed to stow away on sailing ships, and spread to every continent except Antarctica. Black rats eat stored food, and they carry some dangerous diseases. One of their chief enemies – apart from cats and people – is the brown rat, a more aggressive species that is also found indoors.

scavengers included the black kite – a bird of prey with a 1.5 m wingspan, which would sometimes snatch food from people's hands.

Today, we generate even more waste, but because it is collected, it usually ends up out of town. Dumped in landfill sites, it creates massive feeding opportunities for any animals that can reach it. Some of the most successful of these scavengers are gulls. In many cities, they wheel over rubbish dumps in noisy flocks, waiting for a chance to feed. A gull's beak is the perfect implement for this kind of work because it can tear apart plastic bags. Once a gull finds something edible, it swallows it as quickly as possible, because its companions will not hesitate to steal its meal.

NIGHT PATROLS

Herring gulls sometimes breed in towns, but most of them live outside and fly in during the day. But towns and cities are also home to full-time scavengers that do their foraging at night. In North America, one of the most successful is the raccoon. Raccoons are inquisitive animals, which gives them a head start in the search for food. Their nimble front paws are perfect for opening packaging, or for pulling off dustbin lids. Once the lid is off, the raccoon rummages around inside, feeling for anything that it can eat. Raccoons

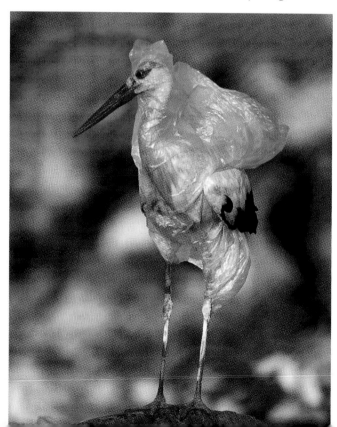

◁ *Sorting through waste can be a dangerous way to find food. This white stork has become wrapped in a plastic bag while feeding on a rubbish dump in Spain. Without help, its chances of survival are slim.*

are quick learners. As well as raiding bins, they can also open doors, and they have even been known to steal food from fridges. Before day breaks, they hide under bridges or in hollow trees, and stay there until night wakes them up once more.

In parts of Europe and North America, the red fox has a similar way of life. It is not such a good climber as the raccoon, nor is it so agile with its paws. But red foxes make up for this by being quick and intelligent, and by having a keen nose for food. They often follow the same route every night, stopping off near fast-food outlets and tearing open rubbish bags. Urban foxes are not total scavengers, and they still have a hunting streak. They catch mice, birds and small insects, but their most important prey is the humble earthworm – an animal that they dig up in gardens and parks.

UNWELCOME VISITORS

Raccoons and foxes can be a nuisance, but some kinds of urban wildlife are much less pleasant to have around. At the top of the unwanted list are the black rat and the brown rat – two rodents that originally came from Asia, but which have spread around the world.

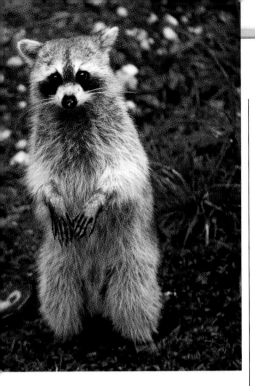

△ *Yards, city parks and camp sites are good feeding grounds for the raccoon, one of the most adaptable mammals in North America.*

Rats can cause serious damage in buildings because they gnaw through anything in their way, and they also spoil stored food. But the greatest danger comes from the diseases they carry, which include the much-feared bubonic plague. Rats can catch the plague, and they pass it on indirectly when rat fleas jump aboard humans instead.

During the 14th century, an outbreak of the plague – known as the Black Death – moved westwards from Asia and killed a quarter of Europe's entire population. In the countryside, villages were abandoned and deserted farms quickly returned to the wild. In towns and cities, matters were even worse. Here, rats, fleas and people were crowded together in insanitary conditions, creating a perfect setting for the disease. In London, about four-fifths of the city's inhabitants perished, while in Italy, some cities locked their gates for weeks and refused to let outsiders enter. When the

horrific epidemic finally died down, Europe's population took nearly three centuries to recover.

The plague returned to Europe in the 1660s, and a further outbreak began in the 1850s, sweeping around the world and claiming at least 100 million lives. Even today, it continues to flare up, but fortunately it is not the threat that it once was. The disease can be treated by antibiotics, and it can be prevented by keeping rats – and their fleas – firmly under control.

URBAN PLANTS

Compared to animals, wild plants have a tougher time in built-up areas, because living space is hard to find. The moment even the smallest piece of ground is cleared, dandelions and other fast-spreading plants move in. Another way of tackling the space shortage is to stay small. Pearlworts can flower when they are just 2 cm high, so they can spend their entire lives tucked away in gaps in the pavement.

◁ *Herring gulls nest on building rooftops, furiously attacking anyone who comes too close to their chicks.*

△ *Hawkweeds and dandelions have deep taproots that help them to survive many of the problems of city life. If they are driven over or cut down, they soon grow back.*

Plants cannot grow through solid brick or concrete, but they are amazingly good at widening any cracks and crevices that they find. As they grow, their roots and stems get thicker, steadily piling on the pressure until the hardest materials start to break up or split apart. When buildings are abandoned, plants soon spring up around them, and their roots start to undermine foundations and walls. One of the most spectacular examples of a plant takeover is at Angkor, in northwest Cambodia. Here, an entire city was smothered by jungle after being abandoned about 600 years ago. Over the centuries, tree roots probed deep into walls, levering apart stone blocks weighing many tonnes.

Even without soil, some plants still get a foothold, as long as there is water to keep them alive. Ragweed seeds have feathery parachutes, and they are often blown up on to roofs, where they settle in gutters and cracks. If they find a corner with dust and dead leaves, they have an

From its nesting site high up on a window ledge, a peregrine falcon looks out over the skyline of New York. The peregrine has one of the biggest ranges of any land bird. Most live on rocky coasts and mountainsides, but some manage to survive among tall buildings in the world's busiest cities. Peregrines dive-bomb other birds in mid-air, and the city pigeon is one of their favourite foods.

△ *Lichens can grow on bare concrete, but old stonework is an even better habitat, because it has a rougher surface.*

even better chance of survival. These rooftop weeds are usually small, but high-rise plants also include shrubs and even trees. One of the most successful is the butterfly bush, or buddleia, which originally comes from China. Its roots penetrate crumbling mortar in walls and rooftops, prising the bricks apart.

FLATLAND
Roofs are difficult places to set up home, but bare walls and pavements are the toughest mini-habitats of all.

After a shower of rain, it can be cool and damp, but after a few hours of sunshine, it is baking hot and totally dry. If a plant starts to grow in surroundings like these, it soon shrivels and dies.

Mosses and lichens are much better at clinging to life in these surroundings. Unlike plants, many of them can survive without water for days or weeks at a time. When it is dry, they shrivel up and turn crisp, but as soon as it rains they soak up moisture and start working again. Mosses usually need a thin layer of dust, but lichens can live on bare concrete and brick. Many lichens are concrete-coloured themselves, so the only way to see them is to get up really close.

These lichens make up the first rung in an unusual urban food chain. They are grazed by tiny animals called springtails, and these in turn are eaten by bright-red spider mites, which look like hyperactive furry dots. The mites are sometimes caught by spiders – top predators in this world without soil.

△ *The butterfly bush thrives on walls and alongside railway tracks, as well as in city gardens. Butterflies find its honey-like smell irresistible.*

GREEN OASES
In a landscape filled with buildings and roads, green spaces are magnets for city wildlife. Parks often have collections of semi-tame animals, but they attract lots of unofficial visitors as well. Squirrels live in the trees, coots set up home on lakes, and city pigeons keep a keen eye out for leftover food. Most of these animals are no different from their country-dwelling relatives, but city pigeons have a more complicated story. Their wild ancestors were birds called rock doves, which were first tamed over 5,000 years ago. During the following centuries, hundreds of different breeds were

◁ *Magnified more than 2,500 times, a house dust mite looks like some form of alien life. These microscopic relatives of spiders are common in almost every home.*

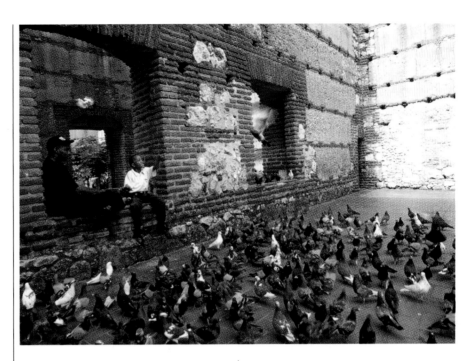

▷ *As soon as they can fly, city pigeons learn their next important lesson – where there are people, there may be food. These pigeons are waiting hopefully for a meal.*

raised, but at the same time, tame pigeons often 'went missing', and took up life on their own. Because these pigeons were used to people, they often headed for towns, creating the flocks that flap around urban areas today.

City pigeons are not everyone's favourite animals, because they pester people for food and splatter droppings wherever they perch. But most urban birds are less pushy and more welcome. All over the world, cities have their local favourites, including blackbirds in Europe, cardinals and chickadees in North America, and cockatoos in Australia. Parks are good places to see them, but so are gardens, because they often have a wide variety of plants. Lots of plants mean plenty of insects and seeds. The big drawback is that gardens also have cats, which kill millions of adult birds and nestlings every year.

Gardens are also good places for seeing butterflies, because many species use them as places to stop and refuel. In spring and summer, most city butterflies are only pausing in transit before they head on towards places where they can breed. But as the days shorten in autumn, somewhere to hibernate becomes their top priority. Butterflies can hibernate successfully in outbuildings and garden sheds, but centrally heated houses are too warm for a successful winter sleep. If they do fly indoors, the best thing to do is to gently pick them up, and put them back outside.

WILDLIFE INDOORS

Many urban animals come indoors by accident, but some spend the whole of their lives inside buildings. These household animals are usually small or microscopic, and most of them are good at surviving in warm surroundings with little or nothing to drink. Some of them eat stored food or fallen crumbs, but the house dust mite lives in household dust and feasts on dead remains, including flakes of human skin, insect scales and the bodies of other mites.

One of the oddest indoor animals is the silverfish – a creature with six short legs and a silvery, scale-covered body, measuring about 1 cm long. At one time, scientists classified it as a primitive insect, but it is so different to the average insect that they have since changed their minds. The silverfish's favourite habitat is in the dark corners of kitchen cupboards and drawers, where it feeds on anything starchy or sweet, including breadcrumbs, flour, grains of sugar, paper and even some kinds of glue. Silverfish have small appetites, so they rarely cause much harm.

The same cannot be said for the clothes moth, which is one of the few kinds of moth that can spend its whole life indoors. The dusty-coloured males are good fliers, and are easy to spot as they flutter about in rooms. Female clothes moths are much less keen on getting airborne, and they scuttle about instead.

Species Profile

Silverfish: *Lepisma saccharina*

This insect-like animal gets its name from its silvery scales and tapering body. It feeds on starchy substances, although it can go for up to three months between meals, and never has to drink. It finds food mainly by taste and touch. Unlike most insects, silverfish never have wings, and they periodically shed their skins even when they are fully grown. They scatter their eggs where they feed.

◁ *A column of pharaoh ants carries food back to its nest. These ants originally came from South America, but they are now common in centrally heated buildings across the globe.*

Once the females have mated, they lay their eggs on anything containing wool, and about ten days later, their caterpillars hatch and start to feed. They can ruin woollen clothes and blankets, but fortunately they cannot digest cotton or synthetic fabrics, so they leave these untouched. Before humans started living indoors, clothes moths led a useful life as scavengers in the wild. Most still do, and they perform a valuable job by breaking down wool and fur after animals have died.

INDOOR SCAVENGERS

Cockroaches were among the world's first insects, and for the last 300 million years they have run about on forest floors. But like clothes moths, they also thrive in houses and other buildings. Cockroaches like rooms that are warm and humid, which is why kitchens suit them best. They feed on almost anything that contains organic matter, from bread to shoe polish and soap, and although they do not spread dangerous diseases, they taint anything that they touch with an unpleasant 'roachy' smell. Female cockroaches carry their eggs in portable cases, and they can breed at a frightening rate. Each one can produce up to 150 young, so a small outbreak of cockroaches can soon turn into a major infestation.

Ants usually nest out of doors, and come inside only when they are foraging for food. But one of the smallest species, called the pharaoh ant, often lives indoors full-time. Unlike most ants, this species makes dozens of nests, which are hidden in out-of-the-way places, including the insides of walls and floors. From here, the workers fan out in a search for food, often using electricity wires or telephone lines as trails. They are only 2 mm long, so they can squeeze through the smallest of crevices. As a result, hardly anything is beyond their reach. Pharaoh ants can be a

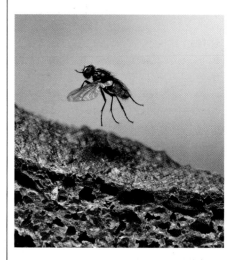

△ *A housefly lands on a slice of bread to feed. Thanks to humans, houseflies are probably the world's most widespread insects.*

△ *This light bulb has attracted lots of moths, plus two moth-eating predators – a gecko and a praying mantis. Mantises sometimes eat young geckos, but this one is large enough to be out of danger.*

serious problem in hospitals because they carry bacteria, and because their hidden nests are difficult to destroy.

IINDOOR PREDATORS

In summer, houseflies and mosquitoes can also be a nuisance indoors. But nature lends a hand in controlling them, because houses are full of predators that catch flying insects. The most important of these hunters are spiders. A typical house is home to hundreds – some actively stalk their prey, but most spin webs and patiently wait for it to come their way.

▷ *Cockroaches are extremely good at sensing vibrations. The slightest movement sends them scuttling for cover.*

The slender daddy-long-legs spider builds untidy webs that hang from ceilings and rafters. Sitting in its web, the spider is easy for humans to see. But insects are not so good at recognizing the spider or its web, and they often get tangled up in its haphazard threads. The house spider has a different hunting technique – it makes a hammock-shaped web in a secluded corner, and hides in a tunnel that reaches into a crack or crevice in the wall. If an insect lands in the web, the spider rushes out, overpowers it, and carries it back to the lair. Male house spiders often leave their webs at night to search for females. During these excursions, they occasionally fall into baths, or unexpectedly sprint across floors. Despite their large size and hairy legs, they are actually harmless, and do a useful service keeping troublesome insects under control.

For spiders, a disadvantage of indoor life is that their webs are often tidied away. When this happens, a spider simply waits until the coast is clear, and then spins a new one in its place.

HUNTING UPSIDE DOWN

Warm parts of the world are the place to see geckos – the largest wild animals that catch their prey indoors. Geckos are unusual lizards that have sticky toe-pads covered with microscopic hairs. Using these,

Species Profile

House spider: *Tegenaria domestica*

This web-building spider is a common indoor animal in many parts of the world. Its webs are strongly built, and they often last for months, trapping lots of dust and dirt as well as prey. Female house spiders spend most of their lives in tunnels connected to their webs, while males leave their webs when they search for a mate. After mating, the male dies, and the female often uses him as a meal.

a gecko can climb up walls and across ceilings, and it can even run upside down. In the wild, geckos usually hunt after dark, but indoor geckos quickly learn that bright lights are good places to catch food. When dusk falls and lights are turned on, they emerge from their hiding places and gather around to feed. Their hunting technique is simple – they stay completely still, and then dart forwards when an insect comes in to land. With their croaky calls and helpful eating habits, these acrobatic lizards make welcome house guests.

GLOSSARY

The following pages explain most of the technical terms that are used in this book.
Where a definition includes words in **bold**, it means that these words have entries of their own.

Abdomen
The rear part of an animal's body, containing the organs that are used for digesting food, getting rid of waste and reproducing.

Adaptation
A feature produced by **evolution** that helps a living thing to survive. Adaptations include physical features, and also different kinds of behaviour.

Alga (plural: **algae**)
Simple, plant-like **organisms** that grow by collecting the energy in sunlight. Most algae live in water. Many are microscopic, but seaweeds, which are the largest algae, can be many metres long.

Amoeba
A single-celled creature that moves by changing shape.

Annual plant
A plant that germinates, flowers and dies within a single growing season.

Antenna (plural: **antennae**)
A long, slender feeler on an animal's head, used to obtain information by touching or smelling. Antennae are always in pairs.

Arthropods
A huge and highly successful group of **invertebrate** animals that have a hard body case, or **exoskeleton**, and legs that bend at flexible joints. Living arthropods include insects, spiders, scorpions and crustaceans, and also centipedes and millipedes.

Bacterium (plural: **bacteria**)
A **microorganism** with a single **cell**. Bacteria are the smallest, simplest and most ancient living things on earth.

Baleen
The fibrous substance that large whales use to sieve food from the water. It hangs down from a whale's upper jaw.

Biennial plant
A plant that lives for two years. During the first year, it germinates and grows. During the second, it flowers, makes seeds and then dies.

Biosphere
All the parts of the world where living things are found.

Blubber
A layer of fat that helps some sea animals to keep warm. Whales, seals, polar bears and penguins all have blubber.

Boreal forest
The great coniferous forest that grows in the far north, close to the Arctic Circle.

Broadleaved tree
A tree that usually has broad, flat leaves. Unlike **conifers**, broadleaved trees are flowering plants.

Browser
A plant-eating animal that feeds on the leaves and shoots of trees and bushes.

Cambium
A layer of **cells** just beneath the surface of a plant's roots and stems. The cells divide to make the plant grow.

Camouflage
A pattern or colour scheme that helps something to blend in with its surroundings. Animals use camouflage to ambush their **prey**, or to avoid being eaten.

Canine teeth
Long, pointed teeth that meat-eating mammals have at the front of their mouths.

Carnivore
Any animal that lives by eating others. The word carnivore is also used for a particular group of mammals that includes cats, dogs and bears. These mammals have specialized meat-eating teeth.

Carpel
One of the female parts of a flower. Carpels contain female **cells**, called ova, which develop into seeds once they have been pollinated.

Cell
A microscopic unit of living matter. Cells are surrounded by membranes, and they contain all the equipment needed to stay alive and to reproduce. Some living things, such as **bacteria**, have just one cell, while others have many millions, specialized to carry out different tasks.

Cellulose
A substance that plants make as a building material.

Chaparral
A kind of shrubland found in California and other parts of the western USA.

Chlorophyll
The green substance that plants use to collect energy from sunlight, so that they can carry out **photosynthesis**.

Chloroplast
A microscopic green structure inside a plant's leaf that contains **chlorophyll**. Chloroplasts carry out **photosynthesis**, which enables plants to grow.

Chromosome
A thread-like chemical package that contains a length of **DNA**. In plants and animals, chromosomes often have a shape like an X.

Chrysalis
A hard case that protects a caterpillar while it turns into a butterfly or a moth.

Cocoon
A silk case spun by an insect or a spider, to protect itself or its **eggs**.

Cold-blooded
Describes an animal whose body stays at the same temperature as its surroundings. Cold-blooded creatures make up most of the animal kingdom.

Colony
A group of individual animals, plants or **microbes** that live together as a single unit. Many colonies look like single living things.

Compound eye
An eye that is divided up into many separate compartments, which work

together to produce an image. Crustaceans and insects have compound eyes.

Conifer
A tree that grows its seeds in cones. Unlike **broadleaved trees**, conifers do not have flowers, and they often keep their leaves all year.

Continental drift
The gradual movement of continents across the earth's surface. Continental drift is driven by heat from deep within the earth, which keeps the crust on the move.

Convergent evolution
The evolution of similar features in **species** that share a similar way of life. Convergent evolution can make unrelated species difficult to tell apart.

Courtship
The behaviour that an animal uses to attract a mate. Male animals use courtship to show that they are fit and healthy.

Cyanobacteria
Bacteria that live in the same way as plants, by collecting the energy in sunlight. Cyanobacteria are also known as blue-green **algae**.

Deciduous tree
A tree that loses all of its leaves for part of the year. Many **broadleaved trees** are deciduous, but not all – in rainforests, broadleaved trees keep their leaves all year round.

Decomposer
Any living thing that feeds on dead remains.

Diatom
A kind of microscopic **alga**. Diatoms have transparent protective cases that are often made of silica.

Digestion
The breaking down of food so that it can be absorbed and used. Animals digest their food after they have swallowed it, but many **microbes** digest food on the spot.

Distribution
All the places in the world where a particular **species** is found.

DNA (deoxyribonucleic acid)
The substance found in living **cells** that makes up **genes**. DNA contains all the chemical instructions needed to assemble a living thing and to make it work.

Echolocation
A way of sensing objects that works by using high-pitched bursts of sound, which bounce back as echoes. Animals that use echolocation include bats, whales and dolphins.

Ecosystem
A **habitat**, together with all the living things that use it as their home.

Egg
A fertilized **cell** that can develop into a new living thing. Eggs are the largest cells in the animal world.

Embryo
A plant or animal at a very early stage of development.

Endemic species
A **species** that is found in one place and nowhere else.

Ephemeral plant
A plant that grows, flowers and dies in a short time. Most ephemeral plants live in deserts and other dry places.

Epiphyte
A plant that grows on trees and other plants.

Evolution
A very slow process of change that enables living things to adapt to the world around them. During evolution, new **species** develop, and existing ones eventually become extinct.

Exoskeleton
A skeleton that supports an animal's body from the outside rather than the inside. Exoskeletons are a common feature in **invertebrates** – **arthropods** have exoskeletons made of separate plates, while many molluscs have shells.

Extinction
The permanent disappearance of a **species**. Extinction happens in nature, but it can also be caused by human activities.

Fertilization
The process that enables a male and a female **cell** to join together, forming a single **egg**.

Filter-feeder
An animal that gets its food by sieving it from water. Filter-feeders include animals in **plankton**, and also the world's largest whales.

Floret
A small flower in a **flowerhead**.

Flowerhead
A collection of flowers growing on a single stem.

Food chain
A food pathway that connects several different **species**. When one species eats another, food and energy move along the chain.

Fossil
The preserved remains of living things. Some fossils are formed by remains

themselves, while others are signs that living things leave behind, such as burrows or footprints.

Fynbos
A kind of shrubland found in southern Africa.

Gene
A chemical instruction that is carried by **DNA**.

Gill
A body-part that animals use to collect oxygen from water. Gills sometimes stick out from an animal's body, but in fish they are usually hidden away inside.

Grazer
A plant-eating animal that feeds mainly on grass.

Grub
A young insect that has very short legs or no legs at all. See **larva**.

Habitat
The surroundings that a particular **species** needs to survive. Most species live in just one habitat, but some can survive in several.

Herbivore
An animal that eats plants.

Hibernation
A deep winter sleep. Animals hibernate so that they can survive a time of year when food is hard to find.

Host
Any living thing that a **parasite** uses as its home and its food.

Hyphae
A network of feeding threads produced by a fungus.

Incubation
Sitting on **eggs** to keep them warm, so they can develop.

Instinct
Any kind of behaviour that is inherited instead of having to be learned.

Invertebrate
Any animal that does not have a backbone.

Larva (plural: **larvae**)
A young animal that looks completely different from its parents, and which changes shape as it grows up.

Lichen
A plant-like **organism** formed by fungi and **algae** living together in a close partnership.

Life cycle
All the steps in the life of a living thing, from the moment it starts life, to the time when it produces young.

Metabolism
All the chemical processes that take place inside a living thing. Some of these processes release energy, while others use it up.

Metamorphosis
A major change in body shape as an animal grows up.

Microbe
See **microorganism**.

Microorganism
Any living thing that is too small to be seen with the naked eye. Microorganisms include **bacteria**, as well as many other forms of life. For several billion years, they were the only living things on earth. Microorganisms are also known as microbes.

Migration
A long journey that animals make to breed or to find food. Most animals migrate along set routes, and are guided by **instinct**.

Mimic
An animal that imitates something else – usually to avoid being eaten. Many mimics imitate leaves, twigs or pebbles, but some imitate poisonous animals.

Molecules
A group of atoms that are linked together. Some molecules have only a few atoms, but molecules made by living things – such as **DNA** and **cellulose** – can have many millions.

Natural selection
The driving force behind **evolution**. Natural selection works by favouring those living things that leave the most young.

Nectar
A sweet, sugary liquid produced by many flowers. Plants make nectar to attract animals. In return for nectar, animal visitors spread the plants' **pollen**.

Nocturnal
Describes an animal that is active mainly or entirely after dark.

Nucleus
The control centre of a **cell**, containing the cell's **genes**.

Nutrient
Any substance that a living thing needs in order to stay alive.

Organism
Any living thing.

Parasite
A living thing that feeds on or inside something else while it is still alive. Unlike a **predator**, a parasite is usually smaller than the thing that it attacks. Parasites often have a complicated **life cycle**.

Perennial plant
A plant that lives for a number of years, instead of for one or two. Trees and shrubs are all perennials.

Petal
A flap in a flower that often helps to attract animal pollinators. In some flowers, petals are separate, but in others they are joined together to form funnels or tubes.

Photosynthesis
A process that works by collecting energy from sunlight and using it to build up carbon-containing chemicals. Plants, **algae** and some **bacteria** use photosynthesis to grow.

Phytoplankton
The plant-like part of **plankton**, made up of **organisms** that need sunlight to grow.

Plankton
Small or microscopic living things that drift near the surface of lakes and oceans. Plankton includes **algae**, and also a wide range of tiny animals that eat algae or each other.

Pollen
The dust-like substance that flowers use to produce seeds. Pollen contains a plant's male **cells**.

Pollination
The movement of **pollen** grains from flower to flower, so that seeds can be formed. Pollen is usually carried by animals or by the wind.

Polyp
An animal that has a tube-shaped body, with a ring of **tentacles** around its mouth. Corals and sea anemones are examples of polyps.

Predator
Any animal that lives by hunting others. Predators are usually larger than their **prey** – unless they hunt in packs – and they are always less common.

Prehensile
Describes something, such as a trunk or a tail, that can wrap around things to hold on to them, or to pick them up.

Prey
An animal that a **predator** hunts as food.

Protists
Single-celled **organisms** that are larger and more complicated than **bacteria**. They include **protozoans** and **algae**.

Protozoan
An animal-like **organism** that is made up of just one **cell**. Protozoans live mainly in water, or in damp **habitats** such as the soil. Some are **parasites** of animals or plants.

Pupa (plural: **pupae**)
A resting stage in the **life cycle** of an insect. Inside the pupa, the young insect's body is broken down, and an adult one is assembled in its place.

Ruminant
A plant-eating mammal that has hooves and a four-chambered stomach. Deer, antelope and cattle are all ruminants.

Seasonal forest
A kind of tropical forest that grows in places that have a wet season and a dry season. It is also known as monsoon forest.

Sepal
An outer flap that protects a flower bud. Unlike **petals**, sepals are normally green,

but in some flowers they are large and brightly coloured.

Species
A single type of living thing. The members of a species can all breed with each other, but they do not normally breed with anything else.

Spiracle
A small opening that lets air into an insect's body.

Spore
A microscopic package of **cells** that is used in reproduction. Most fungi and **algae** reproduce using spores.

Stamen
One of the male parts of a flower. Stamens produce **pollen**, which travels from plant to plant so that seeds can be formed.

Stoma (plural: **stomata**)
A microscopic pore on the surface of a leaf. Stomata let gases flow into and out of leaves, so that plants can carry out **photosynthesis**.

Stromatolite
Rock-like mounds produced by **cyanobacteria** growing in shallow water. Fossilized stromatolites are among the oldest signs of life on earth.

Symbiosis
A partnership that involves two different **species**. By teaming up, each partner often has a better chance of survival. Both partners may be animals, or one may be an animal and one a plant.

Taiga
A Russian word for the **boreal forest**.

Tentacles
Long, fleshy 'feelers' that some animals use to catch their food.

Territory
A space that is claimed by an animal so that it can breed. In most kinds of animals, territories are claimed and defended by males.

Thorax
The middle part of an animal's body. In insects, legs and wings are attached to it.

Toxin
A poison made by a living thing.

Tundra
A cold, treeless **habitat** found in the far north, and sometimes near the summits of high mountains.

Transpiration
The movement of water from a plant's roots, along its stem and out of its leaves. When water reaches the leaves, it evaporates through pores called **stomata**.

Vertebrate
An animal that has a backbone. Vertebrates include fish, amphibians, reptiles, birds and mammals.

Virus
A chemical particle that reproduces by infecting living **cells**.

Warm-blooded
Describes an animal whose body stays at a steady warm temperature. Warm-blooded animals are well insulated, and can stay active even in cold conditions.

WEBSITES

waynesword.palomar.edu/wayne.htm
One of the best plant sites on the web, containing more than 2,000 photos of interesting and unusual plants from all over the world, plus a huge collection of plant myths, legends, facts and figures.

www.bbc.co.uk/nature/wildfacts
Find out about hundreds of different animals at this wildlife site run by the BBC's natural history unit.

www.eia-international.org
The Environmental Investigation Agency (EIA) is an international organization that investigates and exposes environmental crime, from illegal logging to animal smuggling.

www.euronet.nl/users/janpar/virtual/ocean.html
Find out about microscopic life at sea by visiting this 'virtual ocean' page.

www.microscopy-uk.org.uk/mag/indexmag.html?http://
www.microscopy-uk.org.uk/mag/wimsmall/smal1.html
Claiming to be the 'smallest page on the web', this fascinating site is an introduction to the microscopic organisms you can find in a freshwater pond.

www.mbayaq.org
The Monterey Bay Aquarium's website includes the award-winning 'E-quarium' – an online introduction to undersea life.

www.mnh.si.edu/museum/VirtualTour/index.html
The National Museum of Natural History (NMNH) is one of the world's largest museums. This web page opens the door to its collections with a range of virtual tours.

www.nhm.ac.uk/interactive/kids/index.html
Find out more about the natural world by visiting London's Natural History Museum. This regularly updated site includes webcam pictures of animals on the move.

www.sandiegozoo.org
San Diego zoo is famous for its work with endangered animals. Its website features news about animals in captivity and in the wild, updates about the status of threatened species, plus a range of virtual tours.

www.unep-wcmc.org
The World Conservation Monitoring Centre, part of the United Nations, publishes 'Red Lists' of threatened and endangered species from all over the world. Check out Red List species by visiting this website.

INDEX

Page numbers in **bold** refer to main sections.

ACKNOWLEDGEMENTS

The publishers would like to thank the following for permission to reproduce their material. Every care has been taken to trace copyright holders. However, if there have been unintentional omissions or failure to trace copyright holders, we apologise and will, if informed, endeavour to make corrections in any future edition.

Key: b = bottom, c = centre, l = left, r = right, t = top

FLPA – Frank Lane Picture Agency   NGIC – National Geographic Image Collection   OSF – Oxford Scientific Films
Naturepl – Nature Picture Library   NHPA – Natural History Picture Agency   SPL – Science Photo Library

Cover Steve Bloom; **back cover cr** NHPA; **page 1** SPL; **3** NGIC; **4c** SPL; **4bl** Corbis; **5tr** Corbis; **5cl** Corbis; **5b** Corbis; **6** NGIC; **8–9** Getty/Imagebank; **10–11t** SPL; **10cr** SPL; **10–11b** Getty; **11c** SPL; **12c** Getty/Stone; **13b** Getty/Imagebank; **14t** Getty/Imagebank; **14bl** SPL; **15tr** SPL; **15c** SPL; **15bl** SPL; **16cr** Corbis; **16rbc** Getty/Stone; **16br** Corbis; **17tc** SPL; **17cr** SPL; **17rbc** Corbis; **17br** SPL; **18–19c** SPL; **18rbc** SPL; **18rb** Getty/Stone; **19rc** Ardea; **19rbc** Corbis; **19rb** SPL; **20–1** Corbis; **20br** Corbis; **21tl** OSF; **21br** NHPA; **22tl** Getty/Stone; **22tr** Getty/Imagebank; **22cb** Getty/Taxi; **23tc** OSF; **23cr** Getty/Imagebank; **23b** NHPA; **24–5t** Corbis; **24c** Naturepl; **24bl** Corbis; **25tr** Naturepl; **26tl** NGIC; **26–7b** Ardea; **27tr** Corbis; **27br** Corbis; **28–9** Steve Bloom; **28tl** Naturepl; **28tcl** Naturepl; **28tcr** Naturepl; **28tr** Naturepl; **29b** Getty/Stone; **30tr** Corbis; **30cl** Corbis; **30–1** Getty/Imagebank; **31tr** Corbis; **31cr** Corbis; **32–3** Corbis; **32tr** Corbis; **33t** SPL; **33br** Corbis; **38tl** Naturepl; **38bc** Naturepl; **39tl** Corbis; **39cr** FLPA; **39b** Corbis; **40tr** SPL; **40–1** NHPA; **41br** NHPA; **42bl** Getty/Stone; **42br** Getty/Imagebank; **43t** Corbis; **43br** SPL; **44tr** Getty/Stone; **44cr** Corbis; **44b** Corbis; **45tr** Corbis; **45cl** NHPA; **46tl** Corbis; **46bc** Corbis; **46–7** Corbis; **47tc** Naturepl; **47br** Ardea; **48cl** Getty/Stone; **48bl** Naturepl; **48tcr** Corbis; **49cl** SPL; **46tl** NHPA; **49tc** Naturepl; **49crt** Naturepl; **49crb** Naturepl; **50tl** Ardea; **50cr** SPL; **50bl** Naturepl; **51tl** Corbis; **51cr** David Brufford/Harvard University Herbaria; **52tr** Still Pictures; **52cl** Naturepl; **52cr** NHPA; **52bl** Corbis; **53tr** Getty News; **53bl** Corbis; **54tl** Getty/Stone; **54bl** Corbis; **54br** Naturepl; **54–5t** Corbis; **55c** Steve Bloom; **55b** Naturepl; **56–7** SPL; **58cl** SPL; **58–9c** SPL; **58br** SPL; **59t** NGIC; **59cr** NGIC; **60** FLPA/Minden Collection; **61** SPL; **62–3t** SPL; **62bl** SPL; **63br** SPL; **64tl** SPL; **64cr** SPL; **64bl** SPL; **65tr** SPL; **65c** SPL; **65bl** SPL; **66–7** Corbis; **68–9t** SPL; **68bcr** SPL; **69tr** SPL; **69bc** OSF; **69br** OSF; **70tl** SPL; **70bl** SPL; **70–1b** SPL; **71tr** SPL; **71bc** Getty/Imagebank; **72tl** Corbis; **72–3c** Corbis; **72bc** Corbis; **73tl** SPL; **73cr** SPL; **73bc** SPL; **74cl** SPL; **74cr** OSF; **75tl** OSF; **75cr** SPL; **76tr** Corbis; **76bl** SPL; **77tc** SPL; **77cl** Nature Photographers; **77br** Nature Photographers; **78tl** Corbis; **78cr** Corbis; **78–9b** Premaphotos; **79tl** Nature Photographers; **79cr** SPL; **80tr** SPL; **80c** Corbis; **81tl** SPL; **81tr** Corbis; **81br** Premaphotos; **82l** Corbis; **82cr** OSF; **83tl** Premaphotos; **83cr** OSF; **83b** Corbis; **84tl** Getty/Imagebank; **84b** Redcover; **85tr** SPL; **86 inset** Getty/Stone; **86cl** SPL; **86cr** OSF; **86–7t** Corbis; **87tr** OSF; **87b** Corbis; **88–9** Corbis; **90cl** SPL; **90cb** Corbis; **90–1c** SPL; **91tr** Corbis; **91br** SPL; **92tl** SPL; **92cr** Corbis; **93tl** Corbis; **93b** SPL; **94bl** SPL; **94–5** SPL; **95t** SPL; **96tl** Corbis; **96bl** Corbis; **97tr** OSF; **97cl** Steve Shattuck, CSIRO, Australia; **97b** Corbis; **98l** SPL; **98br** Corbis; **99tl** SPL; **99br** SPL; **100cl** Corbis; **100bl** Corbis; **100br** SPL; **100–1** OSF; **101t** OSF; **101cr** OSF; **102cl** SPL; **102–3** Still Pictures; **103t** Woodfall Images; **104tl** Corbis; **104cr** Getty/Imagebank; **104b** OSF; **105tl** OSF; **105c** OSF; **106tr** Corbis; **106cl** Corbis; **106br** OSF; **107bl** Corbis; **107r** Naturepl; **108tl** Corbis; **108br** Getty/Imagebank; **109tl** Corbis; **109cr** OSF; **109b** OSF; **110–1** NGIC; **112tr** NHPA; **112lb** OSF; **112–3** Corbis; **113tr** SPL; **113cl** OSF; **113br** OSF; **114t** OSF; **114b** Robert Brons; **114–5** Corbis; **115t** Corbis; **116tr** OSF; **116tc** SPL; **116bl** SPL; **116bc** SPL; **117tr** Corbis; **117cl** Premaphotos; **117br** SPL; **118tr** SPL; **118cl** Ardea; **118–9b** SPL; **119tc** SPL; **119br** OSF; **120l** Corbis; **120–1** NHPA; **121tl** Corbis; **121tr** NHPA; **121b** Corbis; **122–3** NHPA; **122cr** NHPA; **122bl** NHPA; **123tl** Corbis; **124tl** Naturepl; **124lc** Corbis; **125tl** Corbis; **125** NHPA; **126tr** Corbis; **126cl** NHPA; **126b** SPL; **127tl** Corbis; **127tr** NASA; **128tl** NHPA; **128b** Getty/Taxi; **129tl** Naturepl; **129cl** Corbis; **129b** Steve Bloom; **130t** NGIC; **130cl** OSF; **130br** Corbis; **131t** Steve Bloom; **132tl** NHPA; **132cl** Corbis; **132b** Corbis; **133tl** Corbis; **133cr** Corbis; **133b** Corbis; **134tl** Corbis; **134b** Premaphotos; **135tl** Jens Christian Shou; **135tr** Corbis; **135cl** OSF; **135br** Corbis; **136l** NHPA; **136br** NGIC; **137cr** OSF; **137cl** OSF; **137br** OSF; **138cl** OSF; **138br** Corbis; **138–9** Premaphotos; **139tr** Steve Bloom; **139cr** Getty/Taxi; **140tl** Corbis; **140c** OSF; **140b** Naturepl; **141tl** Corbis; **141c** NHPA; **141br** NHPA; **142cl** OSF; **142–3t** OSF; **142–3b** OSF; **143cr** Naturepl; **143bl** Naturepl; **143bc** Naturepl; **143br** Naturepl; **144tr** Corbis; **144b** Naturepl; **145tr** Getty/Stone; **145cl** OSF; **145cr** Naturepl; **145b** Naturepl; **146–7** Steve Bloom; **148tl** Naturepl; **148bl** Naturepl; **148br** Naturepl; **149tr** Corbis; **150tr** Naturepl; **150b** Corbis; **151c** Naturepl; **151br** Naturepl; **152tl** Getty/Taxi; **152cr** Corbis; **152–3** NGIC; **153br** Steve Bloom; **154l** Naturepl; **155tl** SPL; **155tc** SPL; **155cr** Naturepl; **155bl** OSF; **156tr** Naturepl; **156cl** Steve Bloom; **157** Naturepl; **158bl** Corbis; **158tl** Corbis; **158br** Naturepl; **159tl** Naturepl; **159tr** NHPA; **161–2** Corbis; **164–5** SPL; **164c** FLPA; **164–5b** Steve Bloom; **165t** Ardea; **165c** NHPA; **166t** FLPA; **166cr** Ardea; **166–7b** Corbis; **167** SPL; **167cr** Still Pictures; **168t** NHPA; **168bl** Corbis; **168–9** Corbis; **169** Ardea; **170tl** Corbis; **170c** FLPA; **170c** Corbis; **170–1** Corbis; **171tl** Corbis; **171br** NHPA; **172–3** Polar Institute, Norway; **173 inset** Greenpeace; **174tl** SPL; **174–5** Brian & Cherry Alexander; **175tr** Corbis; **176tl** Still Pictures; **176–7** Naturepl; **176b** Ardea; **177cr** Naturepl; **177b** Naturepl; **178–9** NHPA; **180tr** Steve Bloom; **180–1** Naturepl; **180bl** Corbis; **181bl** Corbis; **182–3t** NGIC; **182–3b** Naturepl; **183cr** NGIC; **183b** NGIC; **184br** Naturepl; **184tl** Corbis; **183–4** NGIC; **185t** Corbis; **185 inset** Naturepl; **186tl** Ardea; **186b** Corbis; **187t** Ardea; **187b** Corbis; **188–9** Corbis; **190tl** NHPA; **190–1** Naturepl; **191tl** Naturepl; **191br** Corbis; **192–3t** Ardea; **192–3b** NHPA; **193tr** Naturepl; **193c** Ardea; **193cr** Ardea; **194l** Corbis; **194b** Getty/Taxi; **195t** NGIC; **195b** Corbis; **196tl** SPL; **196cr** OSF; **196–7t** Corbis; **197cr** Corbis; **197b** NGIC; **198–9** Getty/Imagebank; **200cl** NHPA; **200tr** OSF; **200–1** Corbis; **201tr** Corbis; **202cl** Corbis; **202tr** Corbis; **202–3** OSF; **203t** NHPA; **204–5** Corbis; **204–5b** NHPA; **205r** Derek Hall; **206** Corbis; **207t** SPL; **207bl** FLPA; **207cr** NHPA; **208–9** Corbis; **210t** Corbis; **210bl** Naturepl; **210br** Naturepl; **211tc** Naturepl; **211cl** Naturepl; **211br** Corbis; **212–3t** Ardea; **212–3b** Corbis; **213cr** Corbis; **214tl** Ardea; **214–5b** Naturepl; **215tl** NHPA; **215cr** Corbis; **216tl** Naturepl; **216b** NHPA; **217tl** Naturepl; **217tr** Naturepl; **217b** NHPA; **218tr** Corbis; **219t** Ardea; **219b** Corbis; **220l** NHPA; **220b** Ardea; **221t** Corbis; **221cl** Ardea; **221b** NHPA; **222–3** Corbis; **224–5t** Corbis; **224–5b** Corbis; **225r** Naturepl; **226–7** Steve Bloom; **228tl** FLPA; **228b** NGIC; **228–9t** Corbis; **229r** NHPA; **229b** Ardea; **230t** Corbis; **230br** Ardea; **230br** Ardea; **231t** Corbis; **231b** Corbis; **232t** NHPA; **232l** NHPA; **232br** Still Pictures; **233tr** Corbis; **233b** Still Pictures; **234–5t** Corbis; **234–5b** Ardea; **235tr** Corbis; **236–7** Corbis; **238–9t** NHPA; **238b** Corbis; **239tr** Still Pictures; **239bl** Naturepl; **240tl** Woodfall Images; **240tr** Corbis; **240bl** Naturepl; **241tr** Naturepl; **240–1b** Corbis; **242tl** NHPA; **242c** NHPA; **243l** NHPA; **243br** NGIC; **244tl** NHPA; **244bl** NHPA; **244tr** Naturepl; **245r** NHPA; **246–7t** Corbis; **246–7b** Getty/Stone; **247tr** SPL; **247cr** NHPA; **248cl** Ardea; **248b** Corbis; **248–9t** Naturepl; **249t** Corbis; **249b** Corbis; **250–1** Corbis; **250t** Steve Bloom; **251t** Corbis; **252tl** NHPA; **252tr** Corbis; **252bl** Corbis; **252br** Corbis; **253tl** NHPA; **253b** Corbis; **254–5** Getty/Imagebank; **256tl** NGIC; **256b** Corbis; **256–7t** Corbis; **257** OSF; **257b** NHPA; **258–9t** Corbis; **258–9b** Corbis; **259r** Corbis; **260–1** Getty/Imagebank; **262tl** Still Pictures; **262bl** Corbis; **262cr** Corbis; **263cl** Getty/Imagebank; **263cr** FLPA; **263b** Getty/Stone; **264tl** Corbis; **264b** Corbis; **265t** Corbis; **265bl** OSF; **265br** NHPA; **266c** Corbis; **266–7t** Corbis; **266–7b** NHPA; **267r** Ardea; **268tl** NHPA; **268cr** Naturepl; **269tl** NHPA; **269cr** Corbis; **270bl** SPL; **270cr** Corbis; **271t** Corbis; **272tl** NGIC; **272b** Naturepl; **272–3t** Corbis; **273cl** Corbis; **273b** Ardea; **274–5** Getty/Taxi; **276tl** SPL; **276cr** Corbis; **276bl** SPL; **277tl** Ardea; **277c** Corbis; **277cr** Naturepl; **277br** Naturepl; **278–9t** Corbis; **278–9b** Getty/Stone; **279tr** Corbis; **280tl** NHPA; **280tr** Corbis; **280c** Corbis; **280–1b** NHPA; **281r** Corbis; **282tl** Corbis; **282cr** Edward Parker; **282bl** Corbis; **282tl** NHPA; **283tr** NHPA; **283b** Corbis; **284–5** Ardea; **286tl** NHPA; **286cr** Corbis; **286bl** NHPA; **287tl** NHPA; **287b** NGIC; **287bl** NHPA; **288tl** NHPA; **288cr** Naturepl; **288–9b** Corbis; **289t** Corbis; **290–1t** Corbis; **290–1b** Corbis; **291tr** Corbis; **292tl** NHPA; **292bl** Corbis; **292–3t** Corbis; **293tr** Corbis; **293c** Corbis; **293bl** NHPA; **293br** NHPA; **294–5** Getty/Taxi; **296tl** NHPA; **296–7t** NHPA; **296–7b** Naturepl; **297tr** Corbis; **298–9t** SPL; **298–9b** Corbis; **299tr** Corbis; **300bl** Still Pictures; **300–1t** Corbis; **301tr** Getty/Stone; **301b** NHPA; **302–3** Naturepl; **304tl** SPL; **304bl** SPL; **304–5t** Corbis; **305t** NHPA; **305b** NHPA; **306l** NHPA; **306–7t** NHPA; **306br** NHPA; **307tr** NHPA; **307b** NHPA